C++ Timesaving Techniques For Dummies®

D1535983

The Basic C++ Datatypes

- ✔ int
- ✔ long
- ✔ char
- ✔ float
- ✔ double
- ✔ pointer
- ✔ reference

The Basic STL Datatypes

- ✔ string
- ✔ vector
- ✔ map
- ✔ list
- ✔ iterator
- ✔ dequeue
- ✔ iostream
- ✔ fstream
- ✔ strstream

Modifiers

- ✔ static
- ✔ extern
- ✔ auto

User-Defined Datatypes

- ✔ enumeration
- ✔ struct
- ✔ class
- ✔ union

Components of a Complete Class

void constructor → **1**

copy constructor → **2**

full constructor → **3**

virtual destructor → **4**

operator = → **5**

set method for each data member → **6**

get method for each data member → **7**

clone method → **8**

Ten Simple Rules for Writing C++ Code

1. Check all return codes.
2. Create objects as late as possible.
3. Always use auto_ptr for all allocated objects.
4. Encapsulate all arrays to protect against buffer overruns.
5. Always protect member data from direct access by users.
6. Maintain as little connection between classes as physically possible.
7. Do data validation in separate classes.
8. Separate business logic from programming logic.
9. Always implement your classes within your own namespace to avoid name collisions.
10. Create your own types to implement program-dependent information storage.

For Dummies: Bestselling Book Series for Beginners

C++ Timesaving Techniques For Dummies®

Cheat Sheet

Example of a Complete Class

```cpp
class Complete
{
private:
    bool dirty;        // Keep track of the object state.
private:
    int x;

    // Create an initialization function that
    // can reset all values.
    void Init();

    // Create a copy function that you can use to make
    // clones of an object.
    void Copy( const Complete& aCopy );
public:
    // Always create a default constructor.
    Complete();                                              → 1
    // Always create a copy constructor
    Complete( const Complete& aCopy );                      → 2
    // Always create a full constructor with all accessible
    // members defined.
    Complete( int _x);                                      → 3
    // Always create a virtual destructor.
    virtual ~Complete();                                    → 4

    // Next, define accessors for all data that can be public. If
    // it's not intended to be public, make it a private accessor.
    // First, define all the set methods. The "dirty" flag is not
    // necessary for completeness, but it makes life a LOT easier.

    void setX(const int& _x);                               → 6

    // Now the data get functions. Note that since they cannot modify
    // the object, they are all marked as const.
    int getX(void) const;                                   → 7

    // Implement a clone operator.
    Complete Clone(void);                                   → 8
    // Implement an assigment operator.
    Complete operator=( const Complete& aCopy );            → 5
};
```

Copyright © 2005 Wiley Publishing, Inc.
All rights reserved.

Item 7986-X.

For more information about Wiley Publishing,
call 1-800-762-2974.

For Dummies: Bestselling Book Series for Beginners

C++
Timesaving
Techniques™
FOR
DUMMIES®

C++
Timesaving
Techniques™
FOR
DUMMIES®

by Matthew Telles

WILEY

Wiley Publishing, Inc.

C++ Timesaving Techniques™ For Dummies®

Published by
Wiley Publishing, Inc.
111 River Street
Hoboken, NJ 07030-5774
www.wiley.com

Copyright © 2005 by Wiley Publishing, Inc., Indianapolis, Indiana

Published by Wiley Publishing, Inc., Indianapolis, Indiana

Published simultaneously in Canada

For general information on our other products and services, please contact our Customer Care Department within the U.S. at 800-762-2974, outside the U.S. at 317-572-3993, or fax 317-572-4002.

For technical support, please visit www.wiley.com/techsupport.

Wiley also publishes its books in a variety of electronic formats. Some content that appears in print may not be available in electronic books.

Library of Congress Control Number: 2005920299

ISBN: 0-7645-7986-X

Manufactured in the United States of America

10 9 8 7 6 5 4 3 2 1

1MA/RU/QS/QV/IN

WILEY

About the Author

Matthew Telles is a 20-year veteran of the software-development wars. In his time, he has seen FORTRAN, COBOL, and other dinosaur languages come and go. Currently a senior software engineer for Research Systems, Inc., his days are spent finding and fixing bugs that other people have created. Besides trying to be tactful, he also enjoys working with other developers to teach the techniques he has mastered over his career. With expertise in programming, designing, documenting, and debugging applications, he has reached the pinnacle of a programmer's existence: the ability to write his own bio blurbs for books. The author of seven other programming books, Matt lives in Lakewood, Colorado, and pines away for his beloved DEC 10.

Dedication

This book is dedicated to my friends and family, without whom I couldn't have done it.

Author's Acknowledgments

I would like to acknowledge my employer, Research Systems, for allowing me the time and space to work on this book. In addition, I would like to thank the following people: Carol, for being there and listening; my children, for bringing a ray of sunshine into a gloomy day; and, of course, all of the people behind the scenes as well: the editors, the marketing folk, and that nice guy who kept harassing me for stuff. (Thanks, Chris!)

Publisher's Acknowledgments

We're proud of this book; please send us your comments through our online registration form located at www.dummies.com/register/.

Some of the people who helped bring this book to market include the following:

Acquisitions, Editorial, and Media Development

Project Editor: Christopher Morris

Acquisitions Editor: Katie Feltman

Sr. Copy Editor: Barry Childs-Helton

Technical Editor: John Purdum

Editorial Manager: Kevin Kirschner

Media Development Manager: Laura VanWinkle

Media Development Supervisor: Richard Graves

Editorial Assistant: Amanda Foxworth

Cartoons: Rich Tennant (www.the5thwave.com)

Composition Services

Project Coordinator: Maridee Ennis

Layout and Graphics: Melissa Auciello-Brogan, Denny Hager, Stephanie D. Jumper, Melanee Prendergast, Jacque Roth, Heather Ryan, Janet Seib

Proofreaders: Laura Albert, Laura L. Bowman, John Greenough, Leeann Harney, Arielle Mannelle, Joe Niesen, Carl Pierce, Dwight Ramsey, Brian Walls

Indexer: Ty Koontz

Publishing and Editorial for Technology Dummies

Richard Swadley, Vice President and Executive Group Publisher

Andy Cummings, Vice President and Publisher

Mary Bednarek, Executive Acquisitions Director

Mary C. Corder, Editorial Director

Publishing for Consumer Dummies

Diane Graves Steele, Vice President and Publisher

Joyce Pepple, Acquisitions Director

Composition Services

Gerry Fahey, Vice President of Production Services

Debbie Stailey, Director of Composition Services

Contents at a Glance

Table of Contents

Introduction

C++ is a flexible, powerful programming language with hundreds of thousands of applications. However, the knowledge of how to take advantage of its full potential comes only with time and experience. That's where this book comes in. Think of it as a "cookbook" for solving your programming problems, much as *The Joy of Cooking* is a guide to solving your dinner dilemmas.

C++ Timesaving Techniques For Dummies is a book for the beginning-to-advanced C++ programmer who needs immediate answers to the problems that crop up in the professional software-development world. I assume that you have prior programming experience, as well as experience specifically with the C++ programming language. "Fluff" — like discussions of looping structures or defining variables, or the basics of compiling applications — is kept to a minimum here. Instead, I offer quick, step-by-step instructions for solving specific problems in C++.

Each technique includes example code — which you are welcome to use in your own applications, or modify as you see fit. This is literally a case of "steal this code, please." C++ is a language that lends itself well to component-based design and implementation. This means that you can take a piece from here and a piece from there to implement the solution that you have in mind.

C++ Timesaving Techniques For Dummies is not an operating-system-specific (or even compiler-specific) book. The techniques and code that you find here should work on all compilers that support the standard C++ language, and on all operating systems for which a standard compiler exists. This book is intended to be as useful to the Unix programmer as to the Microsoft Windows programmer, and just as useful for programming with X-windows as it is for .Net.

My goal in writing this book is to empower you with some of the stronger features of C++, as well as some great tips and methods to solve everyday problems, without the headaches and lost time that go with trying to figure out how to use those tools. C++ provides simple, fast, powerful solutions to meet the demands of day-to-day programming — my goal is to save you time while making the tools clear and easy to use.

Saving Time with This Book

The *Timesaving Techniques For Dummies* books focus on big-payoff techniques that save you time, either on the spot or somewhere down the road. And these books get to the point in a hurry, with step-by-step instructions to pace you through the tasks you need to do, without any of the fluff you don't want. I've identified more than 70 techniques that C++ programmers need to know to make the most of their time. In addition, each technique includes code samples that make programming a breeze. Decide for yourself how to use this book: Read it cover to cover if you like, or skip right to the technique that interests you the most.

In *C++ Timesaving Techniques For Dummies,* you can find out how to

✔ **Reduce time-consuming tasks:** I'm letting you in on more than 70 tips and tricks for your C++ system, so you can spend more time creating great results and less time fiddling with a feature so that it works correctly.

✔ **Take your skills up a notch:** You're already familiar with the basics of using C++. Now this book takes you to the next level, helping you become a more powerful programmer.

✔ **Work with the basics of C++ to meet your needs:** I show you how to bend the fundamentals of object-oriented programming and the pre-processor so that your programs work faster and more reliably.

✔ **Improve your skills with types, classes, arrays, and templates:** Fine-tuning your abilities with these elements will improve your programs' functionality and make your code more readable.

✔ **Understand the finer points of input and output:** Improving the way you work with input and output will reduce memory loss and increase speed.

✔ **Use built-in functionality and utilities:** Gaining familiarity with these features will help you get the most out of what C++ already offers.

✔ **Improve your debugging skills:** Getting better at debugging will speed up the whole programming process.

What's Available on the Companion Web Site?

The companion Web site for this book contains all the source code shown for the techniques and examples listed in this book. This resource can save you considerable typing when you want to use the code in your own applications, as well as allowing you to easily refer back to the original code if you modify the things you find here. You can find the site at `www.dummies.com/go/cplusplustfd`.

Obviously, in order to utilize the code in the book, you will need a C++ compiler. The code in this book was all tested with the GNU C++ compiler, a copy of which you will find on the GNU organization's Web site: `www.gnu.org`. This compiler is a public-domain (read: free) compiler that you can use in your own development, or simply to test things on computers that don't have a full-blown commercial development system. The GNU C++ compiler contains all the standard header files, libraries, debuggers, and other tools that C++ programmers expect.

If you already own another compiler, such as Visual Studio, Borland's C++Builder, or another compiler, hey, no worries. The code you find here should work with any of these compilers, as long as you follow the standards for defining header files and including code libraries.

Conventions Used in This Book

When I describe output from the compiler, operating system, or application you're developing, you will see it in a distinctive typeface that looks like this:

```
This is some output
```

Source-code listings — such as the application you're developing and feeding to the compiler to mangle into executable code — will look like this:

```
// This is a loop
for  ( int i=0; i<10; ++i )
    printf("This is line %d\n", i );
```

If you are entering code by hand, you should enter it as you see it in the book, although spaces and blank lines won't matter. Comments can be skipped, if you so choose, but in general, the code is commented as it would be in a production environment.

In general, the code and text in the book should be quite straightforward. The entries are all in list format, taking you step by step through the process of creating source files, compiling them, and running the resulting application. The code is all compiler-agnostic — that is, it doesn't indicate (because it doesn't know) the specific compiler commands you will use for the compiler you have on your machine. Please refer to your compiler's documentation if you have specific questions about the compilation and linking process for your specific compiler or operating system.

What's In This Book

This book is organized into parts — groups of techniques about a common subject that can save you time and help you get your program written fast and running better. Each technique is written to be independent of the others; you need only implement the techniques that benefit you and your users.

Part I: Streamlining the Means and Mechanics of OOP

In this part, you learn the basic concepts of object-oriented programming and how they apply to the C++ programming language.

Part II: Working with the Pre-Processor

The C++ pre-processor is a powerful tool for customizing your application, making your code more readable, and creating portable applications. In this section, you get some handy ways to wring the most out of the pre-processor; some handy techniques explain how to create portable code, and the voice of experience reveals why you should avoid the `assert` macro.

Part III: Types

The C++ language is rich in data types and user-definable types. In this section, we explore using the built-in types of the language, as well as creating your own types that can be used just like the built-in ones. You find techniques in this section that explain structures and how you can use them. You also zero in on enumerations and creating default arguments for methods.

Part IV: Classes

The core of the C++ programming language is the *class*. In this section, you get a look at how to create complete classes that work in any environment — as well as how to perform data validation and manipulation, create properties for your class, and inherit from other people's classes.

Part V: Arrays and Templates

Container classes are a core element of the Standard Template Library (STL), an important part of the C++ programming environment. In this section, you get the goods on working with the various container classes, as well as creating your own containers. Here's where to find out how to iterate over a collection of objects, and how to allocate and de-allocate blocks of objects.

Part VI: Input and Output

It would be a rare program indeed that did not have some form of input and output. After all, why would a user bother to run a program that could not be controlled in some way, or at least yield some sort of useful information? In this section, we learn all about various forms of input and output, from delimited file input to XML file output, and everything in between.

Part VII: Using the Built-in Functionality

One hallmark of the C++ programming language is its extensibility and reusability. Why reinvent the wheel every time you write an application? C++ makes it easy to avoid this pitfall by providing a ton of built-in functionality. In this section, you get to use that built-in functionality — in particular, the C++ library and STL — to implement a complete internationalization class. You also get pointers on avoiding memory leaks, using hash tables, and overriding allocators for a container class.

Part VIII: Utilities

The single best way to learn C++ techniques is to look at the way that other people implement various things. This section contains simple utilities that can sharpen your coding techniques, and it provides valuable code that you can drop directly into your applications. You will find techniques here for encoding and decoding data, converting data into a format that the World Wide Web can understand, and opening a file using multiple search paths.

Part IX: Debugging C++ Applications

One of the most important things to understand about programs is that they break. Things go wrong, code behaves in unexpected ways, and users do things you (and sometimes they) didn't intend.

When these things happen, it is extremely important that you understand how to track down the issues in the code. In this section, you learn valuable techniques for creating tracing macros, tracking down memory leaks, and checking for errors at run-time.

Part X: The Scary (or Fun!) Stuff

This part contains techniques to help you take control of the complexity of your code, and ways you can avoid being intimidated by convoluted code you might run into while working. Not being afraid of your code is the number-one area of importance in programming; this section will aid you in that endeavor.

Icons Used in This Book

Each technique in this book has icons pointing to special information, sometimes quite emphatically. Each icon has its own purpose.

 When there's a way to save time, either now or in the future, this icon leads the way. Home in on these icons when every second counts.

 This icon points to handy hints that help you work through the steps in each technique, or offer handy troubleshooting info.

 These icons are your trail of breadcrumbs, leading back to information that you'll want to keep in mind.

 When you see a Warning icon, there's a chance that your data or your system is at risk. You won't see many of these, but when you do, proceed with caution.

Part I

Streamlining the Means and Mechanics of OOP

Technique

Protecting Your Data with Encapsulation

Save Time By

✔ Understanding encapsulation

✔ Creating and implementing an encapsulated class

✔ Making updates to an encapsulated class

The dictionary defines *encapsulation* as "to encase in or as if in a capsule" and that is exactly the approach that C++ uses. An object is a "capsule" and the information and processing algorithms that it implements are hidden from the user. All that the users see is the functional-level interface that allows them to use the class to do the job they need done. By placing the data within the interface, rather than allowing the user direct access to it, the data is protected from invalid values, wrongful changes, or improper coercion to new data types.

 Most time wasted in application development is spent changing code that has been updated by another source. It doesn't really add anything to your program, but it does take time to change things when someone has modified the algorithm being used. If you hide the algorithm from the developer — and provide a consistent interface — you will find that it takes considerably less time to change the application when the base code changes. Since the user only cares about the data and how it is computed, keeping your algorithm private and your interface constant protects the data integrity for the user.

Creating and Implementing an Encapsulated Class

Listing 1-1 presents the StringCoding class, an encapsulated method of encryption. The benefit of encapsulation is, in effect, that it cuts to the chase: The programmer utilizing our StringCoding class knows nothing about the algorithm used to encrypt strings — and doesn't really need to know what data was used to encrypt the string in the first place. Okay, but why do it? Well, you have three good reasons to "hide" the implementation of an algorithm from its user:

✔ Hiding the implementation stops people from fiddling with the input data to make the algorithm work differently. Such changes may be meant to make the algorithm work correctly, but can easily mess it up; either way, the meddling masks possible bugs from the developers.

✔ Hiding the algorithm makes it easy to replace the implementation with a more workable alternative if one is found.

✔ Hiding the algorithm makes it more difficult for people to "crack" your code and decrypt your data.

The following list of steps shows you how to create and implement this encapsulated method:

1. In the code editor of your choice, create a new file to hold the code for the definition of your source file.

In this example, the file is named ch01.cpp, although you can use whatever you choose.

2. Type the code from Listing 1-1 into your file, substituting your own names for the italicized constants, variables, and filenames.

Or better yet, copy the code from the source file included on this book's companion Web site.

LISTING 1-1: THE STRINGCODING CLASS

```cpp
#include <stdio.h>
#include <string>

class StringCoding
{
private:
    // The key to use in encrypting the string
    std::string sKey;
public:
    // The constructor, uses a preset key
    StringCoding( void )
    {
        sKey = "ATest";
    }
    // Main constructor, allows the user to specify a key
    StringCoding( const char *strKey )
    {
        if ( strKey )
            sKey = strKey;
        else
            sKey = "ATest";
    }
    // Copy constructor
    StringCoding( const StringCoding& aCopy )
    {
        sKey = aCopy.sKey;
    }

public:
    // Methods
    std::string Encode( const char *strIn );
    std::string Decode( const char *strIn );
private:
    std::string Xor( const char *strIn );
};
```

```cpp
std::string StringCoding::Xor( const char *strIn )
{
    std::string sOut = "";

    int nIndex = 0;
    for ( int i=0; i<(int)strlen(strIn); ++i )
    {
        char c = (strIn[i] ^ sKey[nIndex]);
        sOut += c;
        nIndex ++;
        if ( nIndex == sKey.length() )
            nIndex = 0;
    }

    return sOut;
}

// For XOR encoding, the encode and decode methods are the same.
std::string StringCoding::Encode( const char *strIn )
{
    return Xor( strIn );
}

std::string StringCoding::Decode( const char *strIn )
{
    return Xor( strIn );
}

int main(int argc, char **argv)
{
    if ( argc < 2 )
    {
        printf("Usage: ch1_1 inputstring1 [inputstring2...]\n");
        exit(1);
    }

    StringCoding key("XXX");

    for ( int i=1; i<argc; ++i )
    {
        std::string sEncode = key.Encode( argv[i] );
        printf("Input  String : [%s]\n", argv[i] );
        printf("Encoded String: [%s]\n", sEncode.c_str() );
        std::string sDecode = key.Decode( sEncode.c_str() );
        printf("Decoded String: [%s]\n", sDecode.c_str() );
    }

    printf("%d strings encoded\n", argc-1);
    return 0;
}
```

3. Save the source code as a file in the code-editor application and then close the code editor.

4. Compile your completed source code, using your favorite compiler on your favorite operating system.

5. Run your new application on your favorite operating system.

If you have done everything properly, you should see the output shown here in the console window of your operating system:

```
$ ./ch1_1.exe "hello"
Input  String : [hello]
Encoded String: [0=447]
Decoded String: [hello]
1 strings encoded
```

Note that our input and decoded strings are the same — and that the encoded string is completely indecipherable (as a good encrypted string should be). And any programmer using the object will never see the algorithm in question!

Making Updates to an Encapsulated Class

One of the benefits of encapsulation is that it makes updating your hidden data simple and convenient. With encapsulation, you can easily replace the underlying encryption algorithm in Listing 1-1 with an alternative if one is found to work better. In our original algorithm, we did an "exclusive logical or" to convert a character to another character. In the following example, suppose that we want to use a different method for encrypting strings. For simplicity, suppose that this new algorithm encrypts strings simply by changing each character in the input string to the next letter position in the alphabet: An *a* becomes a *b,* a *c* becomes a *d,* and so on. Obviously, our decryption algorithm would have to do the exact opposite, subtracting one letter position from the input string to return a valid output string. We could then modify the Encode method in Listing 1-1 to reflect this change. The following steps show how:

1. Reopen the source file in your code editor.

In this example, we called the source file ch01.cpp.

2. Modify the code as shown in Listing 1-2.

LISTING 1-2: UPDATING THE STRINGCODING CLASS

```
std::string StringCoding::Encode( const char *strIn )
{
    std::string sOut = "";
    for ( int i=0; i<(int)strlen(strIn); ++i )
    {
        char c = strIn[i];
        c ++;

        sOut += c;
    }
    return sOut;

}

std::string StringCoding::Decode( const char *strIn )
{
    std::string sOut = "";
```

```
for ( int i=0; i<(int)strlen(strIn); ++i )
{
    char c = strIn[i];
    c --;

    sOut += c;
}
return sOut;

}
```

3. **Save the source code as a file in the code editor and then close the code editor.**

4. **Compile the application, using your favorite compiler on your favorite operating system.**

5. **Run the application on your favorite operating system.**

You might think that this approach would have an impact on the developers who were using our class. In fact, we can make these changes in our class (check out the resulting program on this book's companion Web site as ch1_1a.cpp) and leave the remainder of the application alone. The developers don't have to worry about it. When we compile and run this application, we get the following output:

```
$ ./ch1_1a.exe "hello"
Input  String : [hello]
Encoded String: [ifmmp]
Decoded String: [hello]
1 strings encoded
```

As you can see, the algorithm changed, yet the encoding and decoding still worked and the application code didn't change at all. This, then, is the real power of encapsulation: It's a black box. The end

users have no need to know how something works in order to use it; they simply need to know what it does and how to make it do its thing.

Encapsulation also solves two other big problems in the programming world:

✔ By putting all the code to implement specific functionality in one place, you know exactly where to go when a bug crops up in that functionality. Rather than having to chase the same code in a hundred scattered places, you have it in one place.

✔ You can change how your data is internally stored without affecting the program external to that class. For example, imagine that in the first version of the code just given, we chose to use an integer value rather than the string key. The outside application would never know, or care.

 If you really want to "hide" your implementation from the user — yet still give the end user a chance to customize your code — implement your own types for the values to be passed in. Doing so requires your users to use your specific data types, rather than more generic ones.

Technique **2**

Using Abstraction to Extend Functionality

Save Time By

- ✔ Understanding abstraction
- ✔ Using virtual methods
- ✔ Creating a mailing-list application
- ✔ Testing applications

The *American Heritage Dictionary* defines the term *abstraction* as "the process of leaving out of consideration one or more properties of a complex object so as to attend to others." Basically, this means that we need to pick and choose the parts of our objects that are important to us. To abstract our data, we choose to encapsulate those portions of the object that contain certain basic types of functionality (base objects) — that way we can reuse them in other objects that redefine that functionality. Such basic objects are called, not surprisingly, *base classes*. The extended objects are called *inherited classes*. Together they form a fundamental principle of C++. Abstraction in C++ is provided through the pure virtual method. A *pure virtual method* is a method in a base class that must be implemented in any derived class in order to compile and use that derived class.

Virtual methods are one of the best timesavers available in C++. By allowing people to override just small pieces of your application functionality — without requiring you to rewrite the entire class — you give them the chance to extend your work with just a small amount of effort of their own. The concept of abstraction is satisfied through the virtual method because the base-class programmer can assume that later programmers will change the behavior of the class through a defined interface. Because it's always better to use less effort, using virtual methods means your code is more likely to be reused — leading to fewer errors, freeing up more time to design and develop quality software.

Creating a Mailing-List Application

This concept is just a little bit abstract (pardon the pun), so here's a concrete example to show you how abstraction really works: Assume you want to implement a mailing list for your company. This mailing list consists of objects (called *mailing-list entries*) that represent each of the people you're trying to reach. Suppose, however, that you have to load the data from one of two sources: from a file containing all the names, or directly from the user's command line. A look at the overall "flow" of this application reveals that the two sides of this system have a lot in common:

To handle input from a file, we need some place to store the names, addresses, cities, states, and zip codes from a file. To handle input from the command line, we need to be able to load that exact same data from the command line and store it in the same place. Then we need the capability to print those mailing-list items or merge them into another document. After the input is stored in memory, of course, we don't really care how it got there; we care only how we can access the data in the objects. The two different paths, file-based and command-line-based, share the same basic information; rather than implement the information twice, we can abstract it into a container for the mailing-list data. Here's how to do that:

1. **In the code editor of your choice, create a new file to hold the code for the definition of the class.**

In this example, the file is named ch02.cpp, although you can use whatever you choose.

2. **Type the code from Listing 2-1 into your file, substituting your own names for the italicized constants, variables, and filenames.**

Better yet, copy the code from the source file on this book's companion Web site.

LISTING 2-1: THE BASEMAILINGLISTENTRY CLASS

```cpp
#include <string>
#include <iostream>
#include <stdio.h>

class BaseMailingListEntry
{
private:
    std::string sFirstName;
    std::string sLastName;
    std::string sAddressLine1;
    std::string sAddressLine2;
    std::string sCity;
    std::string sState;
    std::string sZipCode;
public:
    BaseMailingListEntry(void)
    {
    }
    BaseMailingListEntry( const BaseMailingListEntry& aCopy )
    {
        sFirstName = aCopy.sFirstName;
        sLastName  = aCopy.sLastName;
        sAddressLine1 = aCopy.sAddressLine1;
        sAddressLine2 = aCopy.sAddressLine2;
        sCity = aCopy.sCity;
        sState = aCopy.sState;
        sZipCode = aCopy.sZipCode;
    }

    virtual bool First(void) = 0; // A pure virtual function
    virtual bool Next(void)  = 0; // Another pure virtual function
```

(continued)

LISTING 2-1 *(continued)*

```cpp
    // Accessors
    std::string getFirstName() { return sFirstName; };
    std::string getLastName()  { return sLastName; };
    std::string getAddress1()  { return sAddressLine1; };
    std::string getAddress2()  { return sAddressLine2; };
    std::string getCity()      { return sCity; };
    std::string getState()     { return sState; };
    std::string getZipCode()   { return sZipCode; };

    void setFirstName(const char *strFirstName)
{ sFirstName = strFirstName; };
    void setLastName(const char *strLastName)
{ sLastName = strLastName; };
    void setAddress1( const char *strAddress1)
{ sAddressLine1 = strAddress1; };
    void setAddress2( const char *strAddress2)
{ sAddressLine2 = strAddress2; };
    void setCity(const char *strCity)
{ sCity = strCity; };
    void setState(const char *strState)
{ sState = strState; };
    void setZipCode( const char *strZipCode )
{ sZipCode = strZipCode; };
};
```

Notice that in Listing 2-1, our base class (the ?? class) contains all the data we'll be using in common for the two derived classes (the `File MailingListEntry` and `CommandLineMailing ListEntry` classes), and implements two methods — `First` and `Next`, which allow those derived classes to override the processes of loading the components of the data (whether from a file or the command line).

3. Save the file in your source-code editor.

4. Using your favorite code editor, add the code in Listing 2-2.

You may optionally save this code in a separate header file and include that header file in your main program as well.

LISTING 2-2: THE FILEMAILINGLISTENTRY CLASS

```cpp
class FileMailingListEntry : public BaseMailingListEntry
{
    FILE *fpIn;
public:
    FileMailingListEntry( const char *strFileName )
    {
        fpIn = fopen(strFileName, "r");
    }

    virtual bool ReadEntry(void)
    {
```

```
            char szBuffer[ 256 ];
            fread( szBuffer, sizeof(char), 255, fpIn );
            if ( feof(fpIn) )
                return false;
            setFirstName( szBuffer );
            fread( szBuffer, sizeof(char), 255, fpIn );
            setFirstName( szBuffer );
            fread( szBuffer, sizeof(char), 255, fpIn );
            setAddress1( szBuffer );
            fread( szBuffer, sizeof(char), 255, fpIn );
            setAddress2( szBuffer );
            fread( szBuffer, sizeof(char), 255, fpIn );
            setCity( szBuffer );
            fread( szBuffer, sizeof(char), 255, fpIn );
            setState( szBuffer );
            fread( szBuffer, sizeof(char), 255, fpIn );
            setZipCode( szBuffer );
            return true;
        }
    virtual bool First(void)
    {
        // Move to the beginning of the file, read in the pieces
        fseek( fpIn, 0L, SEEK_SET );
        return ReadEntry();
    }
    virtual bool Next(void)
    {
        // Just get the next one in the file
        return ReadEntry();
    }
};
```

Please note that we do no error-checking in any of this code (that's to avoid making it any larger). A closer look at this object (before moving on to the last object in the group) shows that this class allocates no storage for the various components of the mailing-list entry — nor will you find any accessor functions to retrieve those components. Yet the class is derived from the base class (which implements all this functionality), so we can utilize the storage defined there. This is a really nice feature; it allows us to encapsulate the data in one place and put the "real" functionality in another. You can also see that we've implemented the two required pure virtual functions (First and Next) to make the class read the data from a file.

5. **Save the source file in your source-code re-editor.**

6. **Using the code editor, add the code in Listing 2-3 to your source-code file.**

You may optionally save this code in a separate header file and include that header file in your main program as well.

7. **Save the source file in your source-code editor.**

LISTING 2-3: THE COMMANDLINEMAILINGLISTENTRY CLASS

```cpp
class CommandLineMailingListEntry : public BaseMailingListEntry
{
private:
    bool GetALine( const char *prompt, char *szBuffer )
    {
        puts(prompt);
        gets(szBuffer);

        // Remove trailing carriage return
        szBuffer[strlen(szBuffer)-1] = 0;

        if ( strlen(szBuffer) )
            return true;
        return false;
    }
    bool GetAnEntry()
    {
        char szBuffer[ 80 ];
        if ( GetALine( "Enter the last name of the person: ",
szBuffer ) != true )
            return false;
        setLastName( szBuffer );
        GetALine("Enter the first name of the person: ",
szBuffer );

setFirstName( szBuffer );
        GetALine("Enter the first address line: ", szBuffer );
        setAddress1(szBuffer);
        GetALine("Enter the second address line: ", szBuffer );
        setAddress2(szBuffer);
        GetALine("Enter the city: ", szBuffer );
        setCity(szBuffer);
        GetALine("Enter the state: ", szBuffer);
        setState(szBuffer);
        GetALine("Enter the zip code: ", szBuffer );
        setZipCode( szBuffer);

        return true;
    }

public:
    CommandLineMailingListEntry() {

    }

    virtual bool First(void)
    {
        printf("Enter the first name for the mailing list:\n");
        return GetAnEntry();
    }
    virtual bool Next(void)
```

```
        {
            printf("Enter the next name for the mailing list:\n");
            return GetAnEntry();
        }
    };
```

Testing the Mailing-List Application

After you create a class, it is important to create a test driver that not only ensures that your code is correct, but also shows people how to use your code. The following steps show you how:

1. In the code editor of your choice, reopen the source file to hold the code for your test program.

In this example, I named the test program ch02.cpp.

2. Type the code from Listing 2-4 into your file, substituting your own names for the italicized constants, variables, and filenames.

A more efficient approach is to copy the code from the source file on this book's companion Web site.

LISTING 2-4: THE MAILING-LIST TEST PROGRAM

```
void ProcessEntries( BaseMailingListEntry *pEntry )
{
    bool not_done = pEntry->First();
    while ( not_done )
    {
        // Do something with the entry here.

        // Get the next one
        not_done = pEntry->Next();
    }
}
int main(int argc, char **argv)
{
    int choice = 0;

    printf("Enter 1 to use a file-based mailing list\n");
    printf("Enter 2 to enter data from the command line\n");
    scanf("%d", &choice );

    if ( choice == 1 )
    {
        char szBuffer[ 256 ];
        printf("Enter the file name: ");
        gets(szBuffer);
        FileMailingListEntry fmle(szBuffer);
        ProcessEntries( &fmle );
    }
```

(continued)

LISTING 2-4 *(continued)*

```
else
    if ( choice == 2 )
    {
        CommandLineMailingListEntry cmle;
        ProcessEntries( &cmle );
    }
    else
        printf("Invalid option\n");

    return 0;
}
```

The main function for the driver really isn't very busy — all it's doing is creating whichever type of object you want to use. The ProcessEntries function is the fascinating one because it is a function that is working on a class type that doesn't do anything — it has no idea which type of mailing-list entry object it is processing..Rather, it works from a pointer to the base class. If you run this program, you will find that it works as advertised, as you can see in Listing 2-5.

You could likewise create a file containing all entries that we just typed into the various fields above to

enter those fields into the system. You can do all of this without changing a single line of the ProcessEntries function! This is the power of pure virtual functions, and thus the power of abstraction.

 When you create a set of classes that are all doing the same general thing, look for the common elements of the class and abstract them into a common base class. Then you can build on that common base in the future, more easily creating new versions of the classes as the need arises.

LISTING 2-5: THE MAILING-LIST PROGRAM IN OPERATION

```
Enter 1 to use a file-based mailing list
Enter 2 to enter data from the command line
2
Enter the first name for the mailing list:
Enter the last name of the person: Telles
Enter the first name of the person: Matt
Enter the first address line: 10 Main St
Enter the second address line:
Enter the city: Anytown
Enter the state: NY
Enter the zip code: 11518
Enter the next name for the mailing list:
Enter the last name of the person:
```

Technique 3

Customizing a Class with Virtual Functions

*P*olymorphism (from the Greek for "having many forms") is what happens when you assign different meanings to a symbol or operator in different contexts. All well and good — but what does it mean to us as C++ programmers?

Granted, the pure virtual function in C++ (discussed in Technique 2) is very useful, but C++ gives us an additional edge: The programmer can override *only selected pieces of a class* without forcing us to override the entire class. Although a pure virtual function requires the programmer to implement functionality, a virtual function allows you to override that functionality only if you wish to, which is an important distinction.

Allowing the programmer to customize a class by changing small parts of the functionality makes C++ the fastest development language. You should seriously consider making the individual functions in your classes virtual whenever possible. That way the next developer can modify the functionality with a minimum of fuss.

Small changes to the derived class are called virtual functions — in effect, they allow a derived class to override the functionality in a base class without making you tinker with the base class. You can use this capability to define a given class's default functionality, while still letting end users of the class fine-tune that functionality for their own purposes. This approach might be used for error handling, or to change the way a given class handles printing, or just about anything else. In the next section, I show you how you can customize a class, using virtual functions to change the behavior of a base-class method at run-time.

Customizing a Class with Polymorphism

In order to understand how base classes can be customized using the polymorphic ability offered by virtual functions, let's look at a simple example of customizing a base class in C++.

1. **In the code editor of your choice, create a new file to hold the code for the implementation of the source file.**

   In this example, the file is named ch03.cpp, although you can use whatever you choose.

2. **Type the code from Listing 3-1 into your file, substituting your own names for the italicized constants, variables, and filenames.**

   Better yet, copy the code from the source file on this book's companion Web site.

LISTING 3-1: THE VIRTUAL FUNCTION BASE-CLASS SOURCE CODE

```cpp
#include <string>
#include <stdio.h>

class Fruit
{
public:
    Fruit()
    {
    }

    virtual ~Fruit()
    {
        printf("Deleting a fruit\n");
    }

    virtual std::string Color()
    {
        return "Unknown";
    }

    void Print()
    {
        printf("My color is: %s\n",
        Color().c_str() );
    }
};
```

```cpp
class Orange : public Fruit
{
public:
    Orange()
    {
    }
    virtual std::string Color()
    {
        return "Orange";
    }
};

class Apple : public Fruit
{
public:
    Apple()
    {
    }

    virtual std::string Color()
    {
        return "Reddish";
    }
};

class Grape : public Fruit
{
public:
    Grape()
    {
    }

    virtual std::string Color()
    {
        return "Red";
    }
};

class GreenGrape : public Grape
{
public:
    GreenGrape()
    {
    }

    virtual std::string Color()
    {
        return "Green";
    }
};
```

Testing the Virtual Function Code

Now you should test the code. The following steps show you how:

1. **Open the `ch03.cpp` source file in your favorite source-code editor and add the code in Listing 3-2 to the bottom of the file.**

LISTING 3-2: THE MAIN DRIVER FOR THE VIRTUAL FUNCTION CODE

```
int main(int argc, char **argv)
{
    // Create some fruits
    Apple a;
    Grape g;
    GreenGrape gg;
    Orange o;
    // Show the colors.
    a.Print();
    g.Print()
    gg.Print();
    o.Print();
    // Now do it indirectly
    Fruit *f = NULL;
    f = new Apple();
    f->Print();                         →1
    delete f;
    f = new GreenGrape();
    f->Print();                         →2
    delete f;
}
```

2. **Save the source code in your source-code editor.**

    There are a few interesting things to note in this example. For one thing, you can see how the base class calls the overridden methods without having to "know" about them (see the lines marked →1 and →2). What does this magic is a lookup table for virtual functions (often called the *v-table*) that contains pointers to all the methods within the class. This table is not visible in your code, it is automatically generated by the C++

compiler while generating the machine code for your application. When the linker finds a call to a method that is declared as `virtual`, it uses the lookup table to resolve that method at run-time, rather than at compile-time. For non-virtual methods, of course, the code is much simpler and can be determined at compile-time instead. This means that virtual functions do have some overhead (in terms of memory requirements and code speed) — so if you aren't going to use them in your code, don't declare things as `virtual`. It might seem counter-intuitive to define virtual functions in your code if you are not going to use them, but this is not really the case. In many cases, you can see future uses for the base class that will require that you allow the future developer to override functionality to add new capabilities to the derived class.

3. **Save the source code as a file in the code editor, and then close the editor application.**

4. **Compile the source code with your favorite compiler on your favorite operating system.**

5. **Run the program on your favorite operating-system console.**

If you have done everything properly, you should see the output shown below on the console window:

```
The color of the fruit is: Apple
The color of the fruit is: Red
The color of the fruit is: Green
The color of the fruit is: Orange
The color of the fruit is: Apple
Deleting a fruit
The color of the fruit is: Green
Deleting a fruit
Deleting a fruit
Deleting a fruit
Deleting a fruit
Deleting a fruit
```

As you can see, the direct calls to the code work fine. In addition, you can see that the code that uses a base-class pointer to access the functionality in the derived classes does call the proper overridden virtual methods. This leaves us with only one question remaining, which is how the derived class destructors are invoked and in what order. Let's take a look at that last virtual method, left undiscussed to this point—the virtual destructor in the base Fruit class.

Why Do the Destructors Work?

The interesting thing here is that the destructor for the base class is always called. Because the destructor is declared as virtual, the destructor chains upward through the destructors for the other classes that are derived from the base class. If we created destructors for each derived class, and printed out the results, then if you created a new PurpleGrape GreenGrape class, for example, that was derived from Grape, you would see output that looked like this:

```
PurpleGrape destructing
Grape destructing
Deleting a fruit
```

This output would be shown from the line in which we deleted the PurpleGrapeGreenGrape object. This *chaining* effect allows us to allocate data at each stage of the inheritance tree — while still ensuring that the data is cleaned up appropriately for each level of destructor. It also suggests the following maxim for writing code for classes from which other classes can be derived:

 If you ever expect anyone to derive a class from one you implement, make the destructor for the class virtual, and all manipulation methods virtual as well.

Notice also that the virtual table for a base class can be affected by every class derived from it (as we can see by the GreenGrape class). When I invoke the Print method on a Fruit object that was created as a Grape-derived GreenGrape class, the method is invoked at the Grape class level. This means you can have as many levels of inheritance as you like. As you can see, the virtual-method functionality in C++ is extremely powerful.

To recap, here is the hierarchy for calling the correct Print method when a GreenGrape object is passed to a function that accepts a Fruit object:

1. Fruit::Print is invoked.

2. The compiler looks at the virtual function table (v-table) and finds the entry for the Print method.

3. The method is resolved to be the GreenGrape:: Print method.

4. The GreenGrape::Print method is called.

Technique 4

Inheriting Data and Functionality

Save Time By

- Defining multiple inheritance
- Implementing a configuration file class
- Testing a configuration file class
- Delaying construction
- Error handling with multiple inheritance

In general, the single greatest bit of functionality that C++ has to offer is *inheritance* — the transfer of characteristics from a base class to its derived classes. Inheritance is the ability to derive a new class from one or more existing base classes. In addition to saving some coding labor, the inheritance feature in C++ has many great uses; you can extend, customize, or even limit existing functionality. This Technique looks at inheritance and shows you how to use *multiple inheritance* — a handy (but little-known) capability that combines the best of several classes into a single class for the end user.

To really understand what's going on here, you have to understand something about the way that C++ compilers implement inheritance — and how the language takes advantage of this approach.

Each C++ class contains three sections, each with its own purpose:

- **Storage for the data that belongs to the class:** Every class needs data to work with, and this section of the class keeps the data handy.

- **Jump tables:** These store the static methods of the class so the compiler can generate efficient instructions for calling the internal methods of the class.

- **One optional v-table for virtual methods:** If a class provides no inheritance, there can be an optional v-table, which contains the addresses of any virtual methods in the class. There will never be more than a single virtual table per class, because that table contains the pointers to all of the virtual methods in the class.

 If a virtual method is overridden in a derived class, there's still only one v-table — and it shows the address of the method that belongs to the derived class rather than to the base class. The static method areas repeat for each class.

Okay, but why does inheritance work? Because the compiler generates a "stack" of data, followed by a "stack" of methods, it is no problem at all to implement any number of levels of inheritance. The levels of inheritance define the order of the "stacks." If a class is derived from classes A, B, and C, you will see the stack of methods for A, followed by the ones for B, followed by the ones for C. This way, the compiler can easily convert the derived class into any of its base classes just by selecting a point in the stack to start from. In addition, because you can inherit data from classes that are themselves inheriting from other classes, the whole process just creates a strata of data and methods. This is a good thing, because it means that the class structure easily lends itself to conversions from base class to the derived class.

 The capability to extract pieces of functionality and save them into individual classes makes C++ an amazingly powerful language. If you identify all the individual pieces of functionality in your code and put them in their own base classes, you can quickly and easily build on that functionality to extend your application.

Implementing a ConfigurationFile Class

For the purposes of this example, assume that you want to implement a configuration file class. This class will allow you to store configuration information for your application in an external file and access it in a consistent manner throughout your program source code. I'm just going to explore the idea of creating a single functional class out of "mix-in" classes that do one thing very well and then move on. (As *M*A*S*H* would say, "Thank you, Doctor Winchester.")

When you think about it, configuration files have two basic sets of functionality — a set of properties (representing name and value pairs) and a file manager (which reads and writes those pairs to and from disk). For it all to work right, you must implement the functionality for your class in exactly that way: first the properties, then their management. You should have one base class that implements the property management, and another one that works with the disk file itself.

So, here's how to implement the class:

1. **In the code editor of your choice, create a new file to hold the code for the implementation of the source file.**

In this example, the file is named ch04.cpp, although you can use whatever name you choose.

2. **Type the code from Listing 4-1 into your file, substituting your own names for the italicized constants, variables, and filenames.**

Better yet, copy the code from the source file on this book's companion Web site.

LISTING 4-1: THE PROPERTIES SOURCE CODE.

```cpp
#include <string>
#include <stdio.h>
#include <vector>

class Properties
{
private:
    struct _Prop
    {
        public:
            std::string name;
            std::string value;
        public:
            _Prop operator=(const _Prop&
            aCopy )
            {
                name = aCopy.name;
                value = aCopy.value;
                return *this;
            }

    };

    std::vector< _Prop > sProps;
public:
    Properties(void)
    {
    }
    virtual ~Properties()                    → 1

    {
    }
    Properties( const Properties& aCopy )
    {
        std::vector< _Prop >::const_iterator
        iter;
```

```
    for ( iter = aCopy.sProps.begin();
    iter != aCopy.sProps.end(); ++iter )
        sProps.insert( sProps.end(),
        (*iter) );
}

int NumProperties( void )
{
    return (int)sProps.size();
}
bool GetProperty( int idx, std::string&
name, std::string& value )
{
    if ( idx < 0 || idx >=
    NumProperties() )
        return false;
    name = sProps[idx].name;
    value = sProps[idx].value;
    return true;
}
void AddProperty( const std::string&
name, const std::string& value )
{
    _Prop p;
    p.name = name;
    p.value = value;
    sProps.insert( sProps.end(), p );
}
};
```

Note that this class makes use of the Standard Template Library (STL), which I show you in greater detail in Part V of this book. For now, you can simply assume that the vector class implements a generic array that can be expanded. The vector class requires no minimum number of elements, and can be expanded as far as memory permits.

Our property class will form the basis for a series of property types, all of which could handle different types of properties. In addition, this class can be used as a base for other classes, which need the ability to store property information.

There is really no magic here; you can see that the class simply holds onto property sets and can either add them or give them back to the caller. Note, however, that you have implemented a virtual destructor (see ➜ **1**) for the class — even though nothing in the class needs to be

destroyed just yet. There's no real way of knowing down the line whether this will always be true, so you may as well assume that the destructor will need to do its cleanup work at some point. You are building this class intentionally as a base class for inheritance, however, so it only makes sense to make the destructor virtual. If your destructor is virtual, all derived classes will call the base class destructor as the last part of the destruction process, insuring that all allocated memory is freed.

The next step is to implement the class that manages the file part of the system. For purposes of space, only the write segment of the class is shown in Listing 4-2. However, it would be fairly trivial to implement a ReadAPair method that would retrieve data from a file.

3. **Using your code editor, add the code from Listing 4-2 to your source-code file.**

In this case, we called the file ch04.cpp.

LISTING 4-2: THE SAVEPAIRS CLASS

```
class SavePairs
{
    FILE *fpIn;
public:
    SavePairs( void )
    {
        fpIn = NULL;
    }
    SavePairs( const char *strName )
    {
        fpIn = fopen( strName, "w" );
    }
    virtual ~SavePairs()
    {
        if ( fpIn )
            fclose(fpIn);
    }
    void SaveAPair( std::string name,
    std::string value )
    {
        if ( fpIn )
            fprintf(fpIn, "%s=%s\n",
            name.c_str(), value.c_str());
    }
};
```

Once again, you implement a virtual destructor for your class because it's intended as a base class for inheritance; no point getting specific about what to destroy just yet. You do, however, have a real use for the destructor, because the file pointer that opens in the constructor has to have a corresponding closing instruction (`fclose`) to free the memory and flush the file to disk.

With the virtual destructor in place, the only thing left to do is to combine these two fairly useful classes into a single class that includes the functionality of both and provides a cohesive interface to the end user of the class. We'll call this combined class `ConfigurationFile`.

4. **Using your code editor, add the code in Listing 4-3 to your source-code file.**

LISTING 4-3: THE CONFIGURATIONFILE CLASS

```
class ConfigurationFile : public Properties,
    public SavePairs

{
public:
    ConfigurationFile(void)              ➜ 2
        : SavePairs()
    {
    }
    ConfigurationFile(const char
    *strFileName)                        ➜ 3
        : SavePairs(strFileName)
    {
    }

    virtual ~ConfigurationFile()
    {
        DoSave();
    }

    bool DoSave()                        ➜ 4

    {
        std::string name;
        std::string value;

        for (int i=0; i<NumProperties(); ++i)
        {
            if ( GetProperty( i, name, value
```

```
        ) )
                SaveAPair( name, value );
        }

        return true;
    }
};
```

5. **Save the source code in the code editor.**

There really isn't a lot of code here, but there is a lot to pay attention to. First of all, notice the `DoSave` method. This method, which flushes all of the pairs of property data to disk (see ➜ **4**), calls methods in both of our base classes. You will notice that you don't have to do anything important to get at these methods, they are just a built-in part of the class itself.

Probably the most crucial part of Listing 4-3 is actually a line by itself in one of the constructors. Note the line marked ➜ **3**.

This line is one of the more powerful constructs in C++. Because the `ConfigurationFile` class is derived from the `SavePairs` class, it will automatically call the constructor for the `SavePairs` class before it invokes its own constructor code. Because this is necessary, the base class has to be properly constructed before you can work with the derived class. The compiler calls the default constructor unless you tell it to do otherwise. In this case, you do not want it to call the default constructor (see ➜ **2**), because that would create a `SavePairs` object that had no filename (because it is not assigned in the constructor) and therefore did not open our property file. We want the entire thing to be completely automatic, so we invoke the proper form of the constructor before our `ConfigurationFile` constructor even starts. That generates a little programming peace of mind: As soon as you enter the code for the inherited class, you can be assured that all setup work has been done — which (in this case) also means the file is open and ready to be written to.

Testing the ConfigurationFile Class

After you create a class, create a test driver that not only ensures that your code is correct, but also shows people how to use your code.

1. **In the code editor of your choice, reopen the source file to hold the code for your test program.**

In this example, I named the test program `ch04.cpp`. You could, of course, call this program anything you wanted, since filenames are only human-readable strings. The compiler does not care what you call your file.

2. **Type the code from Listing 4-4 into your file.**

Or better yet, copy the code from the source file on this book's companion Web site.

LISTING 4-4: THE CONFIGURATIONFILE TEST PROGRAM

```
int main(int argc, char **argv)
{
    ConfigurationFile cf("test.dat");
    cf.AddProperty( "Name", "Matt" );
    cf.AddProperty( "Address", "1000 Main
    St" );

}
```

3. **Save the code in the source-code file created in your editor, and then close the editor application.**

4. **Compile the source code with your favorite compiler on your favorite operating system.**

5. **Run the program on your favorite operating-system console.**

If you've done everything properly, you should see the following output from the program on the console window:

```
$ ./a.exe

$ cat test.dat
Name=Matt
Address=1000 Main St
```

As you can see, the configuration file was properly saved to the output file.

Delayed Construction

Although the constructor for a class is all wonderful and good, it does bring up an interesting point. What if something goes wrong in the construction process and you need to signal the user? You have two ways to approach this situation; both have their positives and negatives:

✔ **You can throw an exception.** In general, however, I wouldn't. Throwing exceptions is an option I discuss later, in Technique 53 — but doing so is rarely a good idea. Your users are really not expecting a constructor to throw an exception. Worse, an exception might leave the object in some ambiguous state, where it's unclear whether the constructor has finished running. If you do choose this route, you should also make sure that all values are initialized before you do anything that might generate an exception. (For example, what happens if you throw an exception in a base-class constructor? The error would be propagated up to the main program. This would be very confusing to the user, who wouldn't even know where the error was coming from.)

✔ **You can delay any work that might create an error until later in the processing of the object.** This option is usually more valuable and is worth further exploration.

Let's say, for example, that you are going to open a file in your constructor. The file-opening process could certainly fail, for any number of reasons. One way to handle this error is to check for it, but this might be confusing to the end user, because they would not understand where the file was being opened in the first place and why it failed to open properly. In cases like this, instead of a constructor that looks like this . . .

```
FileOpener::FileOpener( const char
  *strFileName)
{
    fpIn = fopen(strFileName, "r");
}
```

. . . you might instead choose to do the following:

```
FileOpener::FileOpener( const char
  *strFileName)
{
    // Hold onto the file name for later
    use.
    sFileName  = strFileName;
    bIsOpen    = false;
}
bool FileOpener::OpenFile()              → 5
{
    if ( !bIsOpen )
    {
        fpIn = fopen(sFileName.c_str(),
        "r");
        if ( fpIn != NULL )
            bIsOpen = true;
    }
    return bIsOpen;
}
```

Because we cannot return an error from a constructor directly, we break the process into two pieces. The first piece assigns the member variables to the values that the user passed in. There is no way that an error can occur in this process, so the object will be properly constructed. In the OpenFile method (→ 5 in the above listing), we then try to open the file, and indicate the status as the return value of the method.

Then, when you tell your code to actually read from the file, you would do something like this:

```
bool FileOpener::SomeMethod()
{
    if ( OpenFile() )
    {
        // Continue with processing
```

```
    }
    else
        // Generate an error
        return false;
}
```

The advantage to this approach is that you can wait until you absolutely have to before you actually open the file that the class operates on. Doing so means you don't have file overhead every time you construct an object — and you don't have to worry about closing the darn thing if it was never opened. The advantage of delaying the construction is that you can wait until the data is actually needed before doing the time and memory expensive operation of file input and output.

With a little closer look back at the SavePairs class (Listing 4-2), you can see a very serious error lurking there. (Just for practice, take a moment to go back over the class and look for what's missing.)

Do you see it? Imagine that you have an object of type SavePairs, for an example. Now you can make a copy of that object by assigning it to another object of the SavePairs class, or by passing it by value into a method like this:

```
DoSave( SavePairs obj );
```

When you make the above function call, you are making a copy of the obj object by invoking the copy constructor for the class. Now, because you didn't *create* a copy constructor, you have a serious problem. Why? A copy is a bitwise copy of *all elements in the class*. When a copy is made of the FILE pointer in the class, it means you now have two pointers pointing to the same block of memory. Uh-oh. Because you will destroy that memory in the destructor for the class (by calling fclose), the code frees up the same block of memory twice. This is a classic problem that you need to solve whenever you are allocating memory in a class. In this case, you really want to be able to copy the pointer without closing it in the copy. So, what you really need to do is keep track of whether the pointer in question is a copy or an original. To do so, you could rewrite the class as in Listing 4-5:

LISTING 4-5: THE REVISED SAVEPAIRS CLASS

```
class SavePairs
{
    FILE *fpIn;
    bool  bIsACopy;
public:
    SavePairs( void )
    {
        fpIn = NULL;
        bIsACopy = false;
    }
    SavePairs( const char *strName )
    {
        fpIn = fopen( strName, "w" );
        bIsACopy = false;
    }
    SavePairs( const SavePairs& aCopy )
    {
        fpIn = aCopy.fpIn;
        bIsACopy = true;
    }
    virtual ~SavePairs()
    {
        if ( fpIn && !bIsACopy )
            fclose(fpIn);
    }
    void SaveAPair( std::string name,
    std::string value )
    {
        if ( fpIn )
            fprintf(fpIn, "%s=%s\n",
            name.c_str(), value.c_str());
    }
};
```

This code in Listing 4-5 has the advantage of working correctly no matter how it is handled. If you pass a pointer into the file, the code will make a copy of it and not delete it. If you use the original of the file pointer, it will be properly deleted, not duplicated.

This is an improvement. But does this code really fix all possible problems? The answer, of course, is no. Imagine the following scenario:

1. **Create a** SavePairs **object.**

2. **Copy the object by calling the** copy **constructor with a new object.**

3. **Delete the original** SavePairs **object.**

4. **Invoke a method on the copy that uses the file pointer.**

What happens in this scenario? Nothing good, you can be sure. The problem occurs when the last step is hit, and the copied file pointer is used. The original pointer has been deleted, so the copy is pointing at junk. Bad things happen — and your program likely crashes.

A joke that runs around the Internet compares various programming languages in terms of shooting yourself in the foot. The entire joke is easy enough to find, but the part that applies to this subject looks something like this:

C: You shoot yourself in the foot.

C++: You accidentally create a dozen instances of yourself and shoot them all in the foot. Providing emergency assistance is impossible because you can't tell which instances are bitwise copies and which are just pointing at others, saying, "That's me over there."

Many programmers find the joke is too true to be amusing. C++ gives you the (metaphorical) ability to blow off your foot any time you try to compile. There are so many things to think about, and so many possibilities to consider.

 The best way to avoid the disasters of the past is to plan for them in the future. This is nowhere more true than when you're working with the basic building blocks of the system, constructors and destructors. If you do not do the proper groundwork to make sure that your class is as safe as possible, you will pay for it in the long run — each and every time. Make sure that you always implement virtual destructors and check for all copies of your objects in your code. Doing so will make your code cleaner (dare I say "bulletproof"?) and eliminate problems of this sort that would otherwise naturally crop up later.

Technique 5

Separating Rules and Data from Code

Save Time By

- ✔ Using encapsulation to separate rules and data from code
- ✔ Building a data-validation class
- ✔ Testing the data-validation class

One of the biggest problems in the software-development world is maintaining code that we did not design or implement in the first place. Often the hardest thing to do in such cases is to figure out exactly how the code was meant to work. Usually, there is copious documentation that tells you what the code is doing (or what the original programmer *thought* was going on), but very rarely does it tell you why.

The reason is that the business rules and the data that implement those rules are usually embedded somewhere in the code. Hard-coded dates, values — even user names and passwords — can be hidden deep inside the code base. Wouldn't it be nice if there was some way to extract all of that data and those business rules and put them in one place? This really does sound like a case for encapsulation, now doesn't it? Of course it does. As I discuss in Technique 1, encapsulation allows us to insulate the user from the implementation of things. That statement is ambiguous and means quite a few things, so to clarify, let me show you a couple of examples. First, consider the case of the business rule.

When you are creating code for a software project, you must often consider rules that apply across the entire business — such as the allowable number of departments in an accounting database, or perhaps a calculation to determine the maximum amount of a pay raise for a given employee. These rules appear in the form of code snippets scattered across the entire project, residing in different files and forms. When the next project comes along, they are often duplicated, modified, or abandoned. The problem with this approach is that it becomes harder and harder to keep track of what the rules are and what they mean.

Assume, for the moment, that you have to implement some code that checks for dates in the system. (Okay, a date isn't strictly a business rule per se, but it makes a handy example.) To run the check, you could try scattering some code around the entire system to check for leap years, date validity, and so forth, but that would be inefficient and wasteful. Here's why that solution is no solution at all:

Once upon a time, there was a project being done at a very large company. A software audit showed at least five different routines (functions, macros, and inline code) that computed whether a given year was a leap year. This was pretty surprising — but even more surprising was that of those five routines, three were actually wrong. If a bug occurred while the system was calculating whether the current year was a leap year, did the programmer have any idea where to look to solve the problem? Of course not.

In this example, despite the risk of bugs, you still have to determine whether a given date is valid — and whether the given year is a leap year. Your first two basic tasks are to set appropriate defaults for the date, and make sure you can retrieve all the components of the date. The same approach works for any business-rule encapsulation. First, you have to know the pieces of the puzzle that go into the calculations. That way, anyone looking at the code will know exactly what he or she needs to supply. There should be no "hidden" data unless it's being retrieved from an external source. The code should be *plug-and-play;* you should be able to take it from one project to another with minimal changes.

Of course, it's often impossible to completely remove application code from business rules. But that really shouldn't be your goal when you're writing business objects. Instead, you should worry about how those objects are going to be used.

 When you separate the support code from the business rule that it supports, you separate the bugs that can occur into two types: physical errors and logical errors. This alone saves time in tracking down problems. A logical error won't crash a program, but it will cause grief in other ways. A physical error isn't likely to cause you to incorrectly generate checks for billions, but it will crash your application and annoy your users.

Your object should be portable; it is going to be used in multiple projects to support the "date rule." You want your dates to be valid, and you want to be able to extract the components of the date in any project

that might need that data. At the same time, you don't want to give people more than they need, so you aren't going to bother supporting date math, such as calculations for adding days or years to a given date.

 This is another important tip when designing classes for use in C++, whether they are business objects or full-blown application objects. Always keep the code down to a minimum; only include what people need. Do not simply add methods to a class for the sheer joy of adding them. If you bury people in code, they will look for something simpler. There is a common acronym for this in the engineering community, known as "KISS": Keep It Simple, Stupid.

 Always bear the error-handling process in mind when you write reusable objects. Your code is more reusable if it returns error messages instead of throwing exceptions or logging errors to some external source. The reason for this advantage is simple: If you require people to do more than check the return value of a method or function in your code, you force them to do a lot of work that they might not otherwise have to do. People resist doing extra work; they'll avoid your code and use something simpler. (Once again, the KISS principle in action.)

The cDate Class

In order to best encapsulate all of the date information in your program, it is easiest to create a single class that manages date storage, manipulation, and output. In this section, we create a class to do all of that, and call it cDate (for *date class*, of course). With a date class, we are removing all of the rules and algorithms for manipulating dates, such as leap year calculations, date math, and day of week calculations, and moving them into a single place. In addition, we move the date storage, such as how the day, month, and year elements are stored, into one area that the user does not need to be concerned about.

1. **In the code editor of your choice, create a new file to hold the code for the implementation of your source file.**

In this example, that file is named ch05.cpp, although you can use whatever you choose.

2. **Type the code from Listing 5-1 into your file.**

Better yet, copy the code from the source file on this book's companion Web site.

LISTING 5-1: THE cDATE CLASS

```cpp
#include <string>
#include <stdio.h>
#include <time.h>

class cDate
{
private:
    int  MonthNo;
    int  DayOfMonth;
    int  DayOfWeek;
    long YearNo;
protected:
    void GetTodaysDate()
    {
        // First, get the data
        time_t t;
        time(&t);
        struct tm *tmPtr = localtime(&t);

        // Now, store the pieces we care about
        MonthNo = tmPtr->tm_mon;
        YearNo  = tmPtr->tm_year + 1900;
        DayOfMonth = tmPtr->tm_mday;
        DayOfWeek = tmPtr->tm_wday;
    }


    int ComputeDayOfTheWeek() // returns day of week
    {
        int sum_calc;
        int cent_off, year_off, month_off, day_off;
        int year_end;

        year_end = YearNo % 100;     // year in century

// The following calculation calculates offsets for the
// century, year, month, and day to find the name of the
// weekday.
        cent_off = ((39 - (YearNo/100)) % 4 ) * 2;
        year_off = year_end + year_end/4;
```

```
    if (MonthNo == 1)              // January
    {
        month_off = 0;
        if (((YearNo%4) == 0) && ((year_end !=0) ||
        ((YearNo%400) == 0)))
            year_off--;        // leap year
    }
    else if (MonthNo == 2)         // February
    {
        month_off = 3;
        if (((YearNo%4) == 0) && ((year_end !=0) ||
        ((YearNo%400) == 0)))
            year_off--;        // leap year
    }
    else if ((MonthNo == 3) || (MonthNo == 11))
        month_off = 3;
    else if ((MonthNo == 4) || (MonthNo == 7))
        month_off = 6;
    else if (MonthNo == 5)                        // May
        month_off = 1;
    else if (MonthNo == 6)                        // June
        month_off = 4;
    else if (MonthNo == 8)                        // August
        month_off = 2;
    else if ((MonthNo == 9) || (MonthNo == 12))
        month_off = 5;
    else if (MonthNo == 10)                       // October
        month_off = 0;

    day_off = DayOfMonth % 7;    // day offset

    sum_calc = (cent_off + year_off + month_off + day_off) % 7;

    // Using the calculated number, the remainder gives the day
    // of the week
    sum_calc %= 7;

    return sum_calc;

}

int MonthDays( int month, long year )
{
    if ( month < 0 || month > 11 )
        return 0;

    int days[]={31,28,31,30,31,30,31,31,30,31,30,31 };
    int nDays = days[ month ];
```

(continued)

LISTING 5-1 *(continued)*

```
            if ( IsLeapYear( year ) && month == 1)
                nDays ++;
            return nDays;
        }


    public:
        cDate(void)
        {
            // Get today's date
            GetTodaysDate();
        }
        cDate( int day, int month, long year )
        {
            if ( IsValidDate( day, month, year ) )
            {
                MonthNo = month;
                DayOfMonth = day;
                YearNo = year;
                DayOfWeek = ComputeDayOfTheWeek();
            }
        }
        cDate( const cDate& aCopy )
        {
            YearNo = aCopy.YearNo;
            MonthNo  = aCopy.MonthNo;
            DayOfMonth = aCopy.DayOfMonth;
            DayOfWeek = aCopy.DayOfWeek;
        }

        // Accessors
        int Month() { return MonthNo; };
        long Year() { return YearNo; };
        int Day()   { return DayOfMonth; };
        int DayOfTheWeek() { return DayOfWeek; };
        bool IsValidDate(int day, int month, long year);
        bool IsLeapYear( long year );
    };
```

3. In your code editor, add the code in Listing 5-2 to the source-code file for your application. Alternatively, you could create a new file called date.cpp to store all of this information separately.

These are the non-inline methods for the class. You can put them in the same file as your original source code, or create a new source file and add them to it.

LISTING 5-2: NON-INLINE METHODS

```
bool cDate::IsValidDate( int day, int month, long year )
{
    // Is the month valid?
    if ( month < 0 || month > 11 )
        return false;
    // Is the year valid?
    if ( year < 0 || year > 9999 )
        return false;
    // Is the number of days valid for this month/year?
    if ( day < 0 || day > MonthDays(month, year) )
        return false;

    // Must be ok
    return true;
}

bool cDate::IsLeapYear( long year )
{
    int year_end = year % 100;                        // year in century
    if (((year%4) == 0) && ((year_end !=0) || ((year%400) == 0)))
        return true;
    return false;
}
```

Putting this code into a single object and sharing that code among various projects that might need this functionality offers some obvious advantages:

- ✔ If the code needs to be changed, for example, to account for some bug in the leap year calculation, this change can all be done in one place.

- ✔ More importantly, if changes are made to implement a newer, faster way to calculate the leap year or the day of the week, or even to add functionality, none of those changes affect the calling programs in the least. They will still work with the interface as it stands now.

Testing the cDate Class

After you create a class, it is important to create a test driver — doing so not only ensures that your code is correct, but also shows people how to use your code.

1. **In the code editor of your choice, reopen the source file to hold the code for your test program.**

In this example, I named the test program `ch1_5.cpp`.

2. **Type the code from Listing 5-3 into your file.**

Better yet, copy the code from the source file on this book's companion Web site.

LISTING 5-3: THE cDATE CLASS TEST PROGRAM

```
#include <iostream>
using namespace std;

int main(int argc, char **argv)
{
    // Do some testing. First, a valid date
    cDate d1(31, 11, 2004);
    // Now, an invalid one.
    cDate d2(31, 12, 2004);
    // Finally, let's just create a blank one.
    cDate d3;

    // Print them out
    cout << "D1: " << "Month: " << d1.Month() << " Day: " << d1.Day() << " Year: " << d1.Year()
    << endl;
    cout << "D2: " << "Month: " << d2.Month() << " Day: " << d2.Day() << " Year: " << d2.Year()
    << endl;
    cout << "D3: " << "Month: " << d3.Month() << " Day: " << d3.Day() << " Year: " << d3.Year()
    << endl;

    return 0;
}
```

3. Save the source code as a file in your code editor and close the editor application.

4. Compile the source code with your favorite compiler on your favorite operating system.

5. Run the program on your favorite operating system console.

If you have done everything properly, you should see the following output from the program on the console window:

```
$ ./a.exe
D1: Month: 11 Day: 31 Year: 2004
D2: Month: 2011708128 Day: -1 Year:
   2011671585
D3: Month: 8 Day: 7 Year: 2004
```

 Note that the numbers shown in the output may be different on your computer, because they are somewhat random. You should simply expect to see very invalid values.

This, then, is the advantage to working with object-oriented programming in C++: You can make changes "behind the scenes" without interfering with the work of others. You make it possible for people to get access to data and algorithms without having to struggle with how they're stored or implemented. Finally, you can fix or extend the implementations of your algorithms without requiring your users to change all their applications that use those algorithms.

Part II

Working with the Pre-Processor

The 5th Wave   By Rich Tennant

PC DESCENDING A STAIRCASE

"THE ARTIST WAS ALSO A PROGRAMMER AND EVIDENTLY PRODUCED SEVERAL VARIATIONS ON THIS THEME."

Technique 6
Handling Multiple Operating Systems

The problem with the "standard" C++ header files is that they are anything but standard. For example, on Microsoft Windows, the header file for containing all of the "standard" output functions is `stdio.h` — whereas on Unix, the header file is `unistd.h`. Imagine you're compiling a program that can be used on either Unix or Microsoft Windows. The code in all your files might look like this:

```
#ifdef WIN32
#include <stdio.h>
#else
#ifdef UNIX
#include <unistd.h>
#endif
#endif
```

This approach to coding is messy and inefficient: If you get a new compiler that implements the constants for the operating system differently, you will have to go through each and every file to update your code. As an alternative, you could simply include all the files in a single header file — but that would force you to include a lot of header files that you really don't need in many of your program files, which would increase the file bloat and could conceivably cause problems if you need to override some of the standard function names or types. Obviously, clutter is not a very good solution either way.

What if — instead of including the things you don't want and having to compile conditionally around them — you could include only the "right" files for a specific operating system in the first place? That solution would certainly be closer to ideal. Fortunately, the C++ pre-processor offers a perfect way to solve this problem. Read on.

Creating the Header File

In order to be able to conditionally include the pieces of the code we wish to use in our application, we will create a single header file that utilizes pre-compiler defined values to determine the files that are needed. The following steps show you how to create such a file:

1. **In the code editor of your choice, create a new file to hold the code for the source file of the technique.**

In this example, the file is named, `osdefines.h` although you can use whatever you choose. This file will contain the header information.

2. **Type the code from Listing 6-1 into your file, substituting your own names for the italicized constants, variables, and filenames.**

Better yet, copy the code from the source file on this book's companion Web site.

LISTING 6-1: THE HEADER FILE.

```
#ifndef _osdefines_h_
#define _osdefines_h_

// Remove the comment from the WIN32 define
   if you are
// developing on the Microsoft Windows plat-
   form. Remove
// the comment on the UNIX define if you are
   developing
// on the UNIX platform

#define WIN32
// #define UNIX

// Now, define the header files for the
   Windows platform
#ifdef WIN32
#define standard_io_header <stdio.h>
#endif

#ifdef UNIX
#define standard_io_header <unistd.h>
#endif

// Make sure SOMETHING is defined
#ifndef standard_io_header
#error "You must define either WIN32 or
   UNIX"
#endif

#endif // _osdefines_h
```

3. **Save the source code as a file in the code editor and close the code-editor application.**

Testing the Header File

After you create the class, you should create a test driver that not only ensures that your code is correct, but also shows people how to use your code.

Here I show you how to create a test driver that illustrates various kinds of input from the user, and shows how the class is intended to be used.

 Always make sure that you test your code in the scenario most likely for your end user.

1. **In the code editor of your choice, reopen the source file to hold the code for your test program.**

In this example, I named the test program `ch06.cpp`.

2. **Type the code from Listing 6-2 into your file.**

Better yet, copy the code from the source file on this book's companion Web site.

LISTING 2-2: THE MAIN PROGRAM

```
#include "osdefines.h"
#include standard_io_header

#define MAX_VALUES 100
#define STRING(A) #A
#define PASTE(A,B) (A##B)
#define MAKE_SAFE(s) (s==NULL? "NULL" : s )

int main(int argc, char **argv)
{
    int x = 100;

    // We can stringify a variable name
    printf("The value of %s is %d\n",
```

```
STRING(x), x );

 int y = 200;
 int xy = 0;

 // We can use a macro to create a new
    variable.
 PASTE(x,y) = x*y;

 printf("The value of x = %d\n", x );
 printf("The value of y = %d\n", y );

 // The problem is that we can't
    stringify pastes.
 printf("The value of %s = %d\n",
 STRING(PASTE(x,y)), xy );

 char *s1 = NULL;
 char *s2 = "Something";

 printf("String1 = %s\n", MAKE_SAFE(s1));
 printf("String2 = %s\n", MAKE_SAFE(s2));

 return 0;
}
```

3. Save the source file in your code editor and close the code-editor application.

4. Compile the file with your favorite compiler on your favorite operating system.

To verify that your header file will not work unless you define the operating system, comment out both the WIN32 and Unix lines in the `osdefines.h` file. **Try compiling it and you should see an error message like this one:**

```
$ gcc test.cpp
In file included from test.cpp:2:
osdefines.h:23:2: #error "You must define
   either WIN32 or UNIX"
test.cpp:3:10: #include expects "FILENAME"
   or <FILENAME>
```

As you can see, the compiler definitely knows that the operating system is not defined. The next step is to define one of the two constants, depending on the operating system of your choice. There are two different ways to define these constants. You can either put a #define statement at the top of the header file or you can pass the value into the compiler with the –D compile flag. Recompiling the program after this operation should result in no errors — and if that's the case, you know the proper header file is now being included!

 This technique is very easy to implement — and very powerful when you're working with multiple operating systems, compilers, or even libraries. Just keep all system-related data in one header file, and allow the pre-processor to do the rest of your work for you. It is also very valuable, because it allows you to give header files really meaningful names, rather than `stdio.h`. **What, exactly, is a stdio (an s-t-d-i-o?) anyway?**

7

Mastering the Evils of Asserts

Save Time By

- ✔ Defining the problems asserts can cause
- ✔ Compiling with asserts
- ✔ Fixing assert problems

It's hard to talk about the C++ pre-processor without talking about the `assert` macro. This particular macro is used to test a given condition — and, if the condition is not logically true, to print out an error message and exit the program.

Here's where you can get (ahem) assertive with the problem of testing for problems, so a quick look at asserts is in order, followed by a simple technique for using them.

The Assert Problem

The purpose of an `assert` statement is to check for a problem at run-time. `Assert` statements have value during the initial debugging and validation of code, but they have limited value once the program is out in the field. For this reason, you should put in enough assert statements to be sure that the tests of your system will reveal all of the potential problems that you should check for and handle at run-time. Let's look at a simple example of using an `assert` call in your program.

1. **In the code editor of your choice, create a new file to hold the code for the source file of the technique.**

In this example, the file is named `ch07.cpp`, although you can use whatever you choose. This file will contain the source code for our example.

2. **Type the code in Listing 7-1 into your file, substituting your own names for the italicized constants, variables, and filenames.**

Better yet, copy the code from the source file on this book's companion Web site.

LISTING 7-1: USING ASSERTS

```
#include "stdio.h"
#include "assert.h"

int main(int argc, char **argv)
{
    assert( argc > 1 );
    printf("Argument 1 = %s\n", argv[1] );
    return 0;
}
```

3. **Save the source-code file and close the code editor.**

4. **Compile the source file, using your favorite compiler on your favorite operating system.**

If you run this program with no arguments, you will find that it exits abnormally and displays the following error message:

```
$ ./a.exe
assertion "argc > 1" failed: file
    "ch07a.cpp", line 6
Aborted (core dumped)
```

As you can see, the assert macro was triggered properly, and exited the program, which is the expected behavior of the function when it fails. Of course, this isn't exactly what you would normally want the program to do when you fail to enter a value, but it does illustrate the source of the error.

 Crashing a program intentionally, no matter how appealing to the programmer, is no way to deal with the user and will cost you time and effort when dealing with customer support and technical debugging. Save yourself the time up front and deal with the problem correctly instead of aborting the application when an exceptional condition arises.

5. **Recompile the source file with your favorite compiler, using the NDEBUG definition on the command line.**

It is not simply that using an assert to exit a program is ugly. Well, okay, it is, but the worst part is that many compiler environments only define the assert macro when the program is compiled *in debugging mode*. In effect, the assert macro switches into non-operation (yep, off) when the program is compiled for optimized running. With the gcc compiler, you optimize things by compiling with the -DNDEBUG compiler switch. If you compile the program given here with that switch set, however, you get a very different set of output:

```
$ ./a.exe
Argument 1 = (null)
```

The above is the output when you run the program after compiling with the -DNDEBUG flag for the compiler. As you can see, it is very different from the case where the assert macro is enabled.

Note that there was no argument supplied to the program, so we are actually stepping all over memory at this point. Since the array of pointers is filled with the arguments to the application, we are restricted to the number of arguments passed in. If nothing is passed into the program, there will be nothing in the array of arguments, and the pointers in the argv array will be pointing at garbage. Fortunately, we didn't try to do anything with the pointer except print it out, but it could easily have caused a program crash of its own.

Imagine if this code had made it into a production system. The first time that an optimized (often called a "release") build was created, the program would crash as soon as the user ran it without giving the program any arguments on the command line. Obviously, this is not an optimal solution when you are working in the real world. In the next section, I show you how to address this problem.

Fixing the Assert Problem

Assert macros do have value — especially when you're tracking down particularly annoying problems. By littering your code liberally with asserts, you can track down conditions you did not expect. However, those same asserts won't let you simply ignore those pesky conditions you find. To fix the problem, the relevant portion of Listing 7-1 should be rewritten. The following step shows you how. (Note that we are leaving in the assert for debugging purposes — and handling the error appropriately at the same time.)

1. Modify the source code for the test application as in Listing 7-2.

In this case, we called the original source code file ch07.cpp.

LISTING 7-2: FIXING THE ASSERTS PROBLEM

```
#include "stdio.h"
#include "assert.h"

int main(int argc, char **argv)
{
    assert( argc > 1 );
    if ( argc > 1 )
        printf("Argument 1 = %s\n", argv[1]
    );
    return 0;
}
```

What is the difference here? Obviously, if you compile the program in debug (that is, non-optimized) mode and run it with no arguments, the assert is triggered and the program exits, kicking out an error statement as before. If you compile in optimized mode, however, the assert is skipped and the program tests to see whether there are enough arguments to process. If

not, the offending statement that would potentially crash the program is skipped. It's hard, and a little sad, to tell you how many programs were shipped into the world (over the last twenty years or so) containing functions like this:

```
int func( char *s)
{
assert(s != NULL);
strcpy( myBuffer, s);
}
```

This function is intended to copy an input string into a buffer that is supplied by the programmer. That buffer has a certain size, but we are not checking for the maximum allowable number of characters in the input string. If the number of characters coming in is bigger than the number of characters in the myBuffer array, it will cause problems.

As you can imagine, this causes a lot of problems in the real world, because memory that does not belong to the application is being used and assigned values. Asserts are very useful for defining test cases, trapping exceptional errors that you know *could* happen but shouldn't, and finding problems that you really didn't expect to see happen. The nicest thing about asserts is that after you find the problem that it indicates, generally you can use your debugger to figure out exactly what caused the problem — and usually the best approach is to use a stack-trace mechanism. In Technique 62, "Building Tracing into Your Applications," I show you how to build a mechanism like this into your application so that you can find problems like this at run-time.

 Always run your program through a complete test suite, testing for all possible asserts, in an optimized environment. That way, you know the assert calls won't hurt anything when you get the program into the real world.

Technique 8

Using const Instead of #define

Save Time By

- ✔ Comparing #define statements to const statements
- ✔ Using the const statement
- ✔ Understanding errors caused by the #define statement
- ✔ Resolving those errors

Throughout this book, I often use the #define statement to create macros and constant values for use in my programs. It's a useful approach — even so, there are enough downsides that the C++ standards group chose to create a new way to define constants in your application: the const statement. The const statement is used in the following manner:

```
const int MaxValues = 100;
```

If this looks familiar, it's a lot like the way I've been using the #define statement:

```
#define MAX_VALUES 100
```

The difference is that the const construct is defined at the compiler level, rather than at the pre-processor level. With const, the compiler can better optimize values, and can perform type-safe checking.

Here's an example. First, here's how the #define method works. Suppose I write a definition like this:

```
#define NoValues 0
```

and then write a C++ statement that says

```
char *sValues = NoValues;
```

The statement will compile (although some compilers may issue a warning about an unsafe conversion) because the NoValues declaration equates to a string value of NULL. So far, so good — but suppose I now change that value by defining the following (note that any non-null value would illustrate the problem the same way):

```
#define NoValues -99
```

The behavior of the sValues assignment is unpredictable. Some compilers will allow it, assigning a very strange character (whatever –99 is in the character set you are using) to the string. Other compilers will not allow it and will complain bitterly, giving you strange errors to interpret and correct. Either way, the outcome is unpleasant.

Now for the const method. If you wrote

```
const char *NoValues = -99;
```

then you would immediately see how the compiler reacted (by generating a compile error) at the moment you defined the constant. The const construct is *type-safe* — you give it a type, and can assign it only to things of the same, or compatible, types; it won't accept anything else, so its consistency is safe from disruption.

One other compelling reason to use the const construct instead of the #define construct is that the const construct is a legitimate C++ statement that must compile properly on its own. The #define construct is a pre-processor statement — literally pasted into the code by the C++ pre-processor wherever the statement is found. That arrangement can lead to some very strange problems. For example, when a string that is enclosed in quotes is pasted into a given position in the code, the compiler may interpret the quotation marks as enclosing the code around it as well. This may have the effect of commenting out code by making it a literal string rather than a code string.

Using the const Construct

The C++ standard provides a method for fixing the problems caused by the #define statement in the pre-processor. This statement is the const statement, which is handled by the compiler, not the pre-processor, and therefore makes your code easier to understand and debug.

1. **In the code editor of your choice, create a new file to hold the code for the source file of the technique.**

In this example, the file is named ch08.cpp, although you can use whatever you choose.

2. **Type the code in Listing 8-1 into your file.**

Better yet, copy the code from the source file on this book's companion Web site.

Note that in this listing, you can see the effects of both the #define version of the statement and the const version of the statement. The compiler will interpret them differently, as we will see shortly.

LISTING 8-1: USING CONSTANTS

```
#include <stdio.h>

const int MaxValues = 100;
#define MAX_VALUES 100;              → 1

int main(int argc, char **argv)
{
    int myArray[ MaxValues ];
    int myOtherArray[ MAX_VALUES ];

    for ( int i=0; i<MaxValues; ++i )
        myArray[i] = i;
    for ( int i=0; i<MAX_VALUES; ++i )
        myOtherArray[i] = i;

    return 0;
}
```

3. **Compile the application, using your favorite compiler on your favorite operating system.**

Compiling this ordinary-looking program, you will get the following error messages. (This is how it looks on my version of the gcc compiler; yours might look slightly different.)

```
$ gcc ch08.cpp
ch08.cpp: In function `int main(int,
   char**)':
ch08.cpp:9: error: syntax error before `;'
   token
ch08.cpp:13: error: syntax error before
   `;' token
ch08.cpp:14: error: `myOtherArray' unde-
   clared (first use this function)
ch08.cpp:14: error: (Each undeclared iden-
   tifier is reported only once for each
   function it appears in.)
```

The next section describes how to correct these errors.

Identifying the Errors

Looking at the lines that the errors appear on, it is quite unclear what the problem might be. The first line reference is marked with the ➜ **1** symbol.

This certainly looks like a valid line of code — what could the problem be? The answer lies not with the compiler but with the pre-processor. Remember, the pre-processor takes everything that follows the token you define (on the #define line) and faithfully pastes it into the code wherever it finds the token later on. In this case, after the paste occurs, the line itself is converted into

```
int myOtherArray[ 100; ];
```

You can save yourself a lot of time, effort, and trouble by using the proper parts of the language in the proper places. The #define mechanism is wonderful for creating macros, or even for defining constant strings. When it comes to things that are really constant values, use the proper syntax, which is the const keyword.

Note that extra semicolon in the middle of the array definition. That's not legal in C++, and will cause errors. But rather than pointing at the "real" offending line, which is the #define with a semi-colon at the end, the compiler gives you a confusing error about a line that looks just fine.

The #define definition may cause errors, but the const definition of MaxValues has no such problem. What it provides is simply a definition of a value — and you can then use that value anywhere in the program that a literal value or #define constant can be used.

The primary advantage of the constant is that it will always be evaluated properly.

Fixing the Errors

How do we fix these problems in the compiler so that the code does what we want? Let's take a look at some ways in which you can make the code compile and do what you intended, instead of letting the compiler guess incorrectly at what you want.

1. **Reopen the source file in your favorite code editor.**

2. **After the file is open, modify the existing program to fix the compilation errors, as follows.**

    Note that this code replaces the previous code listing, it does not get added to it.

    ```
    int main(int argc, char **argv)
    {
        int xVal = 10;
        int myArray[ xVal ];

        for ( int i=0; i<xVal; ++i )
            myArray[i] = i;

        return 0;
    }
    ```

There is a danger with using this approach. Consider the following:

```
int xVal;
int myArray[ xVal ];
```

Always initialize all variables in your code, even if you don't think you will need them.

In the non-optimized version of the code, xVal is assigned a value of 0 — which allows you to create an array with 0 elements in it. The trouble starts when you run the optimized version: The value of xVal is undetermined, and this code will likely cause a program crash. Try not to do things like this. The best way to fix things like this is to set the compiler warning level to its highest, which will detect uninitialized variables that are used.

Technique 9

Macros and Why Not to Use Them

Save Time By

- ✔ Understanding the drawbacks of macros
- ✔ Using functions instead of macros
- ✔ Avoiding problems with string macros
- ✔ Determining errors when using macros
- ✔ Using macros appropriately

The pre-processor and macros are useful things, but don't go overboard in their use. Aside from the obvious possible disaster (the pre-processor goes berserk and replaces any code in your application with whatever resides in the macro), macros often have side effects that are not clear when they're invoked. Unlike functions — whose side effects can be detected in the debugger — a macro has no such debugging functionality. Because the pre-processor "copies" the macro's code into your application, the debugger really doesn't understand how the macro works. And even though macros allow you to avoid the overhead of pushing data onto the stack and popping it off to invoke a function, the macro increases code size by duplicating the same block of code every time it's used.

Of course, these reasons by themselves aren't enough to make programmers want to avoid using macros. There are much better reasons. For example, consider the min (for "minimum") macro, which many programs define like this:

```
#define min(X, Y)  ((X) < (Y) ? (X) : (Y))
```

Suppose you use the min macro with an argument that does something else — say, like this —

```
next = min (x + y, func(z));
```

The macro expands as follows:

```
next = ((x + y) < (func(z)) ? (x + y) : (func(z)));
```

where x + y replaces X and func(z) replaces Y.

In C++ programming, macros are generally a bad idea unless you are simply tired of typing the same code over and over. Think of them as a keyboard shortcut instead of as a block of code and you will save a lot of time debugging them.

Now, this might not seem like a bad thing. But what if the `func` function has some side effect that occurs when it is called more than once? The side effect would not be immediately apparent from reading the code that shows the function being called twice. But a programmer debugging your program might be stunned if (for example) a function `func` cropped up looking like this, because it would mean that the input value was being changed not once, as it appears, but twice:

```
int func(int &x)
{
    x *= 2;
    return x;
}
```

Obviously, this function accepts a single integer argument by reference. It then multiples this argument by two and returns it. What is the problem here? Well, because the argument is passed by reference, the original argument is changed. This outcome may be what was intended, but it can also cause problems, as in the case of the `min` macro. Instead of having the function return twice the value and compare it, we are actually looking at it compared to four times the argument. You can see from the expanded version of the macro that `z` will be passed into the function two times, and since the function takes its argument by reference, it will be modified in the main program This is very unlikely to be what the programmer originally intended.

Initiating a Function with a String Macro — Almost

Macro issues become subtler when you're allocating and copying strings — which programmers do in C++ all the time. Here's the usual scenario: You have an input string, want to make a copy of it, and store the result in another string. A library function, called `strdup`, does this exact thing. But suppose that you want to copy only a certain number of bytes of the original string into your new string. You couldn't

use `strdup` because it always duplicates the string entirely. Further, assume that in order to conserve memory, you want to remove the original string after copying. This might be done to shrink a string, perhaps, or to make sure something always fits in a particular database field. The following steps show how to create code that does this handy task — implementing it as a macro and then as a function to see what the issues with each might be.

1. **In the code editor of your choice, create a new file to hold the code for the source file of the technique.**

In this example, the file is named `ch09.cpp`, although you can use whatever you choose.

2. **Type the code in Listing 9-1 into your file.**

Better yet, copy the code from the source file on this book's companion Web site.

LISTING 9-1: THE MACRO FILE

```
#include <stdio.h>
#include <string.h>

// This will be our macro version
#define COPY_AND_TRUNC(ns, s) \
    if ( strlen(s) > 20 ) \
    { \
        ns = new char[ 20 ]; \
        memset( ns, 0, 20 ); \
        strncpy( ns, s, 20-1 ); \
    } \
    else \
    { \
        ns = new char[ strlen(s) ]; \
        memset( ns, 0, strlen(s) ); \
        strcpy( ns, s ); \
    } \
    delete s;

int main(int argc, char **argv )
{
    char *s = new char[80];
    strcpy( s, "This is a really long string
to test something");
    char *ns = NULL;
    COPY_AND_TRUNC( ns, s );
```

(continued)

LISTING 9-1 (continued)

```
printf("New string: [%s]\n", ns );
   char *s2 = new char[80];
   strcpy( s2, "This is a really long
   string to test something");
   COPY_AND_TRUNC( s2, s2 );
   printf("New string: [%s]\n", ns );
     return 0;
}
```

Note that you can create a *multiple* line macro by using the backslash ('\') character at the end of the previous line. Doing so expands the macro until it's almost a complete function.

3. Compile the program with your favorite compiler on your favorite operating system.

4. Run the program on your favorite operating system.

If you've done everything properly, you will see the following output:

```
$ ./a.exe
New string: [This is a really lo]
New string: [(null)]
```

Fixing What Went Wrong with the Macro

What happened here? The output of the last function call should have been the same as the first one! This is a serious problem that can be traced to a side effect of the macro. Because the procedure didn't check to see whether input and output were the same, you cannot safely delete the character-pointer buffer that you didn't allocate. However, by following the steps given here, you can rewrite this macro as an equivalent — but safer — function.

1. Reopen the source file in your code editor.

2. Make changes to the source code as shown in Listing 9-2. Note that the lines to be modified are shown at → 1 and → 2. The blocks of code shown here should be added.

LISTING 9-2: THE UPDATED MACRO FILE

```
#include <stdio.h>
#include <string.h>

// This will be our macro version
#define COPY_AND_TRUNC(ns, s) \
    if ( strlen(s) > 20 ) \
    { \
        ns = new char[ 20 ]; \
        memset( ns, 0, 20 ); \
        strncpy( ns, s, 20-1 ); \
    } \
    else \
    { \
        ns = new char[ strlen(s) ]; \
        memset( ns, 0, strlen(s) ); \
        strcpy( ns, s ); \
    } \
    delete s; \
    s = NULL;

char *copy_and_truncate( char *& s )        → 1
{
    char *temp = NULL;
    if ( strlen(s) > 20 )
    {
        temp = new char[ 20 ];
        memset( temp, 0, 20 );
        strncpy( temp, s, 20-1 );
    }
    else
    {
        temp = new char[ strlen(s) ];
        memset( temp, 0, strlen(s) );
        strcpy( temp, s );
    }

    delete s;
    s = NULL;
    return temp;
}


int main(int argc, char **argv )
{
    char *s = new char[80];
    strcpy( s, "This is a really long string
    to test something");
```

```
char *ns = NULL;
COPY_AND_TRUNC( ns, s );
printf("New string: [%s]\n", ns );
char *s2 = new char[80];
strcpy( s2, "This is a really long
string to test something");
COPY_AND_TRUNC( s2, s2 );
printf("New string: [%s]\n", s2 );
char *s3 = new char[80];
strcpy( s3, "This is a really long
string to test something");
s3 = copy_and_truncate( s3 );          ➔ 2
printf("New string: [%s]\n", s3 );


}
```

---

3. **Save the source code in your source-code editor and close the source-code editor application.**

4. **Compile the program using your favorite compiler on your favorite operating system.**

   If you have done everything properly, this time you should see the following output in your console window:

```
$ ./a.exe
New string: [This is a really lo]
New string: [(null)]
New string: [This is a really lo]
```

Note that this time, your function did exactly what you expected it to do. Not only did you not wipe out your pointer, you also did not cause the memory leak that the previous version caused. Okay, imagine having to hassle with macros like that over and over just to get your work done. To avoid all that aggrava-tion, I recommend choosing functions for anything but the very simplest macros. The function shown in the modified code causes no problems, whereas the macros in the initial listing do. This should illustrate the problems caused unintentionally by macros.

Using Macros Appropriately

What are macros good for, then? Remember, a macro is nothing more (and nothing less) than syntactical sugar; it's easy to wind up with too much of a good thing. Using a heap of macros may make reading your coding easier, but you should never modify your code itself with a macro. For example, if you have a particularly complex expression — such as (*iter).c_str() — which can occur when you're using the Standard Template Library (STL) in C++ — you could create a macro that says:

```
#define PTR(x) (*x)
```

Then you can write PTR(x).c_str(), and however often you write it, the definition will be consistent. This isn't a complicated example, but it gives you an idea of when and when not to use macros in your C++ applications. The macro is straightforward, has no side effects, and makes the code easier to read later. These are all good reasons to use a macro.

 If you are trying to generalize a block of code, use templates instead of macros. Your finished source code is more compact that way, and debugging considerations are easier.

Technique 10

Understanding sizeof

The sizeof operator is not technically a part of the pre-processor, but it should be thought of as one. The sizeof operator, as its name implies, returns the size, in bytes, of a given piece of information in your application. It can be used on basic types — such as int, long, float, double, or char * — and on objects, classes, and allocated blocks as well. In fact, anything that is a legitimate type can be passed to the sizeof function.

The sizeof function is extremely useful. If (for example) you want to allocate a block of memory to hold exactly one specific type of data, you can use the sizeof function to determine how many bytes you need to allocate, like this:

```
int bytes = sizeof(block);
char *newBlock = new char[bytes];
memcpy( newBlock, block, bytes );
```

This capability is also useful when you're saving an object into memory while performing a global undo function. You save the state of the object each time it's going to change, and then return it to that saved state by simply copying the block of memory over it. There are other ways to do this task, of course, but this one is simple and very extensible.

In the following sections, I show you what sizeof can and cannot do.

Using the sizeof Function

The sizeof function can be valuable in determining system configurations, sizes of classes, and illustrating many of the internals of the C++ system. The following steps show you how the sizeof function is used, and how it can show you something about the internals of your own code:

1. **In the code editor of your choice, create a new file to hold the code for the source file of the technique.**

   In this example, the file is named ch10.cpp, although you can use whatever you choose.

2. **Type the code from Listing 10-1 into your file.**

Better yet, copy the code from the source file on this book's companion Web site.

LISTING 10-1: THE SIZEOF PROGRAM

```
#include <stdio.h>
#include <string>

class Foo
{
public:
    Foo() {};
    ~Foo() {};
};

class Bar
{
public:
    Bar() {};
    virtual ~Bar() {};
};

class Full
{
    int x;
    double y;
public:
    Full()
    {
    }
    virtual ~Full()
    {
    }
};

class Derived : public Foo
{
public:
    Derived() {};
    ~Derived() {};
};

int main()
{
    int x = 0;
    long y = 0;
    float z = 0;
    double d = 0.0;
    std::string s = "hello";
```

```
    // Basic types
    printf("size of char: %d\n",
    sizeof(char));
    printf("size of char *: %d\n",
    sizeof(char *));
    printf("size of int: %d\n", sizeof(x));
    printf("size of long: %d\n", sizeof(y));
    printf("size of float: %d\n",
    sizeof(z));
    printf("size of double: %d\n",
    sizeof(d));

    printf("size of string: %d\n", sizeof(s)
    );
    printf("size of Foo: %d\n",
    sizeof(Foo));
    printf("size of Bar: %d\n",
    sizeof(Bar));
    printf("size of Full: %d\n",
    sizeof(Full));
    printf("size of Derived: %d\n",
    sizeof(Derived));
}
```

3. **Save the source code as a file in the code editor and then close the editor application.**

4. **Compile the program, using your favorite compiler on your favorite operating system.**

5. **Run the program.**

If you have done everything properly, you should see the following output in your console window:

```
$ ./a.exe
size of char: 1
size of char *: 4
size of int: 4
size of long: 4
size of float: 4
size of double: 8
size of string: 4
size of Foo: 1
size of Bar: 4
size of Full: 16
size of Derived: 1
```

You can see from the output the number of bytes that each of the elements we print up occupy in memory for this program. There are no real surprises here, except for the size of the classes. Let's take a look at what these results mean.

Evaluating the Results

There are some interesting conclusions to be made from this output. For example, although some of the results are not surprising at all (for instance, that the size of a character field is 1 byte), some surprises crop up — for example, the size of a character pointer is the same as any other pointer, which turns out to be the size of a `long`. That means the maximum allowable number of bytes you can allocate using standard pointers is 4 bytes worth — 32 bits. (That's why Microsoft Windows is a 32-bit operating system. But you knew that.)

 You can save a lot of debugging time and design effort by remembering one handy rule: Always check the size of the values you are working with. Rather than hard-code into your application numbers specifically for reading bytes, words, and floating-point values, use the `sizeof` function to get the correct sizes for the compiler, platform, and operating system you are using.

The next surprise is lurking among the objects in the list: The size of a string is shown as 4 bytes, which can't possibly be right — the string it's storing is longer than that. How can that be? The answer is that the `sizeof` function returns the number of bytes directly allocated by the object — that is, the number of bytes occupied by the private and public variables in the object, plus a few bytes for virtual functions (such as those in the `Foo` and `Bar` classes). Notice that even though the `Bar` class has no member variables, it still takes up 4 bytes because it needs the virtual function table (or *v-table*) discussed earlier in Technique 2. Now, why does the `Foo` class take up 1 byte, when it has no virtual methods and no member variables? The answer is that the `sizeof` function is

required to return at least 1 byte for every class. This is to ensure the address of one object will never be the same as the address of another object. If C++ permitted objects to have zero size, the compiler wouldn't be forced to assign those objects a new address in memory. To illustrate, if I wrote the following:

```
Foo f1;
Foo f2;
```

the compiler would be free to make both of these objects point at the same location in memory. This is not desirable, even if neither object had any memory allocated to it. Having two objects with the same location would break too many standard library functions. Any function that compared source and destination (for example) would be broken, even if that breakage caused no real harm. The reason for this is that comparison is done by looking at the addresses the two pointers occupy in memory. If the two addresses are the same, the assumption is that what they point at is the same. If two objects have no data in them, but occupy the same position in memory, they are not the same, even if they seem to be.

The `Bar` class also contains no member variables, but contains a virtual function, and thus pushes the number of allocated bytes to 4. That way of working suggests that there is something very physical about virtual functions, and that you have to incur a memory cost to use that feature.

 Even in programming, there is no such thing as a free lunch.

The `Full` class contains several member variables — a double that takes up 8 bytes, and an integer that takes up 4 — and yet it has 16 allocated bytes. Where do the other 4 bytes come from? You guessed it: from the infamous virtual table, which is created by that virtual destructor. What does this tell us? Even if you don't have a "normal" virtual method, having a virtual destructor still creates a v-table entry — and that means 4 more bytes in the allocation.

The Derived class is puzzling — it looks like it ought to eat up more size than it does. When you look carefully at this class, however, you realize that it contains no virtual function, and neither does the base class from which it is derived. So once again, here is an example of an empty class that takes up a single byte.

Using *sizeof* with Pointers

No discussion of the sizeof function would be quite complete without a look at a common mistake that C++ programmers make when they use the function. Consider the following little program:

```
#include <stdio.h>
#include <stdlib.h>

const char arr[] = "hello";
const char *cp = arr;

main(){

        printf("Size of array %d\n",
                        sizeof(arr));
        printf("Size of pointer %dn",
                        .sizeof(cp));
        return(0);
}
```

Because one statement outputs the size of an array and the other the size of a pointer to that array, you would think that the two printf statements in this little program would display the same values. But they do not. In fact, if you take a look at the output, it looks like this:

```
Size of array 6
Size of pointer 4
```

 The C++ language offers no way to get the size of an array from a single pointer. If you try to use the sizeof operator for that purpose, it will return a valid result but won't give you what you want.

The size of an array is known at compile time and can be displayed by the sizeof function. On the other hand, a pointer is always the size of a pointer, no matter what it's pointing at. Furthermore, if you try to return the size of an array by including the statement sizeof(*cp) where cp is the array, you'll find that the answer is (again) not 6 but 1. Oops. Why is this? Because the expression *cp evaluates to a character, and the size of a single character is always one byte. Be very careful if you're trying to use the sizeof function on pointers — especially if you want to use the result to represent the size of what's being pointed at.

Part III

Types

The 5th Wave   By Rich Tennant

C++ PROGRAMMING

"Before I go on to explain more advanced procedures like the 'Zap-Rowdy-Students-who-Don't-Pay-Attention' function, we'll begin with some basics."

Technique

11

Creating Your Own Basic Types

In C++, types are separated into two regions, basic and user-defined. Basic types are those defined by the language, which generally are modeled on types supported directly by the computer hardware. These types include integers, floating point numbers, and characters. Advanced types, such as strings, structures, and classes, fall into the user-defined region. In this technique, we examine the first region, the basic type. I save the advanced types for the next technique.

How many times have you written a program that required a basic integer variable to be constrained within a given range? You end up duplicating the same code over and over throughout your application, in blocks that look like this:

```
int value = get_a_value();
if ( value < 0 || value > 10 )
{
    printf("invalid input, try again\n");
    return false;
}
```

Of course, after you have shoehorned all these blocks into the code, your boss comes along and tells you that the folks in the accounting department have decided that ten is no longer the magic number — now it's 12. So, you modify all of the code, learning something in the process — namely that you're better off using constants in this situation than variables. Your modifications look like this:

```
const int maxValue = 12;

int value = get_a_value();
if ( value < 0 || value > maxValue )
{
    printf("invalid input, try again\n");
    return false;
}
```

You check the code into your source-code repository and sure enough, the boss comes into your office again. The accountants have requested another change. While the maximum allowable value is still 12, zeroes are not allowed in the accounting system. The smallest value you are permitted to enter is 1. Grumbling, you rewrite the code one more time (taking advantage of what you have learned in the first two experiences) to create something slightly more generic:

```
const int minValue = 1;
const int maxValue = 12;

int value = get_a_value();
if ( value < minValue || value > maxValue
    )
{
    printf("invalid input, try again\n");
    return false;
}
```

Implementing the Range Class

In this technique, I show you a more general way to solve this problem — by using a C++ class. The idea is to just extend the basic type of int to allow for minimum and maximum values. The problem, of course, is that I still want to be able to use other types (such as integers) for comparisons and assignments and the like. The class created in the following steps handles minimum and maximum values, and restricts input within those values.

1. **In the code editor of your choice, create a new file to hold the code for the implementation of the source file.**

In this example, the file is named ch11.cpp, although you can use whatever you choose.

2. **Type the code from Listing 11-1 into your file.**

Better yet, copy the code from the source file on this book's companion Web site.

LISTING 11-1: THE RANGE CLASS

```
#include <stdio.h>
#include <stdlib.h>
#include <limits.h>

class IntRange
{
```

```
private:
    int iMin;
    int iMax;
    int iValue;

    virtual void SetValue( int value )
    {
        if ( value < GetMin() )
            value = GetMin();
        else
            if ( value > GetMax() )
                value = GetMax();
        iValue = value;
    }

public:
    IntRange(void)
    {
        iMin = 0;
        iMax = INT_MAX;
        iValue = iMin;
    }
    IntRange(int min, int max)
    {
        if ( min <= max )
        {
            iMin = min;
            iMax = max;
        }
        else
        {
            iMin = max;
            iMax = min;
        }
        iValue = iMin;
    }
    IntRange( int min, int max, int value )
    {
        if ( min <= max )
        {
            iMin = min;
            iMax = max;
        }
        else
        {
            iMin = max;
            iMax = min;
        }
        SetValue( value );
    }
    IntRange( const IntRange& aCopy )
    {
```

```
        iMin = aCopy.iMin;
        iMax = aCopy.iMax;
        iValue = aCopy.iValue;
    }
    virtual ~IntRange()
    {
    }
    virtual int  GetMin(void)
    {
        return iMin;
    }
    virtual int  GetMax(void)
    {
        return iMax;
    }
    // Define a few operators
    IntRange& operator=(int value)
    {
        SetValue ( value );
        return *this;
    }
    IntRange& operator=(double value)
    {
        SetValue( (int)value );
        return *this;
    }

    virtual int GetValue(void) const
    {
        return iValue;
    }};
```

If you examine this code, you will find that it verifies that the value of an integer variable falls within a certain range. You can define your own minimum and maximum values for the range, and the class will ensure that any value assigned to that variable falls inside that range.

The interesting part of this class is the last part, comprised of the lines below the `Define a few operators` comment. This is where the power of C++'s extensibility shines. I have defined assignment operators so that our class can be used with the built-in types `int` and `double`. Obviously, I could add additional types here, including strings and the like, but this is enough for right now. With this power, you can now use the `IntRange` class to

store your data, sure that the value in the object will always be valid. That's a comfort, and it means there's no longer any reason to write code like the following:

```
int x = get_a_value();
if ( x < min || x > max )
    do_some_error();
```

Instead, I can simply write

```
IntRange myRangeObj(min, max);
myRangeObj = val;
int x = myRangeObj.GetValue();
```

I don't have to check the returned value, because the code requires that it be correct. There is something else that I can do with this class, however, and that is to define external operators for it. Being able to define an external operator is extremely beneficial because it allows users with no access to the source code of the class to create new ways to use the class. This is something absolutely unique to C++; no previous language has anything like it. Without having access to the source code for this class, we can override basic operations (such as less-than, greater-than, or equal-to) in our own code. The ability to add external operators makes it possible to add things the original programmer did not think of for the class operations.

3. **Add the code from Listing 11-2 to your source-code file. This code could easily be added at a later date, in a separate file, by a separate programmer.**

LISTING 11-2: RANGE CLASS OPERATORS

```
bool operator<(const IntRange& aRange, int
    aValue )
{
    return aRange.GetValue() < aValue;
}
bool operator==(const IntRange& aRange, int
    aValue )
{
    return aRange.GetValue() == aValue;
}
```

4. **Save your source-code file and close the code editor.**

Testing the Range Class

After you create a Range class, you should create a test driver that not only ensures that your code is correct, but also shows people how to use your code.

Here I show you how to create a test driver that validates various kinds of input from the user, and illustrates how the Range class, as defined in the previous section, is intended to be used.

1. **In the code editor of your choice, open the existing file to hold the code for your test program.**

In this example, I named the test program ch11_1.cpp.

2. **Type the code from Listing 11-3 into your file.**

Better yet, copy the code from the source file in the ch11 directory of this book's companion Web site.

LISTING 11-2: THE RANGE CLASS TEST DRIVER

```
int main(int argc, char **argv)
{
    IntRange i20(0,20);

    for (int i=1; i<argc; ++i )
    {
        i20 = atoi(argv[i]);
        printf("Setting value to %s, value
        is now %d\n", argv[i],
        i20.GetValue() );
    }
    i20 = 13;
    if ( i20 < 19 )
        printf("The value is under 19\n");
    else
```

```
        printf("The value is over 19\n");

    if ( i20 < 10 )
        printf("The value is under 10\n");
    else
        printf("The value is over 10\n");

    if ( i20 == 13 )
        printf("The value is 13\n");
    else
        printf("The value is NOT 13\n");

    return 0;
}
```

3. **Compile and run the application in the operating system of your choice.**

If you have done everything right, you should see the following output in the shell window on your system:

```
$ ./a.exe 1 2 -1 30
Setting value to 1, value is now 1
Setting value to 2, value is now 2
Setting value to -1, value is now 0
Setting value to 30, value is now 20
The value is under 19
The value is over 10
The value is 13
```

As you can see, the Range class does not allow the values to be assigned outside of the valid entries we defined in our source code.

Notice how the Range class can be used just as if it were a basic type that was a part of the language from the very start! This amazingly powerful technique lets you do just about anything you want (in code, that is). It even makes possible the direct conversion of your own data types into the base type you are extending, in order to pass them directly to functions that expect the basic type.

Technique 12

Creating Your Own Types

Of course, although it is all well and good to create extensions of built-in types, the real goal of programming in C++ is to create new types that the language designers never thought about. For example, imagine that you need to work with a matrix in your program. A *matrix* is simply a two-dimensional array of values. In this technique, I show you how to create a new type, a Matrix class for use in graphics calculations. To do so, it pays to remember that users don't really have to understand how things work behind the scenes; if they can just use those new types as if they were a natural part of the language all along, users are much more likely to use the object and return to it again and again. For the C++ class system, that means our goal is to make the object into something that looks, feels, and acts like a basic type such as integer or float.

Let's start out with the basics of creating a Matrix class. This class will allow you (eventually) to do basic matrix algebra — such as adding two matrices, adding or multiplying a constant to a matrix, and the like. The best syntax for our Matrix class would be one that closely emulates real-world matrices — that is, something like this:

```
Matrix m(10,10);
M[5][5] = 20.0;
```

This code would define a 10 x 10 matrix and allocate space for it. The element at 5,5 would then be set to the value of 20.0, and all other elements would be set to the value of 0.0 (which is the default). We could, for example, create a derived class that implemented an identity matrix, where the diagonal values of the matrix from left to right are set to 1.0 and all other values are set to 0.0.

Immediately, however, we run into a very serious problem. Although it's possible — in fact, fairly easy — to override the [] operator for a class, it is *not* possible to override the operator [][] (or [][][], or any other number of levels of indirection for arrays). Given this limitation, how do we create a class that "looks" like it has a two-dimensional array built into it — and that you can access? The answer lies in some of the magic of C++. To see how it's done, begin building the `Matrix` class by implementing the ability to treat a two-dimensional array as if it were a single object. The next section shows you how.

Creating the Matrix Class

The `Matrix` class allows us to treat a two-dimensional array as if it were a single object. This class looks to the user as if it was a two-dimensional array of values, but it does error checking and allows the user to query the class for basic properties, such as the width and height of the matrix. To do this, the following steps show you how to create two separate classes, one that encapsulates a single row of the matrix, and one that holds arrays of those rows to implement the complete matrix.

1. **In the code editor of your choice, create a new file to hold the code for the implementation of the source file.**

   In this example, the file is named `ch12.cpp`, although you can use whatever you choose.

2. **Type the code from Listing 12-1 into your file.**

   Better yet, copy the code from the source file on this book's companion Web site.

3. **Save the source file.**

LISTING 12-1: THE MATRIX CLASS

```
#include <stdio.h>
#include <math.h>
#include <stdlib.h>
#include <vector>

class Row
{
private:
    std::vector< double > Columns;
public:
    Row( void )
    {
    }
    Row( int size )
    {
```

```
        // Initialize the column
        for ( int i=0; i<size; ++i )
            Columns.insert( Columns.end(),
    0.0 );
    }
    Row( const Row& aCopy )
    {
        std::vector< double >::const_iterator
        iter;
        for ( iter = aCopy.Columns.begin();
        iter !=
aCopy.Columns.end(); ++iter )
        {
            double d = (*iter);
            Columns.insert( Columns.end(),
    d);
        }
    }

    int size()
    {
        return Columns.size();
    }

    double& operator[](int index)
    {
        if ( index < 0 || index > Columns.
        size() )
            throw "Array Index out of
            Bounds";
        return Columns[ index ];
    }
};

class Matrix
{
private:
    std::vector< Row > Rows;
public:
    Matrix ( int rows, int cols )
    {
        for ( int i=0; i<rows; ++i )
        {
            Row r( cols );
            Rows.insert( Rows.end(), r );
        }
    }
    Row& operator[](int index)
    {
        if ( index < 0 || index > Rows.
        size() )
            throw "Array Index out of
            Bounds";
```

```
        return Rows[ index ];
    }

    void Print()
    {
        for ( int r=0; r<Rows.size(); ++r )
        {
            for ( int c=0; c<Rows[r].size();
            ++c )
                printf(" %lf ", Rows[r][c]
                );
            printf("\n");
        }

    }

    int RowCount()
    {
        return Rows.size();
    }
    int ColumnCount()
    {
        if ( Rows.size() )
            return Rows[0].size();
        return 0;
    }

}
```

The code in Listing 12-1 actually does almost nothing — except provide storage space for the matrix and provide methods for getting at that storage space. In this way, the code is a perfect example of object-oriented design and programming: The storage is allocated, the space is managed, and the data is hidden from the user. Otherwise the actual functionality of the object is external to the object (not a good idea). Note the use of two separate classes to allow the *illusion* of multiple array indices. It's worth a closer look at the way this sleight of hand works.

When the user invokes the operator [] on the Matrix class, it really returns a Row object. Of course, this process is transparent to the user, who thinks that he or she is simply operating on a given array element within the matrix. After you obtain a Row element, you then use the operator [] on that object to return individual Column entries in the row.

To the user, it looks like you're using a two-dimensional array. This same technique can be used to implement any number of levels of array you want. Just replace the double entries in the Column class with additional Column objects, and you have a multidimensional array class that can handle virtually any number of dimensions. Considering how little work is needed to manage this trick in the code, it's pretty impressive work.

Of course, the problem here is that although we do have the storage management of the matrix data solved, we don't actually *do* anything with it. Its all very well and good to set individual elements in a matrix, but what people really want are the operations that make matrices what they are — addition, multiplication, and the like. So the real question is, how do we implement this when we have already written the class and added it to the system? That's where C++ saves our hash by letting us implement operators outside a class. In fact, we can do things that the original class designer never even thought about — with no impact on the original design of the class, and no need to modify the code that makes up that class. The next section takes a closer look at an operator that adds two matrices, and shows you how to make it work.

Matrix Operations

After we have the basic class in place to implement the data storage for the matrix, the next step is to implement the functionality to operate on matrices. First, let's add two matrices. The following steps show you how:

1. **Add the code from Listing 12-2 to your source file (or just grab the code from this book's companion Web site):**

These operations are outside of the basic functionality of the class itself, so they are presented as separate listings. You could add them to the original file, create a new file to hold them, or put them in your application source code. For simplicity, I am just tacking them onto the original source file.

LISTING 12-2: THE MATRIX OPERATORS

```
Matrix operator+( Matrix& m1, Matrix& m2 )
{
    // Here, we need to check that the rows
    // and columns of the two are the same.
    if ( m1.RowCount() != m2.RowCount() )
        throw "Adding Matrices: Invalid
        Rows";
    if ( m1.ColumnCount() !=
        m2.ColumnCount() )
        throw "Adding Matrices: Invalid
        Columns";

    Matrix m( m1.RowCount(),
            m1.ColumnCount() );

    for ( int r=0; r<m1.RowCount(); ++ r )
    {
        for ( int c=0; c<m1.ColumnCount();
            ++c )
            m[r][c] = m1[r][c] + m2[r][c];
    }

    return m;
}
```

2. **Save the source-code file.**

Aside from its actual functionality, this little code snippet illustrates some important points. First, because the operator is defined outside the class, we can only use methods defined as public in the class when we're working on the data. Fortunately, as you can see by the code, those methods are all we really need. The "rules" for matrix addition are fairly simple — you just add the same row and column values for each matrix and put the result into the output matrix. Note that because we are returning an object, rather than a reference to an object, we need to worry about copying the object. If you are returning a C++ object, it will automatically invoke the constructor to create the initial object and then the copy constructor to return a copy of the object. Fortunately, the copy constructor is defined for the Matrix **class.**

One problem with operators is that they have no real way to return errors to the calling program. For example, when you write:

```
x = y + z;
```

there is really no way to determine that an error occurred. When we add two integers, we can actually cause all sorts of errors, such as underflows and overflows, but those are mostly hidden from the user. For this reason, the only way that we can indicate to the user that there was a problem is to throw an exception. This is a very hard decision to make in terms of design, because it raises the possibility of exceptions in any line where the end user writes code — as in this example:

```
Matrix m3 = m1 + m2;
```

This line could throw an exception — in which case you'd have to enclose it in a try/catch block — it could bounce you straight out of your application. Obviously, adding two matrices doesn't seem like the kind of thing you should be worrying about crashing your application. We could simply return a blank matrix if the bounds of both matrices were not the same; that would be another choice, but a more complicated one. Now you are getting a result you did not expect from a standard operation. This is one reason for not using overloaded operators; they often have side effects that really don't apply to "standard" types.

Multiplying a Matrix by a Scalar Value

As with the addition of two matrices, we can also multiply a matrix by a scalar value. This operation is actually easier to code than the addition of two matrices, but has an additional side effect that's worth talking about — in a minute. The first order of business is to code the operation. To multiply a matrix by a scalar value, follow these steps:

1. **Using your code editor, reopen the source-code file for this technique and add the contents of Listing 12-3.**

LISTING 12-3: SCALAR MULTIPLICATION

```
Matrix operator*(Matrix& m1, double scalar)
{
    Matrix m( m1.RowCount(),
            m1.ColumnCount() );

    for ( int r=0; r<m1.RowCount(); ++ r )
    {
        for ( int c=0; c<m1.ColumnCount();
            ++c )
            m[r][c] = m1[r][c] * scalar;
    }

    return m;
}
```

2. **Save the source-code file.**

You can then use this code in your program — for example, by writing the following line:

```
Matrix m2 = m1 * 4;
```

This command will work fine, generating a matrix of the appropriate size that is the scalar multiple of the original matrix — and it will multiply all elements by 4. The problem comes in when you try this:

```
Matrix m2 = 4 * m1;
```

Oops. You've reversed the order of the operands — and suddenly there's a problem with the compiler. You get an error that says

```
error: no match for 'operator*' in '4 * m4'
error: candidates are: Matrix
    operator*(Matrix&, double)
```

The reason that you get this error is that the compiler takes the 4 * m1 command and translates it to a call to operator*(int, Matrix& m1). You do not have this method defined.

This is where the apparent magic of C++ gets tricky: C++ allows you to define operators for addition of classes that are as simple to use as adding two numbers (like 1+ 2). It can handle the simple stuff — scalar multiplication of integers, for example — and it understands that numbers can be multiplied in any order. The problem comes in when you try to apply that same concept to your own classes. You have to apply a few tricks of your own; in the next section, I show you how.

Multiplying a Matrix by Scalar Values, Take 2

To resolve this, we need to create a new operator, with virtually the same code, and place the arguments in the opposite order. The following steps show you how:

1. **Using your code editor, reopen the source-code file for this technique and modify the code as you see in Listing 12-4.**

LISTING 12-4: MATRIX MANIPULATION FUNCTIONS

```
Matrix scalar_multiplication( Matrix& m1,
    double scalar )
{
    Matrix m( m1.RowCount(),
            m1.ColumnCount() );

    for ( int r=0; r<m1.RowCount(); ++ r )
    {
        for ( int c=0; c<m1.ColumnCount();
            ++c )
            m[r][c] = m1[r][c] * scalar;
    }

    return m;
}

Matrix operator*(Matrix& m1, double scalar)
{
    return scalar_multiplication( m1, scalar
    );
}
```

(continued)

LISTING 12-4 *(continued)*

```
Matrix operator*(double scalar, Matrix& m1 )
{
    return scalar_multiplication( m1, scalar
    );
}
```

Note that this code replaces the existing `opera-tor*` that we implemented earlier. Remove the existing implementation or you will get a duplicate definition error from the compiler for having two of the same methods defined.

This code allows us to write either:

Matrix m2 = 4 * m1;

Or

Matrix m2 = m1 * 4;

Because the compiler can resolve either order into a valid method, it will allow you to do both in your code. Because the actual multiplication action is the same in either case, we factor out the code that does the "real" work and call it from both methods. This refactoring reduces the total amount of code, and makes it easier to track down problems.

2. **Save the source-code file.**

Testing the Matrix Class

After you create a `Matrix` class, you should create a test driver that not only ensures that your code is correct, but also shows people how to use your code.

Here's the procedure that creates a test driver that validates various kinds of input from the user, and illustrates how the `Matrix` class is intended to be used:

1. **In the code editor of your choice, open the existing file to hold the code for your test program.**

In this example, I named the test program `ch12.cpp`.

2. **Type the code from Listing 12-5 into your file.**

Better yet, copy the code from the source file on this book's companion Web site.

LISTING 12-5: THE MATRIX TEST DRIVER

```
int main()
{
    Matrix m1(5,5);
    Matrix m2(5,5);

    m1[2][2] = 3;                  ➞ 1
    m2[2][2] = 4;
    m2[3][3] = 5;

    Matrix m3 = m1 + m2;           ➞ 2

    printf("Matrix 1:\n");
    m1.Print();
    printf("Matrix 3:\n");
    m3.Print();

    Matrix m4 = m3 * 5;            ➞ 3
    Matrix m5 = 4 * m4;
    printf("Matrix 4:\n");
    m4.Print();
    printf("Matrix 5:\n");
    m5.Print();

}
```

3. **Compile and run the application in the operating system of your choice.**

If you have done everything right, you should see the output from Listing 12-6 in the shell window on your system.

LISTING 12-6: OUTPUT FROM THE MATRIX TEST PROGRAM

```
$ ./a.exe
Matrix 1:
 0.000000  0.000000  0.000000  0.000000
   0.000000
 0.000000  0.000000  0.000000  0.000000
   0.000000
 0.000000  0.000000  3.000000  0.000000
   0.000000
 0.000000  0.000000  0.000000  0.000000
   0.000000
 0.000000  0.000000  0.000000  0.000000
   0.000000
Matrix 3:
 0.000000  0.000000  0.000000  0.000000
   0.000000
 0.000000  0.000000  0.000000  0.000000
   0.000000
 0.000000  0.000000  7.000000  0.000000
   0.000000
 0.000000  0.000000  0.000000  5.000000
   0.000000
 0.000000  0.000000  0.000000  0.000000
   0.000000
Matrix 4:
 0.000000  0.000000  0.000000  0.000000
   0.000000
 0.000000  0.000000  0.000000  0.000000
   0.000000
 0.000000  0.000000  35.000000  0.000000
   0.000000
 0.000000  0.000000  0.000000  25.000000
   0.000000
 0.000000  0.000000  0.000000  0.000000
   0.000000
```

```
Matrix 5:
 0.000000  0.000000  0.000000  0.000000
   0.000000
 0.000000  0.000000  0.000000  0.000000
   0.000000
 0.000000  0.000000  140.000000  0.000000
   0.000000
 0.000000  0.000000  0.000000  100.000000
   0.000000
 0.000000  0.000000  0.000000  0.000000
   0.000000
```

As you can see from the above output, we are displaying the individual matrix objects that are created in the test program. The output shows that the first matrix (m1) displays the data values which we placed into it in the line marked ➜ **1** in the test driver code. The line marked ➜ **2** shows the addition of two matrices, which we then display as Matrix 3. Likewise, the code marked with ➜ **3** indicates the multiplication of a matrix by a scalar value, which is displayed in the output as Matrix 4. If you do the math, you will see that all of the output is correct, indicating that our Matrix class and its manipulation methods are working properly.

As you can see, the matrices display properly and the math is done correctly. We know our test program is correct, and we can use it in the future when we change things.

Technique 13

Using Enumerations

Save Time By

✔ Defining enumerations

✔ Implementing the Enumeration class

✔ Testing the Enumeration class

An *enumeration* is a language type introduced with the C language, which has migrated almost untouched into the C++ language. Enumerations are not true types, as classes are. You can't define operators for enumerations, nor can you change the way in which they behave. As with pre-processor commands, the enumeration command is really more of a syntactical sugar thing, replacing constant values with more readable names. It allows you slightly better readability, but does nothing to change the way your code works. Enumerations allow you to use meaningful names for values, and allow the compiler to do better type checking. The downside of an enumeration is that because it is simply a syntactical replacement for a data value, you can easily fool the compiler by casting invalid values to the enumerated type.

The basic form of an enumeration looks like this:

```
enum <name> {
value1[=number],
value2,
value3,
. . .
valuen
} EnumerationTypeName;
```

where the *<name>* field is the enumeration type we are creating, the *value* parameters are the individual values defined in the enumeration, and *number* is an optional starting point to begin numbering the enumerated values. For example, take a look at this enumeration:

```
enum color {
    Red = 1.
    White = 2.
    Blue
} ColorType;
```

In this example, every time the compiler encounters `ColorType::Red` in our application, it understands the value to be 1, `White` would be 2, and `Blue` 3 (because the numbers are consecutive unless you specify otherwise).

If enumerations actually do not change the logic of your code, why would you bother with them? The primary reason for enumerations is to improve the readability of your code. To illustrate this, here I show you a simple technique involving enumerations you can use to make your code a little safer to use, and a lot easier to understand.

 Enumerations are a great way to have the compiler enforce your valid values on the programmer. Rather than checking after the fact to see whether the value is valid, you can let the compiler check at compile-time to validate that the input will be within the range you want. When you specify that a variable is of an enumerated type, the compiler ensures that the value is of that type, insisting that it be one of the values in the enumeration list.

You might notice that enumerations are a simpler form of the Range validation class we developed in Technique 11. Enumerations are enforced by the compiler, not by your code, and require considerably less effort to implement than a Range checking class. At the same time, they are not as robust. Your mileage may vary, but enumerations are usually used more for readability and maintenance concerns than for validation.

Implementing the Enumeration Class

An enumeration is normally used when the real-world object it is modeling has very simple, very discrete values. The first example that immediately leaps to mind is a traffic light, which has three possible states: red, yellow, and green. In the following steps, let's create a simple example using the traffic light metaphor to illustrate how enumerations work and can be used in your application.

1. **In the code editor of your choice, create a new file to hold the code for the implementation of the source file.**

   In this example, the file is named ch13.cpp, although you can use whatever you choose.

2. **Type the code from Listing 13-1 into your file.**

   Better yet, copy the code you find on this book's companion Web site and change the names of the constants and variables as you choose.

3. **Save the source-code file.**

LISTING 13-1: THE ENUMERATION PROGRAM

```
#include <stdio.h>

typedef enum
{
    Red = 0,
    Yellow,
    Green
} TrafficLightColor;

int ChangeLight( int color )
{
    switch ( color )
    {
        case 1: // Red
            printf("Changing light to RED. Stop!!\n");
            break;
        case 2: // Yellow
            printf("Changing light to YELLOW. Slow down\n");
            break;
        case 3: // Green
```

(continued)

LISTING 13-1 *(continued)*

```
            printf("Changing light to GREEN. Go for it\n");
            break;
        default:
            printf("Invalid light state. Crashing\n");
            return -1;
    }
    return 0;
}

int ChangeLightEnum( TrafficLightColor color )
{
    switch ( color )
    {
        case Red: // Red
            printf("Changing light to RED. Stop!!\n");
            break;
        case Yellow: // Yellow
            printf("Changing light to YELLOW. Slow down\n");
            break;
        case Green: // Green
            printf("Changing light to GREEN. Go for it\n");
            break;
    }
    return 0;
}
```

Testing the Enumeration Class

1. **Add the following code to test the enumeration and validate that it is working properly:**

This code could easily be moved to a separate file. It is placed in one file simply as a convenience. The code illustrates why enumerations are more type-safe than basic integer types, and why you might want to use enumerations over the basic types.

```
int main(int argc, char **argv)
{
    int clr = -1;
    ChangeLight( clr );

    TrafficLightColor c = Red;
    ChangeLightEnum( c );

    return 0;
}
```

2. **Save the source-code file and close the code editor.**

3. **Compile and run the application with your favorite compiler on your favorite operating system.**

If you have done everything right, you should see the following output on the shell window:

```
$ ./a.exe
Invalid light state. Crashing
Changing light to RED. Stop!!
```

 Whenever you use an integer value for input to a function — and that input value is intended to be mapped directly to a real-world set of values — use an enumeration rather than a simple integer. Remember to use meaningful names for your enumeration values to help the application programmers understand what values they are sending to your functions and methods. This will save you time and effort and will make your code more self-documenting, which is always a good thing.

Technique 14

Creating and Using Structures

Save Time By

- Defining structures
- Understanding the advantages of structures over classes
- Implementing structures
- Using derived structures
- Interpreting the output of the structure class

One of the most interesting constructs created for the C programming language was the *structure*. Because it allowed the developer to group a bunch of related data together, and to pass that data around to various functions, the C++ `struct` construct was the beginning of encapsulation for the language.

When the C++ language was being designed, the structure was the primary component — in fact, C++ classes are simply extensions of the structure. The original C++ "compilers" were really translator programs that took C++ code and rewrote it into C, which was then compiled using the standard compiler for that language. This required that all physical parts of the classes be able to be implemented in structures. The C++ `struct` construct, in fact, is a class in which all members are public.

Structures still exist in C++. In fact, a structure is really just a class that makes all of its data members public by default. Contrast that with a standard class, which has all members designated private by default. There is really no difference between

```
struct foo {
    int x;
    int y;
};
```

and

```
class foo
{
 public:
    int x;
    int y;
};
```

Here C++ has anadvantage: You can do more with structures in C++ than you could in C. Structures can contain constructors and accessor methods. They can even contain methods that do not operate on the data of the class itself. You can even have structures derived from other structures. Although the original C++ compilers converted classes into structures, the newer compilers differentiate between the two. A class is still a `struct`, but the interpretation is different. A C++ `struct` is no longer completely backward-compatible with C.

What *can't* you do with structures? For one thing, you can't have virtual methods. Structures do not contain predefined v-tables, so they cannot contain a virtual function. Obviously, that means you can't override methods in the "base structure" for a derived structure. It also means that they cannot have virtual destructors.

 Structures are a great way to use C++ without drawbacks such as huge overhead from classes, overloaded operators, and the like. In addition, because they are fully backward-compatible with C code, structures provide a great interface to existing legacy code. By adding elements like constructors to your structures for initialization, you can get the best of the old world and the new. The constructor allows you to make sure that all of the elements of the structure contain valid values at all times, which was not true of the original C style structure.

Implementing Structures

In this section, I explore the way to implement structures in C++, as well as what you can — and can't — do with them. In this technique, we will look at the original C style structure, the enhanced C++ structure with initialization, and a more complete C++ structure that contains methods.

1. **In the code editor of your choice, create a new file to hold the code for the implementation of the source file.**

In this example, the file is named `ch14.cpp`, although you can use whatever you choose.

2. **Type the code below into your file.**

```
typedef struct classic_c_structure
{
```

```
    int x;
    int y;
} POINT;
```

This will be the "standard" structure as it is implemented in C. Now, let's try the same thing in C++, with a little enhancement to take advantage of what the language offers.

3. **Append the following structure definition to your source-code file, using your favorite code editor:**

```
typedef struct c_plus_plus_structure
{
    int x;
    int y;

    c_plus_plus_structure()
    {
        x = 0;
        y = 0;
    }
} CPP_POINT;
```

The structure listed in the code above is the same as the previous one, but it contains a constructor that will automatically initialize the values within the structure, an otherwise common oversight among programmers.

4. **Append the following structure definition to your source-code file, using your favorite code editor:**

```
typedef struct c_plus_plus_enhanced
{
    int x;
    int y;

    c_plus_plus_enhanced()
    {
        x = 0;
        y = 0;
    }
    void print()
    {
    printf("x = %d\n", x );
    printf("y = %d\n", y );
    }
} CPP_POINTE;
```

In this case, we have simply extended our C++ structure to have another method that allows us to dump the data values of the class.

5. **Append a derived structure to the file. Enter the following code into your code editor.**

This code will show you how derivation is handled in C++ for structures:

```
typedef struct new_struct : public
  CPP_POINTE
{
    int version;

    new_struct()                      → 2
    {
        version = 1;
    }

    void print()
    {
    CPP_POINTE::print();
    printf("version = %d\n",
    version );
    }
} NEW_POINT;
```

6. **Save the source-code file.**

Interpreting the Output

After you have the actual code for your structure implemented, you should test it to illustrate how it is to be used, and to validate that it is working properly.

1. **Add the code from Listing 14-1 to your source-code file, immediately below the structure definitions.**

LISTING 14-1: THE STRUCTURE TEST HARNESS

```
void print_point( CPP_POINTE& p)
{
    p.print();
}

int main(int argc, char **argv)
{
```

```
    POINT p;
    CPP_POINT p1;
    CPP_POINTE p2;
    NEW_POINT p3;

    printf("POINT:\n");
    printf("X: %d\n", p.x);
    printf("Y: %d\n", p.y);

    printf("POINT 1:\n");
    printf("X: %d\n", p1.x);
    printf("Y: %d\n", p1.y);

    printf("POINT 2:\n");
    print_point(p2);

    printf("POINT 3:\n");
    print_point(p3);
}
```

This code simply exercises the various structures that we have defined in the source file. You will be able to see what happens when the initialization process is done and when it is not.

2. **Save the source-code file and close the code editor.**

3. **Compile and run the program, using your favorite compiler on your favorite operating system.**

If you have done everything properly, you should see the following output on your shell window:

```
$ ./a.exe
POINT:
X: 2289768                            → 1
Y: 1627507534
POINT 1:
X: 0
Y: 0
POINT 2:
x = 0
y = 0
POINT 3:
x = 0
y = 0
```

There are a few things to notice here. First of all, you can see why failing to initialize the data values of a structure is a bad idea (see the lines indicated by → **1**). The first point, the classic C-style structure, contains junk code that could easily cause serious problems in an application.

 Always initialize all values in classes or structures to avoid serious problems later in the application.

Imagine how much worse it would be if the structure contained pointers: Pointers that are not initialized to point at something will either be pointing at an invalid part of memory, or worse, to a part of memory that should not be modified.

Notice that when we added a constructor to the structure, our enhanced version called the constructor (→ **2**) automatically for the class, as you would expect. That way the structure elements were initialized without requiring any work from the user. Naturally, you can have constructors that take arguments as well.

 Always implement a constructor for all structures in your C++ code. If you do not, the structure elements will contain random data values.

It's handy to dump the data values for a structure quickly and easily without cluttering the program with `printf` statements — as the third variant of the structure illustrates with its `print()` member function. Of course, we could have easily written a function that accepted a structure of the proper type to print it out (as we did with the second type), but then it would have to appear everywhere the structure was used.

With the derived structure (`new_struct`), there are some interesting things to notice. First, because we can't override the function print within the base class, the structure doesn't print out data that is only in the derived class. This is due to the limitation of no virtual tables in structures. We can, however, pass this structure to anything that accepts its base class — just as we could with a normal class. In this way, the structure "acts" like a class.

 Because the base class members are always public, we can access them from either the structure method itself, or from the external program. This is quite different from a class, where you would have to have accessor methods to get or set the data.

Technique 15

Understanding Constants

Save Time By

- Exploring the uses of constants
- Defining constants
- Implementing constants
- Using the `const` keyword

Pity the poor, misunderstood C++ constant — there are so very many ways to use it, yet so few of them are really understood. By using the constant (or `const` statement) construct in your code, your applications can be made safer, more readable, and more efficient. Yet, programmers are often so overwhelmed by the incredible number of different ways in which they can use constants that they simply avoid the construct completely, allowing the compiler to pick and choose what can change and what cannot in the application. A word to the wise: Allowing the compiler to make choices for you is very rarely a good idea.

 Constants provide a way to self-document your code, as well as a simple way to locate all of the definitions of values in your program. By utilizing constants for your data values, you can make quick, easy, simultaneous changes across the scope of your application. In addition, you can enforce what does and does not change in the methods and functions of your application by using the `const` keyword.

In this technique I explore the various possibilities for working with constants in C++ and what they mean to you as an application developer.

Defining Constants

To best understand how constants work and how you can utilize them in your application, the following steps show you a simple example of defining various kinds of constants. We will be creating a file that contains constants for use as whole numbers, floating point numbers, and character strings. You will see how a constant can directly replace a `#define` value, as well as how the compiler can be used to do type-safe checking of constant assignments.

1. **In the code editor of your choice, create a new file to hold the code for the implementation of the source file.**

In this example, the file is named `ch15.cpp`, although you can use whatever you choose.

2. **Type the code from Listing 15-1 into your file.**

Better yet, copy the code from the source file on this book's companion Web site.

LISTING 15-1: THE CONSTANTS AND THEIR DEFINITIONS

```
#include <stdio.h>
#include <stdlib.h>

// This is a constant value that can be used
// in place of a #define value

const int MaxValues = 100;

// Unlike the #define, you can use a const
// for typesafe constants

const char *StringName = "Matt Telles";
const double Cost = 100.35;
const long MaxLong = 1000000;
```

You can define constants of pretty much any shape or size. Constants can be numbers, strings, characters, or floats. More importantly, the compiler will check for type safety when you assign a constant to another value. For example, you're permitted to assign string values to string constants, like this:

```
string myString = StringName;
```

You are not, however, permitted to assign `MaxLong` values to integers, which would look like this:

```
int iVal = MaxLong; // The compiler will
    complain.
```

3. **Save the source-code file.**

Of course (so far), all adding the constants has really done is give us another way to replace the `#define` statement in our application. The real meat of the C++ constant is giving the compiler directives in your functions and classes, as I show you in the next section.

Implementing Constant Variables

The `const` statement can also be used to tell the compiler that something is not permitted to change, as we will see in this simple technique that relies on another facet of the `const` keyword. Follow these steps to see how it all works:

1. **Append the code from Listing 15-2 to your source-code file.**

LISTING 15-2: A FUNCTION WITH AN IMMUTABLE ARGUMENT

```
// Functions can take constant arguments,
    allowing them
// to guarantee that values don't change.

int func( const int& x )
{
    // We can do this
    int z = x;
    // We cannot do this. Compile Error:
    //x = 10;                              ➔ 1

    return x;
}
```

This function accepts a single argument of type `const int` reference. The `const` modifier indicates to the compiler that the input argument cannot be modified. If you were to uncomment the line marked ➔ **1**, you would see the compiler generate an error telling you that you cannot modify a constant reference.

This example looks at a function that accepts a single-integer argument, the constant x. We are informing both the user of the function and the compiler that this function will never change the value of that argument, even if it is passed in by reference. This information is very important to the compiler; with this knowledge it can optimize your function so that it does not have to pop the value back off the stack and insure that the memory location that it is using will not change. This is possible because this value can be thrown away after the function is done; after all, it could not possibly have changed.

 Proper use of the `const` modifier allows the compiler to generate closer-to-optimal code and generate better warnings, so you can write better applications and have fewer errors to fix in the debugging phase.

Furthermore, because we know that the input is a constant, we can pass in values that are constant. For example, if the reference was not a constant, you'd have to write this:

```
int x = 3;
int myVal = func( x );
```

because the compiler would never allow you to write *this:*

```
int myVal = func(3);
```

When you define the input argument as a constant, however, the compiler is now aware that the actual memory location that's holding your value (in this case, 3) will not change, and it will allow you to pass in the integer value without first assigning it to anything. This arrangement saves a few CPU cycles and some memory — and you don't have to write some silly code that doesn't really do anything.

2. **Using your code editor, append the code from Listing 15-3 to your source-code file.**

This technique illustrates how you can use the `const` keyword within a class to accomplish the same things that it does outside of a class listing.

LISTING 15-3: CONSTANTS IN CLASSES

```
// Classes can have constants in them
const int MaxEntries = 10;
class Foo
{
    int    entries[ MaxEntries ];

public:
    // You can pass in constant references to arguments
    Foo()
    {
    }
    Foo( const Foo& aCopy )
    {
        for ( int i=0; i<MaxEntries; ++i )
            entries[i] = aCopy.entries[i];
    }
    // You can return constant references from methods
    const int * getEntries()
    {

        return &entries[0];
    }
    // You can indicate that a method will NOT change
    // anything in the object
    int getEntry( int index ) const
    {
        return entries[index];
```

(continued)

LISTING 15-3 (continued)

```
    }
    // The two can be combined to say that the return value
    // cannot be changed and the object will not change
    const int& getAConstEntry( int index ) const
    {
        return entries[index];
    }
};
```

---

3. **Save the source-code file and close the code editor.**

As you can see, the const construct is quite versatile. It can be used to indicate a value that is used to replace a number in your code. It can be used to indicate a return value that cannot be changed. It can indicate that a class method accepts an argument that it doesn't change, such as the Copy constructor. Can you imagine writing a Copy constructor that changed the object it copied? That would be a little strange to say the least. Imagine writing something like this:

```
    Foo f1 = f;
```

Then imagine having the f object change out from under you — talk about your basic debugging nightmare. For this reason, it's customary to use a const reference, indicating that you won't change the object being copied. In the same manner, we can pass in values to methods and assure the user that they won't be copied (as in the func function we looked at earlier in Listing 15-2).

Of course, if you can take an input value and assure the user that you will not change it, then the quid pro quo argument is that you must be able to give someone back a value and make sure that they don't change it. This is called returning a const reference. For example, if you have an internal variable, you could create a reference method that gave it back, but only in a read-only fashion. That is what the getEntries method does in Listing 15-3. It returns a const pointer that makes sure that the user doesn't change anything in the program that calls the object.

Finally, you can tell the user that the method you are calling will never change the object. To do so, you simply append the const keyword at the end of the method, which allows your method to be called on const objects. Doing so also allows the compiler to avoid the overhead of having to make copies of objects and such. If the object cannot be changed via the method, there is no reason to worry about making the memory location static.

Testing the Constant Application

After you create the class, you should create a test driver that not only ensures that your code is correct, but also shows people how to use your code.

1. **In the code editor of your choice, open the existing file to hold the code for your test program.**

In this example, I named the test program ch15.cpp.

The next step (for wise programmers, and you know who you are) is to add a simple test driver to the source file so you can take a look at how all this plays out.

2. **Type the code from Listing 15-4 into your file.**

Better yet, copy the code from the source file on this book's companion Web site.

LISTING 15-4: THE TEST DRIVER FOR CONSTS

```
int main(int argc, char **argv)
{
    Foo f;
```

```
    // Note that to get back the entries, we
       MUST define
    // our return type as constant
    const int *entries = f.getEntries();  → 2
    // You can't do this:
    // entries[2] = 2;

    return 0;
}
```

3. **Save the source-code file and close the code editor.**

4. **Compile the application with your favorite compiler on your favorite operating system.**

   Notice that we must use a constant pointer (→ **2**) to access the entries in the class, and that we cannot modify the values in that entry block passed back. The compiler reinforces both these conditions at compile-time.

   Thus you can see how const works in the C++ world — and how you can use it to enforce your application's demands on the end user. (In a *good* way, of course.)

Using the const Keyword

Here's another job for the versatile const keyword: You can use it as a differentiator to determine which method to use; the const keyword is a part of the signature of a method. That means you can have the two methods shown in Listing 15-5 in your class at the same time. The const keyword isn't interpreted by the user, but rather by the compiler to determine which method is being called. If the value is modifiable, it will call the non-const version. If the value cannot be modified, it will call the const version.

LISTING 15-5: USING CONST TO DIFFERENTIATE TWO METHODS

```
    // You can indicate that a method will
       NOT change
    // anything in the object
    int getEntry( int index ) const      → 3
    {
```

```
        return entries[index];
    }
    // Or not, depending on how you feel.
    int getEntry( int index )              → 4
    {
        return entries[ index ];
    }
```

The first of these methods can be used from any object, constant (→ **3**) or otherwise (→ **4**) . The second, on the other hand, can only be used from a non-const object. If you choose to call the second, you have to accept the risk that the user will directly modify the data within your class.

Finally, it is worth pointing out that const is something that can actually be cast away if the user explicitly chooses to do so. So, even if you create the getEntries method (as in Listing 15-3) — which requires you to use a const int pointer to call the method — the programmer can get around this little problem by writing code like that in Listing 15-6.

LISTING 15-6: CASTING AWAY CONST-NESS

```
    // Now, you can break things this way
    int *ent2 = (int *)f.getEntries();    → 5
    ent2[2] = 2;
```

C++ always assumes that the programmer knows what he or she is doing, even if allowing some things to be done incorrectly (which violates the spirit of the language). By doing explicit casting (→ **5**), you can "de-const" a pointer (that is, make a const pointer non-const) and do whatever you want. The compiler assumes that because you did the explicit cast, you knew exactly what the end result would be, and had figured out every possible ramification for the program as a whole. Such trust is touching — but *not* a good idea. If the pointer was defined to be constant in the first place, there was probably a good reason for it. In your own application development, avoid such a technique at all costs.

Technique 16

Scoping Your Variables

The concept of "scope" is fairly unique to the C and C++ languages. *Scope,* also called *lifetime,* is the period of the application during which a variable exists. Some variables can exist for the entire length of the program (and unfortunately, as with some memory leaks, well beyond that length), while others have very short periods — that is, less scope. The length of an object's or variable's lifetime is generally up to the developer, but sometimes you have to keep close watch on when a variable goes out of scope in your own applications.

When implementing classes and objects, scope usually is handled automatically. An object starts to exist when its constructor is invoked, and ceases to exist when its destructor is invoked. Suppose (for example) an object of the Foo class is created on the stack with a command like this:

```
Foo f;
```

The Foo object will be automatically destroyed when the scope it exists in is destroyed. Consider the following example, with three different instances of the Foo class being created on the heap:

```
Foo global_foo; //                                      → 1

int main()
{
    Foo main_foo; //                                    → 2

    for ( int i=0; i<10; ++i )
    {
        Foo loop_foo; //                                → 3

    } //
} //
//
```

As you can see, three different Foo objects are created at different points in the application code. The first one, the global_foo object (indicated at → 1) is created before the application even starts, in the main function.

The second, `main_foo` (indicated at ➔ **2**), is created at the start of the `main` function, and the third, `loop_foo` (indicated at ➔ **3**), exists in the `for` loop in the middle of the `main` function. The `loop_foo` object is created each time the program cycles through the `for` loop — ten times in all.

If we implemented the `Foo` class to tell us when the object was created, and on what line each object was destroyed , we could actually view this information visually and be able to understand the flow of the process.

In the following section, I show you a simple way to do just that.

Illustrating Scope

Identifying an object's starting time and specific code line on-screen is one way to get an idea of its scope. Here's how to make it happen:

1. **In the code editor of your choice, create a new file to hold the code for the implementation of the source file.**

In this example, the file is named `ch16.cpp`, although you can use whatever you choose.

2. **Type the code from Listing 16-1 into your file.**

Better yet, copy the code from the source file on this book's companion Web site.

This code creates a very simple class that self-documents its creation and destruction processes. We will then use this class to see the order in which objects are created and destroyed in a real-world program setting.

LISTING 16-1: ILLUSTRATING SCOPE

```c
#include <stdio.h>
#include <stdlib.h>

class Foo
{
private:
    long _Level;
```

```c
public:
    Foo( long level )
    {
        printf("Creating foo object %ld\n",
        level );
        _Level = level;
    }
    ~Foo()
    {
        printf("Destroying foo object
        %ld\n", _Level );
    }
};
```

3. **Append the following code to your source-code file, using your code editor.**

Here we are simply creating a little test driver that illustrates how the objects are created and destroyed. You could easily place this code in a separate file, but for simplicity we will just add it all to the same file.

This code illustrates the various levels of scope, `global`, `local`, and `loop`, that an object can occupy within an application.

```c
Foo global_foo(0);

int main()
{
    Foo main_foo(1);


    for ( int i=0; i<3; ++i )
    {

        Foo loop_foo(2);

    }
}
```

4. **Save the file and close your code editor.**

5. **Compile and run the application in the operating system of your choice.**

Interpreting the Output

If you have done everything right, you should see the following output in the shell window on your system:

```
$ ./a.exe
Creating foo object 0
Creating foo object 1
Creating foo object 2
Destroying foo object 2
Creating foo object 2
Destroying foo object 2
Creating foo object 2
Destroying foo object 2
Destroying foo object 1
Destroying foo object 0
```

Note that the order in which the variables are destroyed is exactly the reverse of the order in which they were created. This is due to the object's positions in the file: The last object created is the first one destroyed. Paying attention to when objects are created and destroyed in your program helps you optimize the use of memory, and also allows you to control when objects are available. For example, if an object used to create a file requires a filename, instantiating the object before the filename is available doesn't make sense, even if the open method of the object is used well after the fact. Now, consider the following snippet of a program:

```
int main()
{
    Foo *f = new Foo(10);

    // Some other code
}
```

When will the Foo object be created? Obviously, the constructor is called on the line with the new function call. However, it is not at all clear when the object is destroyed. If you were to run the program, you would see the following output:

```
Creating foo object 10
```

There will be no corresponding printout saying that the object was destroyed — because the object is never destroyed. For this reason, you should always be very careful either to create your objects on the heap (using the constructor and no new call), or match your calls to new and delete for the object (in other words, if you allocate an object with new, deallocate it with delete). If you do not delete all objects that you create, you will create memory leaks in your application, which can lead to program crashes, computer slowdowns, and a host of other unpredictable behavior.

An alternative to this approach is the auto_ptr class of the Standard Template Library. This class holds a pointer to a given class, but it does so inside an object allocated on the heap. When the object on the heap goes out of scope, the object is destroyed. As part of that destruction, the pointer is deleted. This is really the best practical use of the scope concept in C++.

17

Using Namespaces

Technique

Save Time By

✔ Resolving name conflicts with namespaces

✔ Creating a namespace application

✔ Testing your namespace application

Once upon a time, there was a language called C. It was a popular language that allowed people to create nice, reusable libraries of code — which they then sold in the marketplace for big bucks. Later on, this language was replaced by a language called C++, which also allowed programmers to create reusable code. Learning from the problems of the past, C++, unlike C, also allowed you to package your code in classes, which solved one of C's very difficult problems: resolving functions with name conflicts. Because it is common to have different functions in different libraries that do similar things, it was inevitable that the names of those functions would be similar. By restricting those methods to different class names, it fixed the problem. Of course, that didn't help when the class names were the same, but we will discuss that problem in just a bit.

Here is how the problem worked: Consider, for example, two libraries that exist in a C-style interface: one performs windowing functions; the other manages documents. In Library One, we have the following function:

```
void SetTitle( char *sTitle )
{
    // Set the title of the window to sTitle
    window->title = sTitle;
}
```

In Library Two, the document library, we have the following function:

```
void SetTitle( char *sTitle )
{
    // Set the file name for the document
    _filename = sTitle;
}
```

Now, both of these functions have the same name and the same signature, but they have very different goals and code to implement them.

Here we have two routines that do the same basic thing (setting a title) with different code — but that isn't the problem. The problem is that the linker in C (and also in C++) can't deal with this situation; it freaks out if two functions have the same name with the same signature. It could handle that if you only wanted one of them, but that obviously would not work. So, with the advent of classes, you'd think all this would be fixed, right? Nope. As with all other things in life, problems don't really go away, they just morph into a different form. Of course, we can fix this problem, it is just a matter of understanding where the problem came from in the first place. The answer, in this case, is to create different classes to wrap the functions.

 Naming classes properly goes a long way toward saving you time when you're trying to link in multiple libraries from different sources. Always preface your classes with a known prefix (such as the company initials) to avoid problems.

Fast-forward a bit to the C++ world. Programmers are still developing libraries, but now these are libraries of *classes,* rather than of simple functions. The basic problem of name conflict has not changed — but our example libraries (now updated in C++) have changed. The windowing library now implements classes to handle the all-new, all-different, *model-view-controller* concept. This concept allows you to work not only with documents but also with views of those documents.

 The concept of a *document* means the data for a displayed window is encapsulated in a class that can load the data from a file, save it to a file, and manipulate it for display purposes.

Meanwhile, over in the document library, we have document classes that store text, formatting information, and preferences for document information. In the document library, the `Document` class is defined like this:

```
class Document
{
private:
    std::string filename;
    std::vector< std::string > lines;
public:
    Document()
    {
    }
```

```
    Document( const char *_filename)
    {
        filename = _filename;
    }
    boolean Read();
    Boolean Write();
};
```

In the windowing library, however, the `Document` class is defined a bit differently:

```
class Document
{
private:
    std::string title;
    std::vector< Window *> windows;
public:
    Document()
    {
    }
    Document( const char *_title );
    void CreateWindow();
};
```

While this is not as simple as the function example, the problem is exactly the same. When push comes to shove, the linker is going to need to resolve two different classes of the same name. This isn't possible, so it is going to complain about it. How do you fix a conflict like this? The answer lies in the concept of C++ *namespaces.*

Namespaces were created in C++ to address just this problem. While you might have a class that is in conflict with another class, it would be extremely unlikely to have an entire library of classes that is in conflict. With proper naming of a namespace, you can avoid the entire problem of class name collision.

Creating a Namespace Application

The basic format of defining a namespace is as follows:

```
namespace <name> {
    // some classes or definitions
};
```

To illustrate how all this works, a quick look at some real code is in order, followed by a tour of the options you can use in your own code to fix name collisions. The following steps show you how:

1. **In the code editor of your choice, create a new file to hold the code for the implementation of the source file.**

In this example, the file is named `ch17.cpp`, although you can use whatever you choose.

2. **Type the code from Listing 17-1 into your file.**

Better yet, copy the code from the source file on this book's companion Web site.

LISTING 17-1: USING NAMESPACES

```
#include <stdio.h>
#include <stdlib.h>
#include <string>

using namespace std;

namespace foo_windowing
{
    class window
    {
    private:
        int window_id;
        string title;
    public:
        window(void)
        {
            window_id = 0;
            title = "";
        }
        window(int id, const char *t)
        {
            window_id = id;
            title = t;
        }
    };

    class document
    {
    private:
        int doc_id;
        string title;
    public:
        document(void)
        {
            doc_id = 0;
            title = "";
        }
        document(int id, const char *t)
        {
            doc_id = id;
            title = t;
        }
    };
}; // End of namespace foo_windowing
```

Before we move on to the next step, let's take a look at the important features of this code that you can adapt to your own programs.

First, notice the `using namespace` statement up there at the top — normally you must fully qualify the names of all classes within any namespace you use. The `string` class for the Standard Template Library happens to "live" within the `std` namespace. When you utilize the `using namespace std` statement, you tell the compiler that you know what you're doing and that it should try the `std::` namespace on anything it cannot immediately recognize. Of course, if you use all available namespaces, you avoid the problem of entering the namespace's name prefix on all your class names — but then you also run into the problem of name collisions again. That's why the compiler makes you qualify the name whenever there's any doubt.

The next step takes a closer look at the second namespace we create (in this case, for the document classes).

3. **Modify your source code in the code editor as shown in Listing 17-2.**

Simply append this code to the end of your current source-code listing.

LISTING 17-2: CREATING A NEW NAMESPACE

```
namespace bar_documents
{
    class document
    {
    private:
        string filename;
```

(continued)

LISTING 17-2 *(continued)*

```
    public:
        document(void)
        {
            filename = "";
        }
        document(const char *fn)
        {
            filename = fn;
        }
    };
        string name()
        {
            return filename;
        }
    };

}; // End of namespace bar_documents
```

4. **Save the source code in the source-code editor.**

As you can see, we have a definite name conflict if we use these two class sets together. They both define a class called document. Worse, the document class in one is very different from the document class in the other. In the first case, our document class represents the data being displayed in a window. In the second case, the

document class represents a file on disk. Fortunately, by placing each of the classes in a different namespace, we can differentiate between the two classes easily so the compiler knows what we're talking about. A real application offers an example in the next section.

Testing the Namespace Application

The following list shows you the steps to create a test driver that validates various kinds of input from the user, and illustrates how namespaces are intended to be used.

1. **In the code editor of your choice, open the existing file to hold the code for your test program.**

In this example, I named the test program ch17.cpp.

2. **Type the code from Listing 17-3 into your file.**

Better yet, copy the code from the source file on this book's companion Web site.

LISTING 17-3: USING NAMESPACES IN AN APPLICATION

```
// Let's default to the bar_documents namespace
using namespace bar_documents;

void print_doc( document& d )
{
    printf("Received file: %s\n", d.name().c_str() );
}

int main( int argc, char **argv )
{
    document d("file1.txt"); // Create a bar_documents document
    foo_windowing::document d1(1, "this is a title");

    // This is okay to do
    print_doc( d );

    // This would not be okay to do
    //print_doc( d1 );
```
→ 1
```
}
```

Here we've inserted a line to make the `bar_docu-ments` namespace *global* — which means we don't have to say `bar_documents::document` everywhere we use the class. In fact (as you can see in the first line of the main program), we simply create a document via a standard usage of the `Document` class. When we want to use the `foo_windowing` namespace classes, however, we still have to fully qualify them as you can see in the second line of the main program. Likewise, we can pass a `bar_documents` document to the function `print_doc`, but we cannot do the same with a `foo_windowing` document. If you uncomment the line that calls `print_doc` with the `foo_windowing` document object, you will get the compile-time error shown in Listing 17-4.

3. **Save your source-code file and close the code editor.**

4. **Compile the file with your favorite compiler on your favorite operating system.**

If you have done everything properly, you will see the following output on your shell window:

```
$ ./a.exe
Received file: file1.txt
```

As you can see from the output, the function that we expected to work with a `bar_documents` namespace document object works properly. If we uncommented the line marked with ➙ **1**, we would get a compile error, since that function does not expect to receive a document object from a different namespace. This is illustrated in Listing 17-4.

 When creating your own reusable classes in C++, always place them within a namespace to avoid name collisions with third-party libraries and other internally developed code.

LISTING 17-4: TRYING TO USE A DIFFERENT NAMESPACE CLASS

```
ch3_5.cpp: In function 'int main(int, char**)':
ch3_5.cpp:74: error: no matching function for call to 'foo_windowing::document
    ::document(const char[16])'
ch3_5.cpp:28: error: candidates are: foo_windowing::document::document(const
    foo_windowing::document&)
ch3_5.cpp:39: error:                 foo_windowing::document::document(int,
    const char*)
ch3_5.cpp:34: error:                 foo_windowing::document::document()
```

18 Technique

Fixing Breaks with Casts

Save Time By

- Defining casts
- Understanding the problems that casts can cause
- Addressing cast-related compiler problems
- Testing your improved code

When you break a bone, the doctor puts it in a cast to make sure that the bone sets properly and keeps the correct shape. C++ has the same notion of casts — and they're used for exactly the same reasons. A cast in C++ explicitly changes a variable or value from one type to another. In this way, we "fix" things by making them the proper type for what we need those values for.

The need for casts comes from the picky nature of the C++ compiler. If you tell it that you're expecting a given function to take an integer value, it will complain if it is given anything *but* an integer value. It might complain (for example) by warning you that there's a lack of precision, like this:

```
int func(int x);

long x=100;
func(x);
```

Here the compiler gripes about this function-call invocation, saying that converting a long integer to a regular one is legal, but you're risking a possible loss of precision. The compiler is right, too. Imagine, for example, that the value of x is 50,000 instead of 100. That number is too big to be stored in a normal integer, so it overflows and the function gets passed a negative number to chew on. Don't believe it? Try the following little programlet:

```
#include <stdio.h>

int func(short int x)
{
    printf("x = %d\n", x );
}

int main(int argc, char **argv)
{
    long x = 10;
    func(x);
    x = 50000;
    func(x);
    return 0;
}
```

Here, because the gcc compiler assumes that int and a long integers are the same thing, we have to use a short int in the function itself for gcc to illustrate the problem.

When you compile and run this program, you see the following output:

```
$ ./a.exe
x = 10
x = -15536
```

Not exactly what we asked for, is it?

If you know that the value of x is never going to exceed the maximum value of an integer, you can safely call the function even with a long integer, as long as you cast it properly:

```
func( (short int)x );
```

The reason that you might want to do something like this is that you don't want to create a new variable, assign the value to it, and then check to make sure that it did not overflow the range of that new variable type. The cast does all of this for you.

Of course, encasing the integer in a cast is considerably more powerful than simply making an integer into a long or a double or anything else. Casting one type to another turns the original variable into a new one, albeit behind the scenes. This is true whether we are casting a variable in the example above, or modifying a variable by casting it to another type.

 If you eliminate all compiler warnings in an application, you can track down problems much more quickly and easily — you're letting the compiler do your work for you. Most compiler warnings, including those requiring casts, need to be addressed immediately, not just ignored. This will save you time in the long run.

In the next section, I show you a more involved example of a cast.

Using Casts

Suppose that you have two base classes, Base1 and Base2. From these two classes, we derive a third class, called Derived. How can you get at functions in the base classes that have the same name in both bases? The answer lies in a cast, as we will see in this example technique. It might seem that we are back to the discussion of name differentiation and namespaces, but this is not the case here. Consider the following layout:

Class 1: Method A

Class 2: Method A

Class 3: Derived from Class 1 and 2.

When we are using Class 3, and refer to Method A, which method do we really mean?

1. **In the code editor of your choice, create a new file to hold the code for the implementation of the source file.**

   In this example, the file is named ch18.cpp, although you can use whatever you choose.

2. **Type the code from Listing 18-1 into your file.**

   Better yet, copy the code from the source file on this book's companion Web site.

LISTING 18-1: USING CASTS

```
#include <stdio.h>
#include <string>

using namespace std;

class Base1
{
private:
    string _name;
    long   _value;
public:
    Base1()
    {
        _name = "";
    }
```

(continued)

LISTING 18-1 *(continued)*

```
Base1( const char *n, long v)
{
    _name = n;
    _value = v;
}
virtual ~Base1()
{
}

string GetName()
{
    return _name;
}
long GetValue()
{
    return _value;
}
void SetName( const char *sName )
{
    _name = sName;
}
void SetValue( long l )
{
    _value = l;
}
};

class Base2
{
private:
    string _fileName;
    long   _fileLength;
public:
    Base2()
    {
        _fileName = "";
        _fileLength = 0;
    }
    Base2( const char *n )
    {
        _fileName = n;
        _fileLength = 0;
    }
    string GetName()
    {
        return _fileName;
    }
    long GetLength()
    {
        return _fileLength;
    }
```

```
void SetName( const char *sName )
{
    _fileName = sName;
}
void SetFileLength( long l )
{
    _fileLength = l;
}
};
```

3. Save the source-code file.

The code in this listing simply defines two classes that happen to share a common method name or two. This is not a problem, of course, because they are defined in different scopes — which means they can be reconciled by the compiler and linker into different entries in the application. In other words, there's no problem. Now, let's create one.

4. Reopen the source-code file with your code editor and add the code from Listing 18-2 to the file.

LISTING 18-2: THE DERIVED CLASS

```
class Derived :public Base1, public Base2
{
public:
    Derived( void )
        : Base1( "AClass", 10 ),
          Base2( "Derived" )
    {
    }
    Derived( const char *name)
        : Base1( name, 0 ),
          Base2( "Derived" )
    {
    }
    void ADerivedMethod()
    {
        printf("In a derived method\n");
    }
};
```

5. Save the source-code file.

This code illustrates a derived class that is built from two base classes. In this case, both of the base classes contain a method of the same name.

We need to find a way to get at the specific method in the base class that we want, which can only be done via casts. Let's look at that now.

If you were to compile and link this program, it would be fine — aside from missing its main function. The compiler would not complain about the Base classes, nor the derived class. There is no problem with deriving a class from two base classes that happen to share a common method name.

The problem comes in when we try to use a *method* from the base classes through the derived class.

6. Append the code from Listing 18-3 to the file to implement a test driver for the code.

LISTING 18-3: THE DERIVED CLASS TEST DRIVER

```
int main()
{
    Derived d;

    d.SetFileLength(100);
    d.SetName( "This is a name" );
    string s = d.GetName();
    return 0;
}
```

7. Save the source-code file and close the code editor.

8. Compile the program using your favorite source-code compiler on your favorite operating system.

You should see output from the compiler resembling that of Listing 18-4:

LISTING 18-4: SAMPLE OUTPUT

```
$ gcc ch3_8.cpp -lstdc++
ch3_8.cpp: In function 'int main()':
ch3_8.cpp:102: error: request for member
   'SetName' is ambiguous
ch3_8.cpp:68: error: candidates are: void
   Base2::SetName(const char*)
```

```
ch3_8.cpp:34: error:                 void
   Base1::SetName(const char*)
ch3_8.cpp:103: error: request for member
   'GetName' is ambiguous
ch3_8.cpp:60: error: candidates are:
   std::string Base2::GetName()
ch3_8.cpp:26: error:
   std::string Base1::GetName()
```

Addressing the Compiler Problems

Now we have an error — so (of course) the question is, how do you get at the Base-class methods when they conflict? Actually you have two ways to do this: Explicitly scope the member function that you want to use, or specifically cast the object so it has the type you want it to be. In this section, I show you how to perform both methods and discuss the consequences of each .

1. Reopen the source-code file from the example (we called it ch18.cpp) and append the code from Listing 18-5.

LISTING 18-5: THE MODIFIED TEST DRIVER CODE

```
int main()
{
    Derived d;

    d.SetFileLength(100);
    /* 1 */ ((Base1)d).SetName( "This is a
       name" );
    /* 2 */ string s = d.Base1::GetName();
       return 0;
}
```

The two alternatives are labeled with comments, between the asterisks, as blocks 1 and 2. The line labeled 1 is the explicit cast; the line labeled 2 is the scoped method call. You can probably see that the second method is somewhat more readable, but both will work just fine. The difference between them, really, is how the lines are interpreted by the compiler. When you cast an object, you are, as far as the compiler is concerned, literally changing its type. When you call the `SetName` method with the cast of the object, the `SetName` method is being called with a `Base1` object, rather than a `Derived` object. What does this mean?

Modifying the classes a bit provides a handy illustration, starting with the next step.

2. **Replace the original definitions of `Base1` and `Base2` with the following code, shown in Listing 18-6.**

LISTING 18-6: THE NEW BASE CLASS LISTINGS

```
class Base1
{
private:
    string _name;
    long   _value;
    virtual void PrintNameChange()
    {
        printf("Changed name to %s\n",
        _name.c_str() );
    }
public:
    Base1()
    {
        _name = "";
    }
    Base1( const char *n, long v)
    {
        _name = n;
        _value = v;
    }
    virtual ~Base1()
    {
    }

    string GetName()
    {
        return _name;
    }
    long GetValue()
    {
        return _value;
    }
    void SetName( const char *sName )
    {
```

```
        _name = sName;
        PrintNameChange();
    }
    void SetValue( long l )
    {
        _value = l;
    }
};
class Derived :public Base1, public Base2
{
    virtual void PrintNameChange()
    {
        printf("Derived: PrintNameChange
        called\n");
    }

public:
    Derived( void )
        : Base1( "AClass", 10 ),
          Base2( "Derived" )
    {
    }
    Derived( const char *name)
        : Base1( name, 0 ),
          Base2( "Derived" )
    {
    }
    void ADerivedMethod()
    {
        printf("In a derived method\n");
    }
};
```

Testing the Changes

After you've made all the changes in the `Base` classes for the objects you're using, the wise next step is to test those changes to make sure the compiler is happy and the code works properly. Here's the drill:

1. **In the code editor of your choice, reopen the existing file to hold the code for your test program.**

In this example, I named the test program `ch18.cpp`.

2. **Type the following code into your file as shown in Listing 18-7.**

Better yet, copy the code from the source file on this book's companion Web site.

LISTING 18-7: THE NEW TEST DRIVER

```
int main()
{
    Derived d;

    d.SetFileLength(100);
    ((Base1)d).SetName( "This is a name" );  → 1
    string s = d.Base1::GetName();
    d.Base1::SetName("This is another name");
    return 0;
}
```

3. **Save the source file in the code editor and close the editor application.**

4. **Compile and link the application on your favorite operating system, using your compiler of choice.**

If you have done everything right, you should see the following output appear on your shell window.

```
$ ./a.exe
Changed name to This is a name
Derived: PrintNameChange called      → 2
```

If you trace through the code, you will see what is going on here:

In the first case, where we physically cast the d object (shown at → **1**) to a Base1 object, the object does not "know" that it is really a Derived object when the virtual method PrintNameChange is called. As a result, the Base class method is used for the cast case (shown at → **2**).

For the second case, where we scoped the method, however, the object is well aware of what it is, and will call the inherited virtual method in the Derived class. This is a very important difference, and can lead to some very subtle logic errors in your program that are very hard to track down and fix. Casts are a very powerful technique in C++, but they are also a serious warning that you are doing something you are not supposed to be doing. If your actions were acceptable in the language, you would not have to explicitly tell the compiler that you are changing the behavior of the code through a cast. This is not a bad thing, but you need to be aware that you are changing behavior. Be sure to understand the side effects of your actions and the possibilities of introducing more problems than you are solving when you use a cast.

 Whenever possible, avoid putting casts in your application. If this is not completely possible, understand fully the warnings that your compiler issues for casts you've made.

Technique 19

Using Pointers to Member Functions

Pointers to member functions are incredibly powerful — and an integral part of the C++ language. If you use them, your code will be easier to understand and expand, and maintenance will be much quicker. In addition, new functionality can be added without having to modify the existing functions in the class. Pointers to member functions help replace complicated switch statements, lookup tables, and a variety of other complicated constructs with a simple, easy-to-implement solution.

However, because they are confusing to implement and syntactically complicated, almost nobody is willing to use the poor things. Nonetheless, the pointer to a member function is a really useful tool in your arsenal of techniques for solving problems with the C++ programming language. The issue, really, is understanding how they work and how to make the compiler understand what you want to do with them.

The first thing to understand is, what exactly *is* a pointer to a member function? In the good old days of C programming, we had plain old function pointers. A *function pointer* was a pointer to a global function, whereas a *pointer to a member function* works only with a class member function; they are otherwise the same thing. Essentially, function pointers allowed you to do this:

```
typedef int (*error_handler)(char *);
```

This statement defined a pointer to a function that accepted a single argument of the *character pointer* type, and returned an integer value. You could then assign a function to this pointer, like this:

```
int my_error_handler(char *s)
{
printf("Error: %s\n", s );
return 0;
}

error_handler TheErrorHandler = my_error_handler;
```

In a library (for example), this is a very useful way to handle errors. You allow each user to set his or her own error handler, rather than simply printing them out, or popping up an error dialog box, or logging the pesky things to a file. This way the end users of the library could trap errors and deal with them — by changing the description, printing out additional debugging information, or whatever else worked for them.

Within your library code, you would then invoke the error handler by writing:

```
(*TheErrorHandler)(theErrorString);
```

obviously checking to see if the `TheErrorHandler` was actually assigned to anything first, or was instead `NULL`.

That was how function pointers were used in C. When C++ arrived, this same kind of functionality was very useful for a variety of tasks and continued to work fine with global functions. However, there was no simple way to implement this functionality since a member function required an object to operate on it, so you couldn't just assign it to a random pointer. You can store a member function pointer anywhere. When it comes to using it, however, you need an object of the class of that member to use it. For example:

```
class Foo
{
    // A member function
    void bar(int x );
    // This defines a type
    typedef void (*ptr_to_member_function)
  (int x ) ;


public:
    ptr_to_member_function p1;
    Foo ()
    {
    // Assign the member function pointer
      p1 = bar;
    }
}

// Later in the code....
Foo::p1(0); // This won't work, since the
            member function requires a
            pointer.
    Foo x;
     x.p1(0); // This will work.
```

With the advent of *member-function pointers,* you could assign a member function to a random pointer, if you didn't mind a bit of strange syntax. You can define these pointers as

```
typedef <return-type> (<classname>::*
    PtrMemberFunc)( <args>) ;
```

Implementing Member-Function Pointers

Let's take a look at a technique for using member-function pointers to implement a simple command processor.

1. **In the code editor of your choice, create a new file to hold the source code for this technique.**

    In this example, I named the test program `ch19.cpp`.

2. **Type the code from Listing 19-1 into your file.**

    Or better yet, copy the code from the source file on this book's companion Web site.

LISTING 19-1: POINTERS TO MEMBER FUNCTIONS

```
#include <stdio.h>
#include <string>
#include <vector>


class Processor
{
    typedef bool
    (Processor::*PtrMemberFunc)( std::string
    ) ;                                        → 1
private:
    std::vector< PtrMemberFunc >
    _functionList;
protected:
    virtual bool ProcessHello(std::string s)
    {
        if ( s == "Hello" )
        {
            printf("Well, hello to you
            too!\n");
            return true;
```

(continued)

LISTING 19-1 (continued)

```
        }
        return false;
    }
    virtual bool ProcessGoodbye( std::
    string s)
    {
        if ( s == "Goodbye" )
        {
            printf("Goodbye. Have a great
            day!\n");
            return true;
        }
        return false;
    }
    virtual bool ProcessOpen( std::string s)
    {
        if ( s == "Open" )
        {
            printf("The door is now open\n");
            return true;
        }
        return false;
    }

public:
    Processor()
    {
        _functionList.insert(
        _functionList.end(),
&Processor::ProcessHello );
        _functionList.insert(
        _functionList.end(),
&Processor::ProcessGoodbye );
        _functionList.insert(
        _functionList.end(),
&Processor::ProcessOpen );
    }
    virtual ~Processor()
    {
    }
    void ProcessCommand( const std::string&
    command )
    {
        std::vector< PtrMemberFunc >::itera-
        tor iter;
        for ( iter = _functionList.begin();
        iter !=
        _functionList.end(); ++iter )
```

```
        {
            PtrMemberFunc ptr = (*iter);
            if ( (this->*ptr)( command ) )
                return;
        }
        printf("Unknown command %s\n",
        command.c_str() );
    }

};
```

3. Save your source code in the editor.

Notice that after you've defined a member-function pointer (see ➔ **1**) , you can use it the same way you'd use a "normal" pointer. In this particular case, we build up an array of pointers and simply chain through them to see whether a given string is processed. Code like this could be easily used for equation parsers, command processors, or anything else that requires a list of items to be validated and parsed. Listing 19-1 is certainly a lot cleaner and easier to extend than code like the following:

```
switch ( command )
{
    case "Hello":
        // Do something
        break;
    // .. other cases
    default:
        printf("Invalid command: %s\n",
        command.c_str() );
        break
}
```

Note that in this case, we need to add a new switch case each time we want to handle a new command. With our array of function pointers, after it is defined and added to the code, the member function does all the work.

Updating Your Code with Member-Function Pointers

Not only is Listing 19-1 cleaner and easier to extend, it is also vastly easier to expand, because you can override whatever functionality you want at the member-function level.

The distinction is worth a closer look, to show you just how useful this technique can be in your application. Imagine that you've implemented this `Processor` object and are merrily using it to process input from the user. Now, suddenly, someone else wants to use the same class — but they want to implement a completely different use for the `Open` command. All the other commands work the same way. Wouldn't it be nice to utilize the same class to do the work — and only override the function that you wanted to change? It turns out that you can. Remember, a pointer to a member function is simply a pointer to whatever will be called when that particular method is invoked on the object. If we override a virtual method in a derived class, it should automatically call that method when we use our new processor. The following steps try that:

1. **Append the code from Listing 19-2 to your source-code file.**

LISTING 19-2: THE COMMAND PROCESSOR CLASS

```
class Processor2 : public Processor
{
protected:
    virtual bool ProcessOpen( std::string s)
    {
        if ( s == "Open" )
        {
            printf("Derived processing of
            Open\n");
            return true;
        }
        return false;
    }
public:
```

```
Processor2()
{
}
};
```

2. **Save your source code in the editor and close the code-editor application.**

Testing the Member Pointer Code

After you create a pointer to a member for a class, you should create a test driver that not only ensures that your code is correct, but also shows people how to use your code.

Here's the classic follow-up — creating a test driver that shows how the class is intended to be used:

1. **In the code editor of your choice, open the existing file to hold the code for your test program.**

In this example, I named the test program ch19.cpp.

2. **Type the code from Listing 19-3 into your file.**

Better yet, copy the code from the source file on this book's companion Web site.

LISTING 19-3: THE TEST DRIVER FOR THE COMMAND PROCESSOR

```
int main(int argc, char **argv )
{
    Processor2 p;

    for ( int i=1; i<argc; ++i )
        p.ProcessCommand( argv[i] );
}
```

3. **Close your source-code file in the editor and close the editor application.**

4. **Compile the source code with your favorite compiler on your favorite operating system, and then run it with the following command:**

```
./a.exe Open Goodbye
```

If you have done everything right, you should see the following output when you run the program with these arguments.

```
Derived processing of Open
Goodbye. Have a great day
```

As you can see, not only have we created a command handler to process the open command, but we have also allowed for standard C++ derivation. In addition, we could easily add additional handlers that process the same command, something that we could not do with the switch statement.

Defining Default Arguments for Your Functions and Methods

Technique 20

Save Time By

- ✓ Simplifying code with default arguments
- ✓ Implementing default arguments in functions and methods
- ✓ Customizing self-defined functions and methods
- ✓ Customizing functions and methods someone else wrote
- ✓ Testing your code

In C++, a failure to call functions or methods properly is a common problem. One solution is to verify all input values when the end user sends them in — but this has the unhappy side effect of creating more errors for the end developer to fix. The problem is that it is harder to screen out bad values than it is to accept only good ones. For an integer value that is supposed to be between 1 and 10, for example, there are ten valid values. However, there are an infinite number of bad integer values that exist outside the range of 1 to 10. Wouldn't it be nice if you could tell the developer what the most likely value is for some of the less-common function arguments? The programmer could then ignore the problematic values by using acceptable defaults. For example, consider the MessageBox function, a standard function used by many Microsoft Windows programmers. This function, which has the following signature, displays a message for the application user to see and respond to.

```
int MessageBox(
    HWND hWnd,
    LPCTSTR lpText,
    LPCTSTR lpCaption,
    UINT uType
);
```

The MessageBox arguments are as follows:

- ✓ **hWnd:** A handle to a Windows window
- ✓ **lpText:** The text to display in the message box
- ✓ **lpCaption:** The caption to put in the title bar of the message box
- ✓ **uType:** The types of buttons (OK, Cancel, Abort, Retry, and so on) to display in the message box.

This is a very handy function and is used nearly universally by Windows programmers to display errors, warnings, and messages. The problem is that it's too easy to forget the order of the arguments. In addition, programmers tend to use the thing over and over in the same ways. This means that the same code is repeated over and over, and changes must be made all over the system when a new way of doing things is desired. It would be nice, therefore, to be able to customize this `MessageBox` function with some defaults, so we could just call it the way we want to. We would have to specify only the values that change, which limits the number of arguments to enter, making it easier to remember the order and easier to avoid error values.

Customizing a function can mean one of two things: If we are the ones writing the function, it means that we can customize the kind of arguments that go into the function and how those arguments are likely to be used. If we didn't write the function in the first place, we can't do those things; we can only "change" the way the function is called by wrapping something about it — that is, placing it inside a new function we created ourselves — one that plays by our rules. We'll look at the first case in a bit; for right now, consider the case of wrapping something around our poor `MessageBox` function to make it easier for the application developer to use.

Customizing the Functions We Didn't Write

One probable use of the `MessageBox` function is to display error messages. Because the end user can do nothing with such an error, there is no reason to display the Cancel button on the message box — even though most applications do just that. In this section, I show you how to create your own variation on the `MessageBox` function — the `ErrorBox` function — which is different from `MessageBox` only in that it puts the word "Error" at the top of the display title bar and it displays only an OK button with the text. There's no real reason to create any new functionality for this function, because, after all, the `MessageBox` function already does everything we want it to do. Our function would look like Listing 20-1.

LISTING 20-1: A CUSTOMIZED MESSAGEBOX FUNCTION

```
int ErrorBox( HWND hWnd, const char *text,
    const char *title = "Error", UINT type =
    MB_OK )
{
    MessageBox(hWnd, text, title, type );
}
```

Okay, we aren't adding much value here, but consider how the function is now called within an application code:

```
// Display an error
ErrorBox( NULL, "You have to first enter a
    file name!");
```

This is certainly a lot easier than the full-blown `MessageBox` call. The advantage, of course, is that you don't *have* to use the shortened version — you can still use the entire thing, like this:

```
ErrorBox(m_hWnd, "The system is very low
    on memory! Retry or Cancel?" "Critical
    Error", MB_RETRY | MB_CANCEL );
```

The shortened version is certainly more readable and consistent, and it saves you time because it offers fewer parameters to update. What if, for example, management decides that the phrasing of your error is too harsh and wants to replace it with `A problem has occurred`? If you're using the long version of this function, the way to solve this problem is to find all calls to the function in your code. With our wrapper function, however, we could eliminate the error in the call itself, and place it into the wrapper function. All errors, for example, could begin with "An error has occurred" and then append the actual error text. Of course, to make things even easier, you could go a step further and allow the function to read data strings from an external file — that capability would allow for internationalization as well.

Customizing Functions We Wrote Ourselves

Of course, simply customizing other people's code isn't always the best approach when adding default arguments. Default arguments are arguments that the function developer provides. If you do not want to specify a value other than the default, you omit the argument entirely. If you wish to change the default for a specific invocation, you may do so. The real point to the practice is to provide the most likely uses of a given argument, while protecting the capability of the user to change (or customize) your defaults.

This technique creates, in a single class, both the functions and methods that allow the user complete control over his or her input — while providing appropriate defaults that make it simple to use the class's methods and functions to accomplish normal operations.

An example is an operation that most programmers do on a regular basis: creating a file. The following steps show you how to create a very simple `File` class that allows opening, reading, writing, and closing files:

1. **In the code editor of your choice, create a new file to hold the code for the implementation of the source file.**

   In this example, the file is named `ch20.cpp`, although you can use whatever you choose.

2. **Type the code from Listing 20-2 into your file.**

   Better yet, copy the code from the source file on this book's companion Web site.

LISTING 20-2: A CLASS WITH METHODS CONTAINING DEFAULT VALUES

```cpp
#include <stdio.h>
#include <string>

class FileHandler
{
private:
    std::string m_fileName;
    FILE        *m_fp;

    static const char *fileName()
    {
        return "log.txt";
    }

public:
    FileHandler( const char *fn = NULL )
    {
        if ( fn )
            m_fileName = fn;
        else
            m_fileName = fileName();
    }
```

(continued)

LISTING 20-2 *(continued)*

```
int open( const char *name = fileName(), const char *mode = "rw" )        → 1
{
    m_fileName = name;
    return open(mode);
}

int open( const std::string& mode )                                        → 2
{
    m_fp = fopen( m_fileName.c_str(), mode.c_str() );
    if ( m_fp == NULL )
        return -1;
    return 0;
}
};
```

3. **Save your file.**

In the constructor, we set the default filename as a NULL pointer. If the user overrides the filename, we use the name they ask for. Otherwise we simply use the internal name returned by the fileName method in our class.

For the first open method (→ 1), we also allow users to override the filename — but this time we directly initialize the filename from the internal method (fileName()). This default value allows the user to call the first open function with no arguments, if they choose.

Working with regular (non-static) methods

Note that this way of calling a method as a default value works only if the method in question is static. You can't do this with a regular method, because regular methods require an object — and this way of calling puts you outside the scope of the object you're using.

For example, we can't do something like the following:

```
virtual const char *filename()
{
    return "log.txt";
}
```

and then use it this way:

```
int open( const char *name = fileName(),
    const char *mode)
```

The compiler will get annoyed, because the fileName method requires a this pointer to operate on. The level at which we're working has no this pointer. Worse, you can't write a command like this one:

```
int open( const char *name = this->
    filename, const char *mode )
```

The reason you can't is simple: The this pointer makes no sense in this case. You aren't inside an object, so you can't tell the outside world to refer to the object you are in. It's an annoyance, but it's one of those things you just get used to. If you find this too much trouble, use the same technique the constructor uses to call the method.

Finally, we have the second open method that can open the file — specifying only the mode we wish. Notice that we can't default this method. Why? If the method had a default argument, there would be no way to tell whether the user meant to call the first or second version of the open method. To illustrate, consider the following series of calls in an application program:

```
FileHandler fh; // Invokes the constructor
fh.open();
```

Now, if we had given the second variant (→ **2**) of the open method a default argument, which version of the open method would be called ? It could be

```
fh.open(name, mode);
```

or it could be

```
fh.open(mode);
```

The compiler has no way of knowing which method the developer originally intended, so it doesn't allow the use of this technique at compile-time.

Of course, we need to add a method to write to the file. There's no way to rationally default the values we want to write out — that's entirely up to the end user of the class — so we won't lift a finger to do so. For a write statement, how could you have any idea what data the end user wanted to write? You couldn't, nor is there any sort of pattern to it.

In your code editor, insert the code shown in Listing 20-3 to your program's source code. (It goes before the closing brace of the class's public part.)

LISTING 20-3: THE FILE WRITE METHOD

```
bool write( const char *string )
{
    bool bRet = false;
    if ( m_fp )
    {
        fputs( string, m_fp );
        bRet = true;
    }
    return bRet;
}
```

Testing the Default Code

It's a good idea to test the class with both default and non-default values, just to see whether your assumptions are valid.

The following steps show you how to create a test driver that will show how the class is intended to be used:

1. **In the code editor of your choice, open the existing file to hold the code for your test program.**

In this example, I named the test program ch20.cpp.

2. **Type the code from Listing 20-4 into your file.**

Better yet, copy the code from the source file on this book's companion Web site.

LISTING 20-4: THE TEST DRIVER FOR THE FILEHANDLER CLASS

```
int main(int argc, char **argv)
{
    FileHandler fh;                          → 3

    if ( fh.open() == -1 )
        printf("Unable to open file. Errno
          %d\n", errno);

    fh.write("This is a test");

    FileHandler fh2("log2.txt");             → 4
    fh.open("w");
    fh.write("This is another test");
}
```

3. **Save the source code and close the source-code editor.**

4. **Compile the code using your favorite compiler on your favorite operating system.**

If you have done everything right, the program should create the log.txt and log2.txt files. These files should be created at → **3** and → **4** in the driver code. The files will contain our output for the FileHandler objects. However, you will quickly find that it did not, in fact, create any files. Depending on your operating system and compiler, you may even get a program crash. So what went wrong?

Fixing the Problem

If you put some debugging statements in the open method with two arguments, you can find the problem very quickly: The open method is called recursively, until the stack is exhausted and the program crashes. Why? Because of the nature of our default arguments, the open function with default arguments calls open again within itself after having assigned the arguments. The best match for the open call in our open method happens to be the method itself! This causes an endlessly recursive loop. So, of course, bad things happen when you call yourself repeatedly in a method. Let's fix that by modifying the open method as in Listing 20-5 (replace the existing method with the new listing code):

LISTING 20-5: THE MODIFIED OPEN METHOD

```
int open( const char *name =
fileName(),const char *mode = "rw+")
{
    m_fileName = name;
    std::string s = mode;
    return open(s);
}
```

Now, if you compile and run the program, you'll find that it runs properly and generates the two files as expected.

Part IV

Classes

The 5th Wave   By Rich Tennant

THE GREAT THING ABOUT OBJECT-ORIENTED PROGRAMMING IS, IT'S MADE SOFTWARE DEVELOPMENT AS EASY AS PUTTING ONE FOOT IN FRONT OF THE OTHER.

Technique 21

Creating a Complete Class

Save Time By

✔ Defining a Complete class

✔ Creating templates for a Complete class

✔ Testing the Complete class

When you are trying to use or reuse a class in C++, there is nothing quite so frustrating as finding that the method that you need is not implemented in that class, or that the method does not work properly when you try to use it in the environment you are using. The reason for this is usually that the programmer who developed the class did not create a Complete class — but what, exactly, does it mean to create one? That's a good question, and this technique will try to answer it.

To do its job, a Complete class must follow a list of specific rules. These rules, in their correct order, are as follows:

1. The class must implement a void constructor.

2. The class must implement a copy constructor.

3. The class must implement a virtual destructor.

4. The class must implement a get method for each data element defined in the class.

5. The class must implement a set method for each data element defined in the class.

6. The class must implement a clone method so it can make a copy of itself.

7. The class must implement an assignment operator.

If you create a class that follows all these rules, you have likely created a Complete class, one that will be reused by programmers over and over again. This will save you time and effort in not having to reinvent the wheel each time that type of code needs to be used in a project.

 Please note that having a set method for a class implies strongly that the set method will check for invalid values. Also, if you have pointers in your class, you should make sure that you initialize them to NULL, copy them properly, and destroy them when they are done. A set method for a pointer ought to take into account that it is acceptable to set the pointer to NULL and not have any memory leaks.

Creating a Complete Class Template

The following steps show you an example of a `Complete` class that you can use as a template for all the classes you implement in the future.

 If you create a template for creating objects and a process for implementing that template for new classes, you avoid many of the problems that haunt C++ programmers. Because the purpose of these techniques is to not only improve your coding skills, but also to insure that you create better software, this is a very valuable

technique that you should insist all developers on your team use in all of their application code. There are no classes that are "too trivial" to benefit from these enhancements.

1. **In the code editor of your choice, open the existing file to hold the code for your test program.**

In this example, I named the test program `ch21.cpp`.

2. **Type the code from Listing 21-1 into your file.**

Better yet, copy the code from the source file on this book's companion Web site.

LISTING 21-1: THE COMPLETE CLASS

```
#include <stdio.h>
#include <string>
#include <string.h>

class Complete
{
private:
    bool dirty;      // Keep track of the object state.                    →1
private:
    int x;
    double y;
    std::string s;
    char *p;

    // Create an initialization function that
    // can reset all values.
    void Init()
    {
        x = 0;
        y = 0;
        s = "";
        if ( p )
            delete p;
        p = NULL;
        dirty = false;
    }

    // Create a copy function that you can use to make
    // clones of an object.
    void Copy( const Complete& aCopy )
    {
        Init();
```

```
            x = aCopy.x;
            y = aCopy.y;
            s = aCopy.s;
            if ( p )
                delete p;
            p = NULL;
            if ( aCopy.p )
            {
                p = new char[ strlen(aCopy.p) ];
                strcpy( p, aCopy.p );
            }
            dirty = true;

    }
public:
    // Always create a default constructor.
    Complete()
    {
        // We need to set the pointer first.
        p = NULL;
        // Now initialize.
        Init();
    }
    // Always create a copy constructor.
    Complete( const Complete& aCopy )
    {
        // We need to set the pointer first.
        p = NULL;
        // Now copy the object.
        Copy( aCopy );
    }
    // Always create a full constructor with all accessible
    // members defined.
    Complete( int _x, double _y, std::string& _s, const char *_p )
    {
        x = _x;
        y = _y;
        s = _s;
        if ( _p )
        {
            p = new char[ strlen(_p) ];
            strcpy ( p, _p );
        }
        else
            p = NULL;
        dirty - true;
    }
    // Always create a virtual destructor.
    virtual ~Complete()
    {
        if ( p )
            delete p;
```

(continued)

LISTING 21-1 *(continued)*

```
    }
    // Next, define accessors for all data that can be public. If
    // it's not intended to be public, make it a private accessor.
    // First, define all the set methods. The "dirty" flag is not
    // necessary for completeness, but it makes life a LOT easier.

    void setX(const int& _x)
    {
        if ( x != _x )
            dirty = true;

        x = _x;
    }
    void setY(const double& _y)
    {
        if ( y != _y )
            dirty = true;
        y = _y;
    }
    // Note that for strings, we always use the easiest base type.
    void setS(const char *_s)
    {
        if ( s != _s )
            dirty = true;
        s = _s;
    }
    void setP( const char *_p)
    {
        if ( p != _p )
            dirty = true;

        // Always clear out a pointer before setting it.
        if ( p )
        {
            delete p;
            p = NULL;
        }

        if ( _p )
        {
            p = new char [ strlen(_p) ];
            strcpy( p, _p );
        }
        else
            p = NULL;
    }

    // Now the data get functions. Note that since they cannot modify
    // the object, they are all marked as const.
```

```
int getX(void) const
{
    return x;
}
double getY(void) const
{
    return y;
}
std::string getS(void) const
{
    return s;
}
// Note: For internal pointers, always return a CONST pointer.
const char * getP(void) const
{
    return p;
}

// Implement a clone operator.
Complete Clone(void)
{
    Complete c;
    c.Copy( *this );
    return c;
}

// Implement an assignment operator.
Complete operator=( const Complete& aCopy )
{
    Copy( aCopy );
    return *this;
}

};
```

3. Save the source file.

 When you are creating your own classes, you should seriously consider using Listing 21-1 as a template. If all classes implemented all their functionality in this manner, they would easily rid the programming world of 10 to 20 percent of all bugs.

Testing the Complete Class

Just writing the class is not enough. You also need to test it. Test cases provide two different uses for developers. First, they provide a way to make sure that you didn't make the code work improperly when you made the change. Secondly, and more importantly, they act as a tutorial for the user of your class. By running your test driver and looking at the order in which you do things, the programmer can discover how to use the code in his or her own program as well as what values are expected and which are error values. It is almost, but not quite, self-documenting code.

How do you go about writing tests for your classes? Well, first you test all the "normal" conditions. One quick way to illustrate is to create a test driver that tests the constructors for the class, like this:

1. In the code editor of your choice, reopen the existing file to hold the code for your test program.

In this example, I named the test program `ch21.cpp`.

2. Type the code from Listing 21-2 into your file.

Better yet, copy the code from the source file on this book's companion Web site.

LISTING 21-2: THE COMPLETE CLASS TEST DRIVER

```
void DumpComplete( const Complete& anObj )
{
    printf("Object:\n");
    printf("X : %d\n", anObj.getX() );
    printf("Y : %lf\n", anObj.getY() );
    printf("S : %s\n", anObj.getS().c_str() );
    printf("P : %s\n", anObj.getP() ?
    anObj.getP() : "NULL" );
}

int main()
{
    // Test the void constructor.
    Complete c1;
    // Test the full constructor.
    std::string s = "Three";
    Complete c2(1, 2.0, s, "This is a test");
    // Test the copy constructor.
    Complete c3(c2);
    // Test the = operator.
    Complete c4=c1;

    DumpComplete( c1 );
    DumpComplete( c2 );
    DumpComplete( c2 );
    DumpComplete( c4 );
}
```

3. Save the source-code file in your editor and close the code-editor application.

4. Compile the application, using your favorite compiler on your favorite operating system.

5. Run the application. You should see the output from Listing 21-3 appear in the console window.

LISTING 21-3: OUTPUT

```
$ ./a.exe
Object:
X : 0
Y : 0.000000
S :
P : NULL
Object:
X : 1
Y : 2.000000
S : Three
P : This is a test
Object:
X : 1
Y : 2.000000
S : Three
P : This is a test
Object:
X : 0
Y : 0.000000
S :
P : NULL
```

As you can see, we get the expected output. The initialized values default to what we set them to in the various constructors and copy functions. It's very hard to overestimate the importance of having unit tests like these. With unit tests, you have a built-in way to verify changes; you have ways to start testing your software; and you have documentation built right in the code. Unit testing is an important portion of such development methodologies as eXtreme Programming (now often called Agile Programming) and the like.

Another important thing to note in our code is the `dirty` flag (shown at → **1** in Listing 21-1) that we have built into the code. The simple `dirty` flag could easily be extracted out into its own small class to manage `dirty` objects — and can be reused across many different classes, as shown in Listing 21-4.

LISTING 21-4: A CHANGEMANAGEMENT CLASS

```
class ChangeManagement
{
private:
    bool dirty;
public:
    ChangeManagement(void)
    {
        dirty = false;
    }
    ChangeManagement( bool flag )
    {
        setDirty(flag);
    }
    ChangeManagement( const ChangeManagement&
    aCopy )
    {
        setDirty(aCopy.isDirty());
    }
    virtual ~ChangeManagement()
    {
    }
    void setDirty( bool flag )
    {
        dirty = flag;
    }
    bool isDirty(void)
    {
        return dirty;
    }
    ChangeManagement& operator=(const
    ChangeManagement& aCopy)
    {
        setDirty( aCopy.isDirty() );
        return *this;
    }
};
```

Okay, why might we want to create a `dirty` flag? Well, for one reason, we could then manage the "dirtiness" of objects outside the objects themselves. We might, for example, have a manager that the `ChangeManagement` class "talked to" to notify it when given objects become dirty or clean (and therefore have to be written to and from disk). This sort of thing would be very useful for a cache manager of objects, when memory is at a premium but disk or other storage space is available.

 Of course, writing unit tests doesn't mean that you have done a complete test. At this point, you've simply validated that the code does what you expected it to do when valid input was given. Never confuse testing with validation. *Validation* shows that the code does what it is supposed to do when you do everything right. *Testing* shows that the code does what it is supposed to do when you do something wrong.

Using Virtual Inheritance

Save Time By

✔ Understanding inheritance

✔ Defining virtual inheritance

✔ Implementing virtual inheritance

✔ Testing and correcting your code

It's no accident that this book devotes some time to understanding how classes are constructed — and how you can inherit from them. Inheritance allows you to save time and effort by providing a ready base of code that can be reused in your own classes. When you are doing class design, however, there are some problems that will cause you pain and consternation. One such problem is in multiple inheritance. While multiple inheritance can solve many problems in class design, it can also cause problems. For example, consider the case of Listing 22-1:

LISTING 22-1: A MULTIPLE INHERITANCE EXAMPLE

```
class Base
{
    char *name;
public:
    virtual const char *Name();
    void setName( const char *n );
}
class A : public Base
{
}
class B : public Base
{
}
class C : public A, public B
{
}
```

Listing 22-1 shows a problem with multiple inheritance that you might not think could ever happen — but it happens nearly all the time. When we have a base class from which all classes in the system inherit information — such as an Object class that stores the name (that is, the type) of the class — we run into the problem of inheriting from the same base class in multiple ways. This situation is often referred to as the "deadly triangle" of object-oriented programming. If you instantiate an object of type C, as in the code shown in Listing 22-1, the compiler and linker won't object — everything appears to work fine. However, the problem comes in when we try to use the methods in the base class `Base`. If we write

```
const char *name = c.Name();
```

then the compiler immediately throws a fit, generating an error for the source-code line. The reason should be obvious: Which `name` method are we calling here? There are two `Base` classes in the inheritance tree for class `C`. Is it the one in the base class `A`, or the one in the base class `B`? Neither is obvious, although we can scope the answer with a little effort:

```
const char *name = c.B::Name();
```

This will fix our compile problem, because the compiler now knows that we mean the `Name` method that is inherited through the class `B` tree.

Unfortunately, this doesn't really solve the problem. After all, our `C` class is not a `B`, nor is it an `A` — it is a `C`, and only that. You might think a dodge like this could "fix" the problem:

```
class C : public A, public B
{
public:
    C()
        : Base("C")
    {
    }
```

Here we explicitly tell the compiler that this is a `C` object and should be used as one. Because the base class constructor takes a name, and that name is used in the `Name` method, it ought to therefore assign the value `C` to the name. The problem is, if you try to compile this mess, you get the error shown in Listing 22-2:

Curses, foiled again; this doesn't solve the problem at all. The compiler is complaining because it does not see which base class we are trying to use. Is it the base class of `A`, or the base class of `B`? This isn't clear, and therefore we cannot simply call the base class constructor.

How, then, can we inherit from two base classes that (in turn) inherit from a common base class? The answer lies in a C++ concept known as *virtual inheritance*. Virtual inheritance combines multiple base classes into a single base class within the inheritance tree, so that there is never any ambiguity.

In Listing 22-1, with two classes inheriting from a common base, the problem occurs because the base class occurs in the inheritance tree twice. Virtual inheritance forces the compiler to create only a single instance of the base class — and to use the data in that single instance wherever the data was last set. This means that the code literally skips the instantiation of the base classes in the two bases (`A` and `B`, in our example) and uses only the instantiation in the last class level, `C`.

LISTING 22-2: COMPILER OUTPUT FOR MULTIPLE INHERITANCE ERROR

```
ch3_11.cpp: In constructor 'C::C()':
ch3_11.cpp:65: error: 'Object' is an ambiguous base of 'C'
ch3_11.cpp:65: error: type 'class Object' is not a direct base of 'C'
ch3_11.cpp: In member function 'void C::Display()':
ch3_11.cpp:70: error: request for member 'Name' is ambiguous in multiple
    inheritance lattice
ch3_11.cpp:23: error: candidates are: virtual const char* Object::Name()
ch3_11.cpp:23: error:                  virtual const char* Object::Name()
```

Implementing Virtual Inheritance

Implementing virtual inheritance in your base classes allows you to create an inheritance structure that will permit all other classes that inherit from your base classes to work properly. The following steps take a look at how we can create an inheritance structure that implements virtual inheritance:

1. **In the code editor of your choice, create a new file to hold the code for the implementation of the source file.**

In this example, the file is named ch22.cpp, although you can use whatever you choose.

2. **Type the code from Listing 22-3 into your file.**

Or better yet, copy the code from the source file on this book's companion Web site.

LISTING 22-3: BASE-CLASS INHERITANCE

```cpp
#include <stdio.h>
#include <string>

class Object
{
private:
    char *name;
public:
    Object(void)
    {
        name=NULL;
    }
    Object(const char *n)
    {
        setName( n );
    }
    virtual ~Object()
    {
        if ( name )
            delete name;
        name = NULL;
    }
    virtual const char *Name()
    {
        return name;
    }
    virtual void setName(const char *n)
    {
        if ( name )
            delete name;
        name = NULL;

        if ( n )
        {
            name = new char[strlen(n)+1];
            strcpy( name, n );
        }
    }
};


class A : public virtual Object        → 1
{
public:
    A()
        : Object("A")
    {
    }
    virtual ~A()
    {
    }
};

class B : public virtual Object        → 2
{
public:
    B()
        : Object("B")
    {
    }
};

class C : public A, public B
{
public:
    C()
    {
    }
    void Display()
    {
        printf("Name = %s\n", Name() );
    }
};

int main(int argc, char **argv)
{
    C c;

    c.Display();
}
```

The keys to the above code are in the lines marked with → **1** and → **2**. These two lines force the compiler to create only a single Object instance in the inheritance tree of both A and B.

3. **Save the code as a file in your code editor and close the editor application.**

4. **Compile the source-code file with your favorite compiler on your favorite operating system, and then run the resulting executable.**

If you have done everything right, you should see the following output:

```
$ ./a.exe
Name = (null)
```

Oops. This is not what we wanted to see. We were expecting the name of the class. That name should be 'C'. The next section fixes that — and gives us the type we really wanted.

Correcting the Code

The problem in our simple example comes about because we assumed that the code would naturally follow one of the two paths through the inheritance tree and assign a name to the class. With virtual inheritance, no such thing happens. The compiler has no idea which class we want to assign the name to, since the values "belong" to the C class, rather than the A and B classes. We have to tell the code what to do. Let's do that here.

1. **Reopen the source-code file created earlier (called ch22.cpp) and edit it in your code editor.**

2. **Modify the constructor for the C class as follows:**
```
C()
     : Object("C")
{
}
```

3. **Recompile and run the program, and you will see the following (correct) output from the application:**
```
$ ./a.exe
Name = C
```

It isn't always possible to modify the base classes for a given object, but when you can, use this technique to avoid the "dread diamond" (having a class derived from two base classes both of which derive from a common base class) — and use classes that have common bases as your own base classes.

 When you're designing a class, keep in mind that if you add a virtual method, you should always inherit from the class virtually. This way, all derived classes will be able to override the functionality of that virtual method directly.

Creating Overloaded Operators

Save Time By

- ✔ Defining overloaded operators
- ✔ Rules for creating overloaded operators
- ✔ Using a conversion operator
- ✔ Using overloaded operators
- ✔ Testing your operator

One of the most fascinating abilities that was added to C++ was the power to actually change the way the compiler interpreted the language. Before C++, if you had a class called, say, Foo, and you wanted to write a method or function to add two Foo objects, you would have to write code similar to the following:

```
Foo addTwoFoos( const Foo&f1, const
Foo& f2)
{
    Foo f3;

    // Do something to add the two foos (f1 and f2)

    return f3;
}
```

Then you could call the function in your application code like this:

```
Foo f1(0);
Foo f2(1);
Foo f3;
f3 = addTwoFoos(f1,f2);
```

Overloaded operators permit you to change the basic syntax of the language, such as changing the way in which the plus operator (+) is used. With the addition of overloaded operators, however, you can now write something like this:

```
Foo operator+(const Foo& f1,
    const Foo& f2 )
{
    Foo f3;

    // Do something to add them

    return f3;
}
```

→ 1

In your code, you can now include statements such as this:

```
Foo f3 = f1+f2;
```

Without the overloaded operator (➜ **1**), this line would generate a compile error, since the compiler knows of no way to add two objects of type `Foo`.

Of course, this power comes with a corresponding price. When you overload operators like this, even the simplest-looking statement can cause problems. Because you can no longer assume that a single line of code results in a single operation, you must step into every line of code in the debugger to trace through and see what is really happening.

Take a look at this simple-looking statement, for example, in which we assign one `Foo` object to another:

```
Foo f1=12;
```

This statement could, conceivably, be hidden within hundreds of lines of code. If an error crops up in the code that processes this simple assignment statement, you have to dig into every one of those lines to find it. So consider: An overloaded operator may be hard to beat for readability. It is more intuitive to say `A+B` when you mean to add two things than to write `add(A,B)`, but it's a debugging nightmare. Weigh very carefully the real need for overloading a particular operator against the pain you can cause someone who's trying to figure out why a side effect in your code caused his program not to work.

Rules for Creating Overloaded Operators

There are four basic rules that you should use when you overload operators in your own classes:

✔ **Make sure that the operator does not conflict with standard usage of that operator.**

This rule is pretty straightforward. If you overload the plus (+) operator, you still expect the operator to do something along the line of adding. You wouldn't expect (for example) to use the plus operator to invert a string; that wouldn't make sense. It would drive anyone trying to understand the code completely batty.

✔ **Make sure that the operator has no unexpected side effects.**

This rule isn't much more complicated. If I'm adding two numbers together, I don't expect the result of the operation to change either number. For example, suppose we wrote something like

```
Foo f1(1);
Foo f2(2);
Foo f3 = f1+f2;
```

After these statements are run, you certainly would expect `f1` to still contain a `1` and `f2` to still contain a `2`. It would be confusing and counterintuitive if you added two numbers and found that `f1` was now `3` and `f2` was now `5`.

✔ **Make sure that an operator is the only way you can implement the functionality without having an adverse impact on the end user and the maintainer of the code.**

This rule is somewhat subjective but easy to understand. If you could easily write an algorithm as a method or function, there would be no reason to overload an operator to perform the algorithm.

✔ **Make sure that the operator and all associated operators are implemented.**

This rule is fairly important — especially from the perspective of a user. For example, if you implement the plus (+) operator, you're going to want to implement the plus-equal operator (+=) as well. It makes no sense to the end user to be able to perform the statement

```
Foo f3 = f1 + f2;
```

without also being able to perform this one:

```
f2 += f1;
```

Unfortunately, the converse operation is not always valid. For example, we might be able to add two strings together easily enough, by appending one to the other. What does subtracting a string from another string mean, though? It could be used to find the string in the first string and extract it, but that really doesn't make a great deal of sense. Therefore, subtraction is not an "associated operator" for strings. This fails both the first and third rules.

Using Conversion Operators

Besides addition, the other sort of operator that often should be implemented for your classes is a *conversion operator*. With it, you can convert a given class into a lot of things. For example, you could convert a string into a character pointer — or a class into an integer for use in other functions. In such cases, you use the conversion operator like this:

```
operator const char *()
```

The `const char *` portion of the operator defines what you are converting the class data into. The `operator` keyword just tells the compiler that you are implementing this as an operator. If you implement the operator given here in your code, you can use the class that implements the code anywhere you would use a `const char *` value. You can do so directly, as in the following lines of code:

```
printf("The value as a string is: %s\n",
    (const char *)myObj);
```

Alternatively, you can do it implicitly by first including these lines of code:

```
void print_a_string( const char *s )
{
    print("string: %s\n", s );
}
```

and then referencing those lines with this line:

```
print_a_string( myObj );
```

The compiler automatically calls your conversion operator "silently" when the object is passed to the `print_a_string` function. The conversion is applied and the `const char *` pointer passed into the function instead of the object. Note that this process does involve some overhead — and if the conversion is to a non-basic type, a temporary object is created — which can cause problems if you are reference-counting (tracking allocations and de-allocations) your objects. You will have a new object created by the compiler that does not appear in your code. Tracing logic that prints out the creation of objects will be confused, and may result in trying to find problems by the end programmer that do not really exist.

Always remember that just because you *can* use C++ functionality, such as overloaded operators, does not mean you *should* or *must* use that capability. Always do what makes the most sense in your programming situation.

Using Overloaded Operators

Overloaded operators are those that have the same name but different numbers or types of arguments. Let's create a few overloaded operators in a class to illustrate this technique in C++.

1. **In the code editor of your choice, create a new file to hold the code for the implementation of the source file.**

In this example, the file is named ch23, although you can use whatever you choose.

2. **Type the code from Listing 23-1 into your file.**

Better yet, copy the code from the source file on this book's companion Web site.

LISTING 23-1: OVERLOADED OPERATORS

```
#include <stdio.h>
#include <string.h>
#include <math.h>
#include <ctype.h>

class MyString
{
    char *buffer;
    int  length;
private:
    void SetBuffer( const char *s )
    {
        if( buffer )
            delete buffer;
        buffer = NULL;
        length = 0;
        if ( s )
        {
            buffer = new char[ strlen(s)+1 ];
            strcpy( buffer, s );
            length = strlen(buffer);
        }
    }
public:
    MyString(void)                        → 1
    {
        buffer = NULL;
        length = 0;
    }
    MyString( const char *s )
    {
        buffer = NULL;
        SetBuffer ( s );
    }
    // Create a string that is blank, of the
        length given.
    MyString( int length )
    {
        buffer = new char[ length+1 ];
        for ( int i=0; i<length; ++i )
            buffer[i] = ' ';
    }
    MyString( const MyString& aCopy )     → 2
    {
        buffer = NULL;
        SetBuffer ( aCopy.buffer );
    }
    virtual ~MyString()                   → 3
    {
        if ( buffer )
            delete buffer;
    }
```

This code implements the various constructors and internal methods that we are going to be using in the class. Note that to be a complete class, we provide the void constructor (→ **1**) and copy constructor (→ **2**), as well as a virtual destructor (→ **3**). In addition, a variety of other constructors allow you to do the complete creation of the object in different ways.

3. **Add the code from Listing 23-2.**

In our case, we only have two different pieces of data in the class: the buffer itself, which holds the string we are encapsulating, and the length of the buffer (for keeping track of valid indexes into the string). Add the code from Listing 23-2 to your source file to implement the accessors.

LISTING 23-2: ACCESSOR METHODS FOR THE MYSTRING CLASS

```
// Accessor methods
    int Length() const
    {
        return length;
    }
    void setLength(int len)
    {
        if ( len != length )
        {
            char *temp = new char[ len+1 ];
            strncpy( temp, buffer, len );
            for ( int i=length; i<len; ++i )
                temp[i] = 0;
            delete buffer;
            buffer = temp;
        }
    }
    MyString& operator=(const MyString&
      aCopy )
    {
        SetBuffer( aCopy.buffer );
        return *this;
    }
    // We can overload the operator= as well
    MyString& operator=(const char *str)
    {
        SetBuffer(str);
        return *this;
    }
```

4. **Add the code from Listing 23-3 to the file.**

This adds the operators for the class. This is an optional step that you might or might not want to add to your own classes.

Listing 23-3 implements some operators for this class. (We'll add conversion operators, indexing operators, an operator to return a sub-string of our string, and some comparison operators so you can see how it all fits together.)

LISTING 23-3: CLASS OPERATORS

```
// Be able to use the object "just as if" it were a string.
    operator const char*()
    {
        return buffer;
    }
    // Be able to iterate through the string using the [] construct.
    // Note that the users can change the string this way. Define a
    // const version of it too, so they cannot change the string.
    char& operator[]( int index )
    {
        // This is probably not the right thing to do, in reality,
        // but if they give us an invalid index, just give them the first byte.
        if ( index < 0 || index > length-1 )
            return buffer[0];
        return buffer[ index ];
    }
    const char& operator[]( int index ) const
    {
        // This is probably not the right thing to do, in reality,
        // but if they give us an invalid index, just give them the first byte.
        if ( index < 0 || index > length-1 )
            return buffer[0];
        return buffer[ index ];
    }
    // Now the fun stuff. Create an operator to return a sub-string of the
    // buffer.
    MyString operator()(int stIndex, int endIndex)
    {
        if ( stIndex < 0 || stIndex > length-1 )
            stIndex = 0;
        if ( endIndex < 0 || endIndex > length-1 )
            endIndex = length-1;
        if ( stIndex > endIndex )
        {
            int temp = stIndex;
            stIndex = endIndex;
            endIndex = temp;
        }
        // Okay, we have valid indices. Let's create the string of the right
        // size.
        MyString s( endIndex-stIndex+1 );
        // Copy the buffer into the string.
        for ( int i=stIndex; i<=endIndex; ++i )
```

```
            s[i-stIndex] = buffer[i];
        return s;
    }
    // Define some comparison operators, case-insensitive.
    bool operator==(const MyString& aString )
    {
        if ( Length() != aString.Length() )
            return false;
        for ( int i=0; i<Length(); ++i )
        {
            char c1 = (*this)[i];
            char c2 = aString[i];
            if ( toupper(c1) != toupper(c2 ) )
                return false;
        }
        return true;
    }
    // Do the same for comparisons to literal strings.
    bool operator==(const char *str)
    {
        if ( Length() != strlen(str) )
            return false;
        for ( int i=0; i<Length(); ++i )
        {
            char c1 = (*this)[i];
            char c2 = str[i];
            if ( toupper(c1) != toupper(c2 ) )
                return false;
        }
        return true;
    }
};
```

Testing the MyString Class

After you create the MyString class, you should create
a test driver that not only ensures that your code is
correct, but also shows people how to use your code.

The following steps show you how to create a test
driver that illustrates how the class is intended to
be used.

1. **In the code editor of your choice, open the existing file to hold the code for your test program.**

In this example, I named the test program ch23.

2. **Type the code from Listing 23-4 into your file.**

Better yet, copy the code from the source file on
this book's companion Web site.

Notice that we can use the operator "[]" on
either side of the equal sign in an expression. If
you use the [] as an l-value, you can actually
directly assign values to the buffer in the code.
However, unlike a "standard" C++ array, the code
actually validates to ensure that the index you
pass in is in the valid range for the internal
buffer. Hence no more buffer overruns — and no
more program crashes!

3. **Save the source code in your code editor.**

LISTING 23-4: THE BUFFER CLASS TEST DRIVER

```c
void print_a_string( const char *s )
{
    printf("The string is: %s\n", s );
}

int main(int argc, char **argv)
{
    MyString s("This is a test");

    printf("The string is: [%s]\n", (const char *)s );
    s[4] = 'm';
    printf("The string is now: [%s]\n", (const char *)s );

    // Get a sub-string of the string.
    MyString sub = s(3,7);
    printf("The sub-string is: [%s]\n", (const char *)sub );

    // We can reset strings to be bigger or smaller.
    sub = "Hello world";
    printf("The sub-string is now: [%s]\n", (const char *)sub );

    if ( sub == "hEllO world" )
        printf("Strings compare\n");
    else
        printf("Strings do NOT compare\n");
    if ( sub == "Goodbye" )
        printf("Strings compare\n");
    else
        printf("Strings do NOT compare\n");
    MyString copy = sub;
    if ( sub == copy )
        printf("Strings compare\n");
    else
        printf("Strings do NOT compare\n");

    print_a_string( sub );
    return 0;
}
```

4. **Compile the source code with your favorite compiler on your favorite operating system.**

5. **Run the resulting program on the operating system of your choice.**

If you have done everything correctly, you should see the following output from the application in the console window.

```
$ ./a.exe
The string is: [This is a test]
The string is now: [Thismis a test]
The sub-string is: [smis ]
The sub-string is now: [Hello world]
Strings compare
Strings do NOT compare
Strings compare
The string is: Hello world
```

As you can see from the output in Listing 23-2, the indexing functions (operator [] and operator ()) properly allow us to retrieve and modify selected pieces of our string. The comparison functions work as well, showing that our overloaded operators are working correctly.

This example really shows the power of overriding operators and creating your own types in C++: You can protect the end user against just about all the problems that have cropped up in years of software development.

Technique 24

Defining Your Own new and delete Handlers

Save Time By

- Implementing new and delete handlers
- Overloading new and delete handlers
- Creating a memory-allocation tracking program
- Testing your program

One basic building block of the C++ language is a set of core keywords for allocating and freeing blocks of memory. The new and delete keywords (for example) were added to the language primarily to support the addition of objects with constructors and destructors — but they're also used to allocate more "generic" blocks of memory, such as character arrays.

The main reason for using the new operator was that it would automatically allocate the needed block of memory, and then call the constructor for the block of memory to initialize it properly. (The old C style alloc/malloc functions couldn't do that.)

The problem with the new and delete operators isn't really in the way they are used; it's that they don't keep track of what is allocated and what is deleted. There are other problems — such as dealing with pools of objects (allowing you to reuse objects without allocating new ones) — but most programmers would agree that the issue of tracking memory allocation is more serious. If you can keep track of exactly when memory is allocated and de-allocated in your application, you will save enormous amounts of time in the debugging process trying to track down memory leaks and overwrites.

Consider, as a good example, the following function, written in C++:

```
int func(int x)
{
    char *ptr = new char[200];                              → 1
    if ( x < 0 || x > 100 )
        return -1;                                         → 2

    // Do some processing of the ptr.

    // De-allocate memory.
    delete ptr;
}
```

This code contains a subtle, but important, memory leak. If you call the function with a value such as 102 passed for x, you will see the problem. The function allocates a block of memory that is 200 bytes long (at → **1**), and then returns without de-allocating the block (at → **2**). That memory is then consumed until the program exits, and is no longer available to the application. This might not seem like such a big problem — unless this routine is called several *thousand* times. Suddenly that 200-byte block becomes a several-*megabyte* memory leak. Not a good outcome at all.

Fortunately, the designers of C++ considered that problems like this could easily crop up. Although they chose not to build in a garbage-collection system, as in Java, they did provide the building blocks for creating your own memory allocation and de-allocation system, and keeping track of such things. To keep track of memory allocation in C++, we need the ability to overload the new and delete handlers in the language. You might think that this would be a complicated affair, but as Technique 23 shows, overloading operators (so they appear to be a basic part of the language) is simple in C++. The new and delete operators are no exception to the overloading process, although you have to go about it a little differently. In this technique, we look at how you can overload the new and delete handlers for the entire system, although the same process can be scaled down to just the class level.

Rules for Implementing new and delete Handlers

There are a few things to note when you are implementing your own new and delete handlers in your application code.

✔ You may not call new and delete within your new or delete handlers. This might seem obvious, but issuing those calls is almost automatic for some developers. In short, new and delete may not be called recursively.

✔ You may not call any methods, functions, or objects that call new or delete within your handlers. If you call a function within a new handler that calls new, you get an instantly recursive call. Following this rule is often harder than it looks. (For example, you cannot use the STL containers because they allocate memory.)

✔ Your new and delete handlers must be very fast. Their code is often called over and over, and must not slow down the application they are being used from.

✔ You cannot change the process in which the new and delete operators are called. That is, you can't return a smaller or larger block than was asked for to the application. Doing so can break many programs.

Overloading new and delete Handlers

With these rules in mind, how can we overload the new and delete operators to keep track of what is being allocated in a given program and report on which allocations were never freed? Let's take a look at an example of that right now.

1. **In the code editor of your choice, create a new file to hold the code for the implementation of the source file.**

In this example, the file is named ch24.cpp, although you can use whatever you choose.

2. **Type the code from Listing 24-1 into your file.**

Better yet, copy the code from the source file on this book's companion Web site.

LISTING 24-1: NEW AND DELETE HANDLERS

```c
#include <stdio.h>
#include <stdlib.h>

typedef struct {
    long    number;
    long    address;
    long    size;
    char    file[64];
    long    line;
} lALLOC_INFO;

lALLOC_INFO *allocations[ 100000 ];
int         nPos = 0;

void AddTrack(long addr,  long asize)
{
    if ( asize == 2688 )
        printf("Found one!\n");
    lALLOC_INFO *info = (lALLOC_INFO *)malloc(sizeof(lALLOC_INFO));
    info->address = addr;
    info->size = asize;
    info->number = nPos;
    allocations[nPos] = info;
    nPos ++;
};

bool RemoveTrack(long addr)
{
    bool bFound = false;

    for(int i = 0; i != nPos; i++)
    {
        if(allocations[i]->address == addr)
        {
            // Okay, delete this one.
            free( allocations[i] );
            bFound = true;
            // And copy the rest down to it.
            for ( int j=i; j<nPos-1; ++j )
                allocations[j] = allocations[j+1];
            nPos --;
            break;
        }
    }
    if ( !bFound )
    printf("Unable to find allocation for delete [%ld]\n",addr);
    return bFound;
};
```

This code keeps track of all allocations — and adds or removes them from a global array as we do our processing. This way, we can track all calls to new or delete within our application — and report on the calls to new that are not matched with a call to delete. Of course, this approach limits how many allocations we are going to track (it's a large, but not infinite, number). We can't dynamically allocate this array without writing a bunch of fancy code that's beyond the scope of this example, so we will use this compromise for now.

3. **Add the code from Listing 24-2 to your source file.**

This code generates a report of what blocks are currently allocated and how big they are. This aids the developer in tracking down the offending code that created the memory leak in the first place. Of course, knowing where the leak occurred doesn't help if the leak happens in a low-level library (because we have no access to the library source code and couldn't modify it if we did), but at least the size will help some. By knowing the size of our allocation, we might be able to map that to a specific block size in the program,

or the size of a given object. This code could easily be moved to a separate utility file but we will include it in the same file for simplicity.

This code simply steps through the list of allocations we have kept track of in the add and remove routines and reports on anything it finds that was not yet freed. This doesn't necessarily mean that the allocation is a leak, though, as we will see. What it means is that at the moment of this particular memory-state snapshot, the allocations in the list have not been freed up.

4. **Add the code from Listing 24-3 to your source file below the remaining code.**

This implements the actual new and delete methods. Once again, we could easily move these to a separate utility file, but it is easier to leave it in one place. This functionality is added separately to indicate how you would append this code to an existing program.

This will implement the actual overload of the new and delete operators. To implement that operation, add the code in Listing 24-3 to your source file.

LISTING 24-2: ALLOCATION REPORT

```
void DumpUnfreed()
{
   long totalSize = 0;
   printf("------------------- Allocations --------------------\n");
   for(int i = 0; i < nPos; i++)
   {
 lALLOC_INFO *pInfo = allocations[i];
   printf("(%ld) ADDRESS %x\t Size: %d unfreed\n",
       pInfo->number, pInfo->address, pInfo->size);
   totalSize += pInfo->size;
   }
   printf("----------------------------------------------------\n");
   printf("Total Unfreed: %d bytes\n\n\n", totalSize);
};
```

LISTING 24-3: OVERLOADED NEW AND DELETE HANDLERS

```
inline void * __cdecl operator new(unsigned int size)
{
    printf("Basic operator new called\n");
    void *ptr = (void *)malloc(size);
    AddTrack((long)ptr, size);
    return(ptr);
};

inline void * __cdecl operator new[](unsigned int size)
{
    printf("Array operator new called\n");
    void *ptr = (void *)malloc(size);
    AddTrack((long)ptr, size);
    return(ptr);
};

inline void __cdecl operator delete(void *p)
{
    printf("Basic operator delete called\n");
    if ( RemoveTrack((long)p) )
        free(p);
};

inline void __cdecl operator delete[](void *p)
{
    printf("Array operator delete called\n");
    if ( RemoveTrack((long)p) )
        free(p);
};
```

5. **Save the source-code file.**

These implementations of the code are nothing special. We simply allocate memory (using the built-in C function `malloc`) and de-allocate the memory by using the `free` function. The code includes some debugging `printf` statements that allow you to show which functions are being called at what time. Within each allocation or de-allocation operator, we call the appropriate tracking function to add or remove this particular allocation from the global array. One thing to note is that this code is actually better than the standard C++ implementation, because it verifies that a given pointer was allocated before it allows it to be freed. You could (for example) cause some mayhem if you were to do this:

```
char *c = new c[100];

// Do some stuff
delete c;

// Do some more stuff
delete c;
```

Expect bad things to happen in a case like this: It's deleting the same pointer twice, which tends to corrupt the stack and destroy all memory in the system. In our system, however, this process is caught and an error message is displayed. Furthermore, the actual pointer is not deleted a second time — so there's no memory corruption in the system and your program does not crash. That's a good enough reason to use a system like this in your production code.

All production code should be tested with a memory-leak tool, or run through code like this to see whether memory is being allocated and freed properly, not freed correctly, or freed more than once.

Testing the Memory Allocation Tracker

In order to see how the allocation tracking code works, it is easiest to create a simple test driver that illustrates the various pieces of the system. Let's create a simple test program to use the new and delete handlers we have created. The following steps show you how:

1. **In the code editor of your choice, open the existing file to hold the code for your test program.**

In this example, I named the test program CH 24.

2. **Type the code from Listing 24-4 into your file.**

Better yet, copy the code from the source file on this book's companion Web site.

3. **Save the source code and close your code editor.**

LISTING 24-4: MEMORY ALLOCATOR TEST DRIVER

```
int main(int argc, char **argv)
{
    DumpUnfreed();
    char *c = new char[200];
    DumpUnfreed();
    char *c2 = new char[256];         → 3
    DumpUnfreed();
    delete c;
    delete c;
    DumpUnfreed();
    int *x = new int[20];
    delete [] x;
    DumpUnfreed();
    Foo *f = new Foo();
    delete f;
    Foo *af = new Foo[5];
    delete [] af;

    Foo *af1 = new Foo[3];
    delete af1;
}
```

4. **Compile the source file, using your favorite compiler on your favorite operating system.**

If you run the resulting executable, the program should give you the output shown in Listing 24-5.

LISTING 24-5: OUTPUT FROM THE MEMORY TRACKING PROGRAM

```
$ ./a.exe
--------------------- Allocations ---------------------
-----------------------------------------------------
Total Unfreed: 0 bytes


Array operator new called
--------------------- Allocations ---------------------
(0) ADDRESS a050648      Size: 200 unfreed
-----------------------------------------------------
Total Unfreed: 200 bytes


Array operator new called
--------------------- Allocations ---------------------
(0) ADDRESS a050648      Size: 200 unfreed
(1) ADDRESS a050770      Size: 256 unfreed
-----------------------------------------------------
```

(continued)

LISTING 24-5 *(continued)*

```
Total Unfreed: 456 bytes


Basic operator delete called
Basic operator delete called
Unable to find allocation for delete [168101448]
-------------------- Allocations --------------------
(1) ADDRESS a050770      Size: 256 unfreed
-----------------------------------------------------
Total Unfreed: 256 bytes


Array operator new called
Array operator delete called
-------------------- Allocations --------------------
(1) ADDRESS a050770      Size: 256 unfreed
-----------------------------------------------------
Total Unfreed: 256 bytes                                       → 4


Basic operator new called
Foo Constructor called
Foo Destructor called
Basic operator delete called
Array operator new called
Foo Constructor called
Foo Constructor called
Foo Constructor called
Foo Constructor called
Foo Constructor called
Foo Destructor called
Foo Destructor called
Foo Destructor called
Foo Destructor called
Foo Destructor called
Array operator delete called
```

There are a lot of interesting things to take out of this technique. First, it gives you a better appreciation of what goes on behind the scenes in a typical C++ program. Second, you can see right away how the allocations and de-allocations are being handled and where the leaks are. In our example, we can see at the end of the program that we have a single memory leak of 256 bytes (at → **4** in Listing 24-5). Note that we print out the current state of the program several times, so it is only the last display that indicates the leak at the end of the program. The others are left in to illustrate how the program is allocating memory. It's obvious, from looking at the program code, that this occurs for the c2 allocation (see → **3** in Listing 24-4). We simply need to add a delete call for the character pointer and all will be copacetic.

The other interesting thing to note in this technique is which C++ new operator is called when. If you allocate a character pointer, for example, it calls the array version of the new operator. This situation is counterintuitive — after all, you're allocating a single character pointer — but it makes sense if you really think about it. It's an array of characters that we happen to treat as a single string, which gives us the array version of the new operator. Likewise, when we allocate a single object, it calls the basic operator for the new allocation.

Before we leave this concept, there's one more potential mess worth looking at. Try adding the following code to the end of your driver application:

```
Foo *af1 = new Foo[3];
delete af1;
```

If you compile this snippet of code at the end of your driver program, and then run the program, you will see the following output:

```
Array operator new called
Foo Constructor called
Foo Constructor called
Foo Constructor called
Foo Destructor called
Basic operator delete called
Unable to find allocation for delete
   [168101480]
```

Looking at the output, you will notice that the constructor for the class was called three times, for the three objects we created. The destructor, however, was only called once. Worse, because the block of memory allocated is actually three separate objects, our deletion routine couldn't find it to delete it.

 Moral: Always call the right version of delete **for the corresponding version of** new.

The new new operator

In C++, there is another version of the new operator called the new in place operator. This operator invokes the constructor for an object and sets it to point to a specific block of memory that is passed into it. If you are implementing a system that uses an embedded processor, where you cannot "really" allocate memory, or if you have an object pool, you might consider such a choice.

 Add a memory tracker to every application you create. You can conditionally compile in the code to see how things are going at any stage of the application-development phase, and can use the resulting reports for quality assurance.

Technique 25

Implementing Properties

Save Time By

- Understanding properties in C++
- Implementing a Property class
- Testing your Property class

If you are accustomed to programming in the "new" languages, such as Java or C#, you are probably already familiar with the concept of properties. Essentially, *properties* are public elements of a class that have their own methods for getting and setting their values. Unlike traditional public values, however, a property cannot be accessed directly by the programmer — even though it looks like it can. A property has set and get functions that are invoked when you attempt to write or read to the property values. C++ has no direct implementation of properties in the language. This is really a shame, because properties save a lot of time for the end user by making it easier to read and write data values within the class.

For example, suppose you have a class named Foo that contains a property called age. This property can be set by the application developer, but only to values within the range of (say) 18 to 80. Now, in a "standard" C++ application, you could define the class with a public member such as in the following:

```
class Foo
{
public:
    Foo()
    {
    }
     int age;
};
```

If you had such a class, you could then write application code to directly set the age property, like this:

```
int main()
{
    Foo f;
    f.age = 22;
}
```

The problem is, you can also set `age` to an invalid value. The restriction is only implemented by the "rule" that an age can't be outside the valid range of 18 to 80. Our code does not enforce this rule, which could easily cause problems in calculations that rely on the rule being obeyed. An invalid assignment might look like this:

```
f.age = 10; // Invalid
```

The ideal solution would be to allow people to directly set the `age` property in this class, but not allow them to set it to values outside the valid range. For example, if a user did so and then added this statement

```
f.age = 10;
```

the age would not be set and would retain its old value. This resistance to unauthorized change is the advantage of a property, instead of allowing the value to change no matter what input value is given. In addition, we can create read-only properties that can be read but not written to. C++ does not offer this capability directly, but it allows us to create such a thing ourselves. A read-only property would

be useful for values that the programmer needs access to, but cannot possibly modify, such as the total memory available in the system. Properties like these save time by making the code easier to read while still maintaining data integrity.

Implementing Properties

Creating a simple class that implements properties for a specific type — in this case, integers — can illustrate this C++ capability. We can then customize the class to allow only specific types of integers, or integer values.

1. **In the code editor of your choice, create a new file to hold the code for the implementation of the source file.**

In this example, the file is named `ch25.cpp`, although you can use whatever you choose.

2. **Type the code from Listing 25-1 into your file.**

Or better yet, copy the code from the source file on this book's companion Web site.

LISTING 25-1: PROPERTY CLASS

```
#include <stdio.h>
#include <string>

class IntProperty
{
    int temp;
    int &iValue;
    bool bWrite;
public:
    void Init()
    {
        bWrite = false;
    }
    IntProperty(void)
        : iValue(temp)
    {
        Init();
    }
```

(continued)

LISTING 25-1 *(continued)*

```cpp
    virtual void set(int i)                                        → 1
    {
        iValue = i;
    }
    virtual int  get(void)                                         → 2
    {
        return iValue;
    }

public:
    IntProperty(int& i)
        : iValue(i)
    {
        Init();
    }
    IntProperty( int i, bool read, bool write )
        : iValue(i)
    {
        Init();
    }
    IntProperty( const IntProperty& aCopy )
        : iValue(aCopy.iValue)
    {
        Init();
    }
    virtual ~IntProperty()
    {
    }


    // Accessors
    int getValue( void )
    {
        return iValue;
    }
    bool getWrite(void)
    {
        return bWrite;
    }
    void setWrite(bool write)
    {
        bWrite=write;
    }


    // Operators
    IntProperty& operator=( int i )
    {
        if( bWrite )
            set(i);
```

```
    else
        printf("Trying to assign to a read-only property\n");

    return *this;
    }
    // Cast to int
    operator int()
    {
        return get();
    }
};
```

This class implements a property according to the C++ standards, and yet works as if it were a Java or C# property. We will be able to read and write to the data value without having to write extra code, but the data values will be validated for the range allowed. To use it, we need to embed it in a class that the end user will interact with. This class will expose the IntProperty object to the end user, but the instance of the IntProperty class within any other class will work with an internal variable of that class. The IntProperty class is really just a wrapper around a reference to a variable, but that variable will be outside the scope of the IntProperty class.

Notice that the set (→ 1) and get (→ 2) methods of the class are internal to the class itself, but are also declared as virtual. That means implementing a derived class that screens out certain data values would be trivial, as we will see in the AgeProperty class later in this technique.

To derive a class from our IntProperty class, we just have to override the get and set methods in the ways we want. To restrict the range of the integer value, for example, we modify the set method to only allow the values we permit. In addition, we must override the operator= method, because operator= is never inherited by a derived class. That's because you could be setting only a portion of the object — which the language won't let you do, so you have to override the operator as well. When you create a

derived class, the operator= would be called for the base class. This would set only the member variables in the base class, and would not set the ones in the derived class. Otherwise, the remainder of the class remains the same.

3. **Add the code from Listing 25-2 to your source file.**

We could simply create a new file to store this new class, but it is easier to just combine them for the purpose of this technique.

In this case, we are going to use the IntProperty in another class.

LISTING 25-2: EXTENDING THE INTPROPERTY CLASS

```
class AgeProperty : public IntProperty
{
private:
    virtual void set(int i)
    {
        if ( i >= 18 && i <= 80 )
            IntProperty::set(i);
    }
public:
    AgeProperty( int &var )
        : IntProperty(var)
    {
    }
    AgeProperty& operator=( int i )
    {
        IntProperty::operator=(i);
        return *this;
    }
};
```

Now, in order to use the class, we need to embed the object as a public member of our encapsulating class, and provide it with a data member that it can access to set and get values. The property class is just a wrapper around a value. Because it contains a reference to a data value outside the class, it can directly modify data in another class. That means that any changes made to the reference in the IntProperty class will be immediately reflected in the underlying class-member variable.

To show how it all fits together, the next section adds a class that makes use of the AgeProperty class.

Testing the Property Class

After we have defined the Property class, we need to test it. The following steps show you how:

1. **In the code editor of your choice, create a new file to hold the code for your test program.**

In this example, I named the test program ch25.cpp.

2. **Put the code from Listing 25-3 into your test-driver file.**

LISTING 25-3: TESTING THE INTVALUE CLASS

```
class TestIntValue
{
private:
    int myInt;
public:
    TestIntValue()
        : i(myInt)
    {
        myInt = 0;
    }

    void Print()
    {
        printf("myInt = %d\n", myInt );
    }

public:
    AgeProperty i;
};
```

This class contains a single integer value, its only data member. The data member is associated with the Property class in the constructor for the class, so any changes to the member variable will be immediately reflected in the Property class and the TestIntValue class at the same time.

Because the data value is used by reference in the Property class, changing the property is the equivalent of changing the original data member directly. We are controlling how the data is changed, while allowing the compiler to generate the code that does the actual data manipulation.

Our class illustrates how the data values change and what they are assigned to at any given moment in time. We will use this class to show off how the property class works.

3. **Add the code from Listing 25-4 to the end of your existing file.**

LISTING 25-4: THE TEST DRIVER CODE

```
int main(int argc, char **argv)
{
    TestIntValue tiv;

    tiv.i = 23;                              → 3
    printf("Value = %d\n", (int)tiv.i );
    tiv.Print();
    tiv.i.setWrite( true );                  → 5
    tiv.i = 23;
    printf("Value = %d\n", (int)tiv.i );
    int x = tiv.i;
    tiv.Print();
    printf("X = %d\n", x );
    tiv.i = 99;
    printf("Value = %d\n", (int)tiv.i );

}
```

4. **Save the source file in your code editor and close the editor application.**

5. **Compile the file with your favorite compiler on your favorite operating system.**

If you have done everything properly, you should see the following output from the application:

```
$ ./a.exe
Trying to assign to a read-only property
Value = 0                                  → 4
myInt = 0
Value = 23                                 → 6
myInt = 23
X = 23
Value = 23
```

The output above illustrates that our property class is working properly. The initial value of the integer is 0, as specified in the constructor. Because the class defaulted to read-only (`setWrite` was not yet called), an attempt to write to the variable (→ **3**) results in no change being made (→ **4**). After we set the `write`

flag to allow changes (→ **5**), we can then assign values to the variable and have it modified in the output (→ **6**).

 Properties are an essential part of languages such as C# and Java, but are not yet a part of the C++ languages. If you get into the habit of thinking about them, however, you can save a lot of time in the long run — for one thing, you won't have to relearn how to use data members for classes. Translating code to and from C++ from the newer languages will become an essential part of mixed language projects in the future, and making it easy to do that translation will save you a lot of time and effort.

Doing Data Validation with Classes

Technique 26

Save Time By

✔ Understanding data validation with classes

✔ Creating a data-validation class

✔ Testing your class

Data validation is one of the most basic and pervasive functions of a computer program. Before you can operate on a given piece of data, you need to know whether or not it is valid. It doesn't matter if it is a date, a time, an age, or a Social Security number; the data you accept into your program will cause problems if it is in an invalid format.

Validating a data type is a perfect form of encapsulation, which makes it a perfect task to assign to a C++ class. Because we encapsulate both the data and the rules for the data type within a class, we can move that class from project to project, anywhere that the data type is needed. This saves time in implementing the class, as well as time and effort in validating and testing the class.

 When you're writing an application, take time to identify the data types you're using. Write classes to validate, save, and load these data types and you will save yourself endless time debugging and extending your applications.

Implementing Data Validation with Classes

Follow these steps to create your own validation classes:

1. **In the code editor of your choice, create a new file to hold the code for your header file.**

   In this example, I call my class ch26.cpp.

2. **Type the code from Listing 26-1 into your file.**

   Better yet, copy the code from the source file on this book's companion Web site.

LISTING 26-1: THE VALIDATION CLASS

```
#include <string>

// Constants used in this validation
#define SSN_LENGTH 9                                          → 1
#define SSN_DELIMITER '-'                                     → 2

// The validator class
class SSNValidator
{
    // Internal member variables
private:
    // This is the actual SSN.
    std::string _ssn;
    // This is the flag indicating validity.
    bool       _valid;

protected:
    bool          IsValid(const char *strSSN);

public:
    // Constructors and destructor
    SSNValidator();
    SSNValidator( const char *ssn );
    SSNValidator( const std::string& ssn );
    SSNValidator( const SSNValidator& aCopy );
    virtual ~SSNValidator();

    // Accessors for this class
    bool          Valid() { return _valid; };
    std::string    SSN()   { return _ssn; };
    void          setSSN( const char *ssn);

    // Operators for this class

    SSNValidator operator=( const char *ssn );
    SSNValidator operator=( const std::string& ssn );
    SSNValidator operator=( const SSNValidator& aCopy );
    operator const char *();

};
```

3. **Save your code in the code editor.**

This will be the definition for our Validator object. This class can then be included in other modules to do validation of the type we are defining. In this example, we are validating a U.S. Social Security Number.

4. **Type the code from Listing 26-2 into your new file.**

Better yet, copy the code from the source file on this book's companion Web site.

LISTING 26-2: SOCIAL SECURITY NUMBER VALIDATOR

```cpp
#include <ctype.h>

bool SSNValidator::IsValid(const char *strSSN)
{
    int i;
    // No NULL values allowed.
    if ( strSSN == NULL )
        return false;
    // Copy the result into a string, removing all delimiters.
    std::string sSSN;
    for ( i=0; i<(int)strlen(strSSN); ++i )
        if ( strSSN[i] != SSN_DELIMITER )
            sSSN += strSSN[i];

    // Must be 9 characters.
    if ( strlen(sSSN.c_str()) != SSN_LENGTH )
        return false;
    // Check to see whether all characters are numeric.
    for ( i=0; i<(int)strlen(sSSN.c_str()); ++i )
        if ( !isdigit( sSSN[i] ) )
            return false;

    // Must be okay.
    return true;
}

// Constructors and destructor
SSNValidator::SSNValidator()
{
    _ssn = "";
    _valid = false;

}

SSNValidator::SSNValidator( const char *ssn )
{
    // Only assign if valid.
    _valid = IsValid( ssn );
    if ( _valid )
        _ssn = ssn;
}

SSNValidator::SSNValidator( const std::string& ssn )
{
    // Only assign if valid.
    _valid = IsValid( ssn.c_str() );
    if ( _valid )
        _ssn = ssn;
}

SSNValidator::SSNValidator( const SSNValidator& aCopy )
```

```
{
    _ssn = aCopy._ssn;
    _valid = aCopy._valid;
}

SSNValidator::~SSNValidator()
{
}

void SSNValidator::setSSN( const char *ssn)
{
    // Only assign if valid.
    if ( IsValid( ssn ) )
    {
        _valid = true;
        _ssn = ssn;
    }
}

// Operators for this class
SSNValidator SSNValidator::operator=( const char *ssn )
{
    // Only assign if valid.
    if ( IsValid( ssn ) )
    {
        _valid = true;
        _ssn = ssn;
    }
    return *this;
}

SSNValidator SSNValidator::operator=( const std::string& ssn )
{
    // Only assign if valid.
    if ( IsValid( ssn.c_str() ) )
    {
        _valid = true;
        _ssn = ssn;
    }
    return *this;
}

SSNValidator SSNValidator::operator=( const SSNValidator& aCopy )
{
    _valid = aCopy._valid;
    _ssn   = aCopy._ssn;
    return *this;
}

SSNValidator::operator const char *()
{
    return _ssn.c_str();
}
```

5. **Save your code and close the code editor.**

The file we just defined will be a real type that you can use in your own applications to store and validate Social Security Numbers (SSNs). You will never again have to write code to check the length of an entry or its contents to see whether it could be a valid SSN value.

> Create a new type for every kind of data you will accept and process in your application. Create a validator for the data type that can be moved from project to project.

Note that we provided constants for both the length of the SSN and its delimiter (see lines marked → **1** and → **2**). This allows you to easily modify the code if the format of the SSN changes over time. Someday you may need to change the SSN to use more digits, or to be formatted with a different delimiter. Preparing for this now saves you huge amounts of time later.

> Never hard-code values into your applications; always use constants that can be easily changed at compile-time.

Testing Your SSN Validator Class

After you create the `Validator` class, you should create a test driver to ensure that your code is correct and show people how to use your code.

Creating a test driver will illustrate the validation of various kinds of input from the user, and will show how the `Validator` class is intended to be used. The driver will contain some basic tests of the class, as well as accepting Social Security Numbers from the user to see whether they are valid or not.

In this example, we create a test driver that does two things. First, it creates a standard battery of tests that illustrates the expected good and bad entries for the type. Second, the test driver allows the programmer to try other styles of entry to see whether the class catches them.

1. **In the code editor of your choice, reopen the file to hold the code for your test program.**

In this example, I named the test program `ch26.cpp`.

2. **Append the code from Listing 26-3 into your test driver file, substituting the names you used for your SSN class definition where appropriate.**

Better yet, copy the code you find from the source file on this book's companion Web site.

LISTING 26-3: THE TEST DRIVER CODE

```
const char *TrueOrFalse( bool value )
{
    if ( value )
        return "TRUE";
    return "FALSE";
}

void DoValidTest( const char *strName, SSNValidator& ssn, bool expected_result )
{
    bool bValid = ssn.Valid();
    printf("%s: Result %s. Expected Result: %s. %s\n", strName,
        TrueOrFalse( bValid ), TrueOrFalse( expected_result ),
        ( bValid == expected_result ? "PASS" : "FAIL" )          );
}
```

```
int main(int argc, char **argv)
{
    if ( argc < 2 )
    {
        printf("Usage: ch3_15 ssn1 [ssn2]...\n");
        exit(1);
    }

    for ( int i=1; i<argc; ++i )
    {
        SSNValidator ssn(argv[i]);
        if ( ssn.Valid() )
            printf("%s is a valid Social Security Number\n",  ssn.SSN().c_str() );
        else
            printf("%s is NOT a valid Social Security Number\n", argv[i] );
    }

    // Do some generic testing.
    SSNValidator ssnNULL( NULL );
    DoValidTest( "NULL Test", ssnNULL, false );
    SSNValidator ssnGood("000-00-0000");
    DoValidTest( "Good Test", ssnGood, true );
    SSNValidator ssnBad("0000a0000");
    DoValidTest( "Bad Test", ssnBad, false );


    return 0;
}
```

3. **Save your test driver file in the code editor and close the code-editor program.**

4. **Compile the test program with your chosen compiler and run it on your chosen operating system.**

Enter command-line arguments, such as

```
123456789 000-00-0000 0909 a12345678
    012-03-3456
```

These are simply forms of the Social Security Number, some valid and some invalid. The first one, containing nine digits and no alphanumeric characters, will be valid. The third argument does not contain nine characters and is therefore invalid. The fourth contains an invalid character (a). The second and fifth entries look valid, but we do not handle the dash character, so they will be deemed invalid by the program.

If your program is working properly, you should see the output from the test driver as shown in Listing 26-4.

LISTING 26-4: OUTPUT FROM THE TEST DRIVER

```
$ ./a 123456789 000-00-000 0909 a12345678
    01-02-2345
123456789 is a valid Social Security Number
000-00-000 is NOT a valid Social Security
    Number
0909 is NOT a valid Social Security Number
a12345678 is NOT a valid Social Security
    Number
01-02-2345 is NOT a valid Social Security
    Number
NULL Test: Result FALSE. Expected Result:
    FALSE. PASS
Good Test: Result TRUE. Expected Result:
    TRUE. PASS
Bad Test: Result FALSE. Expected Result:
    FALSE. PASS
```

As you can see by the output, the program first checks the input arguments from the user. As we expected, only the first input value was valid. All the remaining entries were invalid. The remaining tests simply validate that known conditions work properly.

 I recommend that you create generic test drivers for all your validators, so when changes are made to accommodate new formats, the drivers will be prepared in advance to test them. This will save a lot of time in the long run, and will allow for automated testing.

Technique 27

Building a Date Class

Save Time By

- Creating a generic Date class
- Implementing date functionality into your class
- Testing your class

One of the most common tasks that you will run into as a programmer is working with dates. Whether you are calculating when something is bought or sold, or validating input from the user, your application will probably need to support dates. The standard C library contains various routines for working with dates, such as the `time` and `localtime` functions. The problem, however, is that these routines do not perform adequate validation — and for that matter, they are not easy to use. It would be nice, therefore, to create a single class that implemented all the date functionality that we wanted in our applications. By creating a single class that can be easily ported from project to project, you will save time in the development, design, and testing phases of the project.

Because dates are a fundamental building block of our applications, it makes sense to create a single class that would manipulate them and validate them. If you were to make a list of all of the basic functionality you would like in such a class, you would probably have something like this:

- Validate dates
- Perform date math calculations
- Compute the day of the week
- Return day and month names
- Convert numeric dates to strings

Many other functions exist that would be useful, but these are the most critical in any application. In this technique, we look at the ways you can utilize a `Date` class in your own applications — and how you can implement the functionality needed to do everything on our feature list for a `Date` class.

You can save huge amounts of time by creating classes that not only validate input, but also manipulate it numerically. By creating a class that allows you to add to, or subtract from, a date in your code directly, you do accounting calculations and timing routines in a flash, without any additional coding.

Creating the Date Class

Follow these steps to create your own personal `Date` class:

1. **In the code editor of your choice, create a new file to hold the code for the `Date` class.**

In this example, the file is named `ch27.h`, although you can use whatever you choose.

2. **Type the code from Listing 27-1 into your file.**

Better yet, copy the code you find in the source file on this book's companion Web site. Change the names of the constants and variables as you choose.

LISTING 27-1: THE DATE CLASS DEFINITION

```cpp
#ifndef CH27H_
#define CH27H_
#include <string>

const int MaxMonths = 12;
const int MaxYear   = 9999;

typedef enum
{
    MMDDYYYY = 0,
    DDMMYYYY = 1,
    YYYYMMDD = 2
} DateFormat;

class Date
{
private:
    // Store dates in Julian format.
    long        _julian;
    // The month of the year (0-11)
    int         _month;
    // The day of the month (0-30)
    int         _day_of_month;
    // The day of the week (0-6)
    int         _day_of_week;
    // The year of the date (0-9999)
    int         _year;
    // A string representation of the date
    std::string _string_date;
    // The format to use in the date
    DateFormat  _format;
    // See whether a given date is valid.
    bool IsValid(int m, int d, int y);
    // Compute the day of the week.
    int  DayOfWeek( int m, int d, int y );
    // Convert to Julian format.
    long ToJulian();
    // Convert from a Julian format.
    void FromJulian();
    // Initialize to defaults.
    void Init(void);
    // Make a copy of this date.
    void Copy( const Date& aCopy );

    // Convert to a string.
    const char *ToString();

public:

    // Constructors and destructors
    Date();
    Date( int m, int d, int y );
    Date( const Date& aCopy );
    Date( long julian );
    virtual ~Date();

    // Operators.

    // Assignment operator
    Date operator=( const Date& date );
    // Conversion to Julian date
    operator long();
    // Conversion to a string
    operator const char *();

    // Accessors
    int     Month()      { return _month; };
    int     DayOfMonth() { return
_day_of_month; };
    int     DayOfWeek() { return
_day_of_week; };
    int     Year() { return _year; };
    const char *AsString() { return
_string_date.c_str(); };
    DateFormat Format() { return _format; };

    void setMonth( int m );
    void setDayOfMonth( int _day_of_month );
    void setYear( int y );
    void setFormat( const DateFormat& f );

    // Operations
```

```
// Is a given year a leap year?
bool isLeapYear(int year) const;
// Is this date a leap year?
bool isLeapYear(void) const;
// Return the number of days in a given
month.
int numDaysInMonth( int month, int year
);
// Return the number of days in the cur-
    rent month.
int numDaysInMonth( void );

// Some useful operators for manipula-
    tion
Date operator+(int numDays);
Date operator+=(int numDays);
Date operator-(int numDays);
Date operator-=(int numDays);
};

#endif
```

3. **Save your code in the code editor and close the file.**

The file you just created is the header and interface file for the class. This is what the "public" will see when they want to use our class. Our next task, therefore, is to implement the functionality of the class itself.

4. **In the code editor of your choice, create a new file to hold the code for the implementation of the** Date **class.**

In this example, the file is named ch27.cpp, although you can use whatever you choose.

5. **Type the code from Listing 27-2 into your file.**

Better yet, copy the code from the source file on this book's companion Web site. Change the names of the constants and variables as you choose.

These are all the constants and definitions we will use for our class. The next step is to add the actual implementation.

LISTING 27-2: THE DATE CLASS SOURCE FILE

```
#include "ch27.h"

// Some information we need.
const char *MonthNames[] = {
    "January",
    "February",
    "March",
    "April",
    "May",
    "June",
    "July",
    "August",
    "September",
    "October",
    "November",
    "December"
};

int MonthDays[] =
{
    31, 28, 31, 30, 31, 30, 31, 31, 30, 31, 30, 31
};
```

(continued)

LISTING 27-2 (continued)

```c
char *DayNames[] = {
    "Sunday",
    "Monday",
    "Tuesday",
    "Wednesday",
    "Thursday",
    "Friday",
    "Saturday"
};

#define OCT5_1582        (2299160L)      // "really" 15-Oct-1582
#define OCT14_1582       (2299169L)       // "really"  4-Oct-1582
#define JAN1_1           (1721423L)

#define YEAR             (365)
#define FOUR_YEARS       (1461)
#define CENTURY          (36524L)
#define FOUR_CENTURIES   (146097L)

static int    DaysSoFar[][13] =
        {
        {0, 31, 59, 90, 120, 151, 181, 212, 243, 273, 304, 334, 365},
        {0, 31, 60, 91, 121, 152, 182, 213, 244, 274, 305, 335, 366}
        };
```

Implementing the Date Functionality

After we have the class defined, it is time to implement the actual functionality for that class. In this case, we want to add all of the logic for manipulating and defining dates. Let's do that now.

1. Reopen the Date **class source file (which we called** ch27.cpp**). Add the code from Listing 27-3 to the file.**

LISTING 27-3: THE DATE FUNCTIONALITY

```cpp
void Date::Copy( const Date& aCopy )
{
    _julian = aCopy._julian;
    _month  = aCopy._month;
    _day_of_month = aCopy._day_of_month;
    _day_of_week = aCopy._day_of_week;
    _year = aCopy._year;
    _format = aCopy._format;
    _string_date = aCopy._string_date;
}

void Date::Init()
```

→ 1

```
{
    _julian = 0;
    _month  = 1;
    _day_of_month = 1;
    _day_of_week = 0;
    _year = 2004;
    _format = MMDDYYYY;
    _string_date = AsString();
}

int Date::DayOfWeek( int m, int d, int y)
{
    _day_of_week = ((_julian + 2) % 7 + 1);
        return day_of_week;
}

bool Date::IsValid(int m, int d, int y)
{
    // Check the year.
    if ( y < 0 || y > MaxYear )
        return false;
    // Do the month.
    if ( m < 1 || m > MaxMonths )
        return false;
    // Finally, do the day of the month. First, the easy check...
    if ( d < 1 || d > 31 )
        return false;
    // Now, check the days per THIS month.
    int daysPerMonth = MonthDays[ m ];
    if ( isLeapYear( y ) )
        if ( m == 2 )
            daysPerMonth ++;
    if ( d > daysPerMonth )
        return false;

    // Looks good.
    return true;
}

long Date::ToJulian()
{
    int        a;
    int        work_year=_year;
    long    j;
    int     lp;

    // Correct for negative year  (-1 = 1BC = year 0).

    if (work_year < 0)
            work_year++;

    lp = !(work_year & 3);              // lp = 1 if this is a leap year.
```

→ **2**

→ **3**

(continued)

LISTING 27-3 *(continued)*

```
    j =
        ((work_year-1) / 4)        +          // Plus ALL leap years...
        DaysSoFar[lp][_month-1]     +
        _day_of_month          +
        (work_year * 365L)     +        // Days in years
        JAN1_1              +
        -366;                          // adjustments

    // Deal with Gregorian calendar
    if (j >= OCT14_1582)
    {

        a = (int)(work_year/100);
        j = j+ 2 - a + a/4;            // Skip days that didn't exist.
    }

    _julian = j;
    return _julian;
}

void Date::FromJulian()                                                     → 4
{
    long     z,y;
    short      m,d;
    int      lp;

    z = _julian+1;
    if (z >= OCT5_1582)
    {
        z -= JAN1_1;
        z  = z + (z/CENTURY)  - (z/FOUR_CENTURIES) -2;
        z += JAN1_1;

    }

    z = z - ((z-YEAR) / FOUR_YEARS);       // Remove leap years before the current year.
    y = z / YEAR;

    d = (short) (z - (y * YEAR));

    y = y - 4712;                   // This is our base year in 4713 B.C.
    if (y < 1)
        y--;

    lp = !(y & 3);                  // lp = 1 if this is a leap year.

    if (d==0)
    {
        y--;
        d = (short) (YEAR + lp);
    }
```

```
    m  = (short) (d/30);          // This is a guess at the month.

    while (DaysSoFar[lp][m] >=d)
        m--;                      // Correct guess.

    d = (short) (d - DaysSoFar[lp][m]);

    _day_of_month = d;
    _month = (short) (m+1);
    if ( _month > 12 )
    {
        _month = 1;
        y ++;
    }
    _year = (short) y;
    _day_of_week = DayOfWeek( _month, _day_of_month, _year );
}

Date::Date()
{
    Init();
    ToString();
}

Date::Date( int m, int d, int y )
{
    Init();
    if ( IsValid( m, d, y ) )
    {
        _day_of_month = d;
        _month = m;
        _year  = y;
        _julian = ToJulian();
        ToString();
        _day_of_week = DayOfWeek( _month, _day_of_month, _year );
    }
}

Date::Date( const Date& aCopy )
{
    Init();
    Copy( aCopy );
}

Date::Date( long julian )
{
    Init();
    _julian = julian;
    FromJulian();
    ToString();
}
```

(continued)

LISTING 27-3 *(continued)*

```
Date::~Date()
{
    Init();
}

Date Date::operator=( const Date& date )
{
    Copy( date );
    return *this;
}

// Conversion to Julian date
Date::operator long()
{
    return _julian;
}

// Conversion to a string
Date::operator const char *()
{
    return _string_date.c_str();
}

void Date::setMonth( int m )
{
    if ( m < 0 || m > MaxMonths )
        return;
    _month = m;
}

void Date::setDayOfMonth( int d )
{
    if ( d < 1 || d > 31 )
        return;
    // Now check the days per THIS month.
    int daysPerMonth = MonthDays[ _month ];
    if ( isLeapYear( _year ) )
        if ( _month == 2 )
            daysPerMonth ++;
    if ( d > daysPerMonth )
        return;

    _day_of_month = d;
}

void Date::setYear( int y )
{
    if ( y < 0 || y > MaxYear )
        return;

    _year = y;
}
```

```
void Date::setFormat( const DateFormat& f )
{
    _format = f;
}

bool Date::isLeapYear( void ) const
{
    return  ( (_year >= 1582) ?
                (_year % 4 == 0  &&  _year % 100 != 0  ||  _year % 400 == 0 ):
                (_year % 4 == 0) );
}

bool Date::isLeapYear( int year ) const
{
    return  ( (year >= 1582) ?
                (year % 4 == 0  &&  year % 100 != 0  ||  year % 400 == 0 ):
                (year % 4 == 0) );
}

// Return the number of days in a given month.
int  Date::numDaysInMonth( int m, int y )
{
    // Validate the input.

    // Check the year.
    if ( y < 0 || y > MaxYear )
        return -1;
    // Do the month.
    if ( m < 1 || m > MaxMonths )
        return -1;

    int daysPerMonth = MonthDays[ m ];
    if ( isLeapYear( y ) )
        if ( m == 2 )
            daysPerMonth ++;

    return daysPerMonth;
}

// Return the number of days in the current month.
int  Date::numDaysInMonth( void )
{
    int daysPerMonth = MonthDays[ _month ];
    if ( isLeapYear( _year ) )
        if ( _month == 2 )
            daysPerMonth ++;

    return daysPerMonth;
}

Date Date::operator+(int numDays)
{
```

(continued)

LISTING 27-3 *(continued)*

```
        long j = _julian;
        j += numDays;
        Date d(j);
        return d;
}

Date Date::operator+=(int numDays)
{
        _julian += numDays;
        FromJulian();
        ToString();
        return *this;
}

Date Date::operator-(int numDays)
{
        long j = _julian;
        j -= numDays;
        Date d(j);
        return d;
}

Date Date::operator-=(int numDays)
{
        _julian -= numDays;
        FromJulian();
        ToString();
        return *this;
}

const char *Date::ToString()
{
        char szBuffer[ 256 ];

        switch ( _format )
        {
            case MMDDYYYY:
                sprintf(szBuffer, "%02d/%02d/%02d", _month, _day_of_month, _year );
                break;
            case DDMMYYYY:
                sprintf(szBuffer, "%02d/%02d/%02d", _day_of_month, _month, _year );
                break;
            case YYYYMMDD:
                sprintf(szBuffer, "%02d/%02d/%02d", _year, _month, _day_of_month );
                break;
            default:
                sprintf(szBuffer, "%02d/%02d/%02d", _month, _day_of_month, _year );
                break;
        }

        _string_date = szBuffer;
        return _string_date.c_str();
}
```

Now, this is a lot of code to deal with. Not to worry — the code breaks down into three separate pieces:

▶ **Initialization code** (shown at → **1**) either sets or gets our individual member variables and initializes them to reasonable defaults.

▶ **Validation code** (shown at → **2**) checks to see whether or not the input data is reasonable, given the rules and the current settings.

▶ **Algorithmic code** (shown at → **3** and → **4**) does the actual date manipulation and calculations.

2. **Save the source-code file and close the code editor.**

 Always break your classes into discrete initialization, validation, and calculation pieces. This saves you time by focusing your efforts on what needs to be done, rather than worrying about how to do it.

3. **Compile the test code to make sure that you have all of the code properly entered and correct.**

Testing the Date Class

As with any other utility class, after you have the code written for the class, you must be able to provide a test driver for that class. The following steps show you how to create a test driver that illustrates that the code is working properly — and shows other programmers how to use the class in their own applications.

1. **In the code editor of your choice, create a new file to hold the code for the test driver.**

In this example, the file is named ch27.cpp, although you can use whatever you choose.

2. **Type the code from Listing 27-4 into your file.**

Better yet, copy the code from the source file on this book's companion Web site. Change the names of the constants and variables as you choose.

LISTING 27-4: THE DATE TEST DRIVER CODE.

```
#include <stdio.h>
#include "date.h"

void DumpDate( Date& d )
{
    printf("Date:\n");
    printf("As String: %s\n", d.AsString() );
    printf("Month: %d\n", d.Month() );
    printf("Day   : %d\n", d.DayOfMonth() );
    printf("Day of Week: %d\n", d.DayOfWeek() );
    printf("Year:  %d\n", d.Year() );
    printf("Leap Year: %s\n", d.isLeapYear() ? "Yes" : "No" );
    printf("Number of days in this month: %d\n", d.numDaysInMonth() );
}

int main()
{
    // Initialized date to no values.
    Date d1;
```

(continued)

LISTING 27-4 *(continued)*

```
    // Initialize to the end of the year to test edge cases.
    Date d2(12,31,2004);

    // Print out the dates as strings for testing.
    printf("D1 as string: %s\n", d1.AsString() );
    printf("D2 as string: %s\n", d2.AsString() );

    // Test year wrap and the operator +=.
    d2 += 1;
    printf("D2 as string: %s\n", d2.AsString() );          → 6

    // Test backward year wrap and the operator -=.
    d2 -= 1;
    printf("D2 as string: %s\n", d2.AsString() );

    // Test the assignment operator.
    Date d3 = d2;

    // Check to see whether the class works properly for
    // assigned objects.
    d3 -= 10;
    printf("D3 as string: %s\n", d3.AsString() );

    // Validate the day of the week.
    Date d4 (7,27,2004);
    printf("D4, day of week = %d\n", d4.DayOfWeek() );

    // Test the pieces of the date.
    Date d5;

    d5.setMonth( 11 );
    d5.setDayOfMonth( 31 );
    d5.setYear( 2004 );
    d5.setFormat( YYYYMMDD );

    DumpDate( d5 );

    return 0;
}
```

3. **Save the code as a file in your editor and close the code editor.**

4. **Compile and run the application.**

If you have done everything properly and the code is working correctly, you should see output that looks like this:

```
$ ./a.exe
D1 as string: 01/01/2004          → 5
D2 as string: 12/31/2004
D2 as string: 01/01/2005
D2 as string: 12/31/2004
D3 as string: 12/21/2004          → 7
D4, day of week = 3
Date:
As String: 2004/12/31
```

```
Month: 12
Day  : 31
Day of Week: 0
Year:  2004
Leap Year: Yes
Number of days in this month: 31
```

There are some important things to take away from this output. First, look at the line marked ➔ **5** in the output listing. This line is output for the date object which is defined with the `void` constructor. As you can see, the object is properly initialized with a valid date. Next, let's look at the line marked with ➔ **6**. This line is output after we added one day to the 12/31/2004 date. Obviously, this forces the date to wrap to the next year, which we can verify by looking at the output, showing 01/01/2005. We can also verify, by looking at a calendar, that the date shown at ➔ **7** really does fall on a Tuesday (the 3 in the output). Finally, we run some simple tests to verify that the number of days in the month is correct for December, that the pieces of the date are parsed properly, and that the leap year calculation is correct.

All of this output data allows us to validate that our class works properly and that the functionality can easily be moved from project to project. This will save us a lot of time, and allow us to design our programs with the date functionality already built.

 When you are testing a class, make sure that you exercise all of the functionality in the ways your class is most likely to be used — not just the ways that make sense to you at the time. Our tests verified that the date math, formatting, and accessor methods all worked properly.

Some Final Thoughts on the Date Class

As you can see, our `Date` class is really very useful. However, it could easily be made more useful. For example, you could allow the user to pass in a string to be parsed into its date components, thus solving a common programming problem. Another possible enhancement would be to initialize the default constructor to be the current date. Finally, it would be nice to have the date strings, such as the month and day names, within the class itself and accessible. This would protect them from access by programmers from outside the class. In addition, it could allow us to read them from a file, or get them from some internal resource, to provide internationalization without forcing the end user to know where the data is stored.

 If you store literal string information in a class, make sure that the programmer can replace it from outside the class. This will allow the developers to put in their own descriptions, change the text for internationalization, or just modify the text to fit their needs.

Technique 28

Overriding Functionality with Virtual Methods

Save Time By

✔ Using factory patterns

✔ Building a manager class

✔ Testing the manager class

One of the most common "patterns" of software development is the *factory pattern*. It's an approach to developing software that works like a factory: You create objects from a single model of a particular object type, and the model defines what the objects can do. Generally, the way this works is that you create a factory class that allocates, deallocates, and keeps track of a certain base class of objects. This factory class really only understands how to manage the object type that forms a base for all other objects in the class tree. However, through the magic of virtual methods, it is able to manage all of the objects. Let's take a look at how this works. By creating a single factory, using virtual methods that processes a variety of types of objects, we will save time by not having to reimplement this processing each time we need it.

First, we have a class that manages a given base class of objects — it's called a *factory*. Its uses virtual methods to manage objects — that is, to add new objects, remove them, return them to the user, and report on which ones are in use and not in use.

Next, we have a set of derived classes. These override the functionality of the base class by using virtual methods to accomplish different tasks. As an example, consider the idea of a variety of different kinds of classes to read various types of files. We would have a base class, which might be called a `FileProcessor` class. Our manager would be a `FileProcessorManager` class. The manager would create various `FileProcessors`, based on the file type that was needed, creating them if necessary or returning one that was not currently in use.

 When you implement a common base class, set up an object pool to manage the objects based on it. That way you can always keep track easily of how they are created and destroyed.

Creating a Factory Class

The first step toward managing and processing objects is to create a factory class that works with a generic base class. The following steps show you how to create such a class that utilizes virtual methods to create, add, and delete objects. In this case, we create a base class called Object from which all of our managed objects will be derived.

1. **In the code editor of your choice, create a new file to hold the code for the implementation of the factory code.**

In this example, the file is named ch28.cpp, although you can use whatever you choose.

2. **Type the code from Listing 28-1 into your file.**

Better yet, copy the source file from this book's companion Web site and change the names of the constants and variables as you choose.

LISTING 28-1: THE BASE-CLASS SOURCE CODE

```cpp
#include <stdio.h>
#include <string>
#include <vector>

class Object
{
private:
    std::string _name;
    bool        _inUse;

public:
    Object(void)
    {
        _name = "Object";
        _inUse = false;
    }
    Object( const char *name )
    {
        _name = name;
        _inUse = false;
    }
    Object( const Object& aCopy )
    {
        _name = aCopy._name;
        _inUse = aCopy._inUse;
    }
    virtual ~Object()
    {
    }
    virtual void MarkInUse( bool bFlag )
    {
        _inUse = bFlag;
    }
    virtual bool InUse( void )
    {
        return _inUse;
    }
```

(continued)

LISTING 28-1 *(continued)*

```
    virtual const char *Name(void)
    {
        return _name.c_str();
    }
    virtual void Report() = 0;
};

class MyObject1 : public Object
{
public:
    MyObject1()
        : Object ("MyObject1")
    {
    }
    virtual void Report()
    {
        printf("I am a MyObject1 Object\n");
    }
};

class MyObject2 : public Object
{
public:
    MyObject2()
        : Object ("MyObject2")
    {
    }
    virtual void Report()
    {
        printf("I am a MyObject2 Object\n");
    }
};

class MyObject3 : public Object
{
public:
    MyObject3()
        : Object ("MyObject3")
    {
    }
    virtual void Report()
    {
        printf("I am a MyObject3 Object\n");
    }
};

class Factory
{
private:
    std::vector< Object *> _objects;
```

```
public:
    Factory()
    {
    }
    // Method to add an object to the pool
    virtual void   Add( Object *obj )
    {
        obj->MarkInUse( true );
        _objects.insert( _objects.end(), obj );
    }
    // Method to retrieve an object not in use
    virtual Object *Get( void )
    {
        std::vector< Object *>::iterator iter;

        for ( iter = _objects.begin(); iter != _objects.end(); ++iter )
        {
            if ( (*iter)->InUse() == false )
            {
                printf("Found one\n");

                // Mark it in use
                (*iter)->MarkInUse( true );
                // And give it back
                return (*iter);
            }
        }

        // Didn't find one.
        return NULL;
    }

    virtual void Remove( Object *obj )
    {
        std::vector< Object *>::iterator iter;

        for ( iter = _objects.begin(); iter != _objects.end(); ++iter )
        {
            if ( (*iter) == obj )
            {
                (*iter)->MarkInUse( false );
                break;
            }
        }
    }


    virtual void Report()                                          → 1
    {
        std::vector< Object *>::iterator iter;
```

(continued)

LISTING 28-1 *(continued)*

```
    for ( iter = _objects.begin(); iter != _objects.end(); ++iter )
    {
        if ( (*iter)->InUse() == true )
        {
            printf("Object at %lx in use\n", (*iter) );
        }
        else
        {
            printf("Object at %lx NOT in use\n", (*iter) );
        }
        (*iter)->Report();
    }
    }

};
```

3. Save the file to disk and close the code editor.

4. Compile the application on the operating system of your choice, using your chosen compiler.

 Always implement a method that can report on the state of an object of each class. This allows you to do quick memory dumps at any time, via the factory for each base class. This class can be used by a factory class to report status, and can be overridden via virtual methods to extend that status reporting for derived classes.

Testing the Factory

After you create a class, you should create a test driver that not only ensures that your code is correct, but also shows people how to use your code. The following steps show you how to create a simple test driver to illustrate how the factory class interacts with the derived objects via virtual methods.

1. In the code editor of your choice, open the source file to hold the code for the test driver.

In this example, the file is named ch28.cpp, although you can use whatever you choose.

2. Type the code from Listing 28-2 into your file.

Better yet, copy the code from the source file on this book's companion Web site and change the names of the constants and variables as you choose.

LISTING 28-2: THE TEST DRIVER FOR THE FACTORY OBJECT

```
int main()
{
    // Implement an object factory object
    Factory f;

    // Add some objects to the factory
    MyObject1 *obj1 = new MyObject1;
    MyObject2 *obj2 = new MyObject2;
    MyObject3 *obj3 = new MyObject3;

    f.Add( obj1 );
    f.Add( obj2 );
    f.Add( obj3 );

    // Remove one to simulate the destruc-
tion of an object
    f.Remove( obj1 );

    // Now try to get a new one back.
    Object *pObject = f.Get();
    printf("I got back a %s object\n",
pObject->Name() );
```

```
    // Generate a report to see what is in
use.
    f.Report();

}
```

3. **Save the file and close the code editor.**

4. **Compile the entire program and run it in the operating system of your choice.**

You should see the following output if you have done everything right. Note that depending on your operating system and hardware, the actual numbers shown for addresses will vary.

```
$ ./a.exe
Found one
I got back a MyObject1 object
Object at a050230 in use
I am a MyObject1 Object
Object at a050008 in use
I am a MyObject2 Object
Object at a050638 in use
I am a MyObject3 Object
```

This output shows us that the manager is keeping track of our various base `Object`-derived classes and creating them only when necessary. As you can see, the virtual methods permit us to create the proper type for this particular derived class and to create them as needed.

As you can see, the factory manager can handle all sorts of different kinds of objects — as long as they are derived from a common base class. In addition, our virtual methods can be used to differentiate the objects to let other programmers know what we can do.

Enhancing the Manager Class

One way you might consider enhancing the manager class is to extend it by letting it allocate its own objects. As the code stands, the manager manages only the objects that are added to its list. It cannot create new ones as they are needed. If all of the allocations were done in one place, tracking down problems with memory leaks, allocation errors, and usage patterns would be vastly simpler. This could be done in a variety of ways, from registering a "constructor" function that would be passed to the manager, to adding code to create specific forms of the objects. The latter case is easier, the former case more extensible and flexible.

If you want another bit of programming fun, you can add another good feature to add to the manager: Implement a method that would delete all objects in the class, notifying the objects if necessary. This "clean" method could be called at program shutdown, in order to guarantee that there are no memory leaks in the application. In addition, you could use the `Report` method (shown in Listing 28-1 at ➔ **1**) at various times in your application to ensure that you are not leaving orphan objects in the system that are not eventually de-allocated.

 There is one other way to implement a manager, which is worth a mention. You can create a manager that is a *friend class* to all of the classes it needs to manage. If you use this technique, you should create a method within the managed class that knows how to "clone" itself. This would essentially be a method that allocated a new object, called its copy constructor with itself as an argument, and returned the newly created object to the manager. With this technique, the manager doesn't need to worry about how to create objects; all it has to do is find the ones it manages in its list.

Technique 29

Using Mix-In Classes

Save Time By

- Understanding mix-in classes
- Implementing mix-in classes
- Testing your code

Inheritance is an extremely powerful technique in C++. The problem with inheritance, however, is that you must either give the end-user access to all public methods of a class — or override them privately to "hide" them from use by the end-user. C++ takes an all-or-nothing approach to the derivation of classes with inheritance. This approach is hardly an optimal technique, because removing the undesired functionality from a class that contains many methods would require more work than recreating the class from scratch. For example, if you are inheriting from a class that contains a `print` method, and you do not want that method exposed to the end-user, you must hide the method by creating a new, private version of it. This is not too difficult when there is only one such method, but when there are a dozen of them, it makes more sense to create a new class.

Fortunately, C++ provides an alternative: the *mix-in class*. Here's how it works: The easiest way to limit the functionality you provide from a base class is to use that class as a data member of the inherited class — and to give the end-user access only to the methods you want them to use, instead of providing all methods and removing the ones you don't want used. This approach is particularly useful when you have small classes you want to initialize and restrict (so that only you have access to them), or classes whose overall functionality is more than you feel comfortable providing (or is too complicated for the end-user to deal with). The embedded base class is a mix-in to the inherited class.

Mix-in classes are implemented as data members of the class that provides the overall functionality and are used to extend that functionality. The advantages of the mix-in technique are obvious: It gives the user access to the capabilities you want used, you can restrict what the users have access to, and you can simplify the methods provided by providing your own wrappers with defaults. When your mix-in class is embedded in a class the user may instantiate, you control what methods in the mix-in class are available. To do this, you simply write accessor methods that allow the end-user access to the methods you want them to be using in the mix-in class. This has several advantages. First, you control what access the user has to functionality. Second, if you change the way in which the embedded mix-in class works, the end-user is not impacted. Finally, you can adapt the functionality of the mix-in class to your specific needs, tailoring its behavior within your wrapper methods. Because you do not have to write the entire functionality provided by the mix-in, you save a lot of time, and the usesr get a fully debugged system, saving them time.

Provide access to selected functionality in a class by using that class as a mix-in. You can easily extend your own classes and move information-specific data into a class that handles that data only. This is particularly important when working with classes that encapsulate data that would be easily destroyed, corrupted, or over-written if you provided direct access to the data members.

Implementing Mix-In Classes

Assume you want to add the ability to save data in one of your classes. You could add a base class called Save that permits data to be written to a file. This class would do all the work of managing the output file, writing to it, and closing it. Then you could create a mix-in class to do the save functionality, and then illustrate how that functionality is used in a derived class.

To implement a mix-in class, you simply do the following steps in your own existing class:

1. **In the code editor of your choice, create a new file to hold the code for the implementation of the source file.**

In this example, the file is named ch29.cpp, although you can use whatever you choose.

2. **Type the code from Listing 29-1 into your file.**

Better yet, copy the code from the source file on this book's companion Web site.

LISTING 29-1: THE MIX-IN CLASS

```
#include <stdio.h>
#include <string>

class Save
{
    FILE *fp;
public:
    Save( void )
    {
        fp = NULL;
    }
    Save( const char *strFileName )
    {
        fp = fopen( strFileName, "w" );      → 1
    }
    virtual ~Save()
    {
        if ( fp )
            fclose(fp);                       → 2
    }

    void Write( const char *strOut )          → 3
    {
        if ( fp )
            fprintf(fp, "%s\n", strOut );
    }
    void Write( int i )
    {
        if ( fp )
            fprintf(fp, "%d\n", i );
    }
    void Write( double d )
    {
        if ( fp )
            fprintf(fp, "%ld\n", d );
    }
    FILE *getFilePointer()
    {
        return fp;
    }
};
```

(continued)

LISTING 29-1 (continued)

```
class MyClass
{
private:
    Save s;
public:
    MyClass( void )
        : s("test.txt")                          ➜ 4
    {
        s.Write("Start of MyClass");             ➜ 5
    }
    MyClass( const char *strFileName )
        : s(strFileName)
    {
        s.Write("Start of MyClass");
    }
    virtual ~MyClass()
    {
        s.Write("End of My Class");              ➜ 6
    }
    void Log( const char *strLog )
    {
        s.Write(strLog);
    }
};

int main(int argc, char **argv)
{
    MyClass mc;

    for ( int i=0; i<argc; ++i )
    mc.Log( argv[i] );
    return 0;
}
```

In the above listing, the Save functionality is implemented in a mix-in class, which is used by the MyClass class to give the end-user the ability to save data from the MyClass member variables. Note that the end-user has no access to the Save functionality directly, but instead uses it through the Log method, which utilizes the save functions but does not directly expose them.

3. **Save the source file in your code editor and close the code editor.**

Compiling and Testing Your Mix-In Class

Let's verify that the code works as illustrated and allows you to save data within the MyClass objects. To do this, we will compile and run the program and view the output. The following steps show you how:

1. **Compile the source code with the compiler of your choice on the operating system of your choice.**

    Note that we have implemented all of the file handling functionality — the open (shown at ➜ 1), close (shown at ➜ 2), and save functions of the file — in the mix-in class Save. This class deals with all the operating-system-specific work of dealing with file pointers. Our main class in the example, MyClass, simply works with the mix-in class and assumes that it knows what to do for various combinations of operating systems and environments.

 Always move all operating-system-specific functionality for file systems, memory handling, time functions, and the like, into mix-in classes that you can embed in your code. Doing so ensures that the code is easily portable between different operating systems, compilers, and environments.

2. **Run the program in the operating system shell of your choice.**

If you have done everything properly, you should get no output from the program itself. Instead, you see a file which we defined in the MyClass class at ➜ 4 (called test.txt) generated in the file system, residing in the directory in which you ran the program. This file should contain the output shown in Listing 29-2.

LISTING 29-2: THE TEST.TXT OUTPUT FILE

```
Start of MyClass              → 7
./a
End of My Class               → 8
```

As you can see from the output, the program logs some data of its own, indicating the beginning and end of the class lifespan. In addition, it allows the user to output the arguments to the program.

Because we did not provide any arguments, it simply outputs the name of the executable file, which is the first argument to all programs.

Notice that our class logs its own actions (see → **5** and → **6**, these are shown in the output file at → **7** and → **8**) as well as the actions of the class it is called from. This handy characteristic provides you with an essential debugging log from which you can look at how the program is operating.

Part V

Arrays and Templates

The 5th Wave   By Rich Tennant

Re·al Pro·gram·mers

Real Programmers code in pen.

Creating a Simple Template Class

Save Time By

- Making classes reusable by making them generic
- Comparing void pointers to template classes
- Implementing template classes
- Understanding your output

Because our classes can be reused over and over again in C++, we want to create as general a class as we can so it can be used in the broadest possible variety of applications. For example, it doesn't make much sense to create a class that can print out copyright information for only a specific company, such as

```
(c) Copyright 2004 MySoftwareCompany Inc.
```

It would make a lot more sense to create a class that printed out a copyright symbol, added the company name from an initialization file, and then added the year from passed-in arguments (or from the current year as specified by the computer clock). Allowing data to be inserted from external sources makes the class more generic, which in turn makes it more usable across different applications.

This is the very heart of the C++ construct known as *templates*. A template is, as its name implies, something that can be customized for specific forms of data. For example, consider a class that handled pointers to given data types. The class would have the data type hard-coded into it, and handle only that particular type of pointer. This class would be useful if it handled a specific data type, such as a class named Foo. However, the class would be even more useful if it handled *all* the various data types that can be assigned to pointers. In C, we handled heterogeneous arrays of pointers by using *void pointers,* which were pointers to blocks of memory that did not know what kind of structure, data type, or class the block was meant to be. Unfortunately, with C++, void pointers are ineffective. For example, consider the code in Listing 30-1:

LISTING 30-1: WORKING WITH VOID POINTERS

```
#include <stdio.h>
#include <string.h>

void delete_func( void *obj )
{
    if ( obj )
      delete obj;
}

class Foo
{
    char *s;
public:
    Foo( const char *strTemp )
    {
        printf("Constructor for foo\n");
        s = new char[strlen(strTemp)+1];
        strcpy(s, strTemp);
    }
    virtual ~Foo()
    {
        printf("Destructor for foo\n");
        delete s;
    }
};

int main()
{
    Foo *f = new Foo("This is a test");    → 1
    func(f);
}
```

The above listing illustrates how a pointer can be treated as "generic" — that is, having no type. In the main program (shown at → 1), we create a new Foo object using the standard constructor for the class. This pointer is then passed to the func function, which deletes the pointer, without knowing what type it is. If the destructor for the class were called, we would see two output lines, one for the construction of the class and one for the destruction.

If you were to compile this program and run it, you would see output that said:

```
Constructor for foo
```

with no corresponding destructor call for the object. Why? Because at run-time. the program does not "know" what sort of object obj is in the delete_func function, and therefore cannot call the destructor for the object. In order for the function to "know" what the object it receives is, we must pass it by type. If we are writing a manager of pointers, it would certainly be useful to know what the data types were, so that we could destroy them properly. In order to avoid the problem of void pointers, we could simply derive all objects from a common base type, such as an Object type and then call that destructor for all objects. The problem with this is that it not only introduces overhead in creating the objects, and requires extra space for the base class, it creates problems with multiple inheritance. (For more on multiple inheritance, see Technique 22.) There is really no reason to introduce extra complications when there are simpler approaches possible, and the simpler approach, in this case, is to use C++ *t emplates*. Templates will save you time and effort by reducing the amount of code written and generalizing solutions that can be used across multiple projects.

1. **In the code editor of your choice, create a new file to hold the code for the implementation of the source file.**

In this example, the file is named ch30.cpp, although you can use whatever you choose.

2. **Type the code from Listing 30-2 into your file.**

Better yet, copy the code from the source file on this book's companion Web site.

LISTING 30-2: THE TEMPLATE APPROACH

```
#include <stdio.h>
#include <string.h>
#include <vector>

template <class A>                    → 5
class Manager
{
```

```cpp
   std::vector< A *> _objects;              → 7
public:
   Manager()
   {
   }
   ~Manager()
   {
      Clean();
   }
   void AddInstance( A *pObj )
   {
      _objects.insert( _objects.end(), pObj
);
   }
   void Clean()
   {
      std::vector< A *>::iterator iter;
      for ( iter = _objects.begin(); iter !=
_objects.end(); ++iter )
      {
         delete (*iter);
      }
      _objects.clear();
   }
   A *NewInstance()
   {
      A *pObject = new A;
      AddInstance(pObject);
      return pObject;
   }
   void DeleteInstance(A *obj)
   {
      std::vector< A *>::iterator iter;
      for ( iter = _objects.begin(); iter !=
_objects.end(); ++iter )
         if ( (*iter) == obj )
            _objects.erase(iter);
      delete obj;
   }
};

class Foo
{
   char *s;
public:
   Foo (void)
   {
      printf("Constructor for foo\n");
      const char *strTemp = "Hello world";
```

```cpp
      s = new char[strlen(strTemp)+1];
      strcpy(s, strTemp);
   }
   Foo( const char *strTemp )
   {
      printf("Constructor for foo\n");
      s = new char[strlen(strTemp)+1];
      strcpy(s, strTemp);
   }
   Foo( const Foo& aCopy )
   {
      s = new char[strlen(aCopy.s)+1];
      strcpy( s, aCopy.s );
   }
   virtual ~Foo()
   {
      printf("Destructor for foo\n");
      delete s;
   }
   const char *String()
   {
      return s;
   }
   void setString( const char *str )
   {
      if ( s )
         delete [] s;
      s = new char[strlen(str)+1];
      strcpy( s, str );
   }
};

int main(void)
{
   Manager<Foo> manager;                    → 6

   Foo *f = manager.NewInstance();          → 2
   Foo *f1 = manager.NewInstance();
   Foo *f2 = manager.NewInstance();
   Foo *f3 = manager.NewInstance();
   manager.DeleteInstance( f );             → 4
   manager.Clean();
   return 0;
}
```

3. Save the source file in your code editor and
close the code editor.

4. **Compile the source code with the compiler of your choice on the operating system of your choice.**

   Note that when the program is run, if you have done everything properly, you should see the following output in the shell window:

   ```
   $ ./a.exe
   Constructor for foo            → 3
   Constructor for foo
   Constructor for foo
   Constructor for foo
   Destructor for foo
   Destructor for foo
   Destructor for foo
   Destructor for foo
   ```

The output shows us that the constructor is being called from `NewInstance` (shown at → **2** and then indicated in the output at → **3**), but more importantly that the destructor is properly invoked when we call the `DeleteInstance` method of the manager (shown at → **4**).

As you can see, the manager does understand the `Foo` class type, even though we have not actually used the `Foo` name anywhere in the manager definition. We know this because the manager properly constructs and deletes the objects. How does it do this? Essentially, the `template` keyword (shown at → **5** in the code listing) does all of the work. When the compiler encounters the `template` keyword, it treats the entire block (in this case, the entire class definition) as if it were a giant "macro" (for lack of a better word). Macros, as you might recall from the 'C' preprocessor, substitute a given string for a specific

keyword within the block. Everywhere that the entry in the template (`A`, in our example) appears within the block, it's replaced with whatever the template class is instantiated with (at → **6**). In our main driver, you will see the line:

```
Manager<Foo> manager;
```

This line is expanded by the compiler to replace the `A` with `Foo` everywhere that it appears in the template definition. Unlike macros, however, checking is done at the time the instantiation is created, to insure that the code generated is valid C++. For example, had we omitted a `copy` constructor from the `Foo` class, it would have generated an error in the use of the `Foo` class within an STL vector class, because all maneuvering in the vector is done by copying objects from one place to another. You would have seen an error at the line marked → **7**. The error would have said something about not finding a copy constructor for the class, when the template class vector was expanded by the compiler. For this reason, the compiler first instantiates the entire class, using the class supplied, then compiles the result.

 When you are implementing a template class, put all the code inline in a header file. If you don't, many compilers will only appear to compile the code — but will actually fail in the link phase, since the template instantiation is a one-phase operation. The compiler will not go back and load the code from an external source file.

Technique

31

Extending a Template Class

After you have created a base class that can be used as a template, you can extend that template class by utilizing it in your application. Extending a template class allows the functionality you have defined in the template to be utilized in other ways. There are actually four ways to utilize a template class in your own code. All of them will save you time by allowing you to reuse existing code without having to rewrite it, and to gain the expertise of the original template class writer for your code.

- You can use the actual template class as a template object in your code. To do so, simply use the class with a template argument of your own choice. This is the approach when working with container classes from the Standard Template Library, for example.

- You can use the class you've identified as a template as a member variable in your own object. This means embedding an instance of the template class with a template argument of your own choice in your object.

- To use the template class as a base class for your own object, specify the template argument up front and use it to identify the base class.

- You can use the templated class as a base class for your own inherited class (either a templated class or a non-templated one), allowing the end user to specify one or more template arguments to the class.

This technique looks at all these options and explores the flexibility and power of each one.

 If you choose to implement templates, be aware that they have a high degree of overhead in the code, and they require that all their code be available to the end-user. It's best to implement small template classes and provide them in header files for the end-user to use.

Implementing Template Classes in Code

It does no good to simply discuss the various ways in which you can implement templated classes in your code without concrete examples. Let's look at a few of the various ways in which we can utilize a templated base class in our own applications. Here's how:

1. **In the code editor of your choice, create a new file to hold the code for the implementation of the source file.**

In this example, the file is named ch31.cpp, although you can use whatever you choose.

2. **Type the code from Listing 31-1 into your file.**

Better yet, copy the code from the source file on this book's companion Web site.

LISTING 31-1: USING TEMPLATED CLASSES IN YOUR CODE

```
#include <stdio.h>
#include <string>

// The base template name
template < class A >
class Base
{
    std::string _name;
    A          *_pointer;
public:
    Base(void)
    {
      _name = "Nothing";
      _pointer = NULL;
    }
    Base(const char *strName, A *aPointer )
    {
      _name = strName;
      if ( aPointer )
        _pointer = new A(aPointer);
      else
            _pointer = NULL;
    }
    Base( const Base& aCopy )
```

```
    {
      printf("Copy constructor called\n");
      _name = aCopy._name;
      _pointer = new A(aCopy._pointer);
    }
    virtual ~Base()
    {
      delete _pointer;
    }
    A *Pointer()
    {
      return _pointer;
    }
    std::string Name()
    {
      return _name;
    }
    void setPointer( A *aPointer )
    {
      if ( _pointer )
        delete _pointer;
      _pointer = new A(aPointer);
    }
    void setName( const char *strName )
    {
      _name = strName;
    }
    void Print()
    {
      printf("Base:\n");
      printf("Name = %s\n", _name.c_str());
      printf("Pointer = \n");
      if ( _pointer )
        _pointer->Print();
      else
            printf("Pointer is NULL\n");
    }
};

class Foo
{
private:
    int i;
public:
    Foo(void)
    {
      i = 0;
    }
    Foo ( int iNum )
    {
      i = iNum;
```

```
    }
    Foo( const Foo& aCopy )
    {
        i = aCopy.i;
    }
    Foo ( const Foo* aCopy )
    {
        i = aCopy->i;
    }
    virtual ~Foo()
    {
    }
    int getNumber( void )
    {
        return i;
    }
    void setNumber( int num )
    {
        i = num;
    }
    void Print(void)
    {
        printf("Foo: i = %d\n", i );
    }
};

// Case 1: Using base template as a member variable
class TemplateAsMember
{
    Base<Foo> _fooEntry;
public:
    TemplateAsMember(void)
        : _fooEntry("TemplateAsMember", NULL)
    {
    }
    TemplateAsMember( int intNum )
        : _fooEntry("TemplateAsMember", new Foo(intNum))
    {
    }
    void setNum(int iNum)
    {
        _fooEntry.Pointer()->setNumber ( iNum );
    }
    int getNum(void)
    {
        return _fooEntry.Pointer()->getNumber();
    }
    int multiply(int iMult)
    {
        _fooEntry.Pointer()->setNumber ( _fooEntry.Pointer()->getNumber() * iMult );
    }
    void Print()
```

(continued)

LISTING 31-1 *(continued)*

```
        {
            printf("TemplateAsMember\n");
            _fooEntry.Print();
        }
};

// Case 2: Using the base template as a base
   class
class TemplateAsBase : public Base<Foo>
{
public:
    TemplateAsBase(void)
        : Base<Foo>( "TemplateAsBase", NULL )
    {
    }
    TemplateAsBase(const char *name, Foo
    *pFoo)
        : Base<Foo>( name, pFoo )
    {
    }
    virtual ~TemplateAsBase(void)
    {
    }
    void Print()
    {
        printf("TemplateAsBase:\n");
        Base<Foo>::Print();
    }
};
// Case 3: Using the base template as a base
   class
// for another templated class
template < class A, class B >
class TemplateAsBaseTemplate : public Base<A>
{
private:
    B *_anotherPointer;
public:
    TemplateAsBaseTemplate( void )
        : Base<Foo>( "TemplateAsBaseTemplate",
          NULL )
    {
        _anotherPointer = NULL;
    }
    TemplateAsBaseTemplate( A* anA, B* aB )
        : Base<Foo>( "TemplateAsBaseTemplate",
          anA )
    {
        _anotherPointer = aB;
    }
```

```
    B* getBPointer()
    {
        return _anotherPointer;
    }
    void Print()
    {
        Base<A>::Print();
        if ( _anotherPointer )
            _anotherPointer->Print();
        else
            printf("Another pointer is NULL\n");
    }
};

class AnotherBase
{
private:
    int x;
public:
    AnotherBase()
    {
        x = 0;
    }
    AnotherBase( int i )
    {
        x = i;
    }
    virtual ~AnotherBase(void)
    {
    }
    void Print()
    {
        printf("AnotherBase: x = %d\n", x );
    }
};
```

In Listing 31-1, the code shows how each possible case is addressed and used. We have implemented two "normal" classes, called Foo and AnotherBase, which are used as template arguments to designate the template classes.

Testing the Template Classes

To check whether the code is really working, we need to implement a test driver. The following steps do so for the code in Listing 31-1:

1. **In the code editor of your choice, reopen the source file for the code you just created.**

In this example, the file is named `ch31.cpp`, although you can use whatever you choose.

2. **Append the code from Listing 31-2 to your file.**

Better yet, copy the code from the source file on this book's companion Web site.

LISTING 31-2: THE TEST DRIVER FOR THE TEMPLATED CLASS EXAMPLE

```
int main()
{
    printf("Creating base\n");
    Base<Foo> fooBase;
    printf("Creating template as member\n");
    TemplateAsMember tempMem;
    printf("Creating template as base\n");
    TemplateAsBase tempBase;
    printf("Creating template as base tem-
plate\n");
    TemplateAsBaseTemplate<Foo,AnotherBase>
    tempAsBT;

    fooBase.Print();
    tempMem.Print();
    tempBase.Print();
    tempAsBT.Print();

    return 0;
}
```

3. **Save the source file in your code editor and close the code editor.**

4. **Compile the source code with the compiler of your choice, on the operating system of your choice.**

When the program is run, if you have done everything properly, you should see the following output in the shell window:

```
Creating base
  Void constructor called
  Creating template as member
  Creating base with name
  [TemplateAsMember]
  Creating template as base
  Creating base with name [TemplateAsBase]
  Creating template as base template
  Creating base with name
  [TemplateAsBaseTemplate]
  Base:
  Name = Nothing
  Pointer =
  Pointer is NULL                          → 1
  TemplateAsMember
  Base:
  Name = TemplateAsMember
  Pointer =
  Pointer is NULL
  TemplateAsBase:
  Base:
  Name = TemplateAsBase
  Pointer =
  Pointer is NULL
  Base:
  Name = TemplateAsBaseTemplate
  Pointer =
  Pointer is NULL
  Another pointer is NULL
```

The output from this program shows us that each of the various template instantiations works. As you can see, in each case (see, for example, the line marked ➜ **1**), the constructor was called and the various member variables assigned proper default values. Looking at the examples, it should be clear that each of the various methods arrives at the same conclusion.

 Concrete classes that have been made into templates as a specific form of a class are best suited for extension. This is to say, if you have a template class that accepts a particular type of class for its argument, you are better off extending your template class by creating a form of it as a specific class — and then deriving from that specific class. The reason for this is more human than technical: People usually don't think in terms of templates so much as in terms of class names.

Using Non-class Template Arguments

Looking at the four choices in extending base classes, you will probably notice a few things that suggest particular approaches to the process.

To utilize methods in a base class being used as a template, you must specify which version of the class the template is to use. The reason is that you could conceivably have a class that inherited from multiple classes of the same template, with different types associated with it. This is a good thing because it allows you to segregate specific functionality into separate classes.

Another thing worth noticing is that you may create a templated class that does not require a class as its argument. For example, we could create a template with a numeric argument; the following steps show you how:

1. **In the code editor of your choice, create a new file.**

In this example, the file is named ch31a.cpp, although you can use whatever you choose.

2. **Type the code from Listing 31-3 into your file.**

LISTING 31-3: A TEMPLATE CLASS WITH A NON-CLASS ARGUMENT

```
template <class A>
class LessThanTen
{
    A _element;

public:
    LessThanTen( A entry )
    {
        set ( entry );
    }
    LessThanTen( const LessThanTen& aCopy )
    {
        set( aCopy._element);
    }
    void set( A value )                    → 3
    {
        if ( value > 0 && value < 10 )     → 2
            _element = value;
    }
    A get()
    {
        return _element;
    }

};
```

This code works for a class argument, so long as that class can be compared to an integer. It can also be used for a non-class argument, such as an integer, long integer, or even a floating point value.

With this class shown in Listing 31-3, there is no reason that the template argument should be a class. In fact, it would be implied that a numeric element was used, since the *value* which is passed into the set method is compared to an integral value of 10 (see the line marked → **2**).

3. **Add the following code to your source file to test the integer class. This code will test the template class we just defined above.**

```
int main(void)
{
    LessThanTen<int> ten(3);           → 5
    printf("The value is %d\n",
      ten.get() );
    ten.set( 23 );                     → 4
    printf("The value is now %d\n",
      ten.get() );
    return 0;
}
```

4. **Save the source file in your code editor and then close the code editor.**

5. **Compile the source code with the compiler of your choice, on the operating system of your choice.**

When the program is run, if you have done everything properly, you should see the following output in the shell window:

```
$ ./a.exe
The value is 3
The value is now 3
```

As you can see from the output, the program indeed does properly create a new class that is a templated version of the `LessThanTen` class, using an integer as its template argument. The resulting class contains a method called `set` that takes an integer argument (shown at → **3**) that must be between 0 and 10. Since our value (see → **4**) is not within that range, it is not assigned, and we see that the `print` statement following the assignment still contains the value 3.

Notice that the code works with an integer argument (see the line marked with → **5**), even though the template specifies a class argument. For C++, integers, floating-point numbers, and the like can be considered *first-class* (that is, a basic type) arguments for the purpose of templates. In fact (in this case at least), any argument can be used, so long as the code includes comparison operators greater-than (>) and less-than (<) to ensure that the `set` method works properly.

The ability to use either classes or basic types as template arguments makes the template construct extremely powerful in C++. Because you can write a single class that manages number, character strings, or class values and have it work seamlessly, you save enormous amounts of time and duplicated work.

Creating Templates from Functions and Methods

Technique 32

Save Time By

- Creating function templates
- Creating method templates
- Interpreting your output

Although creating entire classes that are templates is useful, sometimes you just want a single function or method to accept a template argument. For example, if you created a comparison function that used a template for all types, you could then create (say) a `minimum` function that would compare any two data types, including classes, as long as you could tell one was of lesser magnitude than the other. This technique shows how to save time by templatizing only a single function (and later, a single method) of a class.

Implementing Function Templates

A *function template,* or *method template,* is simply a standalone function (inside a class, in the case of a method) that can accept one or more template arguments. Let's take a look at how you would implement function templates in your own code, by creating a generic function that will compute the minimum of two values.

1. **In the code editor of your choice, create a new file to hold the code for the implementation of the source file.**

   In this example, the file is named `ch32.cpp`, although you can use whatever you choose.

2. **Type the code from Listing 32-1 into your file.**

   Better yet, copy the code from the source file on this book's companion Web site.

LISTING 32-1: THE MIN TEMPLATE FUNCTION

```c
#include <stdio.h>
#include <string>

template <class A>
A my_min( const A& val1, const A& val2)                          → 1
{
    if ( val1 == val2 )
        return val1;
    if ( val1 < val2 )
        return val1;
    return val2;
}

bool operator==(const std::string& s1, const std::string& s2)    → 5
{
    int len = s1.length();
    if ( len != s2.length() )
        return false;

    for ( int i=0; i<len; ++i )
        if ( s1[i] != s2[i] )
            return false;

    return true;
}

bool operator <(const std::string& s1, const std::string& s2     → 6
{
    int len = s1.length();
    if ( len > s2.length() )
        len = s2.length();

    for ( int i=0; i<len; ++i )
        if ( s1[i] > s2[i] )
            return false;

    return true;
}

int main(int argc, char **argv)
{
    // First, try it for integers
    int x1 = 100;
    int x2 = 30;
    int xmin = my_min(x1, x2);                                   → 2

    // Now, for floating-point numbers
    float f1 = 12.40;
    float f2 = 4.90;
    float fmin = my_min(f1, f2);
```

(continued)

LISTING 32-1 *(continued)*

```
int xmin2 = my_min(x2, x1);                                    →3

    printf("Xmin = %d\n", xmin);
    printf("Xmin2 = %d\n", xmin2 );
    printf("Fmin = %f\n", fmin );

    // Now that we have implemented the operators,
    // try it for strings.
    std::string s1 = "Hello world";
    std::string s2 = "Goodbye cruel world";

    if ( s1 == s2 )
       printf("Strings are equal\n");
    else
       if ( s1 < s2 )
          printf("string %s is less\n", s1.c_str() );
       else
          printf("String %s is less\n", s2.c_str() );

    std::string smin = my_min( s1, s2 );                       →4
    printf("Min for strings returned: %s\n", smin.c_str() );

}
```

3. **Save the source file in your code editor and close the code editor.**

Note that we have created a templated function called `my_min`, shown at → **1** (it was not called `min`, because that would conflict with a Standard Template Library (STL) function of the same name), which can be used with any data type that supports the equal (=) and less-than (<) operators.

In this case, the source code also implements less-than and equal-to operations for the standard string class in the STL. After we have implemented these operators, we can then instantiate the template for the string class.

4. **Compile the source code with the compiler of your choice on the operating system of your choice.**

When the program is run, if you have done everything properly, you should see the following output in the shell window:

```
$ ./a.exe
Xmin = 30
Xmin2 = 30
Fmin = 4.900000
String Goodbye cruel world is less
Min for strings returned: Goodbye cruel
   world
```

Let's look at this carefully, and see what is going on. We are calling the minimum function, `my_min`, in three locations, shown at the lines marked with → **2**, → **3**, and → **4**. The first line computes the `min` for two integers, the second for two floating point numbers, and the third for two strings.

Although integers and floating point numbers have their own comparison operators (less than, greater than, and so forth) built into the language, strings do not. Therefore, we implement the comparison functions that will be called by `my_min` at the lines marked → **5** and → **6**. After all of this is done, the compiler generates the proper versions of these functions and you see the minimum calculation output shown above.

In this example, the template is automatically generated. Unlike a template class, function templates don't require the programmer to specify the class or type that the template is being implemented for. This saves a lot of time; you don't have to track down where the template was instantiated. The linker is also smart enough, with most modern C++ compilers, to link only in one copy of a given template. This means that if you have multiple calls to a specific templated function in your program, only one will be in the final executable. If your linker is not that smart, you have to force the implementation of a given template in your code.

Creating Method Templates

Similarly, you can also create methods of classes that are themselves templates, even though the class as a whole might not be. You might want to do this as a way to avoid writing a lot of the same code over and over, such as creating a set of assignment methods for different data types.

When you find yourself writing the same method over and over, but specifying a different data type (such as a `set` method or an assignment operator) for each one, immediately think about creating a template method for that operation. This can save you a lot of time.

The following steps show you how to create a method template:

1. **In the code editor of your choice, reopen the source file for the code that you just created.**

In this example, the file is named `ch32.cpp`, although you can use whatever you choose.

2. **Add the code from Listing 32-2 into your file.**

Or better yet, copy the code from the source file on this book's companion Web site.

LISTING 32-2: A CLASS WITH A TEMPLATED METHOD

```cpp
class Foo
{
private:
    std::string _name;
    int         _value;
public:
    Foo(void)
    {
      _name = "Nothing";
      _value = 0;
    }
    Foo(const char *strName, int iValue)
    {
      _name = strName;
      _value = iValue;
    }
    Foo( const Foo& aCopy )
    {
      _name = aCopy._name;
      _value = aCopy._value;
    }
    Foo operator=( const Foo& aCopy )
    {
      _name = aCopy._name;
      _value = aCopy._value;
      return *this;
    }
    // Templatized method to add values
    template < class A >
    void Add( const A& aValue )
    {
      _value += aValue;
    }
    // Templatized method to multiply values
    template < class A >
    void Multiply( const A& aValue )      → 7
    {
      _value = _value * aValue;
    }

    // Method to dump the values
    void Print()
    {
      printf("Name: [%s]\n", _name.c_str()
);
      printf("Value: %d\n", _value );
    }
};
```

(continued)

LISTING 32-2 (continued)

```
int operator*( int iValue, std::string s )
{
    // Convert string to an integer
    int iMult = atoi( s.c_str() );
    // Do the multiplication
    int iResult = iValue * iMult;
    // Return it
    return iResult;
}
```

The above listing shows a class, Foo, which contains a templated method called Multiply (shown at → 7). This method will allow you to multiply various types of data and assign the result to a member variable within the class. Notice also the operator* function that is defined even to multiply our value by a string.

3. **Change the main function of the source file to be as shown in Listing 32-3:**

LISTING 32-3: THE TEST DRIVER FOR THE TEMPLATED METHOD

```
int main(int argc, char **argv)
{
    // First, try it for integers
    int x1 = 100;
    int x2 = 30;
    int xmin = my_min(x1, x2);

    // Now, for floating point numbers
    float f1 = 12.40;
    float f2 = 4.90;
    float fmin = my_min(f1, f2);

    int xmin2 = my_min(x2, x1);

    printf("Xmin = %d\n", xmin);
    printf("Xmin2 = %d\n", xmin2 );
    printf("Fmin = %f\n", fmin );

    // Now that we have implemented the oper
    // ators, try it for strings.
    std::string s1 = "Hello world";
    std::string s2 = "Goodbye cruel world";
```

```
    if ( s1 == s2 )
        printf("Strings are equal\n");
    else
        if ( s1 < s2 )
            printf("string %s is less\n",
s1.c_str() );
        else
            printf("String %s is less\n",
s2.c_str() );

    std::string smin = my_min( s1, s2 );
    printf("Min for strings returned: %s\n",
smin.c_str() );

    Foo f("MyFoo", 10);
    f.Add( 12.0 );
    f.Print();
    f.Multiply( -1 );
    f.Print();
    f.Multiply(std::string("12"));
    f.Print();
}
```

Note that as with template functions, the programmer does not in any way create an instance of the templated member function. The compiler will create instances as needed, by matching up the possible template arguments with the available templates. Naturally, this will only work if the template class definition is available, so once again, the template methods must be in-line defined methods. Because there is no "natural" way in which to multiply a string by an integer, we define a global operator which accepts an integer value and a string, and returns the converted string multiplied by the integer. After this operator is defined, we can then pass in a string to the templated method. (If the operator was not defined, you get a compile error when the template is expanded and the integer multiplication by the input argument is attempted.) There is a quite a bit going on here, obviously.

4. **Compile the source code with the compiler of your choice on the operating system of your choice.**

When the program is run, if you have done everything properly, you should see the following output in the shell window:

```
$ ./a.exe
Xmin = 30
Xmin2 = 30
Fmin = 4.900000
String Goodbye cruel world is less
Min for strings returned: Goodbye cruel
   world
Name: [MyFoo]
Value: 22
Name: [MyFoo]
Value: -22
Name: [MyFoo]
Value: -264
```

→ **8**

The initial part of our output is from the first part of this technique and has not changed. The second part, beginning with the line marked → **8,** shows the result of our templated method. As you can see, we first assign the member variable value the value 10. We then add 12 to it, resulting in the output of 22. Now, we start using the Multiple method. First, we multiply by an integer value of –1, resulting in the output of –22. Then we multiply by a string value of 12, which is converted to an integer using the operator* function we defined, which results in –264 — the value that is printed out.

Note that the string is evaluated to its integer value, 12, and the result multiplied by the current value of –22. This results in a total of –264, which is the value displayed on the console window.

33 Technique

Working with Arrays

Save Time By

- Understanding the vector class
- Implementing array classes
- Working with various algorithms with the vector class

The Standard Template Library (STL) provides access to a number of different forms of storage classes. One of these is the vector class, which allows the programmer to store arbitrary arrays of objects. Unfortunately, the vector class also requires that you "pull in" (link) the entire STL to use it. This can cause significant overhead in your application and can consume large amounts of memory. Because the vector class is a templated class, it copies large chunks of code each time it's used. Although this is normally insignificant for large-scale applications — and well worth the expense of memory and size — it can be quite costly when your applications are smaller or have to operate in more restricted memory areas, as with embedded applications. For this reason, it makes sense to get handy with not only the vector class but also with implementing your own simple array classes that can use restricted memory. This technique shows you how to use vector classes — and techniques for working with various algorithms with the vector class. The next technique, Technique 34, shows you how to use array classes with limited overhead.

Using the Vector Class

The vector class is amazingly powerful and, after you get the hang of it, very easy to use in your own code. Let's look at an example of working with vectors. We will examine how to add data to a vector, step through (iterate) the values in the array, and print out the data in the array. Here's how:

1. **In the code editor of your choice, create a new file to hold the code for the implementation of the source file.**

In this example, the file is named ch33.cpp, although you can use whatever you choose.

2. **Type the code from Listing 33-1 into your file.**

Better yet, copy the code from the source file on this book's companion Web site.

LISTING 33-1: WORKING WITH VECTORS

```
#include <stdio.h>
#include <string>
#include <vector>
#include <iostream>

using namespace std;

template < class A >
void print_array( vector<A> array )
{
   vector<A>::iterator iter;

   for ( iter = array.begin(); iter != array.end(); ++iter )
      cout << (*iter) << "\n";
}

void reverse_array( const vector<string>& arrayIn, vector<string>& arrayOut )
{
   vector<string>::const_iterator iter;

   for ( iter = arrayIn.begin(); iter != arrayIn.end(); ++iter )
   {
      arrayOut.insert( arrayOut.begin(), (*iter) );
   }
}

int main(int argc, char **argv)
{
   vector<string> stringArray;

   // First, add all of the arguments to the
   // array that were passed into the application.
   for ( int i=0; i<argc; ++i )
      stringArray.insert( stringArray.end(), argv[i] );

   // Print them out using an iterator
   vector<string>::iterator iter;
   for (iter = stringArray.begin(); iter != stringArray.end();
        ++iter )
   {
      // This isn't necessary, but illustrates how to get
      // the actual item stored in an array element. Note that
      // the copy constructor will be invoked on this line.
      string s = (*iter);

      cout << "Element: " << s << "\n";
   }
```

→ 1

→ 2

(continued)

Listing 33-1 *(continued)*

```
// Now, we want to remove any element in the array which is the number
// 3
for ( iter = stringArray.begin(); iter != stringArray.end();
    iter ++ )
{
    if ( (*iter) == "3" )
    {
        cout << "Erasing element " << (*iter) << "\n";
        stringArray.erase( iter );
    }
}

// Display the results for the user
printf("Array after removal\n");
print_array( stringArray );

// Next, reverse the array
vector<string> outArray;
reverse_array( stringArray, outArray );
printf("Array after reversal\n");
print_array( outArray );

return 0;
}
```

→ 3

→ 4

3. **Save the source file in your code editor and close the code editor.**

This source code utilizes the power and functionality of the Standard Template Library to do simple array manipulations, including adding new data to an array, reversing the elements in an array, and iterating over the elements in an array.

4. **Compile the source code with the compiler of your choice, on the operating system of your choice.**

When the program is run, if you have done everything properly, you should see the following output in the shell window:

```
    $ ./a.exe 1 2 3 4
Element: ./a
Element: 1
Element: 2
Element: 3
```

```
Element: 4
Erasing element 3
Array after removal
./a
1
2
4
Array after reversal
4
2
1
./a
```

As you can see, the program reads in the arguments from the command line, places them into an array (shown at the line marked → 1), then prints out the array by iterating over each element and printing out the data contained at that array element (shown at → 2). Next, the program removes all values of 3 from the array, illustrating how you can delete from an array (shown at → 3) and leave the rest of the elements in order. Finally, the values in the array are reversed, by copying them into a new array in reverse order (shown at ➔ **4**) and the result is printed out once more.

This example illustrates how easy it is to work with the vector class in the C++ STL — and the result is very powerful. Unfortunately, the class is also quite large. On my system, the resulting executable file takes up over 400KB for this simple little program. This illustrates how the STL pulls in a lot of code when you utilize it. Admittedly, in today's world, 400 KB is not that large, but it's a lot for such a small program.

Technique 34

Implementing Your Own Array Class

After you have learned how to use the STL `vector` class (see Technique 33), it is very instructive to see how you might implement the same sort of class yourself — but with more limited overhead. Here's a look at implementing a simple `vector` class that not only stores strings, but can also insert, delete, and iterate.

Creating the String Array Class

As we saw in Technique 33, the overhead in using the Standard Template Library (STL) is rather high when you want to add only a single array to your program. If you are using multiple array classes, you might as well use the STL, because that way you only have to pay the price (in terms of memory and application size) once. Each array class beyond the first uses negligible space in your application. Let's create a simple string array class that illustrates how easy it is to create array classes for your application that work with specific data types. The following steps show you how:

1. **In the code editor of your choice, create a new file to hold the code for the implementation of the source file.**

In this example, the file is named `ch34.cpp`, although you can use whatever you choose.

2. **Type the code from Listing 34-1 into your file.**

Better yet, copy the code from the source file on this book's companion Web site.

LISTING 34-1: CREATING YOUR OWN STRING ARRAY CLASS

```cpp
#include <stdio.h>
#include <string>

using namespace std;

class MyStringArray
{
    string *_strings;
    int     _numstrings;
    int     _chunksize;
    int     _numused;
    void expand()
    {
        // Allocate a new block
        string *newBlock = new string[ _num-
strings + _chunksize ];
        _numstrings += _chunksize;
        for ( int i=0; i<_numused; ++i )
            newBlock[i] = _strings[i];
        // Delete the old array
        delete [] _strings;
        // Re-assign the pointer
        _strings = newBlock;
    }
public:
    MyStringArray(void)
    {
        _chunksize = 10;
        _strings = new string[ _chunksize ];
        for ( int i=0; i<_chunksize; ++i )
            _strings[i] = "";
        _numstrings = _chunksize;
        _numused = 0;
    }

    MyStringArray( int nSize )
    {
        _chunksize = 10;
        if ( nSize <= _chunksize )
        {
            _strings = new string[ _chunksize
];
            _numstrings = _chunksize;
        }
        else
        {
            _strings = new string[ nSize ];
            _numstrings = nSize;
        }
        _numused = 0;
    }
    virtual ~MyStringArray(void)
    {
        delete [] _strings;
    }
    // Insert at start
    void insert_string( const string& s )
    {
        // See if it will fit.
        if ( _numused == _numstrings )
            expand();
        // It will now fit, move everything up
        for ( int i=_numused; i>=0; --i )
            _strings[i] = _strings[i-1];
        // Put in the new one
        _strings[0] = s;
        _numused ++;
    }
    void append_string( const string& s )
    {
        // See if it will fit.
        if ( _numused == _numstrings )
            expand();
        // Put in the new one
        _strings[_numused] = s;
        _numused ++;
    }
    string remove_at( int idx )
    {
        if ( idx < 0 || idx >= _numused )
            return string("");
        // Save this one
        string ret_string = _strings[idx];
        // And copy all the others after it
back
        for ( int i=idx; i<_numused; ++i )
            _strings[i] = _strings[i+1];
        _numused--;
        return ret_string;
    }
    string get_at(int idx)
    {
        if ( idx < 0 || idx >= _numused )
            return string("");
        return _strings[idx];
    }
    int size()
```

(continued)

LISTING 34-1 *(continued)*

```
    {
        return _numused;
    }
};

int main(int argc, char **argv)
{
    MyStringArray s(5);
    for ( int i=0; i<argc; ++i )
    {
        printf("Appending %s\n", argv[i] );
        s.append_string( argv[i] );        → 1
    }
    printf("Initial String Array:\n");
    for ( int j=0; j<s.size(); ++j )
        printf("String %d = [%s]\n", j,
    s.get_at(j).c_str());
    if ( s.size() > 5 )
    {
        string str = s.remove_at(5);       → 4
        printf("Removed string %s\n",
    str.c_str());
    }
    printf("Final String Array:\n");
    for ( int i=0; i<s.size(); ++i )
        printf("String %d = [%s]\n", i,
    s.get_at(i).c_str());

}
```

When the program is run, if you have done everything properly, you should see the following output in the shell window:

```
$ ./a.exe 1 2 3 4 5 6 7
Appending ./a                              → 2
  Appending 1
  Appending 2
  Appending 3
  Appending 4
  Appending 5
  Appending 6
  Appending 7
  Initial String Array:
  String 0 = [./a]                         → 3
  String 1 = [1]
  String 2 = [2]
  String 3 = [3]
  String 4 = [4]
  String 5 = [5]
  String 6 = [6]
  String 7 = [7]
  Removed string 5
  Final String Array:
  String 0 = [./a]
  String 1 = [1]
  String 2 = [2]
  String 3 = [3]
  String 4 = [4]
  String 5 = [6]
  String 6 = [7]
```

This source code utilizes our simple array functionality to add, remove, and iterate over strings in an open-ended array structure.

Now, our code is not quite as polished as the STL vector class, but it should work just as well. More importantly, when the code is compiled on my system, it produces an executable of less than 100 KB (rather than the 400KB executable of our previous example), the majority of which is the STL string class.

3. Save the source file in your code editor and close the code editor.

4. Compile the source code with the compiler of your choice on the operating system of your choice.

The output from this program is as expected: We append each of the input arguments to our array, watching it grow as we do so. This is illustrated beginning at the lines marked → **1** in the code and → **2** in the output. Next, we print out the array, expecting to see all of the values displayed (see → **3** in the output). As expected, we see all eight data values. Next, the code removes the fifth data element, as shown at → **4** in the code listing. We then print out the array once more, to show that the value was removed and the other data values remain.

Implementing your own array class can save you considerable time in trying to reduce code size, and allows you to use your code in places where it might not otherwise fit due to memory constraints.

As you can see from this output, we can create our own array class that implements the majority of the functionality of the STL vector class at a fraction of the memory and speed needed.

 If memory or speed is an issue, stay away from the Standard Template Library and its array classes; roll your own. You will see marked speed increases, vastly less memory consumption, and greater ease of debugging. If you are not as concerned about memory usage, use the STL: It is already debugged and (no offense) probably better documented than your own classes. In addition, STL code is versatile: Versions of the STL have been ported to nearly all compilers and operating systems.

35

Technique

Working with Vector Algorithms

Save Time By

- ✓ Using the STL's built-in algorithms
- ✓ Using `vector` algorithms
- ✓ Interpreting output

The real power of the Standard Template Library lies not in its ability to simply store and retrieve data in templated form. Rather, it lies in the built-in algorithms you can use on the various storage facilities in the STL. Although the container classes do an excellent job of holding onto the data you put into them, the templated algorithms allow you to work with that data, sorting it, searching it, and converting it into other forms.

 When you need to search, process, or remove specific items from a group, strongly consider the STL storage classes rather than creating your own classes to do the same work. You can manipulate any of them with well-proven and debugged algorithms.

The STL includes algorithm functions for iterating over collections, finding specific entries, removing specific entries, and sorting the entries in collections — to name but a few. In this technique, we look at the ways to manipulate data efficiently in a collection, using the algorithms available for vectors. In this technique, we will examine ways in which to sort, search and remove items in an STL container. These algorithms are available for any of the STL container classes, using the same names in each case. Although we will focus on the `vector` class in this technique, the same algorithms will work with stacks, maps, queues, and all of the rest of the STL containers. Using these algorithms will save you time in doing the most likely tasks required of applications today.

Working with Vector Algorithms

If you are presented with an array, or vector, of data, certain functions are almost always going to be requested by the user. The ability to sort the data according to its value is one of them. Another requirement is almost certainly going to be the ability to find a given data value in the vector. Finally, inserting and removing data are essential for any array. Let's take a look at techniques for doing all of these tasks, using the STL `vector` class and the STL algorithms. Here's how:

1. **In the code editor of your choice, create a new file to hold the code for the implementation of the source file.**

In this example, the file is named ch35.cpp, although you can use whatever you choose.

2. **Type the code from Listing 35-1 into your file.**

Better yet, copy the code from the source file on this book's companion Web site.

LISTING 35-1: USING THE STL ALGORITHMS WITH THE VECTOR CLASS

```cpp
#include <stdio.h>
#include <string>
#include <vector>
#include <algorithm>

bool contains_c( const std::string& s )
{
    for ( int i=0; i<s.length(); ++i )
        if ( s[i] == 'c' )
            return true;
    return false;
}
int main(int argc, char **argv)
{
    // First, create a vector out of all
    // of the input strings

    std::vector< std::string > elements;
    for ( int i=0; i<argc; ++i )                                              → 1
        elements.insert( elements.end(), argv[i] );

    // Print out the elements.
    printf("Original list:\n");
    std::vector< std::string >::iterator iter;
    for ( iter = elements.begin(); iter != elements.end(); ++iter )
        printf("Element %s\n", (*iter).c_str() );

    // Now, sort the elements.
    std::sort( elements.begin(), elements.end() );                           → 2

    // Print them out again.
    printf("Sorted list:\n");
    for ( iter = elements.begin(); iter != elements.end(); ++iter )
        printf("Element %s\n", (*iter).c_str() );
```

(continued)

LISTING 35-1 *(continued)*

```
// Find a specific element, if it exists.
std::vector< std::string >::iterator ptr_iter;

ptr_iter = std::find( elements.begin(), elements.end(), "Hello");
if ( ptr_iter != elements.end() )
    printf("Found the element %s\n", (*ptr_iter).c_str() );
else
    printf("Didn't find the requested element\n");

// If we found it, remove it from the list.
if ( ptr_iter != elements.end() )
    elements.erase( ptr_iter );

// And relist them.
printf("Altered list:\n");
for ( iter = elements.begin(); iter != elements.end(); ++iter )
    printf("Element %s\n", (*iter).c_str() );

// See how many times "Why" is in the list.
int cnt = std::count( elements.begin(), elements.end(), "Why" );
printf("Found %d entries with the name \'Why\'\n", cnt );

// Remove entries only if they contain the letter 'c'
std::remove_if( elements.begin(), elements.end(), contains_c );
printf("Final list:\n");
for ( iter = elements.begin(); iter != elements.end(); ++iter )
    printf("Element %s\n", (*iter).c_str() );

return 0;
}
```

➝ 3

3. **Save the source file in your code editor and close the code editor.**

This source code utilizes the power and functionality of the Standard Template Library to do simple array manipulations. Adding items, removing them, counting the number that match a given string, searching, and sorting the array are all illustrated.

4. **Compile the source code with the compiler of your choice on the operating system of your choice.**

When the program is run, if you have done everything properly, you should see the output shown in Listing 35-2 in the shell window.

LISTING 35-2: OUTPUT FROM THE VECTOR ALGORITHM PROGRAM

```
$ ./a.exe Hello Goodbye Why What Iditarod
  Alpha Why Me Accord
Original list:
Element ./a
Element Hello
Element Goodbye
Element Why
Element What
Element Iditarod
Element Alpha
Element Why
Element Me
Element Accord
Sorted list:
Element ./a
Element Accord
Element Alpha
Element Goodbye
Element Hello
Element Iditarod
Element Me
Element What
Element Why
Element Why
Found the element Hello
Altered list:
Element ./a
Element Accord
Element Alpha
Element Goodbye
Element Iditarod
Element Me
Element What
Element Why
Element Why
Found 2 entries with the name 'Why'
Final list:
Element ./a
Element Alpha
Element Goodbye
Element Iditarod
Element Me
Element What
Element Why
Element Why
Element Why
```

The output breaks down into several steps, matching the program steps. First, we input the data from the command line and store it into the original list, as it is marked in the output. This occurs at the line → **1** in the code listing. Next, we sort the list, using the STL `sort` algorithm (shown at → **2** in the code listing). This single line of code sorts the entire array, comparing each element to the next and swapping them into place. The data is then output with the header sorted list. Our next task is to locate a specific string, in this case `"Hello"`, within the array (see → **3**). If it is found, that element is removed and the array is printed out once more, using the title altered list. Our next task is to count the number of times a given string (`"Why"`) appears in the list and print out that value. Finally, we remove all the items beginning with the letter `c` and print the list. All of this takes place in but a handful of lines of code, illustrating just how powerful and time saving the STL algorithms can be.

As you can see, with a minimum of code, we accomplished a rather large amount of functionality. For this reason alone, you should strongly consider using the STL `vector` class in your own code.

The `vector` class implements numerous algorithms for sorting, searching, and manipulation. You can write a single function with multiple algorithms to process large amounts of data — or even selected portions of data — simply by using iterators and the algorithm functions.

Technique 36

Deleting an Array of Elements

Using the `delete` function with arrays can be one of the most confusing constructs in C++. When do you need to delete a single element, as opposed to an entire array of elements? What happens if you don't use the proper deletion method with the proper allocation method? Deleting a single element, when you allocate an array of elements, results in the failure of destructors to be called. Not deleting an element you allocate results in memory leaks and potential system crashes. In general, the correct deletion method must be matched with the proper invocation of the new method. Failure to do this matchup will result in memory leaks that are very hard to trace — which will eventually crash your application with enough use. If you do the work up front of matching correct allocations and de-allocations, you will save a lot of time during the debugging and maintenance process.

 Always match up the allocation with the deletion of elements in your application. When in doubt, use the delete array operations (`delete [] array`) rather than the "normal" deletion operation (`delete array`) to make sure your arrays are properly deleted. Even for non-class elements, failure to delete arrays properly can cause memory leaks. Note, however, that calling `delete []` when you have allocated a pointer with new `<Type>` will cause a crash.

Examining Allocations of Arrays and Pointers

The only real way to understand exactly how allocations and de-allocations work is to look at an example of working with allocating single objects, with and without pointers, in either single objects or arrays of objects. Let's do that right now, with a short example program.

1. **In the code editor of your choice, create a new file to hold the code for the implementation of the source file.**

In this example, the file is named `ch36.cpp`, although you can use whatever you choose.

2. **Type the code from Listing 36-1 into your file.**

Better yet, copy the code from the source file on this book's companion Web site.

LISTING 36-1: ALLOCATING OBJECTS WITH AND WITHOUT POINTERS

```c
#include <stdio.h>
#include <vector>

class NoPointer
{
    int x;
public:
    NoPointer()
    {
        printf("NoPointer: Void Constructor
called\n");
        x = 0;
    }
    NoPointer( int num )
    {
        printf("NoPointer: Full constructor
called\n");
        x = num;
    }
    NoPointer( const NoPointer& aCopy )
    {
        printf("NoPointer: Copy constructor
called\n");
        x = aCopy.x;
    }
    virtual ~NoPointer()
    {
        printf("NoPointer: Destructor
called\n");
    }

    NoPointer operator=( const NoPointer&
aCopy )
    {
        printf("NoPointer: operator=
called\n");
        x = aCopy.x;
        return *this;
    }
    void setX( int num )
    {
        x = num;
    }
    int getX (void)
    {
        return x;
    }
};

class PointerClass
{
    char *ptr;
public:
    PointerClass()
    {
        printf("PointerClass: Void Constructor
called\n");
        ptr = NULL;
    }
    PointerClass( const char *str )
    {
        printf("PointerClass: Full constructor
called\n");
        ptr = new char[ strlen(str)+1 ];    →1
        strcpy( ptr, str );
    }
    PointerClass( const PointerClass& aCopy )
    {
        printf("PointerClass: Copy constructor
called\n");
        if ( aCopy.ptr )
        {
        ptr = new char[ strlen(aCopy.ptr)+1 ];
            strcpy( ptr, aCopy.ptr );
        }
        else
            ptr = NULL;
    }
    virtual ~PointerClass()
    {
        printf("PointerClass: Destructor
called\n");
        delete [] ptr;                       →2
    }

    PointerClass operator=( const
PointerClass& aCopy )
    {
        printf("PointerClass: operator=
called\n");
        if ( aCopy.ptr )
        {
        ptr = new char[ strlen(aCopy.ptr)+1 ];
            strcpy( ptr, aCopy.ptr );
        }
        else
            ptr = NULL;
```

(continued)

LISTING 36-1 *(continued)*

```cpp
        return *this;
    }
    void setPtr( const char *str )
    {
        if ( str )
        {
      str = new char[ strlen(str)+1 ];
            strcpy( ptr, str );
        }
        else
            ptr = NULL;
    }
    const char *getPtr (void)
    {
        return ptr;
    }
};

int main()
{
    // Just create one of each to see what
        happens.
    printf("Creating np\n");
    NoPointer *np = new NoPointer(5);
    printf("Creating pc\n");
    PointerClass *pc = new
    PointerClass("Hello");
    printf("Deleting np\n");
    delete np;
    printf("Deleting pc\n");
    delete pc;

    // Now, create an array of them.
    printf("Creating npa\n");
    NoPointer *npa = new NoPointer[5];        ➔ 3
    printf("Creating pca\n");
    PointerClass *pca =
    new PointerClass[5];                      ➔ 4

    // Delete them.
    printf("Deleting npa\n");
    delete npa;
    printf("Deleting pca\n");
    delete pca;

    // Now, do it the right way.
    printf("Creating npa2\n");
    NoPointer *npa2 = new NoPointer[5];
    printf("Creating pca2\n");
    PointerClass *pca2 = new PointerClass[5];
```

```cpp
    // Delete them.
    printf("Deleting npa2\n");
    delete [] npa2;
    printf("Deleting pca2\n");
    delete [] pca2;

    // See what happens with a vector.
    printf("Creating vector of
    PointerClass\n");
    std::vector< PointerClass > *pcv = new
    std::vector<PointerClass>;

    for ( int i=0; i<5; ++i )
    {
        PointerClass pc;
        pcv->insert(pcv->end(), pc );
    }

    printf("Deleting vector of
    PointerClass\n");
    delete pcv;

}
```

As you can see from the above code listing, we have created two different sorts of classes. The first class, NoPointer, is a simple class that contains only basic member variables, with no pointers stored in the member data of the class. The second class, PointerClass, contains pointer data that is allocated when an instance of the class is constructed and de-allocated when the instance is freed. If you look at line ➔ **1**, you will see how the ptr member variable is allocated in the constructor for the PointerClass. That ptr member variable should be de-allocated at line ➔ **2** if all goes well in the class.

3. Save the source file in your code editor and close the code editor.

4. Compile the source code with the compiler of your choice on the operating system of your choice.

When the program is run, if you have done everything properly, you should see the output shown in Listing 36-2 in the shell window.

LISTING 36-2: THE OUTPUT FROM THE ALLOCATION EXAMPLE

```
$ ./a.exe
Creating np
NoPointer: Full constructor called
Creating pc
PointerClass: Full constructor called
Deleting np
NoPointer: Destructor called
Deleting pc
PointerClass: Destructor called
Creating npa                                    → 7
NoPointer: Void Constructor called
NoPointer: Void Constructor called
NoPointer: Void Constructor called
NoPointer: Void Constructor called
NoPointer: Void Constructor called
Creating pca
PointerClass: Void Constructor called
PointerClass: Void Constructor called
PointerClass: Void Constructor called
PointerClass: Void Constructor called
PointerClass: Void Constructor called
Deleting npa                                    → 5
NoPointer: Destructor called
Deleting pca                                    → 6
PointerClass: Destructor called
Creating npa2
NoPointer: Void Constructor called
NoPointer: Void Constructor called
NoPointer: Void Constructor called
NoPointer: Void Constructor called
NoPointer: Void Constructor called
Creating pca2
PointerClass: Void Constructor called
PointerClass: Void Constructor called
PointerClass: Void Constructor called
PointerClass: Void Constructor called
PointerClass: Void Constructor called
Deleting npa2
NoPointer: Destructor called
NoPointer: Destructor called
NoPointer: Destructor called
NoPointer: Destructor called
NoPointer: Destructor called
Deleting pca2
PointerClass: Destructor called
PointerClass: Destructor called
PointerClass: Destructor called
PointerClass: Destructor called
PointerClass: Destructor called
Creating vector of PointerClass
PointerClass: Void Constructor called
PointerClass: Copy constructor called
PointerClass: Destructor called
PointerClass: Void Constructor called
PointerClass: Copy constructor called
PointerClass: Copy constructor called
PointerClass: Destructor called
PointerClass: Destructor called
PointerClass: Void Constructor called
PointerClass: Copy constructor called
PointerClass: Copy constructor called
PointerClass: Copy constructor called
PointerClass: Destructor called
PointerClass: Destructor called
PointerClass: Destructor called
PointerClass: Void Constructor called
PointerClass: Copy constructor called
PointerClass: Destructor called
PointerClass: Void Constructor called
PointerClass: Copy constructor called
PointerClass: Copy constructor called
PointerClass: Copy constructor called
PointerClass: Copy constructor called
PointerClass: Copy constructor called
PointerClass: Destructor called
PointerClass: Destructor called
PointerClass: Destructor called
PointerClass: Destructor called
PointerClass: Destructor called
Deleting vector of PointerClass
PointerClass: Destructor called
PointerClass: Destructor called
PointerClass: Destructor called
PointerClass: Destructor called
PointerClass: Destructor called
```

The important part of this output is shown in the lines marked with → **5** and → **6** As you can see, we are de-allocating the pointers that we allocated in the code at lines marked → **3** and → **4**. In both cases, we have allocated an array of objects. If you look at the output, you will see that the constructor for the class is called multiple times (see lines starting with → 7) but that the destructor is called only once. This introduces an immediate memory leak in the application.

Always place debugging `print` statements in your constructors and destructor to verify that you have called each the proper number of times and in the proper manner.

37 Technique

Creating Arrays of Objects

Save Time By

- ✔ Understanding the various ways to create arrays of objects
- ✔ Declaring arrays on the stack
- ✔ Creating objects on the heap
- ✔ Using STL container classes to create arrays
- ✔ Interpreting your output

C++ offers three different ways to create arrays of objects, using the language constructs and the Standard Template Library (STL):

- ✔ **Declaring arrays on the stack:** This method, using the [] construct, creates a static array that exists from the point at which it is allocated. You create a static array by writing

  object-type array[*num-elements*];

  where *object-type* is the class of the object you wish to create an array of, and the number of elements in the array is represented by the *num-elements* parameter. The advantage to this approach is that the array size is known at compile time, and the program will be loaded with the proper amount of memory. The problem with this approach is that the array exists only as long as the array is in scope. When the array variable goes out of scope, the array is destroyed.

- ✔ **Creating objects on the heap:** This approach has the advantage of allowing you to control exactly when the array is created or destroyed — but a disadvantage is that it will not automatically "clean up" (de-allocate) after you. If you fail to de-allocate an array (or if you de-allocate it in the wrong way), you create a memory leak in your program. You create an object on the heap by writing

  object-type object;

- ✔ **Using STL container classes to create arrays:** (We could quibble over whether the various container classes in the STL constitute separate methods of creating arrays, but for the sake of this technique, we'll just consider the use of all of the various container classes as a single approach.) The advantage of this method is that it does not create the objects until they are actually inserted into the container class — and it automatically destroys those objects when the container class goes out of scope. Containers can be dynamically created on the stack so you can control the scope of objects in the container as well. Two disadvantages to this method: The increase in overhead is significant, and the container classes require you to implement a number of methods in your classes — such as copy constructors, assignment operators, and virtual destructors — to avoid memory leaks. You create an STL container class by writing:

```
vector<object-type> array;
```

This technique looks at the various advantages and disadvantages of creating objects in these three different ways. By understanding how you can most easily create an array of objects in your code, you will save time when writing, debugging, and optimizing your code.

The following steps take you through all three techniques for object-array allocation in a single example:

1. **In the code editor of your choice, create a new file to hold the code for the implementation of the source file.**

In this example, the file is named ch37.cpp, although you can use whatever you choose.

2. **Type the code from Listing 37-1 into your file.**

Better yet, copy the code from the source file on this book's companion Web site.

LISTING 37-1: CREATING AN ARRAY OF OBJECTS

```cpp
#include <stdio.h>
#include <string>
#include <vector>

class Foo
{
    std::string _str;
public:
    Foo(void)
    {
        printf("Foo: Void constructor\n");
        _str = "";
    }
    Foo ( const char *s )
    {
        printf("Foo: Full constructor
[%s]\n", s);
        _str = s;
    }
    Foo( const Foo& aCopy )
    {
        printf("Foo: Copy constructor\n");
        _str = aCopy._str;
    }
    virtual ~Foo()
    {
        printf("Foo: Destructor\n");
    }
    Foo operator=(const Foo& aCopy)
    {
        _str = aCopy._str;
        return *this;
    }
    std::string String()
    {
        return _str;
    }
    void setString( const char *str )
    {
        _str = str;
    }
};

int main()
{
    printf("Creating array via new\n");
    Foo *f = new Foo[2]("Hello");          → 1
    printf("Creating array on heap\n");
    Foo f1[3];                             → 2

    // Create a vector
    printf("Creating vector of foo\n");
    std::vector<Foo> fooVector;            → 3

    printf("Adding objects to vector\n");
    Foo f2;
    Foo f3;
    Foo f4;
    fooVector.insert( fooVector.end(), f2 );
    fooVector.insert( fooVector.end(), f3 );
    fooVector.insert( fooVector.end(), f4 );

    printf("Deleting array on heap\n");
    delete [] f;
}
```

Looking at the above code listing, you can see that there are three different arrays defined in the program. At ➤ **1**, we allocate an array from the stack, using the new operator. At ➤ **2**, we allocate an array on the heap, using the standard array syntax of C++. Finally, at ➤ **3**, we see how the Standard Template Library vector class is used to define an array of objects.

3. **Save the source file in your code editor and close the code editor.**

4. **Compile the source code with the compiler of your choice on the operating system of your choice.**

When the program is run, if you have done everything properly, you should see the output shown in Listing 37-2 in the shell window.

LISTING 37-2: OUTPUT FROM THE ARRAY-ALLOCATION PROGRAM

```
$ ./a.exe
Creating array via new            ➤ 4
Foo: Full constructor [Hello]
Foo: Full constructor [Hello]
Creating array on heap            ➤ 5
Foo: Void constructor
Foo: Void constructor
Foo: Void constructor
Creating vector of foo            ➤ 6
Adding objects to vector
Foo: Void constructor
Foo: Void constructor
Foo: Void constructor
Foo: Copy constructor
Foo: Copy constructor
Foo: Copy constructor
Foo: Destructor
Foo: Copy constructor
Foo: Copy constructor
Foo: Copy constructor
Foo: Destructor
Foo: Destructor
Deleting array on heap            ➤ 7
Foo: Destructor
Foo: Destructor
Foo: Destructor
Foo: Destructor
Foo: Destructor
Foo: Destructor
Foo: Destructor
```

```
Foo: Destructor
Foo: Destructor                   ➤ 8
Foo: Destructor
Foo: Destructor
```

As you can see, the static array is created at the point at which the compiler finds the code for it. The dynamic array is created at the point at which the new operator is used to allocate it, and the vector array does not begin to allocate space for the objects until they are inserted into the vector. Take a look at a breakdown of the lines shown in Listing 37-2:

✔ ➤ **4** This line shows the point at which the array is allocated with new. As you can see, two constructor calls are made, indicating that two objects were created and put into the array. Note that because we gave the new operator a constructor argument, it calls the full constructor for the class.

✔ ➤ **5** This line shows where we allocated a block of objects on the heap, using standard C++ array syntax. Note that the void constructor is used for these objects, initializing all three of them (one for each array element).

✔ ➤ **6** This line shows where we used the Standard Template Library vector class to store objects. No objects were created in this call. We then allocate several objects on the heap and add them to the vector. Notice that the objects are copied into the vector using the copy constructor to create new instances of the class.

✔ ➤ **7** Here we delete the array that we allocated with the new call. There should be two objects deleted in this process and the output shows that there are, in fact, two objects destroyed.

✔ ➤ **8** This line shows the final destruction of the objects that were allocated in the array on the heap.

If you count the total number of destructor calls at the end of the output listing, you will see that there are 11 of them. This might not seem obvious from the fact that we allocated only eight objects in the main program (two in the new array, three in the heap array, and three in the vector). However, because the copy constructor was invoked three times, three additional objects were created, making a total of 11.

 If you take a look at the output from the program (in Listing 37-2), you see that the vector class does significant manipulation of the data in the vector — that's to store it efficiently and make room for new objects. Therefore, if your objects require a lot of overhead for their creation and destruction, the vector class is not a good choice for a container. You would be better off pre-allocating a large number of the objects — and using that array, whether static or dynamic, to store your information.

One important thing to notice in the code is that we always use the delete [] method for de-allocating arrays of objects. If you replace the delete [] method with a simple delete call, you will find that the code does not call the destructor for each member of the array, and that memory leaks can easily occur. This risk of memory leakage is particularly important if you store pointers to objects in your array, and access them through any sort of base class.

Working with Arrays of Object Pointers

Save Time By

- Understanding arrays of object pointers
- Implementing arrays of object pointers
- Interpreting output

Although simple arrays of objects are easy to work with, arrays of pointers that indicate objects are slightly more complicated to handle. The syntax for creating and deleting these arrays is a little more difficult; heterogeneous arrays of pointers that point to a common base object require a bit more work — and this technique guides you through what must be done. C++ allows you to store pointers to all related classes — that is, those derived from a common base — in a single array, while keeping track of their types and sizes. This can save you a lot of time, by allowing you to place all of the related objects in a single array while processing them differently using their derived types.

You can save a lot of time by storing all objects that derive from a common base in a single array for access — as long as you have a way to access the objects consistently. If you do so, you must use a virtual destructor in the base class to insure that all de-allocations are done properly. If you do not do this, the destructors for the derived classes will not be called, and potential memory leaks can occur.

Creating an Array of Heterogeneous Objects

If you are working with a batch of different classes, all derived from a single base class, it can be advantageous to store them all in one place. For one thing, you only have one array to work with. For another, because the objects are all related, it is likely that you will be doing the same processing on them all at the same time. Let's look at an example of creating a heterogeneous array that stores multiple classes of objects.

1. **In the code editor of your choice, create a new file to hold the code for the implementation of the source file.**

   In this example, the file is named ch38.cpp, although you can use whatever you choose.

2. **Type the code from Listing 38-1 into your file.**

   Better yet, copy the code from the source file on this book's companion Web site.

LISTING 38-1: CREATING AN ARRAY OF OBJECT POINTERS

```c
#include <stdio.h>
#include <string.h>


class Base
{
   char *ptr;
public:
   Base(void)
   {
      ptr = NULL;
   }
   Base( const char *str )
   {
      setString( str );
   }
   virtual ~Base()
   {
      printf("Base::~Base called\n");
      delete ptr;
   }
   void setString( const char *str )
   {
      ptr = new char[strlen(str)+1];
      strcpy( ptr, str );
   }
   const char *getString()
   {
      return ptr;
   }
};


class Derived : public Base
{
private:
   int _num;
public:
   Derived(void)
      : Base("DerivedVoid")
   {
     _num = 0;
   }
   Derived( int nVal )
      : Base("DerivedFull")
   {
     _num = nVal;
   }
   virtual ~Derived()
   {
      printf("Derived::~Derived called\n");
   }
```

```c
   void setVal( int nVal )
   {
      _num = nVal;
   }
   int getVal ( void )
   {
      return _num;
   }
};

const int NumElements = 3;

int main(void)
{
   Base **bArray = new Base*[10];           ➜ 1

   for ( int i=0; i<NumElements; ++i )
      bArray[i] = new Derived(i);           ➜ 2

   // Print them out
   for ( int j=0; j<NumElements; ++j )
      printf("Object %s - %d\n", bArray[j]-
>getString(), ((Derived *)bArray[j])-
>getVal());

   // Delete them
   for ( int i=0; i<NumElements; ++i )
      delete bArray[i];

   delete [] bArray;
   return 0;
}
```

The above code listing illustrates how we create an array of pointers and store data in that array. As you can see at ➜ **1**, allocating an array of pointers is no different than allocating any other sort of array in C++. The difference here is that while the array space is allocated, no actual objects are created. This is because we are allocating space for pointers to the objects, not objects themselves. The actual allocation of objects and the space they consume is illustrated at the line marked ➜ **2**. Note that even though we have an array of Base pointers, we can create and store Derived pointers in the array, since they are a derived form of Base.

3. Save the source file in your code editor and close the code editor.

4. Compile the source code with the compiler of your choice on the operating system of your choice.

When the program is run, if you have done everything properly, you should see the following output in the shell window:

```
$ ./a.exe
Object DerivedFull - 0
Object DerivedFull - 1
Object DerivedFull - 2
Derived::~Derived called
Base::~Base called
Derived::~Derived called
Base::~Base called
Derived::~Derived called
Base::~Base called
```

The output here illustrates that the array of pointers is created as we expected. The string stored in the Base class was created from the Derived constructor, which is what we anticipated. The destruction of the objects does chain upward to call both the Base class and Derived class destructors. In short, this code works exactly as advertised.

The ability to work with an array of heterogeneous pointers is quite powerful in C++, because it means that you need not know what sort of object you are working with. Had we created virtual methods for getting and setting the values in the Base class, we would not even have to cast the object in the printf in the main function.

Technique 39

Implementing a Spreadsheet

One of the most famous (or perhaps infamous) applications to help make the personal computer popular was the spreadsheet — nothing more than a grid of cells arranged in rows and columns — in other words, a two-dimensional array. Spreadsheets have more functionality than simple arrays (for example, you can build in formulae), but at its heart, a spreadsheet is an array of rows and columns. This technique uses the Standard Template Library (STL) to set up and implement a spreadsheet shell. The result can easily be used to create a real spreadsheet implementation. Spreadsheets are common elements of applications these days, from doing presentations of data to what-if analysis. By having a generic spreadsheet class that you can drop into your next project, you will find that you save a lot of time in both the design and implementation phase of the project.

 The implementation shown here isn't designed to work with or interpret formulae, but it will do everything else. If you want a complete spreadsheet that can handle formulae, all you need to do is incorporate a simple expression parser.

The basics of the spreadsheet are three elements: the column (or cell), the row, and the sheet itself. Each column contains a piece of data and the information for formatting that piece of data for display. The column contains methods to copy itself, clear itself out, and modify the data or formatting information in itself. The row is simply an array of columns that makes up a single row of the spreadsheet. The Row class needs to be able to modify any existing column in the row, as well as add new columns and remove columns. A row should be able to return the contents of any given column within that row so that the end user can modify the contents directly.

Finally, the Spreadsheet class will contain an array of rows. This array knows nothing about the individual columns in the sheet, nor does it know anything about formatting or data. This data encapsulation is consistent with the object-oriented paradigm, certainly, but is also important in terms of being able to easily modify the basic layers of the system with minimal change to the upper layers.

When you're implementing a complex system, you can save immense time by breaking it down into the most discrete simple components you can make. This way, when change is needed later on, the amount of required effort is smaller and the ripple effect throughout the system is minimal.

Creating the Column Class

The first element of the spreadsheet is the column. Let's build a simple class that maintains information about the column, and contains methods to work with that information. Here's how:

1. **In the code editor of your choice, create a new file to hold the code for the implementation of the source file.**

   In this example, the file is named ch39.cpp, although you can use whatever you choose.

2. **Type the code from Listing 39-1 into your file.**

   Better yet, copy the code from the source file on this book's companion Web site.

LISTING 39-1: THE COLUMN CLASS

```cpp
#include <stdio.h>
#include <string>
#include <vector>

class Column
{
    std::string _format;
    std::string _value;
public:
    Column(void)
    {
        _format = "%s";
        _value = "";
    }
    Column( const char *format, const char
    *value )
    {
        _format = format;
        _value = value;
    }
    Column( const Column& aCopy )
    {
        _format = aCopy._format;
        _value = aCopy._value;
    }
    virtual ~Column()
    {
    }
    Column operator=( const Column& aCopy )
    {
        _format = aCopy._format;
        _value = aCopy._value;
        return *this;
    }
    Column operator=(const char *value)
    {
        _value = value;
        return *this;
    }

    void setValue( const char *value )
    {
        _value = value;
    }
    std::string getValue( void )
    {
        return _value;
    }
    void setFormat( const char *format )
    {
        _format = format;
    }
    std::string getFormat( void )
    {
        return _format;
    }
    virtual std::string getFormattedString
( void ) const                          → 1
    {
        char szBuffer[ 100 ];
        sprintf(szBuffer, _format.c_str(),
        _value.c_str());
        std::string sRet = szBuffer;
        return sRet;
    }
};
```

This code implements the most basic element of the spreadsheet system, the column. As you can see, we implement a complete class by adding methods for the constructors, destructors, assignment operators, and accessor methods. It also implements a virtual method (shown at → 1) for returning the contents of the column in a formatted manner. Doing so allows other column types to be defined later on down the line, if you so desire.

3. **Save your file in your code editor.**

The next step is to implement the Row class that will hold an array of columns.

Creating the Row Class

After we have created a Column class, the next thing to do is to create a Row class that contains the columns we wish to store in the spreadsheet. You can think of the Column class as the data for a single cell, and the Row class as a list of cells for a given row.

1. **Append the code from Listing 39-2 to the end of your file.**

LISTING 39-2: THE ROW CLASS

```cpp
class Row
{
    std::vector< Column > _columns;

    void Copy( const Row& aCopy )
    {
        std::vector< Column >::const_
          iterator iter;
        for ( iter = aCopy._columns.begin();
          iter != aCopy._columns.end();
          ++iter )
            _columns.insert( _columns.end(),
            (*iter) );
    }
public:
    Row(void)
    {
    }
```

```cpp
    Row( unsigned int numColumns )
    {
        for ( int i=0; i<numColumns; ++i )
        {
            Column c;
            _columns.insert( _columns.end(),
  c );
        }
    }
    Row( const Row& aCopy )
    {
        Copy( aCopy );
    }
    Row operator=( const Row& aCopy )
    {
        Copy( aCopy );
    }
    Column& operator[]( int idx )          → 3
    {
        if ( idx < 0 || idx > _columns.
          size()-1 )
            throw "Row: Index out
              of range";                   → 2
        return _columns[ idx ];
    }

    int NumColumns( void )
    {
        return _columns.size();
    }
    void Clear()
    {
        std::vector< Column >::iterator
          iter;
        for ( iter = _columns.begin();
          iter != _columns.end(); ++iter )
            (*iter).setValue( "" );
    }
    void Print() const
    {
        std::vector< Column >::const_
          iterator iter;
        for ( iter = _columns.begin();
          iter != _columns.end(); ++iter )
            printf("%s ",
  (*iter).getFormattedString().c_str() );
        printf("\n");
    }
};
```

Note that the `Row` class does not do anything with the columns, except to store them and give the end-user access to the ones they want. Note also that we use exception handling (shown at → **2**) to deal with the exceptional cases of array indices out of bounds. There are no good defaults possible here, so we just assume that it is a fatal error to ask for an invalid column number.

One thing that could be changed here is that the `Row` class does not handle resizing. Instead, the `Row` class simply assumes that the array of columns is always being instantiated from scratch. To properly resize a row, you would need to create a new array of columns of the right size, and then copy the existing columns into that row.

2. **Save your file.**

The final step of the process of implementing the class is to put together the actual `Spreadsheet` class. The next section shows how.

Creating the Spreadsheet Class

Finally, we come to the important part for the end-user: the `Spreadsheet` class itself. A spreadsheet, of course, is simply a list of the rows that make up the sheet, which in turn is a list of the columns that make up each row. Our spreadsheet will always be "square" — that is, it will contain an equal number of columns in each row.

1. **Append the code from Listing 39-3 to the end of your file.**

LISTING 39-3: THE SPREADSHEET CLASS

```
class Spreadsheet
{
    int            _cols;
    std::vector< Row > _rows;
    std::string    _name;

    void _BuildSheet( int nRows, int nCols )
    {
        // If there is anything already
           here, remove it.
```

```
        _rows.erase(_rows.begin(),
        _rows.end());
        // Now, add in the rows.
        for ( int i=0; i<nRows; ++i )
        {
            Row row(nCols);
            _rows.insert( _rows.end(),
               row );
        }
    }
    void _InternalSetRows( const unsigned
      int nRows )
    {
        _BuildSheet( nRows, _cols );
    }
    void _InternalSetCols( const unsigned
      int nCols )
    {
        // Save the number of rows, so we
           can rebuild it.
        int nRowCount = _rows.size();
        // Set the number of columns.
        _cols = nCols;
        // Now rebuild the rows.
        _BuildSheet( nRowCount, nCols );
    }
    void Copy( const Spreadsheet& aCopy )
    {
        _InternalSetCols( aCopy.
          NumColumns() );

        std::vector< Row >::const_iterator
          iter;
        for ( iter = aCopy._rows.begin();
          iter != aCopy._rows.end(); ++iter )
            _rows.insert( _rows.end(),
              (*iter) );

        _name = aCopy._name;
    }
public:
    Spreadsheet(void)
    {
    }
    Spreadsheet( const char *name )
    {
        _name = name;
    }
    Spreadsheet( const char *name, unsigned
      int nRows, unsigned int nCols )
    {
```

(continued)

LISTING 39-3 (continued)

```
        _name = name;
        _InternalSetCols( nCols );
        _InternalSetRows( nRows );
    }
    Spreadsheet( const Spreadsheet& aCopy )
    {
        Copy( aCopy );
    }
    Spreadsheet operator=( const
     Spreadsheet& aCopy )
    {
        Copy( aCopy );
        return *this;
    }
    Row& operator[]( int idx )            → 4
    {
        if ( idx < 0 || idx > _rows.
          size()-1 )
            throw "Spreadsheet: Index out of
              range";
        return _rows[idx];
    }
    Spreadsheet operator()(int r1, int c1,
     int r2, int c2)
    {
        Spreadsheet ret;

        // Assign the pieces.
        ret.setNumColumns( c2-c1+1 );
        ret.setNumRows( r2-r1+1 );

        // Now copy over the chunk they want.
        try
        {
            for ( int r = r1; r <= r2; ++r )
                for ( int c = c1; c <= c2;
                  ++c )
                    ret[r-r1][c-c1] =
                      (*this)[r][c];
        }
        catch ( ... )
        {
            throw "Spreadsheet: Index out of
              range";
        }
        return ret;
    }
    void setNumColumns( int nCols )
    {
        _InternalSetCols( nCols );
    }
    void setNumRows( int nRows )
```

```
    {
        _InternalSetRows( nRows );
    }
    int NumColumns() const
    {
        return _cols;
    }
    int NumRows() const
    {
        return _rows.size();
    }
    void setName( const char *name )
    {
        _name = name;
    }
    std::string getName( void ) const
    {
        return _name;
    }

    void Print() const
    {
        std::vector< Row >::const_iterator
          iter;
        printf("Sheet: %s\n", _name.c_str()
          );
        for ( iter = _rows.begin(); iter !=
          _rows.end(); ++iter )
        {
            (*iter).Print();
        }
    }

    void Clear()
    {
        std::vector< Row >::iterator iter;
        for ( iter = _rows.begin(); iter !=
          _rows.end(); ++iter )
            (*iter).Clear();
    }
};
```

As I mentioned earlier in this technique, the spreadsheet is really just a holder of rows, which in turn are a holder of columns. The Column class is the only one that "understands" what the data being stored looks like, or how it is formatted, or how it will be displayed. The Spreadsheet class provides access to the individual rows in the sheet, without any knowledge of how the columns are stored in each row.

2. **Save the source file in the source-code editor and close the editor application.**

Testing Your Spreadsheet

To see that the code is really working, implement a test driver for the code. The following steps show you how:

1. **In the code editor of your choice, reopen the source file for the code that you just created.**

In this example, the file is named ch39.cpp, although you can use whatever you choose.

2. **Append the code from Listing 39-4 to the end of your file.**

Better yet, copy the code from the source file on this book's companion Web site.

LISTING 39-4: THE SPREADSHEET TEST DRIVER

```
int main(int argc, char **argv)
{
    Spreadsheet s1("Sheet1", 10, 10 );

    // Initialize the spreadsheet.
    for ( int i=0; i<s1.NumRows(); ++i )
        for ( int j=0; j<s1.NumColumns();
            ++j )
        {
            s1[i][j] = "*";
            s1[i][j].setFormat("%6s");
        }

    // Set some values.
    s1[5][4] = "Hello";                    → 5
    s1[0][0] = "Begin";

    // Display it so that the user can see it.
    s1.Print();

    // Get a slice of the spreadsheet.
    Spreadsheet s2 = s1(0,0,3,3);
    s2.setName("Sheet 2");
    s2.Print();

    // Change a column, so we know that it
        works.
    s2[2][2] = "!";
    s2.Print();

    // Now, clear out the original sheet and
        display it.
    s1.Clear();
    s1.Print();

}
```

When the program is run, if you have done everything properly, you should see the output from Listing 39-5 in the shell window.

LISTING 39-5: THE OUTPUT FROM THE SPREADSHEET TEST DRIVER APPLICATION

```
Sheet: Sheet1
  Begin      *       *       *       *       *       *       *       *       *
     *       *       *       *       *       *       *       *       *       *
     *       *       *       *       *       *       *       *       *       *
     *       *       *       *       *       *       *       *       *       *
     *       *       *       *       *       *       *       *       *       *
     *       *       *       *    Hello      *       *       *       *       *
     *       *       *       *       *       *       *       *       *       *
     *       *       *       *       *       *       *       *       *       *
     *       *       *       *       *       *       *       *       *       *
     *       *       *       *       *       *       *       *       *       *
```

(continued)

LISTING 39-5 *(continued)*

```
Sheet: Sheet 2
  Begin       *       *       *
        *     *       *       *
        *     *       *       *
        *     *       *       *
Sheet: Sheet 2
  Begin       *       *       *
        *     *       *       *
        *     *       !       *
        *     *       *       *
Sheet: Sheet1
```

The output shown indicates the state of the spreadsheet at the time it is displayed. An asterisk (*) is shown in any cell that contains no data, while cells that do contain data are shown with the data value. For example, you will see the string Hello in the center of Sheet1, which was placed there at ➜ **5** in the code listing for the main driver. Likewise, the top left corner of Sheet1 contains the string Begin, which was placed there at the following line in the driver program.

We could easily use this spreadsheet class to store data, display it for the user, or manipulate data that is contained in a row/column definition.

The asterisks are simply placeholders to show where the actual column data should be. As you can see, the data values that we set in our test driver show up where they're supposed to.

You can't truly implement a two-dimensional array in C++, since there is no operator [][]. However, if you look at the code, you can see a way to implement an operator that returns another class that implements the same operator. The spreadsheet class implements an operator[] (shown by the ➜ **4** in Listing 39-3) which returns the row requested by the index. The row class then implements the operator[] (shown by the ➜ **3** line in Listing 39-2) to return the column requested by the index. That's why [row][col] = *value* works.

Part VI

Input and Output

The 5th Wave   By Rich Tennant

Re·al Pro·gram·mers

INVALID CODE
YOU @*!*
WALNUT BRAIN!

Real Programmers strive to insult users
with error messages.

Technique 40

Using the Standard Streams to Format Data

Save Time By

- Understanding stream classes
- Formatting data with stream classes
- Understanding your output

If you've been programming in C++ for a long time, you're probably used to outputting data with the printf, fprintf, and sprintf functions that date back to the C programming days. It is now time to take the plunge into using the stream components of the standard C++ library, because these components will save you lots of time and heartache. The stream components support input, output, and formatting for data in C++ applications. Like the printf, fprintf, and sprintf functions, streams exist to write to the console, to files, and to format data into strings. Unlike the aforementioned functions, streams are type-safe and extensible, which saves you time by reducing the amount of code you need to write and the amount of debugging you need to do to find problems in output.

The stream components save time by being type-safe, well written, and comprehensive. If you use streams instead of more specific output functions, you will find that your code is smaller, easier to understand, and more portable.

Although most programmers are aware that you can input and output data through the stream classes, most are unaware that the stream classes have a wealth of formatting functionality built into them.

In this technique, I show you how to work with the formatting functionality of the stream classes, how to extract data from a stream, and how to output columns and change floating point precision for data.

Working with Streams

In order to understand just how a stream component can be used in your application to save time and effort, let's take a look at a simple example of a stream being used in an application. In this case, we will create some data in our program, and then output that data to the user. In addition, we will examine how to extend the stream class by creating our own output control.

1. **In the code editor of your choice, create a new file to hold the code for the implementation of the source file.**

In this example, the file is named ch40.cpp, although you can use whatever you choose.

2. **Type the code from Listing 40-1 into your file.**

Better yet, copy the code from the source file on this book's companion Web site.

LISTING 40-1: USING STREAMS

```
#include <stdio.h>
#include <iostream>
#include <sstream>
#include <vector>

using namespace std;

void PrintDoubleRow( int numElements, double
   *dArray, ostream& out )
{
    // First, set up some elements of the
       ostream.

    // Set the output floating point preci-
       sion to 2 decimal places.
    out.precision(4);
    // Only show the decimal point if it is
       not a whole number.
    out << showpoint;

    for ( int i=0; i<numElements; ++i )
    {
        // Set each column to be 8 spaces.
        out.width(8);
        // Output the float.
        out << dArray[i];
    }

    out << endl;
}

template < class A >
ostream& operator<<( ostream& out,
   vector< A >& dVector )
{
```

→ 4

```
    vector<A>::iterator iter;
    for ( iter = dVector.begin(); iter !=
      dVector.end(); ++iter )
    {
        out.width(8);
        out << (*iter);
    }
    out << endl;
    return out;
}

int main(int argc, char **argv)
{
    double dArray[20];
    int    nCount = 0;

    // See whether they gave us any on the
       command line.
    if ( argc > 2 )
    {
        for ( int i=1; i<argc; ++i )
        {
            stringstream str;
            double number;

            str.setf(ios::fixed,
             std::ios_base::floatfield);
            str.width(0);
            str.precision(4);
            str << argv[i];
            str >> number;
            dArray[nCount] = number;
            nCount++;
        }
    }
    else
    {
        // Prompt the user for input.
        bool bDone = false;
        while ( !bDone )
        {
            char szBuffer[80];
            cout << "Enter a number (or a
               dash (*) to quit): ";
            memset( szBuffer, 0, 80 );
            cin >> szBuffer;
            if ( szBuffer[0] == '*' )
                bDone = true;
            else
            {
```

```
            stringstream str;
            double number;

            str.setf(ios::fixed,
               std::ios_base::float-
               field);
            str.width(0);
            str.precision(4);
            str << szBuffer;
            str >> number;
            dArray[nCount] = number;
            nCount++;
         }
      }
   }
   PrintDoubleRow( nCount, dArray,
   cout );                                     → 1

   // Now display it as a vector.
   vector< double > dVector;                    → 2
   for ( int i=0; i<nCount; ++i )
      dVector.insert( dVector.end(),
         dArray[i] );
   cout << "Vector: " << endl;
   cout << dVector << endl;                      → 3
}
```

Let's take a look at what is going on here. First, we create a standard array of double values and put data received from the user into the array. That array is then printed out using the standard stream class (see → **1**). Next, we are creating an "array" using the Standard Template Library vector class (see → **2**). We then print that vector out using a stream shown at → **3**. But wait, how does this work? Vectors are not among the standard supported types for streams. If you look at the templated function marked with → **4**, you will see that we have created an overloaded operator that takes a vector object and outputs it to a stream. The compiler will match up our overloaded operator along with the streaming of the vector, and make sure that it all works properly. Note also the use of the width and precision methods of the stream class to set the output width of each column in the vector properly, and only output the right number of decimal points.

3. Save the source-code file in the code editor and close the editor application.

4. Compile the application in your favorite compiler, on your favorite operating system.

If you have done everything right, when you run the application with the following command-line input:

```
1 2 3 4
```

you should see the following output from the application on the console window:

```
$ ./a.exe 1 2 3 4
   1.000   2.000   3.000   4.000
Vector:
   1.000   2.000   3.000   4.000
```

As you can see, the output is the same for both the array and vector classes. We can also see that the width of the columns is fixed at eight characters, as we specified in the width method of the stream. Finally, note that the number of decimal points is fixed at three for each entry, once again as specified in the precision method.

Alternatively, you can enter the data at the prompt. To do so, run the program with no input arguments, and then enter the values when prompted from the user. In this case, you should see the following output from the program in the console window:

```
$ ./a.exe
Enter a number (or a dash (*) to quit): 1
Enter a number (or a dash (*) to quit): 2
Enter a number (or a dash (*) to quit): 3
Enter a number (or a dash (*) to quit): 4
Enter a number (or a dash (*) to quit): *
   1.000   2.000   3.000   4.000
Vector:
   1.000   2.000   3.000   4.000
```

The output from the program is the same, the only difference is how the data got into the system. Note again that the width of the columns is still fixed and the number of decimal points is still what we specified.

Technique 41

Reading In and Processing Files

Save Time By

- ✔ Reading in files with stream classes
- ✔ Processing files with stream classes
- ✔ Creating a test file
- ✔ Interpreting your output

Processing files in C++ is really the same as processing any other sort of input or output. Unlike similar functions in C, however, the file-processing functions in C++ allow you to use the same code for processing data — from either the keyboard or a file. This generality makes it considerably easier to write code that is easy to test, run, and maintain. And, of course, when code is faster to write and easier to test, it saves you time in the project.

 If you use stream classes instead of C-style file functions to access data, you will find the code quicker to write and test — and errors easier to trap. See Technique 40 for more on using stream classes.

This technique shows you how to use the file-stream classes to read in — and process — a simple preferences file. I also tell you how this method compares to the old style of doing things, so that you can easily drop in this code wherever you are using the older C-style functions.

1. **In the code editor of your choice, create a new file to hold the code for the implementation of the source file.**

In this example, the file is named ch41.cpp, although you can use whatever you choose.

2. **Type the code from Listing 41-1 into your file.**

Better yet, copy the code from the source file on this book's companion Web site.

LISTING 41-1: THE FILE-READING CLASS

```
#include <stdio.h>
#include <string.h>

#include <fstream>
#include <ios>
#include <iostream>
#include <string>
#include <vector>
```

```
using namespace std;
// The old fashioned way

class Entry
{
private:
    char *strName;
    char *strValue;

    void Init()
    {
        strName = NULL;
        strValue = NULL;
    }
public:
    Entry()
    {
        Init();
    }
    Entry( const char *name, const char *value )
    {
        Init();
        setName( name );
        setValue ( value );
    }
    Entry( const Entry& aCopy )
    {
        Init();
        setName( aCopy.strName );
        setValue( aCopy.strValue );
    }
    ~Entry()
    {
        if ( strName )
            delete [] strName;
        if ( strValue )
            delete [] strValue;
    }
    Entry operator=( const Entry& aCopy )
    {
        setName( aCopy.strName );
        setValue( aCopy.strValue );
        return *this;
    }
    void setName(const char *name)
    {
        if ( strName )
            delete [] strName;
        strName = new char[strlen(name)+1 ];
        strcpy( strName, name );
    }
    void setValue( const char *value )
```

(continued)

LISTING 41-1 *(continued)*

```
    {
        if ( strValue )
            delete [] strValue;
        strValue = new char[strlen
          (value)+1 ];
        strcpy( strValue, value );
    }

    const char *getName( void )
    {
        return strName;
    }
    const char *getValue( void )
    {
        return strValue;
    }
};


bool OpenFileAndReadOld( const char
    *strFileName, Entry* array, int
    nMaxEntries, int *numFound )
{
    FILE *fp = fopen ( strFileName, "r" );
    if ( fp == NULL )
        return false;
    int nPos = 0;
    while ( !feof(fp) )
    {
        char szBuffer[ 257 ];          → 1
        memset( szBuffer, 0, 256 );
        if ( fgets( szBuffer, 256, fp ) ==
          NULL )
            break;

        // Look for the position of the '='
          sign.
        char *str = strstr(szBuffer, "=");
        if ( str )
        {
            // First, get the name.
            char szName[256];
            memset( szName, 0, 256 );
            strncpy(szName, szBuffer,
              strlen(szBuffer)-strlen(str) );

            // Now, get the value.
            char szValue[256];
            memset( szValue, 0, 256 );
            strncpy(szValue, str+1,
              strlen(str)-1 );
            if ( szValue[strlen(szValue)-1]
              == '\n' )
```

```
                szValue[strlen(szValue)-1]
                  = 0;

            Entry e( szName, szValue );
            if ( nPos < nMaxEntries )
            {
                array[ nPos ] = e;
                nPos ++;
            }
        }
    }

    *numFound = nPos;

    fclose(fp);

    return true;
}
```

The code in Listing 41-1 does things the old-fashioned way (C-style), using *file-based* functions. Trying it with streams creates reusable operators along the way. That's next.

3. Now, append the code in Listing 41-2 to the source file using your favorite source-code editor.

LISTING 41-2: USING STREAMS FOR FILE READING

```
// Various operators used by the
  application.

ifstream& operator<<( string& sIn, ifstream&
  in )                                → 3
{
    while ( !in.eof() )
    {
        char c;
        in.get(c);
        if ( in.fail() )
            return in;
        sIn += c;
        if ( c == '\n' )
            return in;
    }

    return in;
}
```

```
string operator-( string& sIn,                         Entry e(name.c_str(),
    char cIn )                           → 4               value.c_str());
{                                                       entries.insert( entries.end(),
    string sOut = "";                               e );
    for ( int i=0; i<sIn.length(); ++i )           }
        if ( sIn[i] != cIn )                    }
            sOut += sIn[i];
    return sOut;
}                                               in.close( );
                                                return true;
bool OpenFileAndReadNew( const char
    *szFileName, std::vector< Entry >&      }
    entries )
{
    ifstream in;
    in.open( szFileName );
```

As you can see, the code is much easier to understand and maintain in the stream version. Readability is important in coding because it takes less time for the maintenance programmer to read and understand your objective. The stream versions of the code form their own description of what we are trying to do, improving on the confusing C-style functions. More importantly, if we want to test the functions from the keyboard, it is trivial to pass in the standard input object instead of a file. The code can cope with both types of input.

```
    if ( in.fail() )
    {
        printf("Unable to open file %s\n",
         szFileName );
        return false;
    }

    // Process the file
    while ( !in.eof() )
    {
        // Get an input line
        string sLine = "";
        sLine << in;                     → 2

        // Skip comments
        if ( sLine.length() && sLine[0]
           == '#' ) continue;
```

To understand just how simple the stream version is compared to the older version, take a look at two similar segments of the code. The line marked → 1 in the original listing shows how we read a line in from the input source. The corresponding line in the updated stream version is marked → 2. Note that the stream version is not only smaller and easier to read, but also it handles problems the original code did not. For example, the string class can handle an almost infinite number of characters, whereas the buffer used in the original code is fixed in size. Likewise, the stream version automatically enters the number of characters into the string class, which makes checking for blank lines simple. Finally, checking for substrings in stream classes is considerably easier than using the clunky old strstr function that required you to check for NULL returns and end of string comparisons.

```
        // Remove all carriage returns and
            line feeds
        sLine = sLine - '\n';
        sLine = sLine - '\r';

        // Now, extract the pieces
        int ePos = sLine.find_first_of
           ('=', 0);
        if ( ePos != string::npos )
        {
            // Copy the name
            string name =
              sLine.substr(0,ePos);
            string value =
              sLine.substr(ePos+1);
```

4. Save the source code as a file in the code editor.

Notice the operators that are defined in this block of code (shown at the lines marked → **3** and → **4**). These provide a standard way to retrieve a single line of a file into a string object — and a fast, efficient way to remove a character from a string. The nicest thing about C++ operators is that they can be defined externally to the class they manipulate, so they don't require that the original classes be modified. This is a good way to extend functionality without derivation or modification.

Testing the File-Reading Code

After you have created the file-reading functionality, you should create a test driver that not only ensures that your code is correct, but also shows people how to use your code.

The following steps show you how to create a test driver that illustrates how the two methods for inputting data (`OpenAndReadFileOld` and `OpenAndReadFileNew`) are used — and what the output of each will be.

1. **In the code editor of your choice, reopen the existing file to hold the code for your test program.**

   In this example, I named the test program `ch 41.cpp`.

2. **Append the code from Listing 41-3 into your file.**

   Better yet, copy the code from the source file on this book's companion Web site.

LISTING 41-3: THE FILE-READ TEST DRIVER

```
int main( int argc, char **argv )
{
    if ( argc < 2 )
    {
        printf("Usage ch5_3 filename\n");
        exit(1);
    }

    Entry entries1[50];
    int   num = 0;
```

```
    printf("Old Way:\n");
    if ( OpenFileAndReadOld( argv[1],
      entries1, 50, &num ) == false )
    {
        printf("Error processing file %s\n",
          argv[1] );
        exit(1);
    }
    for ( int i=0; i<num; ++i )
    {
        cout << "Entry " << i << endl;
        cout << "Name: " <<
          entries1[i].getName() << endl;
        cout << "Value: " <<
          entries1[i].getValue() << endl;
    }

    printf("New Way:\n");
    std::vector< Entry > entries2;
    if ( OpenFileAndReadNew( argv[1],
      entries2 ) == false )
    {
        printf("Error processing file %s\n",
          argv[1] );
        exit(1);
    }
    std::vector< Entry >::iterator iter;
    int nPos = 0;
    for ( iter = entries2.begin();
    iter != entries2.end(); ++iter )
    {
        cout << "Entry " << nPos << endl;
        cout << "Name: " <<
          (*iter).getName() << endl;
        cout << "Value: " <<
          (*iter).getValue() << endl;
        nPos ++;
    }
}
```

This simple program just allows us to read in a test file in two different ways, using both the old-style C functions and the new-style stream functions. We then print out the values to compare them. Note that the old-style function requires that we use a fixed-size array, while the stream version uses the newer vector class to allow for an almost-infinite number of entries.

3. **Save the source-code file and close the source editor application.**

Creating the Test File

In order to use the test driver, we need some input data for the driver to process. Let's create a simple test file that contains data that we can read in to compare the old-and new-style functions of input and output.

1. **In the code editor of your choice, create a text file for testing the application.**

   In this case, I used the name test.txt for the test file.

2. **Type the following text into the test file:**

   ```
   Config1=A config string
   Config2=100
   Config3=Another line

   # This is a comment
   Config4=A.$5
   ```

3. **Save the test file and close the code-editor application.**

4. **Compile and run the program with your favorite compiler and operating system.**

If you have done everything properly, you should see the following output from the program on your console window:

```
$ ./a.exe test.txt
Old Way:                              → 5
Entry 0
Name: Config1
Value: A config string
Entry 1
Name: Config2
```

```
Value: 100
Entry 2
Name: Config3
Value: Another line
Entry 3
Name: Config4
Value: A.$5
New Way:                              → 6
Entry 0
Name: Config1
Value: A config string
Entry 1
Name: Config2
Value: 100
Entry 2
Name: Config3
Value: Another line
Entry 3
Name: Config4
Value: A.$5
```

As you can see by the output of our program, both the old and new ways of processing the data work the same. All of the entries shown under the Old Way output line were read in using the old-style C functions, while the output shown under the New Way output line were read in using the new-style streams. By using this simple program, therefore, we can easily convert old-style applications to the new-style functions quickly and easily, saving time and effort.

No functional difference exists between the old-style C functions and the new-style C++ streams. To see this, compare the lines shown at → **5** and at → **6**. Leaving out the additional operators that can be reused anywhere, however, makes the new-style code that handles streams considerably smaller and easier to read; by comparison, the old-style code is cumbersome and confusing.

Technique 42

How to Read Delimited Files

Save Time By

- Understanding standard delimited files

- Creating generic classes for reading or loading standard delimited files into your application

- Testing your output

There are a lot of ways to store data in file systems. One of the most popular is a standard *delimited file,* in which the individual fields of the records are separated by known delimiters. There are numerous examples of this, from comma separated values (CSV) to XML files to fixed-size records that include null bytes. The capability to load delimited data into your application is very valuable — and it makes your application considerably easier to use.

 Extracting the input and output of data formats into separate classes will not only make the classes more reusable across applications, it will also save you lots of time when trying to load known formats into new applications.

This technique builds some generic classes that aid loading and parsing delimited files. I have to make a few assumptions here, although each of these assumptions is fairly easy to adapt if you need to change the logic. The assumptions are as follows:

- The files contain only delimiters that separate fields. That is, no fields in the file contain delimiters.

- The records exist one per line. This is really just a convenience; it would be easy enough to check for an end-of-record signature other than the end-of-line character.

- The fields can vary in size.

Reading Delimited Files

Because the need to read delimited files is such a common problem in the software development world, it makes sense to build a generic method for reading them. By doing this, we save a lot of time because we are able to move the code to read the files from project to project. For example, you can create a generic class that can be used to read any sort of delimited files and test it with a variety of input.

1. **In the code editor of your choice, create a new file to hold the code for the implementation of the source file.**

In this example, the file is named `ch42.cpp`, although you can use whatever you choose.

2. **Type the code from Listing 42-1 into your file.**

Better yet, copy the code from the source file on this book's companion Web site.

LISTING 42-1: READING A DELIMITED FILE

```cpp
#include <stdio.h>
#include <string>
#include <vector>
#include <iostream>
#include <fstream>

// Avoid having to type out std:: for all
// STL classes.
using namespace std;

// This class manages a list of delimiters.
class Delimiters                          → 1
{
private:
    // Array of possible delimiters. Use a
      vector,
    // since the characters could include
      NULL byte
    // or other characters that string can't
      handle.
    vector< char > _delimiters;

protected:
    virtual void Copy ( const Delimiters&
      aCopy )
    {
        vector<char>::const_iterator iter;
        for ( iter =
          aCopy._delimiters.begin(); iter !=
          aCopy._delimiters.end(); ++iter )
            _delimiters.insert( _delimiters.
                end(), (*iter) );
    }
public:
    Delimiters(void)
    {
    }
    Delimiters( const char *delimiterList )
    {
        for ( int i=0;
  i<strlen(delimiterList); ++i)
        {
            _delimiters.insert( _delimiters.
                end(), delimiterList[i] );
        }
    }
    Delimiters( const Delimiters& aCopy )
    {
        Copy ( aCopy );
    }
    Delimiters operator=( const Delimiters&
      aCopy )
    {
        Copy( aCopy);
    }
    virtual ~Delimiters(void)
    {
    }

    // Clear out the entire list.
    virtual void Clear()
    {
        _delimiters.erase( _delimiters.
            begin(), _delimiters.end() );
    }
    // Add a delimiter to the list.
    virtual void Add( char c )
    {
        _delimiters.insert( _delimiters.
            end(), c );
    }
    // See whether a given character is in
      the list.
    virtual bool Contains( char c )
    {
        vector<char>::const_iterator iter;
        for ( iter = _delimiters.begin();
          iter != _delimiters.end(); ++iter )
            if ( c == (*iter) )
                return true;
        return false;
    }
    // Remove a given delimiter.
    virtual bool Remove( char c )
    {
        vector<char>::iterator iter;
        for ( iter = _delimiters.begin();
          iter != _delimiters.end(); ++iter )
            if ( c == (*iter) )
            {
```

(continued)

LISTING 42-1 *(continued)*

```cpp
                    _delimiters.erase( iter );
                    return true;
            }
        return false;
    }

};

// This class manages the data for a given row of a
// delimited file.
class DelimitedRow                              → 2
{
private:
    vector< string > _columns;
protected:
    virtual void Copy( const DelimitedRow& aCopy )
    {
        vector<string>::const_iterator iter;
        for ( iter = aCopy._columns.begin(); iter != aCopy._columns.end(); ++iter )
            _columns.insert( _columns.end(), (*iter) );
    }
public:
    DelimitedRow(void)
    {
    }
    DelimitedRow( const char *col )
    {
        Add( col );
    }
    virtual ~DelimitedRow()
    {
    }
    virtual void Add( const char *col )
    {
        _columns.insert( _columns.end(), col );
    }
    int NumColumns( void )
    {
        return _columns.size();
    }
    string getColumn( int index )
    {
        if ( index < 0 || index > NumColumns()-1 )
            return string("");
        return _columns[index];
    }
};
```

```
// This class will handle a single delimited file.
class DelimitedFileParser                    → 3
{
private:
    string                  _fileName;
    Delimiters              _delim;
    ifstream                _in;
    vector<DelimitedRow>    _rows;
protected:
    virtual void Copy( const DelimitedFileParser& aCopy )
    {
        _fileName = aCopy._fileName;
        _delim    = aCopy._delim;

        vector<DelimitedRow>::const_iterator iter;
        for ( iter = aCopy._rows.begin(); iter != aCopy._rows.end(); ++iter )
            _rows.insert( _rows.end(), (*iter) );
    }
    virtual void _ParseLine( string sIn )
    {
        // Given a delimiter list, and an input string, parse through
        // the string.
        DelimitedRow row;
        string sCol = "";
        for ( int i=0; i<sIn.length(); ++i )
        {
            if ( _delim.Contains( sIn[i] ) )
            {
                row.Add( sCol.c_str() );
                sCol = "";
            }
            else
                sCol += sIn[i];
        }
        row.Add( sCol.c_str() );
        _rows.insert( _rows.end(), row );

    }

public:
    DelimitedFileParser(void)
    {
    }
    DelimitedFileParser( const char *fileName, const char *delimiters )
        : _delim( delimiters )
    {
        Open( fileName );
    }
    DelimitedFileParser( const DelimitedFileParser& aCopy )
    {
        Copy ( aCopy );
    }
```

(continued)

LISTING 42-1 (continued)

```
virtual ~DelimitedFileParser()
{
    _in.close();
}
virtual bool Open( const char
  *fileName )
{
    _fileName = fileName;
    _in.open( _fileName.c_str() );
    return !_in.fail();
}
virtual bool Parse()
{
    // Make sure the file is open.
    if ( _in.fail() )
    {
        return false;
    }

    while ( !_in.eof() )
    {
        string sIn = "";

        while ( !_in.eof() )
        {
            // Get an input line.
            char c;
            _in.get(c);
            if ( _in.fail() )
                break;
            if ( c != '\r' && c !=
              '\n' )
                sIn += c;
            if ( c == '\n' )
                break;
        }
        // Parse it.
        if ( sIn.length() )
            _ParseLine( sIn );

    }

    return true;
}
int NumRows()
{
    return _rows.size();
}
DelimitedRow getRow( int index )
{
    if ( index < 0 || index >=
```

```
    NumRows() )
            throw "getRow: index out of
              range";
        return _rows[index];
    }
};
```

This code implements a generic parser and container of delimited files. By specifying the delimiter between fields, the end-of-record indicator, and the source filename, you can then use this class to read in and retrieve all of the individual fields in the file.

As you can see from the code, the entire application is made up of three classes, each of which manages a specific part of the process. The process has three parts: file management (shown at ➔ **3**), data storage (shown at ➔ **2**), and delimiter management (shown at ➔ **1**).

3. **Save the source file in the source-code editor and close the editor application.**

 Always separate the individual components of a process into separate classes. That way you can easily modify one piece of the process without affecting the rest of the system. More importantly, you can reuse smaller components in other applications without having to pull in the entire system.

Testing the Code

After you have created the functionality, you should create a test driver that not only ensures that your code is correct, but also shows people how to use your code.

The following steps show you how to create a test driver that illustrates how the file parser is used — and what the output will be.

1. **In the code editor of your choice, reopen the existing file to hold the code for your test program.**

In this example, I named the test program `ch42.cpp`.

2. **Append the code from Listing 42-2 into your file.**

   Better yet, copy the code from the source file on this book's companion Web site.

LISTING 42-2: THE DELIMITER TEST DRIVER

```
int main(int argc, char **argv)
{
    if ( argc < 2 )
    {
        printf("Usage ch5_2
<delimitedFile>\n");
        exit(1);
    }

    DelimitedFileParser fileParser( argv[1],
      ":" );

    fileParser.Parse();

    printf("%d Rows found\n",
      fileParser.NumRows() );
    for ( int i=0; i<fileParser.NumRows();
      ++i )
    {
        DelimitedRow row =
          fileParser.getRow(i);
        printf("Row: %d\n", i );
        for ( int j=0; j<row.NumColumns();
          ++j )
            printf("Column %d = [%s]\n", j,
              row.getColumn(j).c_str() );
    }

}
```

3. **Save the source-code file and close the code-editor application.**

4. **Create a test file for testing the application in the text editor of your choice.**

   This file is used for input to the application and contains the delimited records.

   In this case, I used the name `test_delimited.txt` for the test file.

5. **Type the following text into the test file:**

   ```
   Line 1:Column 2:This is a
      test:100:200:300
   Line 2:Column 2:This is another
      test:200:300:400
   ```

6. **Save the test file and close the code-editor application.**

7. **Compile and run the program with your favorite compiler and operating system.**

If you have done everything properly, you should see the following output from the program on your console window:

```
$ ./a.exe test_delimited.txt
2 Rows found
Row: 0
Column 0 = [Line 1]
Column 1 = [Column 2]
Column 2 = [This is a test]
Column 3 = [100]
Column 4 = [200]
Column 5 = [300]
Row: 1
Column 0 = [Line 2]
Column 1 = [Column 2]
Column 2 = [This is another test]
Column 3 = [200]
Column 4 = [300]
Column 5 = [400]
```

As you can see from the output, the parser properly determines that there are two records in the test file that we gave it for input. Each of the input lines contains five columns of data, separated by a colon (:) character. By telling the parser that the delimiter is a colon, it then breaks each line into individual columns and returns that data to the user as a `DelimitedRow` object in a vector of such objects.

This class can now be moved from project to project, in any situation where we need to read in a delimited file and use the individual components of each record (or line) in the file. This saves us time in implementing the functionality over and over, and saves us effort because the code will already be debugged.

Technique 43

Writing Your Objects as XML

Save Time By

- ✔ Comparing XML code to C++ code
- ✔ Using XML to store and restore data to and from C++ classes
- ✔ Creating an XMLWriter class
- ✔ Testing your XMLWriter class
- ✔ Interpreting your output

The current buzzword of the programming world is *XML* and *XML compatibility*. XML, which stands for eXtended Markup Language, is really just a variant of the SGML display language (from which HTML was also derived) that has been optimized for data storage instead of for display.

It's no surprise that the capability to output data as XML code has become very important in the programming world. Because the structure of XML is so much like the structure of C++ — in terms of hierarchical display and classes and attributes — you can easily use XML to store and restore data to and from C++ classes.

The general format of an XML structure is as follows:

```
<xml>
    <structure-name>
        <element-name>
            value
        </element-name>
    </structure-name>
</xml>
```

As you can see, it looks very much like a C++ class structure with a structure name as the name of the class and an element name as the name of each piece of member data of that class. Here's an example:

```
Class Foo
{
    int x; // We can think of the semicolon as </int>
    // And so forth
};
```

In the above class definition, we have an object name (class `Foo`), an element (`int`), and a value for that element (`x`). This maps quite directly into the XML general schema. The initial definition was a true XML object, whereas this definition is a true C++ class. Yet you can see how one maps to the other. We could write the above class as

```
<Foo>
   <int> x </int>
</Foo>
```

and, as you can see, the two map quite well. By storing data in XML format, we make it possible to read the data not only into C++ applications, but also into any other applications that understand the XML format, such as databases. Storing data in a known, standard format saves time by eliminating the need to write translators for your data formats, and by allowing you to use existing applications with your data. In this example, we will look at how to write out a C++ class in XML format, and then how to read back in that XML data to a C++ class.

Creating the XML Writer

The first step in the process is to add the ability to write out the data for our class in XML format. We will call the element that does this processing an XMLWriter object. Let's look at a generic way to create an XMLWriter that will save us time by allowing us to apply this functionality to all objects in our system.

1. **In the code editor of your choice, create a new file to hold the code for the definition of the class.**

In this example, the file is named ch43.cpp, although you can use whatever you choose. This file will contain the class definition for the needed automation object.

2. **Type the code from Listing 43-1 into your file.**

Better yet, copy the code from the source file on this book's companion Web site.

LISTING 43-1: THE XML WRITER CLASS

```
#include <stdio.h>
#include <string>
#include <vector>
#include <fstream>
```

```
using namespace std;

// Class to manage the storage of the XML
   data.

class XMLElement
{
private:
    string _name;
    string _value;
    vector< XMLElement > _subElements;
protected:
    virtual void Init()
    {
        _name = "";
        _value = "";
        _subElements.erase(
    _subElements.begin(), _subElements.end()
    );
    }
    virtual void Copy( const XMLElement&
      aCopy )
    {
        setName( aCopy.getName().c_str() );
        setValue ( aCopy.getValue().c_str()
    );

        vector< XMLElement >::const_
          iterator iter;
        for ( iter =
          aCopy._subElements.begin();
                iter !=
          aCopy._subElements.end();
                   ++iter )
            _subElements.insert
    ( _subElements.end(), (*iter) );
    }
public:
    XMLElement( void )
    {
        Init();
    }
    XMLElement( const char *name, const
      char *value )
    {
        setName( name );
        setValue( value );
    }
    XMLElement( const char *name, int
      value )
    {
```

(continued)

LISTING 43-1 *(continued)*

```cpp
        setName( name );
        char szBuffer[10];
        sprintf(szBuffer, "%d", value );
        setValue( szBuffer );
    }
    XMLElement( const char *name, double
      value )
    {
        setName( name );
        char szBuffer[10];
        sprintf(szBuffer, "%lf", value );
        setValue( szBuffer );
    }

    XMLElement( const XMLElement& aCopy )
    {
        Copy( aCopy );
    }
    virtual ~XMLElement()
    {
    }
    XMLElement operator=( const XMLElement&
      aCopy )
    {
        Copy( aCopy );
        return *this;
    }

    // Accessors
    void setName( const char *name )
    {
        _name = name;
    }
    void setValue( const char *value )
    {
        _value = value;
    }
    string getName( void ) const
    {
        return _name;
    }
    string getValue( void ) const
    {
        return _value;
    }
```

```cpp
    // Sub-element maintenance.
    void addSubElement( const XMLElement&
      anElement )
    {
        _subElements.insert( _subElements.
          end(), anElement );
    }
    int numSubElements( void )
    {
        return _subElements.size();
    }
    XMLElement& getSubElement( int index )
    {
        if ( index < 0 || index >=
          numSubElements() )
            throw "getSubElement: index out
              of range";
        return _subElements[ index ];
    }
};

// Class to manage the output of XML data.
class XMLWriter
{
private:
    ofstream _out;
public:
    XMLWriter( void )
    {
    }
    XMLWriter( const char *fileName )
    {
        _out.open(fileName);
        if ( _out.fail() == false )
        {
            _out << "<xml>" << endl;
        }
    }
    XMLWriter( const XMLWriter& aCopy )
    {
    }
    virtual ~XMLWriter()
    {
        if ( _out.fail() == false )
        {
            _out << "</xml>" << endl;
        }
        _out.close();
    }
```

```
void setFileName( const char *fileName )
{
    _out.open(fileName);
    if ( _out.fail() == false )
    {
        _out << "<xml>" << endl;
    }
}
virtual bool Write( XMLElement& aRoot )
{
    if ( _out.fail() )
        return false;

    // First, process the element.
    _out << "<" <<
aRoot.getName().c_str() << ">" << endl;

        // If there is a value, output it.
        if ( aRoot.getValue().length()
          != 0 )
            _out << aRoot.getValue().c_str()
              << endl;

        // Now, process all sub-elements.
        for ( int i=0;
i<aRoot.numSubElements(); ++i )
            Write( aRoot.getSubElement(i) );

        // Finally, close the element.
        _out << "</" <<
aRoot.getName().c_str() << ">" << endl;

    }
};
```

This listing illustrates the basics of our XML writing functionality. Each element of an XML object will be stored in an XMLElement object. The writer (XMLWriter class) then processes each of these elements to output them in valid XML format.

3. Save the source-code file and close your editor application.

4. Compile the application with your favorite compiler, on your favorite operating system, to verify that you have made no errors.

Testing the XML Writer

After you create the class, you should create a test driver that not only ensures that your code is correct, but also shows people how to use your code.

The following steps show you how to create a test driver that illustrates various types of data elements, and will illustrate how the class is intended to be used.

1. In the code editor of your choice, reopen the source file for your test program.

In this example, I named the test program ch43.cpp.

2. Type the code from Listing 43-2 into your file.

Better yet, copy the code from the source file on this book's companion Web site.

LISTING 43-2: THE XMLWRITER TEST CODE

```
class XmlTest
{
private:
    int iVal;
    string sVal;
    double dVal;
public:
    XmlTest()
    {
        iVal = 100;
        sVal = "Test";
        dVal = 123.45;
    }
    ~XmlTest()
    {
    }
    XMLElement getXML(void)
    {
        XMLElement e("XmlTest", "");
        e.addSubElement(
          XMLElement("iVal", iVal) );
        e.addSubElement(
          XMLElement("sVal", sVal.
          c_str()) );
        e.addSubElement(
          XMLElement("dVal", dVal) );
        return e;
```

(continued)

LISTING 43-2 *(continued)*

```
    }
};

class XmlSuperClass                              → 1
{
    XmlTest xt;                                  → 2
    int     count;
public:
    XmlSuperClass()
    {
        count = 1;
    }
    ~XmlSuperClass()
    {
    }
    XMLElement getXML()
    {
        // First, do ourselves
        XMLElement e("XmlSuperClass", "");
        e.addSubElement(
           XMLElement("count", count) );

        // Now the sub-object
        e.addSubElement( xt.getXML() );

        return e;
    }
};
 void TestWriter1(void)
 {
     XMLElement ele1("Sub-Element1", "123");
     XMLElement ele2("Sub-Element2", "234");
     XMLElement subele1("Sub-Sub-Element1",
     "345");
     XMLElement subele2("Sub-Sub-Element2",
     "456");
     XMLElement root("Root", "");

     ele1.addSubElement( subele1 );
     ele2.addSubElement( subele2 );
     root.addSubElement( ele1 );
     root.addSubElement( ele2 );

     XMLWriter writer("test.xml");
     writer.Write( root );
 }
```

```
void TestWriter2(void)
{
    XmlSuperClass xsc;
    XMLWriter writer("test2.xml");
    XMLElement e = xsc.getXML();
    writer.Write( e );
}


int main()
{
    TestWriter1();
    TestWriter2();
    return 0;
}
```

3. **Save the source-code file and close the editor application.**

4. **Compile the application, using your favorite compiler on your favorite operating system.**

If you have done everything properly, running the application results in the creation of two files, test.xml and test2.xml. If you look at the contents of these files, you should see the following:

```
test.xml:
$ cat test.xml
<xml>
<Root>
<Sub-Element1>
123
<Sub-Sub-Element1>
345
</Sub-Sub-Element1>
</Sub-Element1>
<Sub-Element2>
234
<Sub-Sub-Element2>
456
</Sub-Sub-Element2>
</Sub-Element2>
</Root>
</xml>
```

```
test2.xml:
$ cat test2.xml
<xml>
<XmlSuperClass>                    → 3
<count>
1
</count>
<XmlTest>                          → 4
<iVal>                             → 5
100
</iVal>
<sVal>
Test
</sVal>
<dVal>
123.450000
</dVal>
</XmlTest>
</XmlSuperClass>
</xml>
```

If we look at the class hierarchy shown in the application source code, we see that the main class, XmlSuperClass (shown at → 1), contains both standard data elements (count, an integer) and embedded objects (XmlTest, shown at → 2). In the XML output, we see these elements at the lines marked → 3 and → 4. Note how the embedded class contains its own elements (shown at → 5 in the output list) which are children of both the XmlTest and XmlSuperClass classes.

The code shows that both cases work fine — the simple case of using the XMLElement and XMLWriter classes, and the embedded case of outputting an entire C++ class with an embedded C++ object.

Technique 44

Removing White Space from Input

Although it might not seem like a big deal, dealing with white space in input from either files or the console can be a major pain in the neck for C++ programmers. After all, white space isn't empty; it has to be accounted for. When you want to store a user name in your database, for example, do you really want to store any leading and trailing spaces, tabs, or other non-printing characters? If you do so, the users will then have to remember to type those spaces in again whenever they log in to your application. While this might be a useful security condition, it seems unlikely that anyone would remember to add either leading or trailing spaces to a user name or password in an application.

For this reason, if you give your code the capability to strip off leading and trailing spaces from a given string with no fuss — and return that string to the calling application — you save a lot of time and hassle. This technique looks at creating that exact capability. The following steps show you how:

1. **In the code editor of your choice, create a new file to hold the code for the implementation of the source file.**

   In this example, the file is named ch44.cpp, although you can use whatever you choose.

2. **Type the code from Listing 44-1 into your file.**

   Better yet, copy the code from the source file on this book's companion Web site.

LISTING 44-1: THE WHITE SPACE REMOVAL CODE

```
#include <string>
#include <ctype.h>

// Nobody wants to have to type std:: for
// all of the STL functions.
using namespace std;
```

```cpp
string strip_leading( const string& sIn )
{
    string sOut;

    // Skip over all leading spaces.
    unsigned int nPos = 0;
    while ( nPos < sIn.length() )
    {
        if ( !isspace(sIn[nPos]) )
            break;
        nPos ++;
    }

    // Now we have the starting position of
    // the "real" string. Copy to the end...
    while ( nPos < sIn.length() )
    {
        sOut += sIn[nPos];
        nPos ++;
    }

    // ...and give back the new string,
    // without modifying the input string.
    return sOut;
}

string strip_trailing( const string& sIn )
{
    string sOut;

    // Skip over all trailing spaces.
    int nPos = sIn.length()-1;
    while ( nPos >= 0 )
    {
        if ( !isspace(sIn[nPos]) )
            break;
        nPos --;
    }

    // Now we have the ending position of
    // the "real" string. Copy from the
    // beginning to that position...
    for ( int i=0; i<=nPos; ++i )
        sOut += sIn[i];
```

→ 1

```cpp
    // ...and give back the new string,
    // without modifying the input string.
    return sOut;
}

int main(int argc, char **argv )
{
    if ( argc > 2 )
    {
        printf("Removing Leading Spaces\n");
        for ( int i = 1; i < argc; ++i )
        {
            printf("Input String: [%s]\n",
              argv[i] );
            string s = argv[i];
            s = strip_leading( s );
            printf("Result String: [%s]\n",
              s.c_str() );
        }
        printf("Removing Trailing
          Spaces\n");
        for ( int i = 1; i < argc; ++i )
        {
            printf("Input String: [%s]\n",
              argv[i] );
            string s = argv[i];
            s = strip_trailing( s );
            printf("Result String: [%s]\n",
              s.c_str() );
        }
        printf("Removing both leading and
          trailing\n");
        for ( int i = 1; i < argc; ++i )
        {
            printf("Input String: [%s]\n",
              argv[i] );
            string s = argv[i];
            s = strip_trailing( strip_
              leading(s) );
            printf("Result String: [%s]\n",
              s.c_str() );
        }
    }
    else
    {
```

(continued)

LISTING 44-1 (continued)

```
        bool bDone = false;
        while ( !bDone )
        {
            char szBuffer[ 80 ];
            printf("Enter string to fix: ");
            gets(szBuffer);
            printf("Input string: [%s]\n",
              szBuffer );

            // Strip the trailing carriage
              return.
            if ( strlen(szBuffer) )
                szBuffer[strlen(szBuffer)-1]
                = 0;
            if ( !strlen(szBuffer) )
                bDone = true;
            else
            {
                string s = szBuffer;
                s = strip_leading( s );
                printf("After removing
                  leading: %s\n", s.c_str() );
                s = strip_trailing( s );
                printf("After removing
                  trailing: %s\n", s.c_str()
                  );
            }
        }

        return 0;
    }
```

3. **Save the source-code file and close the editor application.**

4. **Compile the application with your favorite compiler on your favorite operating system.**

If you have done everything properly, and you run the program with the following command-line options, you should see the following output in your console window:

```
$ ./a "   this is a test   " " hello   "
  "    goodbye"
Removing Leading Spaces
Input String: [   this is a test   ]        → 2
Result String: [this is a test   ]          → 3
Input String: [ hello   ]
Result String: [hello   ]
Input String: [    goodbye]
Result String: [goodbye]
Removing Trailing Spaces
Input String: [   this is a test   ]
Result String: [   this is a test]          → 4
Input String: [ hello   ]
Result String: [ hello]
Input String: [    goodbye]
Result String: [    goodbye]
Removing both leading and trailing
Input String: [   this is a test   ]
Result String: [this is a test]             → 5
Input String: [ hello   ]
Result String: [hello]
Input String: [    goodbye]
Result String: [goodbye]
```

Stripping any trailing white space from a string is a simple endeavor. You just find the last white space character and truncate the string at that point. Stripping leading white space, on the other hand, is a more complicated problem. As you can see at the line marked → **1** in the source listing, you must create a separate string to use for the return value of the strip_leading function. This string is then built-up by finding the first non-blank character in the input string and then copying everything from that point to the end of the string into the output string. The output string is then returned to the calling application *sans* leading white space.

In the output, we see that each string is input into the system, then the various white space characters in the front and back of the string are removed. In each case, the string is output to the user to view how it is modified. For example, if we look at the input line at → **2**, we see that it contains both leading and trailing spaces. When the strip_leading function is applied, we get the result shown at → **3**, which is the same string with no leading spaces. When the strip_trailing function is applied, we get the result shown at → **4**, which is the same string with no trailing spaces. Finally, we apply both of the functions at the same time, and get the result shown at → **5**, which has neither leading nor trailing spaces.

You can also test the application by typing in data from the prompt by running the application with no input arguments. Here is a sample of what the test looks like in that form:

```
$ ./a.exe
Enter string to fix:    this is a test
Input string: [   this is a test ]
After removing leading: this is a test
After removing trailing: this is a test
Enter string to fix:
Input string: []
```

As you can see, input from either the command line or from user entries (whether from the keyboard or a file) can contain white space. This white space must be removed to look at the "real" strings in many cases, and these functions will save you a lot of time by doing it for you automatically.

Creating a Configuration File

Configuration files are a basic part of any application that needs to be portable across various operating systems. Because of differ-ences in binary formats and "endian" concerns (placement of the most significant byte), configuration files are normally stored in text for-mat. This is somewhat problematic, as it requires the application to be able to load, parse, and work with the entries in a configuration file, while interpreting the data that is stored there. Because the format is text, you must worry about the user modifying the text files, changing them so that they are no longer in a valid format, and the like. It would make sense, therefore, if there were a standard interface to a configuration file, and a standard format for using text-based configuration files. This would allow you to use a standard format in all of your applications, saving you time and effort.

This technique shows you how to develop a method for storing data in the simplest possible fashion in a configuration file (text based), while still allowing the users to store the kinds of data they need. A typical entry in one of our configuration files would look like this:

```
# This is a comment
Value = "    This is a test"
```

The first line of the entry is a comment field — ignored by the parser — that tells any reader of the configuration file why the specific data is stored in this key (and how it might be interpreted or modified). The sec-ond line is the value itself, which is made up of two pieces:

✔ The keyword that we are defining, in this case `Value`.

✔ The complete string assigned to this value, with embedded and possi-bly leading spaces. In this case, our value string is `"    This is a test"`. Note that when read in, the string will contain leading spaces, as the user wished. Note that the only reason that we store these spaces is that they are contained in quotation marks, indicating the user wished to keep them. If the spaces were simply on the leading and trailing edges of strings in the entry without quotation marks, we would remove them.

The capability to configure applications is the hallmark of a professional program. If you build in the configuration options from the start of the design (rather than hacking on some configurations at the end of the process), the result is a much more robust and extensible application. Even if you add new options later on, the basis for the code will already be there.

Creating the Configuration-File Class

The configuration-file class encapsulates the reading, parsing, and storing of the data in the text-based configuration file. The following steps show you how to build a stand-alone class that can simply be moved from application to application, allowing you to save time and have a consistent interface.

1. **In the code editor of your choice, create a new file to hold the definition for your configuration-file class.**

In this example, the file is named `ConfigurationFile.h`, although you can use whatever you choose.

2. **Type the code from Listing 45-1 into your file.**

Better yet, copy the code from the source file on this book's companion Web site.

LISTING 45-1: THE CONFIGURATION FILE'S HEADER FILE

```
#ifndef _CONFIGURATIONFILE_H_
#define _CONFIGURATIONFILE_H_

#include <string>
#include <vector>
#include <fstream>
#include <map>
#include <list>

using namespace std;
```

```
class ConfigurationFile
{
public:
    ConfigurationFile(const char
    *strFileName);
    virtual ~ConfigurationFile(void);
    bool read(void);

    bool    hasValue( const char *key );
    string getValue( const char *key );
    void    setValue( const char *key, const
    char *value );

protected:
    virtual void    get_token_and_value();
    virtual char
    eat_white_and_comments(bool traverse_
    newlines=true);
    virtual bool
    advance_to_equal_sign_on_line();
    virtual void    makeLower
    (string &instring);

protected:
    fstream         m_in;
    string          m_token;
    string          m_value;
    string              m_sConfigFile;
    typedef pair <string, string>
    String_Pair;
    map<string, string> m_ConfigEntries;
};

#endif
```

This file contains the definition of the class; it contains no code for manipulating the data. The header file acts as the interface for other applications to use the class, as we will see. It is best to separate your actual implementation code from your definition, as this helps emphasize the encapsulation concept of C++.

3. **Save the source-code file.**

4. **In the code editor of your choice, create a new file to hold the definition for the configuration-file class.**

In this example, the file is named
ConfigurationFile.cpp, although you can use
whatever you choose.

5. Type the code from Listing 45-2 into your file.

LISTING 45-2: THE CONFIGURATION FILE SOURCE CODE.

```cpp
#include "ConfigurationFile.h"
#include <errno.h>
#include <algorithm>
#include <sstream>
#include <iostream>
#include <string>

template <class T>
bool from_string(T &t,
                 const std::string &s,
                 std::ios_base &
   (*f)(std::ios_base&))
{
   std::istringstream iss(s);
   return !(iss>>f>>t).fail();
}


class StringUtil                        → 1
{
public:
   StringUtil() {}
   ~StringUtil() {}

   // Find the given string in the source
      string and replace it with the
   // "replace" string, everywhere
      instances of that string exist.
   static void findandreplace( string&
source, const string& find, const string&
   replace )
   {
      size_t j;
      for (;(j = source.find( find ))
        != string::npos;)
      {
         source.replace( j,
            find.length(), replace );
      }
   }
```

```cpp
// The following function returns a
   string with all-uppercase characters.
static string makeUpper( const string&
   instring)
{
   string temp=instring;
   transform( temp.begin(), temp.end(),
     temp.begin(), ::toupper );
   return temp;
}


// The following function returns a
   string with all-lowercase characters.
static string makeLower( const string&
   instring)
{
   string temp;
   transform( temp.begin(), temp.end(),
     temp.begin(), ::tolower );
   return temp;
}

static bool contains( const string&
   source, const char *find )
{
   return ( 0!=strstr(source.
     c_str(),find) );
}

static string pad( const string&
instring, char padchar, int length )
{
   string outstring = instring;

   for ( int i=(int)outstring.length();
i<length; ++i )
      outstring += padchar;

   return outstring;
}

// Trim the given characters from the
   beginning and end of a string.
// the default is to trim whitespace.
   If the string is empty or contains
// only the trim characters, an empty
   string is returned.
static string trim( const string
   &instring,
                     const string
&trimstring=string(" \t\n"))
```

```
    {
        if (trimstring.size()==0) return
          instring;

        string temp="";
        string::size_type begpos=instring.find_first_not_of (trimstring);
        if (begpos==string::npos)
        {
            return temp;
        }
        else
        {
            string::size_type endpos=instring.find_last_not_of (trimstring);
            temp=instring.substr(begpos,
endpos-begpos+1);
        }
        return temp;
    }

    // Convert the string to an int. Note that a string exception is thrown if
    // it is invalid.
    static int toInt(const string & myInString)
    {
        int i=0;
        string inString = trim(myInString);

        if( !from_string<int>(i, inString, std::dec) )
        {
            string exceptionText = "StringUtils::toInt() - Not an integer: " + inString;
            throw exceptionText;
        }

        // Time to run some more checks.
        for (unsigned int j=0; j < inString.length(); j++)
        {
            if ( !isNumeric(inString[j]) )
            {
                if (j==0 && inString[j] =='-')
                {
                    continue;
                }
                else
                {
                    string exceptionText = "StringUtils::toInt() - Not an integer: " +
                        inString;
                    throw exceptionText;
                }
            }
        }
    }
```

(continued)

LISTING 45-2 *(continued)*

```cpp
        return (i);
    }

    // Convert the string to an int. Note:
A string exception is thrown if
    // it is invalid.
    static float toFloat(const string & myInString)
    {
        float f=0;
        string inString = trim(myInString);

        if( !from_string<float>(f, inString, std::dec) )
        {
            string exceptionText = "StringUtils::toFloat() - Not a float: " + inString;
            throw exceptionText;
        }

        // Now it runs some more checks.
        int dec_count=0;
        for (unsigned int j=0; j < inString.length(); j++)
        {
            if ( !isNumeric(inString[j]) )
            {
                if (j==0 && inString[j] =='-')
                {
                    continue;
                }
                else if (inString[j]=='.')
                {
                    dec_count++;
                    if (dec_count > 1)
                    {
                        string exceptionText = "StringUtils::toFloat() - Not a float: " +
                            inString;
                        throw exceptionText;
                    }
                    continue;
                }
                else
                {
                    string exceptionText = "StringUtils::toFloat() - Not a float: " + inString;
                    throw exceptionText;
                }
            }
        }


        return (f);
    }
```

```
// Returns true if the character is numeric.
static bool isNumeric(char c)
{
    return ('0' <= c && c <= '9');
}


// Replace environment variables in the string with their values.
// Note: environment variables must be of the form ${ENVVAR}.
static string substituteEnvVar( const string &myInString )
{
    string outString="";
    char variable[512];

    const char *s = myInString.c_str();
    while(*s!=0)
    {
        if (*s=='$' && *(s+1)=='{')
        {
            // When you've found beginning of variable, find the end.
            strcpy(variable,s+2);
            char *end = strchr (variable,'}');
            if (end)
            {
                *end='\0';
                char *cp = (char *)getenv(variable);
                if (cp)
                    outString += (char *) getenv(variable);
                s = strchr(s,'}');
            }
            else
            {
                outString += *s;
            }

        }
        else
        {
            outString += *s;
        }
        s++;
    }

    return outString;

}


};
```

(continued)

LISTING 45-2 *(continued)*

```
ConfigurationFile::ConfigurationFile( const char *strConfigFile )                    ➔ 2
{
    if ( strConfigFile )
        m_sConfigFile = strConfigFile;
}

ConfigurationFile::~ConfigurationFile()
{
}

bool ConfigurationFile::read()                                                        ➔ 3
{
    m_in.open(m_sConfigFile.
  c_str(),ios::in);

    if (m_in.fail())
    {
        return false;
    }
    while (!m_in.eof())
    {
        //----------------------------------------------------------
        // Get a token and value.
        // This gives values to member vars: m_token and m_value.
        //----------------------------------------------------------
        get_token_and_value();

        if ( m_token.length() )
            m_ConfigEntries.insert( String_
  Pair(m_token, m_value) );

    }
    m_in.close();

    return true;

}

void ConfigurationFile::get_token_and_
    value(void)
{
    char token[1024];
    char ch;
    bool found_equal=false;

    int i=0;
    eat_white_and_comments();
    while(!(m_in.get(ch)).fail())
    {
        if ((ch != '\t'))
        {
```

```
            if ( (ch == '=') || (ch == ' ') || (ch == '\n') || (ch == '\r') ||
                (ch == '\t'))
            {
                if (ch == '=')found_equal=true;
                break;
            }
            token[i++]=ch;
        }
    }

    if (i==0)
    {
        // It didn't find a token, in this case.
        m_token="";
        m_value="";
        return;
    }

    // Null-terminate the token that was found.
    token[i++]='\0';
    m_token = token;
    makeLower(m_token);

    // Advance to the equal sign, if need be.
    if (!found_equal)
    {
        if (!advance_to_equal_sign_on_line())
        {
            // The token had no value.
            m_token="";
            m_value="";
            return;
        }
    }

    // Get the token's value.
    i=0;
    char c = eat_white_and_comments(false);

    if ( c != '\n' )
    {
        i=0;
        while(!(m_in.get(ch)).fail())
        {
            if ((ch == '\t') || (ch == '\r') ||  (ch == '\n') || (ch == '#') )
            {
                while (ch!='\n')
                {
                    if (m_in.get(ch).fail()) break;
                }
```

(continued)

LISTING 45-2 *(continued)*

```
                break;
            }
            else
            {
                token[i++]=ch;
            }
        }
    }

    if (i==0)
    {
        // This token had no value.
        m_value="";
    }
    else
    {
        token[i++]='\0';
        m_value=token;

        // Remove leading/trailing spaces.
        m_value = StringUtil::trim(m_value);
        // Strip leading and trailing quotes, if there are any.
        if ( m_value[0] == '"' )
            m_value = m_value.substr( 1 );
        if ( m_value[ m_value.length() -1 ] == '"' )
            m_value = m_value.substr( 0, m_value.length()-1 );
    }

}

bool
ConfigurationFile::advance_to_equal_sign_on_line()
{
    char ch;
    bool found_equal=false;

    while ( !(m_in.get(ch)).fail() )
    {
        if ((ch=='\r')||(ch=='\n')) break;
        if (ch == '=')
        {
            found_equal=true;
            break;
        }
    }

    return found_equal;
}


char
ConfigurationFile::eat_white_and_comments
```

```
  (bool traverse_newlines)
{
  char ch;
  bool in_comment;

  in_comment = false;
  while (!(m_in.get(ch)).fail())
    if (ch == '#')
      in_comment = true;
    else if (ch == '\n')
    {
      in_comment = false;
      if (!traverse_newlines)
      {
          return(ch); // Stop eating.
      }
    }
    else if ((!in_comment) && (ch != ' ') &&
(ch != '\t') && (ch != '\r'))
      {
        m_in.putback(ch);
        return 0;
      }

  return 0;
}

void ConfigurationFile::makeLower
   (string &instring)
{
  for(unsigned i=0; i < instring.size();
   i++)
  {
      instring[i] = tolower(instring[i]);
  }
}

bool ConfigurationFile::hasValue( const char
   *key )                            → 4
{
    bool bRet = false;
    std::string sKey = key;
    makeLower( sKey );
    if ( m_ConfigEntries.find( sKey.c_str()
) != m_ConfigEntries.end() )
    {
        bRet = true;
    }
    return bRet;
}

string ConfigurationFile::getValue( const
   char *key )
{
    std::string sKey = key;
    makeLower( sKey );
    if ( m_ConfigEntries.find( sKey.
c_str() ) != m_ConfigEntries.end() )
    {
        std::map<string, string>::iterator
          iter;
        iter =
m_ConfigEntries.find(sKey.c_str());
        return (*iter).second;
    }
    return "";
}

void ConfigurationFile::setValue( const char
   *key, const char *value )
{
    std::string sKey = key;
    makeLower( sKey );

    m_ConfigEntries[sKey] = value;
}
```

Our source code above breaks down into three general pieces. First, we separate out all of the utility routines that work with strings and characters and place them in the StringUtil utility class (shown at the line marked with → **1**). Next, we have the actual configuration-file class, shown at the line marked with → **2**. This class manages the storage and processing of the file. The processing is done in the read function, shown at → **3**, and the storage functions begin with the line marked → **4**. As you can see, the routine simply reads in a line from the input file and separates it into two pieces, divided by an equal sign. Comments, which are lines that are either blank or marked with a pound sign ('#') are ignored. Everything to the left of the equal sign is considered to be the "tag," while everything to the right of the equal sign is considered to be the "value." Tag and value pairs make up the configuration data. The retrieval routines work by allowing the user to see if a given tag is defined, and if so to retrieve its value.

6. **Save the source file in the source code editor.**

Setting Up Your Test File

After you create any class, you should create a test driver that not only ensures that your code is correct, but also shows people how to use your code.

The following steps show you how to create a test driver that illustrates how the class is intended to be used:

1. **In the code editor of your choice, reopen the source file to hold the code for your test program.**

In this example, I named the test program ch45.cpp.

2. **Type the code from Listing 45-3 into your file.**

Better yet, copy the code from the source file on this book's companion Web site.

LISTING 45-3: THE CONFIGURATION-FILE TEST CODE

```
#include <stdio.h>
#include "ConfigurationFile.h"

int main( int argc, char **argv )
{
    if ( argc < 3 )
    {
        printf("Usage: ch5_7 config-file-
name arg1 [arg2 .. ]\n");
        printf("Where:      config-file-
name is the name of the configuration
file\n");
        printf("            arg1 .. argn
are the values to print out\n");
        return -1;
    }

    ConfigurationFile cf(argv[1]);
    if ( cf.read() == false )
    {
        printf("Unable to read configuration
file\n");
        return -2;
    }
```

```
    for ( int i=2; i<argc; ++i )
    {
        if ( !cf.hasValue( argv[i] ) )
        {
            printf("Value %s NOT found in
configuration file\n", argv[i] );
        }
        else
        {
            string s = cf.getValue
( argv[i] );
            printf("Key %s = [%s]\n",
argv[i], s.c_str() );
        }
    }

    return 0;
}
```

3. **Save the source-code file in the code editor.**

4. **In the code editor of your choice, create a new text file to hold the actual configuration test file for your test program.**

In this example, I named the test input data file input.cfg.

5. **Type the following text into your file:**

```
Color=Blue                          → 5
Name=Matt                           → 6
Address="      "
City="Denver, CO"                   → 7
ZipCode=80232
#This is a comment
```

Testing the Configuration-File Class

Now that everything's set up, the following steps show you how to put it all together and go for a test drive:

1. **Compile and run the source-code file (which we called** ch45_7.cpp) **along with the configuration-class file (which we called** ConfigurationFile.cpp) **in your favorite compiler, on your favorite operating system.**

2. **Run the program.**

If you have done everything right, you should see the following output in your console window:

```
$ ./a.exe input.cfg Color Name City State
Key Color = [Blue]
Key Name = [Matt]
Key City = [Denver, CO]
Value State NOT found in configuration
     file                                  → 8
```

Looking at the input file, you can see that the values of Color, Name, and City are all entries (on the left-hand side of the equal sign). For those keys, the values are Blue, Matt, and Denver, CO. These items are shown at the lines marked with → **5**, → **6** and → **7**. The test driver simply reads the configuration file using our configuration-file class and then displays the various key and value pairs. The test driver then exercises the full functionality of the retrieval code by looking for a value (State) that is not in the configuration file, and the code properly displays an error as shown by the line marked with → **8**. From this output, and the test driver code, you can see exactly how the configuration-file class was meant to be used, making it excellent documentation for the developer. You can also see from the listing that the output is what we were expecting, which makes it a good unit test. All in all, it shows just how you can save time and effort by using a standardized configuration format and using this class to read it.

Part VII

Using the Built-In Functionality

BIKER I.S. GUYS

TATTOOS

"Remember—I want the bleeding file server surrounded by flaming workstations with the word 'Motherboard' scrolling underneath."

Technique 46

Creating an Internationalization Class

Save Time By

- ✔ Understanding internationalization
- ✔ Building language files
- ✔ Reading an international file
- ✔ Creating a string reader
- ✔ Testing your code

Once upon a time, if you were programming in the United States, you tailored your applications only for English-speaking Americans. Your main concern was the code that implemented the algorithms that were in your application; if you had an error message to display, you'd write a message that vaguely expressed the error and the user would just have to deal with it — no matter what language he spoke or how confusing the error message was. Fortunately, those days of usability-challenged code are over. Experts now create messages and indicators for applications so users can best understand what is going on. The error messages themselves are usually tailored to specific customer bases. Most importantly, however, our code is no longer directed only towards English-speaking Americans. Applications are distributed around the world, and need to work in any language, with any alphabet set. The capability to display messages in any language is known as *internationalization*.

You can't simply bolt an internationalization feature onto your program — you have to design that capability in from the beginning. You can't just translate messages on the fly, either; you have to know up front what the message is going to say. For this reason, creating a system that supports internationalization is important.

The process of internationalization is really threefold:

1. Identify all of the text that needs to be displayed in the various languages. Place this text into a single file, along with identifiers that can be used within the application to display the text.

2. Convert the text into a format that can be shipped easily with the application.

3. Provide a method to access all this content.

Only by doing all this can we save time when creating applications in multiple languages. If you write applications with any sort of regional or international appeal, eventually you must internationalize them. By building in this support up front — and giving the application the capability to load those literal strings from external sources — you not only save time later on, but also save huge amounts of space in your application memory. This approach also allows you to customize your error messages and display prompts directed to different age and regional groups. This is the procedure we will be using in this technique to illustrate how to save time and effort up front by creating a single way in which to internationalize your applications.

Building the Language Files

Before you can display text, you need to be able to build files that contain the language data. You

don't want to store all possible languages in your application because that would cause the memory requirements to go through the roof. So we store our languages in compressed-text format by squeezing out the returns and spaces between the items of data. These steps show you how:

1. **In the code editor of your choice, create a new file to hold the code for the source file of the technique.**

In this example, the file is named ch46.cpp, although you can use whatever you choose. This file will contain the class definition for our automation object.

2. **Type the code from Listing 46-1 into your file.**

Better yet, copy the code from the source file on this book's companion Web site.

LISTING 46-1: THE STRINGENTRY CLASS

```cpp
#include <stdio.h>
#include <string>
#include <vector>
#include <iostream>
#include <fstream>

using namespace std;

#define VERSION_STRING "Version 1.0.0"

class StringEntry
{
private:
    unsigned long _id;
    string        _strEntry;
    unsigned long _offset;
    unsigned long _length;
protected:
    void Init()
    {
        setID ( 0 );
        setString( "" );
```

```
        setOffset( 0 );
        setLength( 0 );
    }
    void Copy( const StringEntry& aCopy )
    {
        setID ( aCopy.ID() );
        setString( aCopy.String() );
        setOffset( aCopy.Offset() );
        setLength ( aCopy.Length() );
    }
public:
    StringEntry(void)
    {
        Init();
    }
    StringEntry( unsigned long id, const char *strIn )
    {
        Init();
        setID( id );
        setString( strIn );
        // For now, assign the length to just be the length
        // of the string.
        setLength( strlen(strIn) );
    }
    StringEntry( const StringEntry& aCopy )
    {
        Copy( aCopy );
    }
    StringEntry operator=( const StringEntry& aCopy )
    {
        Copy( aCopy );
    }

    unsigned long ID() const
    {
        return _id;
    }
    string String() const
    {
        return _strEntry;
    }
    unsigned long Offset() const
    {
        return _offset;
    }
    unsigned long Length() const
    {
        return _length;
    }
```

(continued)

LISTING 46-1 *(continued)*

```
    void setID( unsigned long id )
    {
        _id = id;
    }
    void setString( const char *strIn )
    {
        _strEntry = strIn;
    }
    void setString( const string& sIn )
    {
        _strEntry = sIn;
    }
    void setOffset( unsigned long offset )
    {
        _offset = offset;
    }
    void setLength( unsigned long length )
    {
        _length = length;
    }

    virtual void write( ofstream& out )
    {
        // Get the current output position.
        setOffset( out.tellp() );
        // Write out the string.
        const char *strOut = String().c_str();
        out << strOut;
    }

    virtual void dump( ostream& out )
    {
        out << "StringEntry:" << endl;
        out << "ID    : " << ID() << endl;
        out << "String: [" << String().c_str() << "]" << endl;
        out << "Length: " << Length() << endl;
        out << "Offset: " << Offset() << endl;
    }

};

class StringWriter
{
private:
    vector< StringEntry >    _entries;
    string                   _fileName;
    string                   _outputFileName;
```

```cpp
string get_line( ifstream& in )
{
    string sOut = "";
    char   cLastChar = 0;
    while ( !in.eof() )
    {
        // Read in a character at a time. If we hit end of line,
        // and the last character is NOT \, we are done.
        char c;
        in.get(c);
        if ( in.fail() )
            break;
        if ( c == '\n' )
        {
            // We found a return. See whether the last thing was a backslash.
            if ( cLastChar != '\\' )
                break;
            else
            {
                // Remove the backslash.
                sOut = sOut.substr(0, sOut.length()-1);
            }
        }
        sOut += c;
        cLastChar = c;
    }
    return sOut;
}

virtual bool ProcessLine( const string& sIn )
{
    // There has to be a colon (:).
    int nColonPos = sIn.find_first_of( ':' );
    if ( nColonPos == string::npos )
        return false;

    // Get the pieces.
    string sNumber = sIn.substr(0, nColonPos);
    string sValue  = sIn.substr( nColonPos+1 );

    // Add it to our list.
    StringEntry se( atol(sNumber.c_str()), sValue.c_str() );
    _entries.insert( _entries.end(), se );

    return false;
}
```

(continued)

LISTING 46-1 *(continued)*

```
        virtual bool Load()                                              → 1
        {
            // Try to open the input file.
            ifstream in(_fileName.c_str());
            if ( in.fail() )
                return false;

            // Read in the first line for version information.
            string sLine = get_line(in);
            if ( strcmp( sLine.c_str(), VERSION_STRING ) )
                return false;

            for ( int i=0; i<10; ++i )
            {
                if ( in.fail() )
                    break;
                sLine = get_line(in);
                // Ignore blank lines.
                if ( sLine.length() == 0 )
                    continue;

                // Ignore comments.
                if ( sLine[0] == '#' )
                    continue;

                if ( ProcessLine( sLine ) )
                    printf("Invalid input: %s\n", sLine.c_str () );
            }
        }

    public:
        StringWriter( void )
        {
        }
        StringWriter( const char *inputFileName, const char *outputFileName )
        {
            _fileName = inputFileName;
            _outputFileName = outputFileName;
            Load();
        }
        virtual bool Save( void )                                        → 2
        {
            // If there are no entries, abort.
            if ( _entries.size() == 0 )
                return false;

            // Try to open the output file.
            ofstream out( _outputFileName.c_str() );
            if ( out.fail() )
                return false;
```

```
        // Okay, process each of them.
        vector< StringEntry >::iterator iter;
        for ( iter = _entries.begin(); iter != _entries.end(); ++iter )
        {
            // Write out the entry.
            (*iter).write( out );
        }

        // Now, process the index file.
        string indexFileName = _outputFileName + ".idx";
        ofstream out2(indexFileName.c_str());
        if ( out2.fail() )
        {
            printf("Unable to open index file %s for output\n", indexFileName.c_str() );
            return false;
        }
        for ( iter = _entries.begin(); iter != _entries.end(); ++iter )
        {
            // Write out the entry.
            out2 << (*iter).Offset() << ", " << (*iter).Length() << ", " << (*iter).ID() << endl;
        }
        return true;
    }

};

int main(int argc, char **argv)
{
    if ( argc < 3 )
    {
        printf("Usage: StringEntry input-file output-file\n" );
        printf("Where: input-file is the file containing the string definitions\n");
        printf("       output-file is the final generated file name\n");
        return(-1);
    }
    StringWriter s(argv[1], argv[2]);
    if ( s.Save() == false )
        printf("Error generating file\n");

    return 0;
}
```

The code above breaks down into a storage class (StringEntry), a writing class (StringWriter), and a test driver that illustrates how to use the code. The test driver expects two arguments: a file that contains the string definitions and an argument that specifies the name of the file to create for an output file. The input file simply consists of ID numbers (integer values) followed by a colon and then the string to encode into the output file. Each entry in the definition file is read, parsed, and placed into a StringEntry object. This all happens in the Load function of the StringWriter class shown at ➜ **1**. After the entire input file is parsed, it is written to the output format in the `Save` method of the `StringWriter` class, shown at ➜ **2**. The result of running this program should be a language file that can then be used by your application for international uses.

3. **Save the source code in your code editor.**

Creating an Input Text File

After we have created the application to read the text file and convert it into an international language file, the next step is to test the application by creating a simple text file that contains strings we will use in the final international language file. The following steps show you how to do that by creating a very small text file we can use for testing the application:

1. **In the code editor of your choice, create a new file to hold the text for the test language file we will be using.**

In this example, the file is named `test.in.eng`, although you can use whatever name you choose. This file will contain the strings we wish to place in the output international language file.

2. **Type the following text into your file, substituting your own values wherever you choose.**

Better yet, copy the code from the source file on this book's companion Web site.

```
Version 1.0.0
# This is a comment
# This is another comment \
   but it is very very long
1:Hello                                  ➜ 3
2:Goodbye
3:Why me?
4:English
5:French
```

3. **Compile the source file with your favorite compiler, on your favorite operating system.**

In this example, the source file was called `StringEntry.cpp`; however, you may call it anything you like.

4. **Run the application on the operating system of your choice, using the input file as an argument to the application.**

If you have done everything correctly, you will see the following output in the console window, and will have two files created in the file system (called `my.eng` and `my.eng.idx`):

```
$ ./a.exe test.in.eng my.eng

The my.eng file will look like this:
$ cat my.eng
HelloGoodbyeWhy me?EnglishFrench         ➜ 4

The my.eng.idx file will look like this:
$ cat my.eng.idx
0, 5                                     ➜ 5
5, 7
12, 7
19, 7
26, 6
```

As you can see from the two outputs shown above, after the writer is finished with the input text file, it is no longer truly in readable format. The strings are concatenated in a binary output format, with a secondary file containing indices that indicate where each string starts and ends. For example, the input file contains the string shown in the listing at ➜ **3** This string is then written to the binary output file, `my.eng`, at ➜ **4** The index for this particular entry is shown in the `my.eng.idx` file at ➜ **5** The first entry in the index indicates the position in the file (0-based). As you can see, the string we are looking at begins at the first position of the output file. The second entry in the index indicates the length of the string, in this case five. So, we go to position zero, count off five characters and that will be our first string. And, as you can see, that is in fact the string `Hello`.

Reading the International File

After we have created the file and the index file for it, the next step is to build a reader that reads the strings in the various languages. The reader uses a two-step process to achieve this: First it reads in the index file so that it knows where all the strings are in the file, and then it loads a string to be read. The following steps show you how to do this.

 Strings take up a large amount of the memory of an application and provide clues for hackers. For example, error messages may indicate where the processing for security is handled in the code. By finding these strings in the program executable file, the hacker can then determine where to make patches to "crack" your program to not require a license. When extracting all of the text for a system into external files, you should either encrypt the text to make it secure, or at least have it removed from the portion of the program that it describes. This will save you a lot of time in securing — as well as debugging — your application, by eliminating at least one type of problem from the released product.

1. **In the code editor of your choice, create a new file to hold the code for the source file of the technique.**

In this example, the file is named ch46_1.cpp, although you can use whatever you choose. This file will contain the class definition for our automation object.

2. **Type the code from Listing 46-2 into your file.**

Better yet, copy the code from the source file on this book's companion Web site.

LISTING 46-2: THE STRINGREADER CLASS

```cpp
#include <stdio.h>
#include <vector>
#include <string>
#include <iostream>
#include <fstream>
#include <sstream>

using namespace std;

class StringIndex
{
private:
    unsigned long _offset;
    unsigned long _length;
    unsigned long _id;
protected:
    virtual void Init()
    {
        setOffset(0);
        setLength(0);
        setID(0);
    }
public:
    StringIndex(void)
    {
        Init();
    }
    StringIndex( unsigned long offset, unsigned long length, unsigned id )
```

(continued)

LISTING 46-2 *(continued)*

```
{
    Init();
    setOffset( offset );
    setLength( length );
    setID( id );
}
StringIndex( const StringIndex& aCopy )
{
    setOffset( aCopy.getOffset() );
    setLength( aCopy.getLength() );
    setID ( aCopy.getID() );
}
virtual ~StringIndex()
{
}
StringIndex operator=( const StringIndex& aCopy )
{
    setOffset( aCopy.getOffset() );
    setLength( aCopy.getLength() );
    setID ( aCopy.getID() );
    return *this;
}

void setOffset( unsigned long offset )
{
    _offset = offset;
}
void setLength( unsigned long length )
{
    _length = length;
}
void setID( unsigned long id )
{
    _id = id;
}
unsigned long getOffset( void ) const
{
    return _offset;
}
unsigned long getLength( void ) const
{
    return _length;
}
unsigned long getID( void ) const
{
    return _id;
}
```

```
    virtual void dump( void )
    {
        cout << "StringIndex: " << endl;
        cout << "Offset: " << getOffset() << endl;
        cout << "Length: " << getLength() << endl;
        cout << "ID     : " << getID() << endl;
    }
};




class StringReader
{
private:
    string _fileName;
    vector< StringIndex > _indices;
protected:
    virtual bool Load(void)
    {
        string indexFileName = _fileName + ".idx";
        ifstream in(indexFileName.c_str());
        if ( in.fail() )
            return false;

        // Read in each line.
        while ( !in.eof() )
        {
            string sIn = "";

            while ( !in.eof() )
            {
                // Get an input line.
                char c;
                in.get(c);
                if ( in.fail() )
                    break;
                if ( c != '\r' && c != '\n' )
                    sIn += c;
                if ( c == '\n' )
                    break;
            }

            if ( sIn.length() == 0 )
                break;

            // Okay, we have a line. Now, parse it.
            istringstream iss(sIn.c_str());
```

(continued)

LISTING 46-2 (continued)

```
            char c;
            long lLength = 0;
            long lOffset = 0;
            long lID = 0;
            // Parse the line, eating the comma
            iss >> lOffset >> c >> lLength >> c >> lID;

            StringIndex si(lOffset, lLength, lID);
            si.dump();
            _indices.insert( _indices.end(), si );
        }


        return true;
    }
    virtual string _loadString( const StringIndex& si )
    {
        ifstream in(_fileName.c_str());
        in.seekg( si.getOffset() );
        string retStr;
        for ( int i=0; i<si.getLength(); ++i )
        {
            char c;
            in.get(c);
            if ( in.fail() )
                break;
            retStr += c;
        }
        return retStr;
    }
public:
    StringReader(void)
    {
    }
    StringReader( const char *fileName )
    {
        _fileName = fileName;
        Load();
    }
    StringReader( const StringReader& aCopy )
    {
        _fileName = aCopy._fileName;
        vector< StringIndex >::const_iterator iter;
        for (iter = aCopy._indices.begin(); iter != aCopy._indices.end(); ++iter )
            _indices.insert( _indices.end(), (*iter) );
    }
    string getString( long id )
```

→ 6

```
        {
            // First, see if we have this id.
            vector< StringIndex >::const_iterator iter;
            for (iter = _indices.begin(); iter != _indices.end(); ++iter )
                if ( (*iter).getID() == id )
                    return _loadString( (*iter) );
            return string("");
        }
};
```

3. Save the source code as a file in your editor and close the editor application.

Testing the String Reader

After you create a class, you should create a test driver that not only ensures that your code is correct, but also shows people how to use your code.

The following steps show you how to create a test driver that illustrates how to read a language file, and shows how the class is intended to be used:

1. In the code editor of your choice, reopen the source file to hold the code for your test program.

In this example, I named the test program `ch46a.cpp`.

2. Type the code from Listing 46-3 into your file.

Better yet, copy the code from the source file on this book's companion Web site.

LISTING 46-3: THE STRINGREADER TEST DRIVER

```
int main(int argc, char **argv)
{
    if ( argc < 3 )
    {
        printf("Usage: ch6_1 string-file-name id1 [id2, ..]\n");
        printf("Where: string-file-name is the name of the compressed string file to use\n");
        printf("       id1..etc are the ids to display\n");
        return -1;
    }

    StringReader sReader(argv[1]);

    for ( int i=2; i<argc; ++i )
    {
        int id = atoi(argv[i]);

        string s = sReader.getString( id );
        printf("String %d: [%s]\n", id, s.c_str() );
    }
    return 0;
}
```

3. Save the source-code file in the code editor.

4. Compile and run the source file with your favorite compiler on your favorite operating system.

If you have done everything right, running the application with the arguments shown should produce the following result on your console window:

```
$ ./a.exe my.eng 2 3 5 9
String 2: [Goodbye]
String 3: [Why me?]
String 5: [French]
String 9: []
```

 You will also see the diagnostics, which are not shown, for the application. If you do not wish to view the diagnostics, comment out the dump method call shown at line → **6** in Listing 46-2.

By looking at the output above, we can see that when we read data back in from the language file, using the indices we have defined in the program, we get back the same strings that we put there in the original language text file. This shows that the program is working properly and that we are getting the language data directly from the file — not from strings embedded in the application.

Hashing Out Translations

Technique 47

The *hash table* is one of the most valuable constructs in the Standard Template Library. Hash tables are data structures that contain two types of values, usually key-value pairs. A hash table is used anytime you want to either replace one value with another, or map a given key to a given value. (As you may imagine, it's a commonly used encryption tool.)

One of the most useful things that you can do with a hash table is to store and look up existing values and replace them with new ones. For example, in a translation application, it would be nice to be able to build a dictionary of words and their resulting translations. The ability to retrieve information based on a key-value pair can save a lot of time in an application. For example, a search and replace feature could use this functionality. Alternatively, you could use this functionality to implement a command parser, with a mapping of strings to integer values. Using hash tables can save you a lot of time in translating one type of input to another in your applications. In this technique, we will look at that exact problem and how to solve it in your application code.

Creating a Translator Class

We will use the hash table function to create a class that "translates" text by replacing certain keywords in the text with other words. Imagine that we want to replace all occurrences of the word *computer* with the word *pc,* for example. This type of conversion is commonly referred to as a *filter,* because it takes input and filters it to a new output format. In this section we will create the `Translator` class, which will store the text we wish to replace, along with the text we wish to insert in the place of the original.

1. **In the code editor of your choice, create a new file to hold the code for the source file of the technique.**

In this example, the file is named ch47, although you can use whatever you choose.

2. **Type the following code from Listing 47-1 into your file.**

Better yet, copy the code from the source file on this book's companion Web site.

LISTING 47-1: THE TRANSLATOR CLASS

```
#include <stdio.h>
#include <string>
#include <map>
#include <fstream>
#include <iostream>

using namespace std;

class Translator
{
private:
    string    _fileName;
    map<string,string>    _dictionary;    → 2
protected:
    void Clear()
    {
        _dictionary.erase(
    _dictionary.begin(), _dictionary.end() );
    }
    bool Load( const char *fileName )      → 1
    {
        ifstream in(fileName);
        if ( in.fail() )
            return false;

        // Just read in pairs of values.

        while ( !in.eof() )
        {
            string word;
            string replacement;
            in >> word;
            if ( word.length() )
            {
                in >> replacement;
                _dictionary[word] = replace-
                    ment;
```

```
        }
    }

    return true;
}
public:
    Translator( void )
    {
    }
    Translator( const char *fileName )
    {
        Clear();
        setFileName( fileName );
    }
    Translator( const Translator& aCopy )
    {
        Clear();
        setFileName( aCopy.getFileName() );
    }
    Translator operator=( const Translator&
      aCopy )
    {
        Clear();
        setFileName( aCopy.getFileName() );
    }
    void setFileName( const string&
      sFileName )
    {
        _fileName = sFileName;
        Load(_fileName.c_str());
    }
    string getFileName( void ) const
    {
        return _fileName;
    }
    string replace( string in )            → 3
    {
        map<string,string>::iterator iter;

        iter = _dictionary.find( in );

        if ( iter != _dictionary.end() )
        {
            return iter->second;
        }
        return in;
    }
};
```

This code simply manages the translation operations. The code consists of three basic functions:

▶ The class manages an input file that contains the mappings of old text to the new text we wish to replace it with. (See ➜ **1**.)

This method takes a filename, attempts to open it, and reads in the data pairs if the open operation was successful.

▶ The class manages the storage of the mappings in a hash table. (See ➜ **2**.)

This is done by the hash table, represented by the Standard Template Library map class.

▶ The class replaces a given string with the string desired in the final output. (Shown at ➜ **3**.)

Note that we simply pass in each string and replace it if it is found in the hash table. If it is not, we return the original string. This allows the application to save time by not bothering to check if the string needs to be replaced or not.

3. **Save the source code as a file in your code editor.**

This dictionary will do all the work of loading data from a translation file and replacing individual words with specified translated words. For example, consider the idea of replacing all occurrences of the word *good* with the word *bad*. If we were given the input string *good day, I am having a good time at this goodly party,* we would translate this into *bad day, I am having a bad time at this goodly party*. Note that we only replace full matches, not text that appears anywhere in the input string. The class now exists, the only thing we need to do is use it.

Testing the Translator Class

After you create the dictionary, you should create a test driver that not only ensures that your code is correct, but also shows people how to use your code.

The following steps show you how to create a test driver that illustrates various kinds of input from the user, and shows how the class is intended to be used:

1. **In the code editor of your choice, reopen the source file to hold the code for your test program.**

In this example, I named the test program ch47.cpp.

2. **Append the code from Listing 47-2 into your file.**

Better yet, copy the code from the source file on this book's companion Web site.

LISTING 47-2: THE TRANSLATOR CLASS TEST DRIVER

```
int main()
{
    Translator t("translate.txt");        ➜ 4
    printf("Enter some text to translate:
      ");
    string in;

    bool bDone = false;
    while ( !bDone )                      ➜ 5
    {
        char c;
        cin.get(c);
        if ( c == '\n' )
            bDone = true;
        else
            in += c;
    }

    printf("Initial string: %s\n",
      in.c_str() );

    // Break it down into words.
    string word;
    for ( int i=0; i<in.length(); ++i )
    {
        if ( in[i] == ' ' )
        {
            if ( word.length() )          ➜ 6
            {
                string sOut = t.replace(
                  word );
                cout << sOut << " ";
            }
```

(continued)

LISTING 47-2 *(continued)*

```
            word = "";
        }
        else
            word += in[i];
    }
    if ( word.length() )                    → 7
    {
        string sOut = t.replace( word );
        cout << sOut << " ";
    }


}
```

The code above simply reads input from the keyboard, breaks it down into words, and then calls the translator to replace any portions of the string that need to be translated from our input file. The translator operates on a file called `translate.txt`, as shown at → **4**. You can easily change this filename, or even pass one in on the command line, if you wish. Each line is read from the keyboard, one character at a time, until a carriage return is encountered. (See → **5**.) Finally, we parse the input line until we encounter a space (shown at → **6**) or the end of the string (shown at → **7**). When this happens, we replace the "word" we have parsed by calling the `replace` method of the translator.

3. **Save the source-code file in the editor and then close the editor application.**

4. **Compile the source file, using your favorite compiler on your favorite operating system.**

5. **In your code editor, create a translation-text file.**

This file will contain the pairs of words to be used in the translation file; each pair consists of a word and the translated version of that word. I called mine `translation.txt`, but you can call it whatever you like.

6. **Put the following text into the `translation.txt` file:**

```
good bad
insult dis
talk jive
```

You can place any words you want in the file. The first word will be replaced by the second word in any sentence you input into the system.

7. **Run the program on your favorite operating system.**

If you have done everything properly, you should see output resembling this:

```
$ ./a.exe
    Enter some text to translate:
    Initial string: you are so good to
      talk and not insult me
    you are so bad to jive and not dis
      me
```

48 Technique

Implementing Virtual Files

These days, application data can be very large and can consume a lot of your memory. Depending on your application footprint and target operating system, loading the entire application file into memory at one time may be impossible. Memory shortages are common with embedded systems, and with hand-held devices, where only a limited amount of memory is available to share between numerous applications. There are a number of ways to handle such conditions, from reading in only as much data as you can and not storing the remainder, to limiting the data to chunks and forcing the user to select which chunk they want. None of these solutions, however, is quite as elegant to either the developer or the end-user as the *virtual file*. A virtual file is a window into the file you are trying to process. It appears to end-users as if they're seeing the whole file at once — but they're really seeing just one small piece of it at a time. If you build virtual views of your files into your application up front, you save time in the long run, because you won't have to go back and redesign your applications when the files become larger than you were expecting.

 The capability to provide a virtual window into a file not only conserves memory, it also conserves speed. By loading only a small chunk of the file at any given moment, you can load immense files in no time and all, and page through them very quickly. This method is used by many large text editors.

Creating a Virtual File Class

In order to manage virtual files, we will need two different classes. First, we will need a single class that manages a given chunk of data from the file. This class will manage the data in that chunk, as well as keep track of where that particular piece of data was read from the file and how big it is. After this, we need to have a manager that keeps track of all of those chunks of data, allocating new objects to manage the individual pieces that are read in, and deleting the pieces that are no longer used. Let's create a few classes to do that now.

1. **In the code editor of your choice, create a new file to hold the code for the source file of the technique.**

In this example, the file is named ch48.cpp, although you can use whatever you choose. This file will contain the class definition for our virtual file manager objects.

2. **Type the code given in Listing 48-1 into your file.**

Better yet, copy the code from the source file on this book's companion Web site.

LISTING 48-1: THE VIRTUAL FILE MANAGER CLASSES

```cpp
#include <iostream>
#include <string>
#include <vector>
#include <fstream>

using namespace std;

class FileChunk
{
private:
    string   _chunk;
    long    _offset;
    long    _length;
    bool    _inuse;
    long    _accesses;
protected:
    void Clear()
    {
        _offset = -1;
        _length = -1;
        _chunk = "";
        _inuse = false;
        _accesses = 0;
    }
    void Copy( const FileChunk& aCopy )
    {
        _offset = aCopy._offset;
        _length = aCopy._length;
        _chunk = aCopy._chunk;
        _inuse = aCopy._inuse;
    }
    bool Read ( ifstream& in, long pos, long length )
    {
        _offset = pos;
        _chunk = "";
        _length = 0;

        // Seek to the position in the stream.
        in.seekg( pos );
        if ( in.fail() )
            return false;
```

→ 1

```
            // Read up to the end of the file or the last of the length
            // bytes.
            for ( int i=0; i<length; ++i )
            {
                char c;
                in.get(c);
                if ( in.fail() )
                    break;
                _length ++;
                _chunk += c;
            }
            _inuse = true;
    }
public:
    FileChunk( void )
    {
        Clear();
    }
    FileChunk( ifstream& in, long pos, long length )
    {
        Clear();
        Read( in, pos, length );
    }
    FileChunk( const FileChunk& aCopy )
    {
        Clear();
        Copy( aCopy );
    }
    FileChunk operator=( const FileChunk& aCopy )
    {
        Clear();
        Copy( aCopy );
        return *this;
    }

    // Accessors
    long Offset()
    {
        return _offset;
    }
    long Length()
    {
        return _length;
    }
    string& Chunk()
    {
        _accesses ++;
        return _chunk;
    }
    bool InUse(void)
    {
        return _inuse;
```

(continued)

LISTING 48-1 *(continued)*

```
    }
    void setOffset( long offset )
    {
        _offset = _offset;
    }
    void setLength( long length )
    {
        _length = length;
    }
    void setChunk( const string& chunk )
    {
        _chunk = chunk;
    }
    long AccessCount( void )
    {
        return _accesses;
    }
    bool Load( ifstream& in, long offset, long length )
    {
        Clear();
        return Read( in, offset, length );
    }
};

const int kChunkSize = 128;

class FileChunkManager
{
private:
    int          _numChunks;
    FileChunk    *_chunks;
    ifstream     _in;
    string       _fileName;
protected:
    FileChunk *findChunk( long theOffset )
    {
        for ( int i=0; i<_numChunks; ++i )
        {
            if ( _chunks[i].InUse() == true )
            {
                long offset = _chunks[i].Offset();
                long length = _chunks[i].Length();
                if ( theOffset >= offset && theOffset <= offset+length )
                    return &_chunks[i];
            }
        }
        return NULL;
    }
    FileChunk *addChunk( long theOffset )
```

→ **2**

```
    {
        for ( int i=0; i<_numChunks; ++i )
        {
            if ( _chunks[i].InUse() == false )
            {
                if ( _chunks[i].Load( _in, theOffset, kChunkSize ) )
                    return &_chunks[i];
            }
        }
        return NULL;
    }
    FileChunk *getLeastRecentlyAccessed()
    {
        int idx = 0;
        long access = _chunks[0].AccessCount();

        for ( int i=0; i<_numChunks; ++i )
        {
            if ( _chunks[i].InUse() == true )
            {
                if ( _chunks[i].AccessCount() < access )
                {
                    idx = i;
                    access = _chunks[i].AccessCount();
                }
            }
        }
        return &_chunks[idx];
    }

public:
    FileChunkManager(void)
    {
        _numChunks = 0;
        _chunks = NULL;
    }
    FileChunkManager( const char *fileName, int nMaxChunks )
    {
        _numChunks = nMaxChunks;
        _chunks = new FileChunk[ nMaxChunks ];
        _fileName = fileName;
        _in.open( fileName );
    }
    FileChunkManager( const FileChunkManager& aCopy )
    {
        _numChunks = aCopy._numChunks;
        _chunks = new FileChunk[ _numChunks ];
        for ( int i=0; i<_numChunks; ++i )
            _chunks[i] = aCopy._chunks[i];
        _fileName = aCopy._fileName;
        _in.open( _fileName.c_str() );
    }
```

(continued)

LISTING 48-1 *(continued)*

```
    virtual ~FileChunkManager( void )
    {
        delete [] _chunks;
    }

    char operator[]( long offset )
    {
        // Find which chunk this offset is in.
        FileChunk *chunk = findChunk( offset );
        if ( chunk == NULL )
        {
            // There are none. See whether we can add one.
            chunk = addChunk( offset );
        }
        // If we have one, just get the data from it.
        // Otherwise, we have to go dump one.
        if ( !chunk )
        {
            chunk = getLeastRecentlyAccessed();
            chunk->Load( _in, offset, kChunkSize );
        }

        // Finally, extract the piece we need.
        int pos = offset - chunk->Offset();
        return chunk->Chunk()[pos];
    }

    // Dump the function to illustrate what is in the chunks.
    void Dump(void)
    {
        for ( int i=0; i<_numChunks; ++i )
        {
            printf("Chunk %d: %s\n", i, _chunks[i].InUse() ? "In Use" : "NOT Used" );
            printf("Offset: %ld\n", _chunks[i].Offset() );
            printf("Length: %ld\n", _chunks[i].Length() );
            if ( _chunks[i].InUse() )
                printf("String: [%s]\n", _chunks[i].Chunk().c_str() );
        }
    }
};
```

The code above shows the two basic classes: the FileChunk and FileChunkManager classes. The FileChunk class, shown at ➤ **1**, manages a single chunk of data in the file. This data includes the offset within the file, the file object itself, and the text from that location in the file. It also stores the length of the chunk that was actually read in, since some chunks at the end of the file could be smaller than the full size block. The second class,

the FileChunkManager class, shown at ➤ **2**, maintains an array of FileChunk objects, keeping track of which ones are in use and what their offsets are. When a block of the file is requested, the manager object looks through its list to see if there is a block that has that data in it and if so, requests that particular text from that particular object.

3. **Save the source file in the code editor.**

Testing the Virtual File Class

After you create a class, you should create a test driver that not only ensures that your code is correct, but also shows people how to use your code.

The following steps show you how to create a test driver that illustrates various kinds of input from the user, and shows how the class is intended to be used:

1. **In the code editor of your choice, reopen the source file to hold the code for your test program.**

In this example, I named the test program ch48.

2. **Type the code shown in Listing 48-2 into your file.**

Better yet, copy the code from the source file on this book's companion Web site.

LISTING 48-2: THE VIRTUAL FILE CLASS TEST DRIVER

```
int main(int argc, char **argv)
{
    if ( argc < 2 )
    {
        printf("Usage: ch6_3 filename\n");
        printf("Where: filename is the file
            to load\n");
    }


    FileChunkManager fcm( argv[1], 5 );
    for ( int i=0; i<4096; ++i )
    {
        char c = fcm[i];
    }

    fcm.Dump();

    return 0;
}
```

3. **Save the source-code file in your code editor and close the editor application.**

4. **Compile the entire application with your favorite compiler on your favorite operating system.**

5. **Run the application.**

You will need to pass in a filename for the program to manage. For this example output, I used the actual text file representing the program, ch48.cpp.

If you have done everything properly, you should see the output shown in Listing 48-3 when you run the application on a given program.

LISTING 48-3: OUTPUT FROM THE TEST DRIVER

```
Chunk 0: In Use
Offset: 3999
Length: 128
String: [
        int pos = offset - chunk->Offset();
        return chunk->Chunk()[pos];
    }

    // Dump function to illustrate what is
        in the chunks.
]
Chunk 1: In Use                                  → 3
Offset: 129
Length: 128
String: [ate:
    string    _chunk;
    long      _offset;
    long      _length;
    bool      _inuse;
    long      _accesses;
protected:
    void Clear()
    {
        _offset = -1;]
Chunk 2: In Use
Offset: 258
Length: 128
String: [et = -1;
        _length = -1;
        _chunk = "";
        _inuse = false;
        _accesses = 0;
    }
    void Copy( const FileChunk& aCopy )
```

(continued)

LISTING 48-3 *(continued)*

```
      {
            _offset ]
Chunk 3: In Use
Offset: 387
Length: 128
String: [offset = aCopy._offset;
        _length = aCopy._length;
        _chunk = aCopy._chunk;
        _inuse = aCopy._inuse;
      }
    bool Read( ifstream& in]
Chunk 4: In Use
Offset: 516
Length: 128
String: [& in, long pos, long length )
      {
          _offset = pos;
          _chunk = "";
          _length = 0;

          // Seek to the position in the
             stream
      in.se]
```

The output above indicates how each chunk of the file is read in and in what order. You can see how the individual chunks were read in, such as the one shown at the line marked with ➜ **3**. You can see that the chunk consists of a block of text 128 bytes long, starting at position 129. This chunk is marked "In Use," indicating that the manager is still processing from that chunk.

the chunk consists of a block of text 128 bytes long, starting at position 129. This chunk is marked "In Use," indicating that the manager is still processing from that chunk.

As you can see from the above output, the file is read in chunks, and those chunks are not specifically in position order. There are never more than 512 bytes in use at any given time, but it appears to the user as if the entire file is available for use.

Improving Your Virtual File Class

While the virtual file class is certainly useful as it stands, there are a number of improvements that could be made to it, such as these:

- ✔ The size of each chunk could be made configurable.

- ✔ The simple algorithm that determines which chunk to throw away when all available chunks have been used could be enhanced.

Several chunks of the file's data could be pre-loaded at startup to minimize the startup time for reading pieces.

> Always keep a list of possible improvements along with your classes as you write them. When you come back to the class — or someone else takes it over — it will have a built-in to-do list that enhances it and raises its value.

Using Iterators for Your Collections

Save Time By

- ✔ Using collections
- ✔ Understanding iterators
- ✔ Manipulating collections with iterators
- ✔ Interpreting your output

Collections are at the heart of the Standard Template Library (STL). They form the basis for the reusability of all reuse in your classes — and allow you to treat large groups of data in both ordered and unordered fashions. Without collections, coding would be a lot more of a problem — we'd have to write up our own arrays, linked lists, and the like. You can certainly still write your own array classes or even use static arrays, but these classes would not have the years of testing and usage collections have, which means more bugs, more design problems, and an overall slower development process. By using the classes in the STL for containers, you save time by not having to develop your own classes, and by not having to debug code you have just written to implement your own container.

To interface with collections of any sort, the STL offers a generic tool called the *iterator*. Iterators are very useful, very simple tools that allow you to get at any piece of a collection, manipulate it, and print out the values of the container's data elements. Pretty handy, but iterators are capable of much more than this — as demonstrated in this technique. An iterator, as its name implies, allows you to "iterate over" (or move through) a collection of data. For example, when writing standard C++ arrays, we might produce some code that looks like this:

```
int array[20];
for ( int i=0; i<20; ++i )
    printf("Array element %d = %d\n", i, array[i] );
```

This code works for a normal array, because all of the elements in the array are guaranteed to be contiguous in member. With the STL containers, that guarantee does not exist. The STL containers manage buckets of data, which may be scattered around in memory. With an iterator class, however, we can treat our STL collections just as if they were like the code above.

 If you are using collections in your applications, make sure you define an iterator that has access to those collections. That iterator will give you a standardized way of working with the data without requiring you to do a lot of extra work.

In this technique I show you an example of using container collections in the STL and how to use iterators with those collections. I explore several different types of collections, from vectors (arrays) to maps and linked lists. In all cases, we can iterate over these collections using the same kinds of iterators. I explain how to move forward and backward through the collections, as well as how to insert and remove things from the various container types. Finally, I examine some of the cooler things about iterators, such as swapping elements and using iterators on files. The following steps get you started:

1. **In the code editor of your choice, create a new file to hold the code for the source file of the technique.**

In this example, the file is named ch49.cpp, although you can use whatever you choose. This file will contain the class definition for the needed automation object.

2. **Type the code from Listing 49-1 into your file.**

Better yet, copy the code from the source file on this book's companion Web site.

LISTING 49-1: ITERATING OVER THE COLLECTION CLASSES IN THE STL

```
#include <iostream>
#include <string>
#include <vector>
#include <map>
#include <list>
#include <fstream>
#include <algorithm>
#include <iterator>
#include <set>

using namespace std;

int main( int argc, char **argv )
{
    // Add a bunch of items to each type.
    char *names[] = {
        "Matt",
        "Sarah",
        "Rachel",
        "Jenny",
        "Lee",
        "Kim",
        NULL
    };

    // First, do the vector.
    vector< string > nameArray;
    for ( int i=0; names[i]; ++i )
    {
        nameArray.insert( nameArray.end(), names[i] );
    }
```

```
// Next, load the map.
map< char, string > nameMap;
for ( int i=0; names[i]; ++i )
    nameMap[ names[i][0] ] = names[i];

// The linked list is next.
list< string > nameList;
for ( int i=0; names[i]; ++i )
{
    nameList.insert( nameList.end(), names[i] );
}

// Sets are popular.
set<string, greater<string> > nameSet;
for ( int i=0; names[i]; ++i )
{
    // Try inserting them twice to see what happens.
    nameSet.insert( nameSet.end(), names[i] );
    nameSet.insert( nameSet.end(), names[i] );
}

// Now, iterate over them.
for ( int i=0; i<nameArray.size(); ++i )
    printf("Array[%d] = %s\n", i, nameArray[i].c_str() );

map<char, string>::iterator iter;
int idx = 0;
for ( iter = nameMap.begin(); iter != nameMap.end(); ++iter )
{
    printf("Map Entry[%d]:\n", idx);
    printf("Key        : %c\n", (*iter).first );
    printf("Value      : %s\n", (*iter).second.c_str() );
    idx ++;
}

printf("Set:\n");
set<string, greater<string> >::iterator set_iter;
for ( set_iter = nameSet.begin(); set_iter != nameSet.end(); ++set_iter )
{
    printf("Set Entry: %s\n", (*set_iter).c_str() );
}


printf("Original List:\n");
list<string>::iterator list_iter;
for ( list_iter = nameList.begin(); list_iter != nameList.end(); ++list_iter )
{
    printf("List Entry: %s\n", (*list_iter).c_str() );
}
```

→ 1

(continued)

LISTING 49-1 (continued)

```
    // Iterators can be used to remove items.
    for ( list_iter = nameList.begin(); list_iter != nameList.end(); ++list_iter )
    {
        if ( (*list_iter) == "Matt" )
        {
            // Note, once we delete something, the iterator is no longer
            // valid.
            nameList.erase( list_iter );
            break;
        }
    }

    printf("Final List:\n");
    for ( list_iter = nameList.begin(); list_iter != nameList.end(); ++list_iter )
    {
        printf("List Entry: %s\n", (*list_iter).c_str() );
    }

    // You can also iterate in reverse.
    printf("In reverse\n");
    list<string>::reverse_iterator riter;
    for ( riter = nameList.rbegin(); riter != nameList.rend(); ++riter )
    {
        printf("List Entry: %s\n", (*riter).c_str() );
    }

    // Iterators can be used to swap two elements.
    iter_swap (nameList.begin(), --nameList.end());
    printf("Swapped:\n");
    for ( list_iter = nameList.begin(); list_iter != nameList.end(); ++list_iter )
    {
        printf("List Entry: %s\n", (*list_iter).c_str() );
    }


    // Finally, you can iterate over streams.
    ifstream in("ch6_4.cpp");
    istream_iterator<string> cinPos(in);

    for ( int i=0; i<10; ++i )
    {

        if (cinPos != istream_iterator<string>())
        {
            cout << *cinPos++;
        }
        cout << endl;
    }
    cout << endl;

    return 0;
}
```

→ 2

→ 3

The code above shows the various ways in which we can iterate over the collection classes in the STL. For example, at → **1**, you see the iteration over a map collection. Maps are normally accessed by referring to given elements in them, but, as you can see here, they can also be listed in order using iterators. Line → **2** shows how we can iterate over a collection in reverse — that is, by starting at the end and working our way back to the beginning — simply by changing the type of iterator we use. Note that even though we are going backwards through the container objects, we still increment the iterator. This means that we could write a single block of code to iterate over a collection and then select the iterator we wish to use for direction without having to change any of the code.

3. Save the source-code file in your editor and close the editor application.

4. Compile the application, using your favorite compiler on your favorite operating system.

5. Run the program on your favorite operating system.

If you have done everything properly, you should see the output shown in Listing 49-2 in your console window.

LISTING 49-2: OUTPUT FROM THE ITERATOR TEST

```
Array[0] = Matt
Array[1] = Sarah
Array[2] = Rachel
Array[3] = Jenny
Array[4] = Lee
Array[5] = Kim
Map Entry[0]:
Key          : J
Value        : Jenny
Map Entry[1]:
Key          : K
Value        : Kim
Map Entry[2]:
Key          : L
Value        : Lee
Map Entry[3]:
```

```
Key          : M
Value        : Matt
Map Entry[4]:
Key          : R
Value        : Rachel
Map Entry[5]:
Key          : S
Value        : Sarah
Set:
Set Entry: Sarah
Set Entry: Rachel
Set Entry: Matt
Set Entry: Lee
Set Entry: Kim
Set Entry: Jenny
Original List:
List Entry: Matt
List Entry: Sarah
List Entry: Rachel
List Entry: Jenny
List Entry: Lee
List Entry: Kim
Final List:                          → 4
List Entry: Sarah
List Entry: Rachel
List Entry: Jenny
List Entry: Lee
List Entry: Kim
In reverse
List Entry: Kim
List Entry: Lee
List Entry: Jenny
List Entry: Rachel
List Entry: Sarah
Swapped:                             → 5
List Entry: Kim
List Entry: Rachel
List Entry: Jenny
List Entry: Lee
List Entry: Sarah
#include
<iostream>
#include
<string>
#include
<vector>
#include
<map>
#include
<list>
```

The output shown in Listing 49-2 shows that our test program is running properly. We can see, from ➞ **4**, that the entry Matt was removed from the list. Likewise, we can see from ➞ **5** that the Rachel and Lee entries in the list were swapped. This indicates that our code works properly.

As you can see, the iterator is an extremely powerful tool. Not only can it be used on all sorts of various collections, but it also allows you to treat a stream as simply a collection of data (shown in Listing 49-1 at ➞ **3**). (Of course, when you think about it, that's exactly what a stream is.) The stream is passed to the stream iterator, which then allows us to step through the file one character at a time jumping to whatever position they wish in the file by incrementing or decrementing the iterator.

Be careful with iterators

Here are a couple of important caveats when you're using iterators:

- ✔ If you remove items from the collection using an iterator, you cannot assume that the iterator you used remains usable afterwards. Iterators maintain internal state, so they are "pointing at" an invalid item in the container. After you have removed items, close the iterator and reset an iterator for the collection again.

- ✔ Iterators come in two forms, const and non-const. Use const iterators for constant collections, to ensure that no data is modified.

Technique 50

Overriding the Allocator for a Collection Class

Save Time By

- ✔ Exploring memory allocators
- ✔ Using memory allocators
- ✔ Implementing a memory allocator with an existing framework of classes
- ✔ Interpreting output

One of the real strengths of the Standard Template Library (STL) is that you can configure classes to fit your specific needs. For example, you can put any class you need in a given template, so long as the class follows certain basic rules. Or you can change the way in which memory is allocated for the collection — you could allocate memory from a static heap for a given collection, for example, or perhaps make the memory persistent through the allocation mechanism (that is, not allow memory to be moved around on the system). These two examples, specifically, would allow you to utilize the STL in an embedded system. Whatever you can dream up for your system to use, the STL can handle.

The purpose of memory allocators is to provide the container classes with a class-independent way of getting memory to use for storage of objects. For example, when I define an array in standard C++, such as this:

```
int array[20];
```

I request 20 words of storage from the compiler. Likewise, I can dynamically allocate a block of memory, like this:

```
int *array = new int[20];
```

In this case, I have dynamically requested the same 20 words of storage, but this time from the operating system itself, rather than from the compiler. Within the STL, however, the problem is more complicated. How do we allocate blocks of memory when we don't know exactly how big those blocks will be? This is what allocators do for us; they allow us to allocate blocks of memory within the STL containers.

The capability to replace the way memory is allocated can be very important if you are working in a memory-constrained environment, or one in which memory is allocated in a special way. This capability spares you from having to change the underlying code to make your classes work. By implementing custom allocators in your applications, you can trace allocations, look for errors in your code, and switch things out speedily should the occasion arise. This technique takes a look at the basics of implementing your own allocator for the STL — and using it with the existing framework of classes. Because we can change the allocator for the STL container classes, we can configure them to work in different environments, such as embedded systems, different operating systems, or even hand-held devices that allocate memory in a completely different way. By understanding how to change the allocation of memory, you will save time in debugging complicated memory, errors, or in porting your code from system to system.

Creating a Custom Memory Allocator

In order to explore the way in which memory is allocated in the STL, let's create a simple skeleton that

will allow us to override the default memory allocator for a container class. This will show you how the allocation process works, and allow you to have a template from which you can create your own allocators, should the need arise. Understanding this process will save you enormous time in figuring out memory allocators, which are not particularly well documented in the STL documentation.

1. **In the code editor of your choice, create a new file to hold the code for the header file of the technique.**

   In this example, the file is named ch50.h, although you can use whatever you choose. This file will contain the class definition for your allocator.

2. **Type the code from Listing 50-1 into your file.**

   Better yet, copy the code from the source file on this book's companion Web site.

LISTING 50-1: THE ALLOCATOR CLASS DEFINITION FILE

```
#ifndef _ALLOCATOR_H_
#define _ALLOCATOR_H_

#include <limits>
#include <iostream>

using namespace std;

template <class T>
class MyAlloc {
    public:
      // Type the definitions.
        typedef T          value_type;
        typedef T*         pointer;
        typedef const T* const_pointer;
        typedef T&         reference;
        typedef const T& const_reference;
        typedef std::size_t    size_type;
        typedef std::ptrdiff_t difference_type;


      template <class U>
      struct rebind {
          typedef MyAlloc<U> other;
      };
```

```cpp
        // Return the address of values.
        T* address (T& value) const {
            return &value;
        }

        /* Constructors and destructor
         * have nothing to do because the allocator has no state.
         */
        MyAlloc() throw()
        {
        }
        MyAlloc(const MyAlloc&) throw()
        {
        }

        template <class U>
        MyAlloc (const MyAlloc<U>&) throw()
        {
        }

        ~MyAlloc() throw() {
        }

        // Return maximum number of elements that can be allocated.
        size_t max_size () const throw()
        {
            return numeric_limits<std::size_t>::max() / sizeof(T);
        }

        // Allocate but don't initialize num elements of type T.
        T* allocate (size_t num, const void* = 0)
        {
            // Print message and allocate memory with global new.
            cerr << "allocate " << num << " element(s)"
                      << " of size " << sizeof(T) << std::endl;
            T* ret = (T*)(::operator new(num*sizeof(T)));
            cerr << " allocated at: " << (void*)ret << std::endl;
            return ret;
        }
```
→ 1
```cpp
// Initialize elements of allocated storage p with value value.
        void construct (T* p, const T& value)
        {
            // Initialize memory with placement new.
            new((void*)p)T(value);
        }
```
→ 2
```cpp
        // Destroy elements of initialized storage p.
        void destroy (T* p)
        {
            // Destroy objects by calling their destructor.
            p->~T();
        }
```
→ 3

(continued)

LISTING 50-1 *(continued)*

```
    // Deallocate storage p of deleted elements.
    void deallocate (T* p, size_t num)                              → 4
    {
        // Print message and deallocate memory with global delete.
        cerr << "deallocate " << num << " element(s)"
                    << " of size " << sizeof(T)
                    << " at: " << (void*)p << std::endl;
        ::operator delete((void*)p);
    }
};

// Return that all specializations of this allocator are interchangeable.
template <class T1, class T2>
bool operator== (const MyAlloc<T1>&,
                const MyAlloc<T2>&) throw() {
    return true;
}
template <class T1, class T2>
bool operator!= (const MyAlloc<T1>&,
                const MyAlloc<T2>&) throw()
{
    return false;
}

#endif
```

The listing above does not actually do anything; it simply implements the class definition for our allocator. We have overriden four methods that really matter here:

▶ allocate, shown at ➔ 1. This method is called to specifically allocate a block of memory. In our case, we simply return a block of memory while printing some diagnostic information.

▶ construct, shown at ➔ 2. This method is called to create a new object given a block of memory. Fortunately, C++ allows for a specialized version of the new operator, called the *in-place new* that allows you to construct an object within a pre-allocated block. This allows us to use the block allocated by the allocate method.

▶ destroy, shown at ➔ 3. This method is not intended to de-allocate the block of memory,

because it could be reused in the container later on. Instead, it simply invokes the destructor directly for the class.

▶ deallocate, shown at ➔ 4. This method frees up the allocated block that was allocated in the allocate method. Once again, we added some diagnostics here.

3. **Save and close the source file in the editor.**

4. **In the code editor, create a new file to hold the code for the source file of the technique.**

In this example, the file is named ch50.cpp, although you can use whatever you choose. This file will contain the test code for using the allocator.

5. **Type the code from Listing 50-2 into your file.**

Better yet, copy the code from the source file on this book's companion Web site.

LISTING 50-2: THE TEST DRIVER FOR THE CUSTOM ALLOCATOR

```cpp
#include <vector>
#include "Allocator.h"

class MyBuffer
{
private:
    char *_buffer;
    int   _length;

    virtual void Init()
    {
        setBuffer( NULL );
        setLength( 0 );
    }
    virtual void Message( const char *msg )
    {
        cout << "MyBuffer: " << msg << endl;
    }

public:
    MyBuffer( void )
    {
        Message("Void Constructor");
        Init();
    }
    MyBuffer( int length, const char
      *inBuffer )
    {
        Message("Full Constructor");
        setLength( length );
        setBuffer( inBuffer );
    }
    MyBuffer( const MyBuffer& aCopy )
    {
        Message("Copy Constructor");
        setLength ( aCopy.getLength() );
        setBuffer( aCopy.getBuffer() );
    }
    virtual ~MyBuffer( void )
    {
        Message("Destructor");
        if ( _buffer )
            delete [] _buffer;
    }

    MyBuffer operator=( const MyBuffer&
      aCopy )
    {
        Message("operator=");
        setLength ( aCopy.getLength() );
        setBuffer( aCopy.getBuffer() );
        return *this;
    }
    virtual void setLength( int length )
    {
        _length = length;
    }
    virtual void setBuffer( const char
      *buffer )
    {
        if ( buffer )
        {
            _buffer = new
              char[strlen(buffer)+1];
            memcpy( _buffer, buffer,
              strlen(buffer) );
        }
        else
            _buffer = NULL;
    }
    virtual int getLength( void ) const
    {
        return _length;
    }
    virtual const char *getBuffer( void )
      const
    {
        return _buffer;
    }
};


int main()
{
    std::vector<MyBuffer, MyAlloc<MyBuffer>
    > myVector;

    const char *s1 = "Hello world";
    const char *s2 = "Goodbye cruel world";
    const char *s3 = "Hello again world";

    MyBuffer m1(strlen(s1), s1);
    MyBuffer m2(strlen(s2), s2);
    MyBuffer m3(strlen(s3), s3);

    myVector.insert( myVector.end(), m1 );
    myVector.insert( myVector.end(), m2 );
    myVector.insert( myVector.end(), m3 );
}
```

Our test driver simply exercises some of the more basic constructs of a container, creating a few new objects and adding them to a vector. The vector is destroyed when it goes out of scope. We added some diagnostic print messages to illustrate when the various pieces of code in the MyBuffer class are called.

6. **Save the source file in the editor and close the editor application.**

7. **Compile the application with the compiler of your choice on your favorite operating system.**

If you have done everything right, you should get something similar to the output shown in Listing 50-3 when you run the program in your console window.

LISTING 50-3: OUTPUT FROM THE TEST DRIVER

```
$ ./a.exe
MyBuffer: Full Constructor          → 5
MyBuffer: Full Constructor
MyBuffer: Full Constructor
allocate 1 element(s) of size 12    → 6
  allocated at: 0xa050768
MyBuffer: Copy Constructor
allocate 2 element(s) of size 12
  allocated at: 0xa050788
MyBuffer: Copy Constructor
MyBuffer: Copy Constructor
MyBuffer: Destructor
deallocate 1 element(s) of size 12 at:
    0xa050768
allocate 4 element(s) of size 12
  allocated at: 0xa0507d0
MyBuffer: Copy Constructor          → 7
MyBuffer: Copy Constructor
MyBuffer: Copy Constructor
MyBuffer: Destructor
MyBuffer: Destructor
deallocate 2 element(s) of size 12 at:
    0xa050788                       → 8
MyBuffer: Destructor
MyBuffer: Destructor
MyBuffer: Destructor
MyBuffer: Destructor
MyBuffer: Destructor
MyBuffer: Destructor
deallocate 4 element(s) of size 12 at:
    0xa0507d0
```

The display shows the allocator doing its job, telling us just when everything is being allocated and destroyed. The messages we placed in the constructor are printed out (seen at → **5**) from the construction in our main program. The allocator memory allocation is shown at → **6**. This corresponds to the call to insert in the vector called myVector in the main function. As each item is placed into the array, a new object is allocated by the allocate method and then the object is copied into that block, as shown at → **7**. Finally, the vector goes out of scope and the deallocate method is called, as shown at → **8**. This calls the destructors for the class, as shown in the output.

Always build a debugging version of allocation (with diagnostic printouts) for your programs so you can track memory leaks (and overall memory usage).

Technique 51

Using the auto_ptr Class to Avoid Memory Leaks

Save Time By

✔ Preventing memory leaks caused by overwritten pointers

✔ Introducing the `auto_ptr` class

✔ Implementing the `auto_ptr` class

✔ Interpreting the output

There are numerous products on the market for detecting and resolving memory leaks. And in this book, I have included several techniques for discovering memory leaks as well. However, the best way to handle memory leaks is to not have them in the first place. Defensive programming techniques can avoid memory-leak problems and save you immense amounts of time and trouble in the long-run.

 Rather than try to find and fix problems as they occur, you'd be better off utilizing techniques that avoid the problem in the first place. This way you have more time to spend on solving problems directly related to user interaction and needs and less time to worry about trivial problems that must be fixed before you can get to those issues.

One of the most insidious memory leak issues is that of pointers that are overwritten or failed to de-allocate. If a pointer is not de-allocated, a memory leak will occur. If enough memory leaks occur, your program will not be able to allocate new memory and will likely crash. With overwritten pointers, the memory that they point at is not the same memory that was allocated. As a result, the original memory is not de-allocated, which causes the memory leak problem. Alternatively, the overwritten pointer may point at something important in memory, and when it is dereferenced and used to modify that memory, it will cause a program crash. The STL provides a wonderful tool for avoiding this particular problem: the `auto_ptr` class. This class ensures that a pointer is always deleted when its work is done, even if it has been copied over, ignored, or transferred to an orphan object. This technique explores how to use the `auto_ptr` class to avoid problems in your own code.

Using the auto_ptr Class

The `auto_ptr` class makes code cleaner by removing the need to check for allocations and de-allocations of objects all over your code. Let's look at the steps necessary to use the `auto_ptr` class in your own code. Essentially, there is only one real "step" involved, which is to wrap an allocated pointer in an `auto_ptr` template object. We will see how the object is allocated and then freed when the `auto_ptr` template object goes out of scope.

1. **In the code editor of your choice, create a new file to hold the code for the technique.**

   In this example, the file is named ch51.cpp, although you can use whatever you choose. This file will contain the source code for our classes.

2. **Type the code from Listing 51-1 into your file.**

   Better yet, copy the code from the source file on this book's companion Web site.

LISTING 51-1: USING THE AUTO_PTR CLASS WITH YOUR OWN FUNCTIONS

```
#include <iostream>
#include <memory>

using namespace std;

class Tracker
{
private:
    static int _allocations;
    static int _frees;
public:
    Tracker( void )
    {
        _allocations ++;
    }
    Tracker( const Tracker& aCopy )
    {
        _allocations ++;
    }
    ~Tracker()
    {
        _frees ++;
    }

    static int Allocations()
    {
        return _allocations;
    }
    static int Frees()
    {
        return _frees;
    }
    static void reset()
    {
        _allocations = 0;
        _frees = 0;
```

```
    }
    static void report()
    {
        cout << "Tracker Class:" << endl;
        cout << "Allocations: " << _alloca-
            tions << endl;
        cout << "Frees: " << _frees << endl;
    }
};

int Tracker::_allocations = 0;
int Tracker::_frees = 0;

void func1()
{
    Tracker t1;
    Tracker *t2 = new Tracker();
    Tracker t3 = *t2;
    Tracker t4 = t1;

    t2 = new Tracker();              ➙ 1
}

void func2()                         ➙ 2
{
    Tracker t1;
    auto_ptr<Tracker> t2( new Tracker );
    Tracker t3 = *t2;
    Tracker t4 = t1;

    t2.reset( new Tracker );
}

void call_an_exception_function()
{
    throw 1;
}

void func3()                         ➙ 3
{
    Tracker *t = new Tracker;

    call_an_exception_function();

    delete t;
}

void func4()
{
    auto_ptr<Tracker> t(new Tracker);   ➙ 4
```

```
        call_an_exception_function();
}

int main(void)
{
    cout << "Running function 1:" << endl;
    func1();
    Tracker::report();                          ➜ 5
    Tracker::reset();                           ➜ 6

    cout << endl;
    cout << "Running function 2:" << endl;
    func2();
    Tracker::report();
    Tracker::reset();

    cout << endl;
    cout << "Running function 3:" << endl;
    try
    {
        func3();
    }
    catch ( ... )
    {
    }

    Tracker::report();
    Tracker::reset();

    cout << endl;
    cout << "Running function 4:" << endl;
    try
    {
        func4();
    }
    catch ( ... )
    {
    }

    Tracker::report();
}
```

Our test code illustrates two separate ways in which memory can be leaked:

► You can forget to de-allocate a pointer, as shown in the func1 function at ➜ **1**. In this case, we are simply allocating a new

object and never freeing the object, which creates a memory leak. The function called func2, labeled ➜ **2**, shows the same code using an auto_ptr class rather than a plain allocation.

► You can allocate and free an object, but because the function calls something that throws an exception, the de-allocation line will never be run and a memory leak will occur. This more subtle memory leak is shown in function func3 at ➜ **3**. Function func4 shows the same basic code using an auto_ptr template instead, as shown in the line marked ➜ **4**.

3. **Save the source code in your editor and close the editor application.**

4. **Compile the application using your favorite compiler on your favorite operating system.**

5. **Run the application in the console window.**

If you have done everything right, the application should give you the output shown in Listing 51-2.

LISTING 51-2: OUTPUT FROM THE auto_ptr TEST PROGRAM

```
$ ./a.exe
Running function 1:
Tracker Class:
Allocations: 5
Frees: 3

Running function 2:
Tracker Class:
Allocations: 5
Frees: 5

Running function 3:
Tracker Class:
Allocations: 1
Frees: 0

Running function 4:
Tracker Class:
Allocations: 1
Frees: 1
```

As you can see from the output, the class Tracker tracks how many times the various constructors are called, and how many times the destructor is called in each run. The report is done via the Tracker class report method, as shown in Listing 51-1 at ➔ **5**. Note that we reset the count each time, using the reset function as shown at ➔ **6**. In an ideal situation, with no memory leaks, the numbers for allocations and frees should be the same. For functions func1 and func3, the allocation and free numbers are not the same, indicating a memory leak. For functions func2 and func4, the auto_ptr cases, the allocations and frees match up, indicating that there was no memory leak.

The functions we invoke here (func1, func2, func3, and func4) show the various ways in which memory can be leaked in an application. As you can see, the "normal" way of doing things results in numerous insidious memory leaks that are hard to track down. Compare the auto_ptr cases, which, even with exceptional events, always free their memory.

Rules for using the auto_ptr class

There are no free lunches in the programming world, and the auto_ptr class is no exception to that rule. There are certain times you should not use an auto_ptr, and certain rules you must understand — such as the following:

✔ You cannot use auto_ptrs in standard template collections such as the STL. Because the STL does not follow the standard rules for copying objects, auto_ptrs will not be destroyed properly. The designers of the STL made this choice and actually created templates that would not compile with auto_ptrs.

✔ If you copy an auto_ptr, you must not use the original again, as the pointer is transferred from one object to the other.

✔ The copy constructor for an auto_ptr is completely different than the copy constructor for a normal object or pointer. Do not treat them equivalently. Auto_ptr copy constructors transfer control of the pointer they contain, they do not make copies of it.

Other than that, the class is really a godsend for programmers. When you are working with pointers, use the auto_ptr class early and often in your programming applications.

Avoiding Memory Overwrites

Save Time By

- ✔ Understanding memory overwrites
- ✔ Preventing memory overwrites in arrays and allocated blocks
- ✔ Protecting your data
- ✔ Interpreting the output

Memory overwrites are a bane of the C++ programmer. A *memory overwrite* occurs when you write to an area outside an allocated block. This is bad, since you are writing to a block of memory that you may or may not own, but certainly did not intend to modify. For example, if we have a C++ statement that says

```
char line[10];
```

and we then write something that says

```
line[11] = 'a';
```

we have overwritten a valid part of memory and might cause problems in the application later on. Unfortunately, memory overwrites like this are somewhat hard to track down without specialized tools and software. Alternatively, of course, you can simply avoid writing outside the valid bounds of an array or allocated block, but that is a bit easier said than done. The real problem here is that when we write to position 11 of the ten-block array, we have overwritten something in memory. That something could be another variable, it could be the return address for a function, or it could be a pointer that was previously allocated. None of these are good things. You need to stay within the memory allotment that you have requested for a memory block.

This technique looks at a way to use the C++ coding concepts to protect the data we are working with from being overwritten. This is a basic concept of encapsulation in C++: If you have data, you need to make sure that the data is used properly. That means not assigning values outside a valid range; it also means not overwriting bounds that have been established.

Creating a Memory Safe Buffer Class

The most common memory overwrite case occurs when strings are copied and assigned values. This error, which typically shows up with the use of the C functions strcpy and memcpy, occurs because the functions do not "know" how big a string is, so they cannot protect against the string boundaries being overwritten. In order to fix this problem, we will create a class that understands its own boundaries and only allows the correct number of characters to be written to or copied into the object. In this way, we will create a generic buffer class that can be safely used to store strings in all of your applications, saving you time in implementing the class and in debugging memory overwrites. Here's how:

1. **In the code editor of your choice, create a new file to hold the code for the technique.**

In this example, the file is named ch52.cpp, although you can use whatever you choose. This file will contain the source code for our classes.

2. **Type the code from Listing 52-1 into your file.**

Better yet, copy the code from the source file on this book's companion Web site.

LISTING 52-1: THE BUFFER CLASS

```cpp
#include <iostream>
#include <fstream>

using namespace std;

class Buffer
{
private:
    char *_buffer;
    long _length;

    virtual void Init()
    {
        _buffer = NULL;
        _length = 0;
    }
    virtual void Clear()
    {
        if ( _buffer )
            delete [] _buffer;
        Init();
    }
public:
    Buffer(void)
    {
        Init();
    }
    Buffer( const char *buffer, int length )
    {
        Init();
        SetBuffer( buffer, length );
    }
    Buffer ( int length )
    {
        _buffer = new char[length];
        _length = length;
        set( 0 );
    }
    Buffer( const Buffer& aCopy )
```

```
{
    Init();
    SetBuffer( aCopy._buffer, aCopy._length );
}
virtual ~Buffer()
{
    if ( _buffer )
        delete [] _buffer;
}
Buffer operator=(const Buffer& aCopy )
{
    Clear();
    SetBuffer( aCopy._buffer, aCopy._length );
    return *this;
}
Buffer operator=(const char *buffer )
{
    Clear();
    SetBuffer( buffer, strlen(buffer) );
    return *this;
}
char& operator[]( int index )
{
    if ( index < 0 || index >= _length )
        throw "Buffer: Index out of range";
    return _buffer[ index ];
}
Buffer operator()(int st, int end)
{
    // Validate the pieces.
    if ( st < 0 || st >= _length )
        throw "Buffer: Start index out of range";
    if ( end < 0 || end >= _length )
        throw "Buffer: End index out of range";
    Buffer b( _buffer+st, end-st+1 );
    return b;
}

void set( char c )
{
    for ( int i=0; i<_length; ++i )
        _buffer[i] = c;
}

virtual void SetBuffer( const char *buffer, int length )
{
    _buffer = new char[ length ];
    for ( int i=0; i<length; ++i )
        _buffer[i] = buffer[i];
    _length = length;
}
void empty()
```

→ **4**

(continued)

LISTING 52-1 *(continued)*

```
        {
            set( 0 );
        }
        int Length() const
        {
            return _length;
        }

};

ostream& operator <<( ostream& out, Buffer &b )
{
    for ( int i=0; i<b.Length(); ++i )
        out << b[i];
    return out;
}

void func1()                                                              → 1
{
    char *buffer = new char[10];
    strcpy( buffer, "This is a really long string");
    cout << "Func1: [1]" << buffer << endl;
    memset( buffer, 0, 11 );
    cout << "Func1: [2]" << buffer << endl;
    strcpy( buffer, "This is a short string");
    buffer[ 12] = 0;
    cout << "Func1: [3]" << buffer << endl;
}

void func2()                                                              → 2
{
    Buffer b(10);
    try
    {
        b = "This is a really long string";
        cout << "Func2: [1]" << b << endl;
        b.set( 0 );
        cout << "Func2: [2]" << b << endl;
        b[12] = 0;
        cout << "Func2: [3]" << b << endl;
    }
    catch ( ... )                                                         → 3
    {
        printf("Exception caught\n");
    }
}

int main()
{
    func1();
    func2();
}
```

The two functions shown above illustrate the memory overwrite problem, first as addressed by the standard C++ allocation of arrays (func1, shown at → **1**) and then using our Buffer class to handle the problem (func2, shown at → **2**). In each case, we allocate a character buffer of ten characters. In the func1 case, we then copy a string that is much longer than ten characters into the buffer. This causes a memory overwrite and could easily crash your program. However, because standard C++ has no way of detecting this, you will not see the problem immediately. In the second case, func2, we are using our Buffer class, which detects the problem as soon as you try to copy the larger string into the small allocated buffer and report it.

3. **Save the source code in your code editor and close the editor application.**

4. **Compile the application, using your favorite compiler on your favorite operating system.**

5. **Run the application in the console window.**

If you have done everything right, you should see something similar to this output from the application:

```
$ ./a.exe
Func1: [1]This is a rel
Func1: [2]
Func1: [3]This is a sh
Func2: [1]This is a really long string
Func2: [2]
Func2: [3]
```

Note that you may see different output on different operating systems, depending on how the error occurs and whether or not it is visible. For func1, we see that the string does not get set to what we expect it to. You might see the string "This is a really long string" which would be even worse. In the func2 case, however, we never assign the strings that are too long, because an exception is thrown and the code properly handles it.

As you can see, in the "pure" C-style access code (shown at → **1**), there are no checks to see whether the programmer overwrites the buffer that is allocated. Obviously, in your own code it would not be quite as straightforward to find the problem. There do not appear to be any problems with the code here; everything prints out and continues processing properly. However, damage has been done to structures in memory — and these might or might not show up as program crashes. Worse, you might give the user incorrect output upon which they may make invalid decisions.

In the second case, C++ style (shown at → **2**), you can see that the code protects against overwrites and throws an exception (shown at the line marked → **4** and caught at the line marked → **3**) when an invalid write occurs. This allows the programmer to immediately find where the problem happened and to fix it quickly and easily.

Technique 53

Throwing, Catching, and Re-throwing Exceptions

C++'s exception handling ability is a feature that differentiates it from virtually all older programming systems. As with Java, C#, and other modern programming languages, C++ offers the ability to jump out of the middle of a block of code when an exceptional event occurs.

The concept of an *exception handling* is really quite simple. In older programming languages, when errors occurred, an error code was sent to the calling application, which could — and often did — simply ignore it. Exception handling changes this. It forces the application developer to consider in advance what could go wrong in the lower-level code, and to provide routines to contend with any errors that crop up. Now when an error — that is, an *exception* — occurs, the program passes control to the appropriate predefined routine. Error handling ensures that errors aren't ignored; they're dealt with.

This technique takes a closer look at throwing and catching exceptions. First, we examine throwing an exception and logging it in a generic fashion. Logging errors is important because it allows you to provide a complete debugging log that can be used to see what went wrong when a problem occurs. This will save you time and effort in debugging your application, and results in better code for the end-user.

Throwing and Logging Exceptions

In order to best understand how to use exception handling in your own applications, let's look at a simple example of throwing exceptions in which those exceptions are logged to an output error file that can be used for debugging purposes. To do this, we will need two different types of classes.

- ✔ We need a class to hold the information about what went wrong. This class will contain the line number where the error occurred and information detailing the nature of the error.

- ✔ We need a class that will manage the process of catching the exception and logging the information into an error log.

The following steps show you how this is done:

1. **In the code editor of your choice, create a new file to hold the code for the technique.**

In this example, the file is named ch53.cpp, although you can use whatever you choose. This file will contain the source code for our classes.

2. **Type the code from Listing 53-1 into your file.**

Better yet, copy the code from the source file on this book's companion Web site.

LISTING 53-1: THE EXCEPTION HANDLING CLASSES

```cpp
#include <iostream>
#include <string>
#include <fstream>
#include <stdio.h>

using namespace std;


class ExceptionClass                                                → 1
{
    string _message;
    string _file;
    long   _line;
public:
    ExceptionClass(void)
    {
        _message = "Unknown Exception";
    }
    ExceptionClass( const char *msg, const char *fileName, long lineNo )
    {
        _message = msg;
        _file    = fileName;
        _line    = lineNo;
    }
    ExceptionClass( const ExceptionClass& aCopy )
    {
        _message = aCopy._message;
        _file    = aCopy._file;
        _line    = aCopy._line;
    }

    void setMessage(const char *msg, const char *fileName, long lineNo )
    {
        _message = msg;
        _file    = fileName;
        _line    = lineNo;
    }
```

(continued)

LISTING 53-1 *(continued)*

```
    virtual string Report(void) const
    {
        string out;
        out = "Exception reported in file ";
        out += _file.c_str();
        out += " at line ";
        out += _line;
        return out;
    }
    virtual ostream& Report( ostream& out ) const
    {
        out << "Exception reported in file " << _file.c_str() << " at line " << _line << endl;
        out << _message.c_str() << endl;
        return out;
    }
};

class ExceptionCatcher                                                      ➔ 2
{
private:
    string          _message;
    ofstream    _logFile;
    string          _fileName;
public:
    ExceptionCatcher( void )
    {
        string msg = "Startup";
        LogMessage( msg );
    }
    ExceptionCatcher( const char *fileName )
        : _logFile( fileName )
    {
        string msg = "Startup";
        msg += " [";
        msg += fileName;
        msg += "]";
        LogMessage( msg );
    }
    ExceptionCatcher( const ExceptionCatcher& aCopy )
        : _logFile ( aCopy._fileName.c_str() )
    {
        _fileName = aCopy._fileName;
        _message = aCopy._message;
        string msg = "Startup";
        msg += " [";
        msg += _fileName;
        msg += "]";
        LogMessage( msg );
```

```
    }
    ExceptionCatcher( const ExceptionClass& exception )
    {
        _message = exception.Report();
    }
    virtual ~ExceptionCatcher()
    {
        string msg = "Shutdown";
        LogMessage( msg );
    }
    virtual void LogMessage( string msg )
    {
        if ( !_logFile.fail() )
            _logFile << msg.c_str() << endl;
    }
    virtual void LogMessage( const ExceptionClass& exception )
    {
        if ( !_logFile.fail() )
        {
            exception.Report( _logFile );
        }
    }
};

void process_option( int x )
{
    if ( x < 2 || x > 8 )
        throw "Invalid Input to process_option";

    int z = 10 / x;

    cout << "Properly processed option " << x << endl;
}

int func1( int x)
throw( ExceptionClass )
{
    ExceptionClass ec;
    try
    {
        switch ( x )
        {
            case 0:
                cout << "You selected the first option" << endl;
                break;
            case 1:
                cout << "You selected the second option" << endl;
                break;
            case 2:
                process_option( x );
```

(continued)

LISTING 53-1 *(continued)*

```
                    default:
                        ec.setMessage( "Invalid Option", __FILE__, __LINE__ );
                        throw ec;
                }

    }

    catch ( const char *msg )
    {
        string sErr = "Unknown Error: ";
        sErr += msg;
        ec.setMessage( sErr.c_str(), __FILE__, __LINE__ );
        throw ec;
    }

    return 0;
}

int main(int argc, char **argv)
{
    if ( argc < 2 )
    {
        cout << "Usage: ch6_9 <inputs>" << endl;
        cout << "Where: inputs is a series of numbers" << endl;
        return -1;
    }

    ExceptionCatcher catcher("errors.log");

    // Process the inputs.
    for ( int i=1; i<argc; ++i )
    {
        int iVal = atoi( argv[i] );
        try
        {
            func1(iVal);
        }
        catch ( ExceptionClass& ec )
        {
            ec.Report( cout );
            catcher.LogMessage( ec );
        }

        catch ( ... )
        {
            cout << "Caught an exception" << endl;
        }
    }

    return 0;
}
```

→ 3

The purpose of this code is to illustrate how to handle an error, log the error to an output file, and then utilize the information in that file to see what really went wrong. Our test driver simply allows the user to enter several options from the command line and then passes them to a selector function that decides what to do based on that input. If the input is within range, it is processed. Otherwise, an exception object is built indicating what problem occurred and where. In this case, our error object will show all times in which the user entered a value outside the valid range. To do this, we use the `ExceptionClass` class, shown at ➔ **1**. This class simply holds the error information, and allows the application to retrieve it. It also provides a reporting function to format the information in a user readable way and to print it out. The second class, the `ExceptionCatcher` (shown at ➔ **2**) just takes the information from the `ExceptionClass` object and prints it to the file specified in its constructor. Note that when an error occurs, it is propagated up to the main program, and caught at ➔ **3**.

3. **Save the source code in your code editor and then close the editor application.**

4. **Compile the application, using your favorite compiler on your favorite operating system.**

5. **Run the application in the console window.**

If you have done everything right, you should see the following output from the application:

```
$ ./a.exe 1 2 3
You selected the second option
Properly processed option 2
Exception reported in file ch53.cpp at
   line 138
Invalid Option
Exception reported in file ch53.cpp at
   line 138
Invalid Option
```

 Note that the filename shown will vary depending on the program name you have chosen and the operating system you are working on.

In addition, you will have a file in your file system called `errors.log`. This file should contain the following entries in it:

```
$ cat errors.log
Startup [errors.log]
Exception reported in file ch53.cpp at
   line 138
Invalid Option
Exception reported in file ch53.cpp at
   line 138
Invalid Option
Shutdown
```

The output above indicates that there were errors detected in the program, which is to be expected because we gave the input invalid values. For the values that were understood, the message `Properly processed option` followed by the option number is displayed. For all other values, an exception is generated and the error `Invalid Option` is displayed.

Dealing with Unhandled Exceptions

Exception handling is a good thing, but sometimes an exception type pops up that you were not expecting. This is particularly problematic when you're working with third-party libraries that either change over time or poorly document the exception types they throw. There is obviously nothing you can do about an exception type that you know nothing about — but you can at least stop your program from behaving badly when one *is* thrown.

The following steps show you an example of an exception that isn't handled properly (a divide-by-zero error) and how you can use the built-in set_terminate function to deal with it before it can lead to memory leaks and the like in your application. The set_terminate function defines a user-implemented function that will be called before the program exits. This function can be used to de-allocate any allocated blocks of memory or to close any open files or to do any other last minute handling that needs to be done to make your program shut down cleanly.

1. **In the code editor of your choice, reopen the source file to hold the code for the technique.**

In this example, the file is named ch53.cpp, although you can use whatever you choose.

2. **Add the code from Listing 53-2 into your file.**

Better yet, copy the code from the source file on this book's companion Web site.

LISTING 53-2: USING SET_TERMINATE IN YOUR APPLICATION

```cpp
int *gAllocatedBuffer = NULL;

void term_func()
{
    cout << "term_func() was called by terminate().\n";

    // Do our global cleanup here.
    delete [] gAllocatedBuffer;

    // We MUST call exit, because the terminate routine will abort
    // otherwise.
    exit(-1);
}

int func2( void )
{
    set_terminate( term_func );
    try
    {
        int i = 10;
        int j = 0;
        int x = 0;

        if ( j != 0 )
            x = i / j;
        else
            throw "Error: Division by Zero!";
    }
    catch ( ExceptionClass& ec )
    {
        cout << "Exception Caught" << endl;
    }
}
```

➙ 4

Also, remember to add a call to `func2` in your main function so that we can look at the output of the program. After you do this, you will see that when the `func2` function is invoked, it causes a divide-by-zero error (shown at **→ 4** in Listing 53-2), which would normally crash the program without freeing the allocated `gAllocatedBuffer` memory block back to the operating system. Instead, we check for the error, throw an exception that is caught by the compiler-generated code, and then call the termination function.

Note that we are throwing an exception that contains a character string, but catching only the exceptions of type `ExceptionClass`. The two will not match — which means the code for catching the exception will be bypassed.

3. Save the source code in your code editor and then close the editor application.

4. Compile the application, using your favorite compiler on your favorite operating system.

5. Run the application in the console window.

If you have done everything right, you should see the following output from the application:

```
$ ./a.exe 1 2 3
You selected the second option
Properly processed option 2
Exception reported in file ch6_9.cpp at
    line 138
Invalid Option
Exception reported in file ch6_9.cpp at
    line 138
Invalid Option
term_func() was called by terminate().
```

Note that the `term_func` was called because an unhandled exception was generated by the code and never caught by the application code. If we did not install our own termination function, the program would simply exit and you would never see the `term_func` function call in the output.

Re-throwing Exceptions

One of the most annoying things about traditional error handling in C and C++ is that it forces you to lose a lot of lower-level information. For example, if you call a function to read a record, which in turn calls a function to move to the record in the file, which in turn calls a function to seek to the offset in the file (which causes an error), some potentially useful lower-level information (the fact that the offset was invalid) is lost at the top level. All you know is that the function to read a record failed, and possibly that it failed in the move routine. You still have to sit down with a debugger and step all the way down into the lowest-level functionality to see what really happened in the code. We can fix this by chaining errors from the lowest level to the uppermost level of an application. This chaining effect is accomplished by rethrowing exceptions.

 Exception handling is a sure way to make sure that an error is handled in an application. If you design your application (from the ground up) to use exception handling, you save time later on by simplifying the debugging and maintenance phase of the system.

With exception handling, however, you can pass the information up the chain so the highest-level function can report all the data for a given error from the bottom level to the top.

In order to pass information from a lower level of the application to a higher one, you must catch exceptions, append to them and rethrow them. In the following list, I show you exactly how you do that, from generating the initial exception to catching it and adding to it to pass it to a higher level.

1. **In the code editor of your choice, reopen the source file to hold the code for the technique.**

In this example, the file is named ch53.cpp, although you can use whatever you choose.

2. **Add the code from Listing 53-3 into your file.**

Or better yet, copy the code from the source file on this book's companion Web site.

LISTING 53-3: PASSING EXCEPTIONS TO A HIGHER LEVEL

```
int read_file( long offset )
    throw(string)
{
    if ( offset < 0 || offset >= 100 )
        throw string("read_file: Invalid offset");      ➜ 5
    return 0;
}

int read_record( long record )
    throw(string)
{
    if ( record < 0 || record > 10 )
        throw string("read_record: invalid record number");
    long offset = record * 10;
    try
    {
        read_file( offset );
    }
    catch ( string msg )
    {
        string sMsg = "record_record: unable to go to offset\n";   ➜ 6
        sMsg += msg;
        throw sMsg;
    }
    return 0;
}

int func3(long recno)
{
    try
    {
        read_record( recno );
    }
    catch ( string s )
    {
        cout << "func 3: Error in read:" << endl;
        cout << s.c_str() << endl;                        ➜ 7
    }
    catch ( ... )
    {
        cout << "func 3: Unknown error in read:" << endl;
    }
    cout << "End of func3\n";
}
```

In this example, we first catch an error at the lowest level, the read_file function, and generate an exception that is thrown to the read_record function, as shown at ➔ **5**. This error is then caught in the read_record function, but the fact that the read_record function fails trying to read the data is added and the error is then rethrown, as shown at ➔ **6**. The error is then caught at a higher level, in the func3 function (as shown at ➔ **7**), and the results are displayed for the user.

3. **In the main function, modify the code to call our new function, adding a call to func3 wherever you would like in the code, as follows:**

```
//func2();

cout << "Func3 [1]" << endl;
func3(2);
cout << "Func3 [2]" << endl;
```

```
func3(10);
cout << "Func3 [3]" << endl;
func3(20);
```

Note that the func2 call has been commented out, because it exits the program. This is easy to overlook; if your program never hits the func3 calls, it's probably because you forgot to comment out this line.

4. **Save the source code as a file in your code editor and then close the editor application.**

5. **Compile the application using your favorite compiler on your favorite operating system.**

6. **Run the application in the console window.**

If you have done everything right, you should see the output from the application as shown in Listing 53-4.

LISTING 53-4: UPDATED OUTPUT FROM THE EXCEPTION HANDLING PROGRAM

```
$ ./a.exe 1 2 3
You selected the second option
Properly processed option 2
Exception reported in file ch6_9.cpp at line 138
Invalid Option
Exception reported in file ch6_9.cpp at line 138
Invalid Option
Func3 [1]
End of func3
Func3 [2]
func 3: Error in read:                                                    ➔ 8
record_record: unable to go to offset
read_file: Invalid offset
End of func3
Func3 [3]
func 3: Error in read:
read_record: invalid record number
End of func3
```

As you can see from the line marked with → **8** in the above output listing, the function `func3` generates the entire error string, rather than a simple notation that an error occurred. From this, we can see how much more useful it is to see the entire history of what went wrong rather than simply that an error occurred.

Some caveats about exception handling

While exception handling is a wonderful thing and deals with many of the problems that are inherent in our C++ programs today, there are a few issues you should be aware of before you leap into using it everywhere.

✔ Exception handling is not cheap; it costs you speed and processing power. Every time you throw an exception, the entire stack must be unwound, all proper destructors called, and the proper handler found and called.

✔ Exception handling can result in unintended memory leaks if an exception is thrown at the wrong moment. For example, consider the following:

```
void func(char *strIn)
{
    char *buffer = new char[80];
    if ( strIn == NULL )
      throw "Bad input";

    // Process input

    delete [] buffer;
}
```

If you call this function with a `NULL` pointer, it causes a memory leak because the buffer array is never de-allocated.

✔ Never use an exception type whose `copy` constructor could throw an exception. This includes strings, and some STL container classes. Always make sure that the copy constructor is exception-safe before using it. If you do not follow this rule, you will cause problems with recursive error handling.

✔ Some C++ compilers cause the exception object to be deleted twice. Make sure that any exception class you write is safe: Clear out all pointers in the destructor.

Enforcing Return Codes

Technique 54

Failing to handle errors is the single biggest reason for program failure — and that's what creates the need for debugging and maintenance. If you eliminate the source of failures, you will give yourself more time for developing better classes of applications and better features for your users. In this technique, I show you how to combine return codes with exception handling to avoid these failures.

In C++, methods and functions can return a *status code* that says whether the function succeeded, failed, or was left in some in-between state. For example, we might have a function that returns a status code indicating where the method is in processing data. The status code returned may look something like this:

```
int get_status(void)
{
    switch ( current_status )
    {
        case NotProcessing:
                return -1;
        case InProcessing:
                return 1;
        case ProcessingComplete:
                return 0;
    }
    return -99;
}
```

Now, in this example, if the function returns a value of -99, obviously something very bad is going on — because we have no idea what state the object might have reached. Normally, if the status code were -99, we would want to stop processing immediately — and possibly exit the program. Unfortunately, there is no way for the developer of the function to force the developer using the function to check the return status code to make sure that they know something has gone wrong. Wouldn't it be nice if there was a way to ensure that the programmer looked at the return code to see if it was invalid or not?

As it turns out, you can make sure that the developer checked the return codes. By using the following steps, you can force the return code to be checked; if the code isn't checked, you can throw an exception. This is really the best of all possible worlds. Exception handling is a very sure way to force the developer to handle errors, but it also has a large overhead in terms of processing speed and CPU usage. Return codes, on the other hand, have low overhead, but you can't really be sure that the developer will ever look at them. By combining the two approaches, you can be absolutely sure that errors are handled, which eliminates most of the run-time problems that crop up for end-users. There is some overhead involved here, due to the exception-handling addition, but that overhead is mitigated by the fact that the exceptions will not be thrown if the error is properly checked.

1. **In the code editor of your choice, create a new file to hold the code for the technique.**

In this example, the file is named `ch54.cpp`, although you can use whatever you choose. This file will contain the source code for our classes.

2. **Type the code from Listing 54-1 into your file.**

Better yet, copy the code from the source file on this book's companion Web site.

LISTING 54-1: THE RETURN CODE CLASS

```cpp
#include <iostream>
#include <string>

using namespace std;

template < class T >
class RetValue
{
    T _value;
    bool _checked;
public:
    RetValue( void )
    {
        _checked = false;
    }
    RetValue( const T& t )
    {
        _value = t;
        _checked = false;
    }
    RetValue( const RetValue& aCopy )
    {
        _value = aCopy._value;
        _checked = false;
    }
    virtual ~RetValue(void)
    {
        if ( !_checked )
            throw "Error: Return value not checked!!";
```

→ 1
→ 2

→ 3

```
}
bool operator==( const T& t)
{
    _checked = true;
    return t == _value;
}
bool operator!=( const T& t)
{
    _checked = true;
    return t != _value;
}
bool operator <( const T& t)
{
    _checked = true;
    return _value < t;
}
bool operator <=( const T& t)
{
    _checked = true;
    return _value <= t;
}
bool operator >( const T& t)
{
    _checked = true;
    return _value > t;
}
bool operator >=( const T& t)
{
    _checked = true;
    return _value >= t;
}
operator T()
{
    _checked = true;
    return _value;
}
bool operator!()
{
    _checked = true;
    return !_value;
}
T operator&( const T& t )
{
    _checked = true;
    return _value & t;
}
T operator|( const T& t )
{
    _checked = true;
    return _value | t;
}
bool IsChecked()
```

→ 7

(continued)

LISTING 54-1 *(continued)*

```
        {
            return _checked;
        }
        T& Value()
        {
            return _value;
        }
};

RetValue<int> func( int iValue )
{
    if ( iValue == 34 )
        return RetValue<int>(1);
    if ( iValue == 35 )
        return RetValue<int>(2);

    return RetValue<int>(0);
}

RetValue<int> func2(int iValue)
{
    RetValue<int> ret = func(iValue);
    if ( ret )
        return ret;

    return RetValue<int>(0);
}

class MyReturnValue
{
    string _message;
public:
    MyReturnValue( void )
    {
        _message = "";
    }
    MyReturnValue( const char *msg )
    {
        _message = msg;
    }
    MyReturnValue( const MyReturnValue& aCopy )
    {
        _message = aCopy._message;
    }
    MyReturnValue operator=( const MyReturnValue& aCopy )
    {
        _message = aCopy._message;
        return *this;
    }
    string Message(void)
    {
        return _message;
```

```
    }
    string operator=( const string& msg )
    {
        _message = msg;
        return _message;
    }
    bool operator==( const MyReturnValue& aValue )
    {
        return _message == aValue._message;
    }
    bool operator<( const MyReturnValue& aValue )
    {
        return _message < aValue._message;
    }
};

int main()
{
    try
    {
        if ( !func( 34 ))
            printf("Success!!\n");
        if ( func(35) & 2 )
            printf("Error 35\n");
        RetValue<int> t1 = 5;
        int x = 5;
        int y = 3;
        printf("5 == 5? %s\n", t1 == x ? "Yes" : "No" );
        printf("5 == 3? %s\n", t1 == y ? "Yes" : "No" );
        int iVal = t1;

        printf("Calling func2\n");
        func2(34);
    }
    catch ( ... )
    {
        printf("Exception!\n");
    }

    try
    {
        RetValue<MyReturnValue> rv1 = MyReturnValue("This is a test");
        MyReturnValue rv = rv1;
        string s = rv.Message();
        printf("Return Value: %s\n", s.c_str() );

    }
    catch ( ... )
    {
        printf("Exception in MyReturnValue\n");
    }

    return 0;
}
```

→ 4

→ 5

→ 6

The base class here, RetValue, implements a templated return code class that can accept any sort of data to use as the "real" return code for functions and methods. This code is stored in the class as a member variable, as shown at ➜ **1**. Below that is another member variable called checked, which is used to see whether or not the return code has ever been compared to anything. (See ➜ **2**.) The user can trigger this by comparing the value of the return code using any of the standard boolean operators (such as equal, not equal, less than, greater than, and so forth). After any of these operators is used, the return code knows that the developer using the return code has checked it in some way, and allows the program to continue. If the return code object goes out of scope without the error being checked, an exception will be thrown, as shown at ➜ **3**. Because the class is templated, you can store anything you want in the class member data. We illustrate this by creating our own class, called MyReturnValue and returning it from a function.

3. **Save the source code in your code editor and then close the editor application.**

4. **Compile the application, using your favorite compiler on your favorite operating system.**

5. **Run the application in the console window.**

If you have done everything right, you should see the following output from the application:

```
$ ./a.exe
Error 35
5 == 5? Yes
5 == 3? No
Calling func2
Exception!
Return Value: This is a test
```

The output from this little test program shows that when we check an error, such as the not (!) operator comparison at ➜ **4** or the logical and (&) operator at ➜ **5**, there is no exception generated by the code. However, if a function that returns a RetValue

template object, such as func2, is called, as shown at ➜ **6**, and the return value is not checked, there will be an exception generated.

As you can see, if the user does not choose to check a return value, the destructor for the class throws an exception when the object goes out of scope. This forces the application developer to deal with the problem, one way or the other. If the developer does not handle the exception, it terminates the program. If the developer does handle the exception, he will immediately realize where the return code was not handled.

What's especially handy about this technique is that it also illustrates how you can override virtually every possible comparison operation for an object (such as the operator== shown at ➜ **7**). By checking the various operations, we know whether the user did something like this:

```
if ( method_with_return_code() ==
   BadReturn)
{
}
```

instead of something like this:

```
int myRet = method_with_return_code();
```

In the first case, the user is actually checking to see if the value was equal to something. In the second case, they are assigning the value to another variable that might never be checked. By looking at how the user accesses our return value, we can know whether they really checked the return code or not. This is where the overloaded operators come in; we set the checked flag in the overloaded operator and therefore we know whether the result was really looked at.

In addition, you have to worry about things like passing return codes up the chain from low-level methods to higher level ones. If the user makes a copy of the object to add a result or check the current result, we want to know about it. They might then pass a copy of the object to a higher level calling routine. The copy constructor for the class is a bit different from others you may have seen or coded; it does not simply assign all of the member variables to be the same as the object it copies. Instead, it copies the value of the return code, and then makes sure that the flag indicating that the return value was checked is reset to unchecked, because otherwise the user could simply copy the object into another return code and never look at the "real" status value.

Make sure that the errors you return to the user are as descriptive as possible, including as much information as you can. After all, you want your users to be able to actually do something about the trouble.

55 Technique

Using Wildcards

Save Time By

- ✔ Using wildcard characters to search
- ✔ Implementing a class that uses wildcard characters
- ✔ Testing your wildcard class

If you have ever searched for files on a computer, you have probably used wildcards. Wildcards, in this sense, are characters used in search strings that stand not for themselves but for a broad range of characters. The idea of finding all of the files that match a given pattern is rather common in the computer world. So is the idea of searching files for strings that match wildcard patterns. For example, if you must find a file but can't quite recall the name of that file — all you remember is that it began with the word convert or conversion or something similar — using a wildcard would be a great solution. Searching for the word convert only pulls up files that began with that specific word. Searching for conv*, on the other hand, gives you a much broader selection of files. The asterisk (*) wildcard character represents any group of zero or more characters. This means the resulting list from your search would include files that began with conv and then ended in any group of zero or more characters, such as

```
Convert
Conversion
Conversation
```

and the like.

Because they match zero or more characters, asterisks are useful wildcards, but they have their limitations. Using the asterisk, the pattern A*B matches AB, AbasdhB, and AbB. It does not match ABC nor AajhaBajksjB.

Wildcards represent a powerful capability that finds all the words that match a given root. Even better, wildcards also allow you to match words when you aren't quite sure of the spelling. For example, what if you're looking for the word conscious, but you can't recall how to spell it — does it have an *s* in the middle or not? Wildcards allow you to search for the term anyway; you just search for con?cious. The question mark (?) wildcard represents any single character (or none at all); the pattern A?B matches both AB and AbB. So the expression con?cious matches the word conscious whether or not it included an *s* in that position.

 Often users want to be able to use wildcards to filter data. If you give them this capability, you can save yourself a lot of time in supporting them. Appropriately used, wildcards can help make life a bit easier for everyone.

The question-mark and asterisk characters are common wildcards — but not the only ones. In the SQL language, for example, you use a percent sign (%) instead of an asterisk to match multiple characters. For this reason, when you design a class that permits wildcards in search strings, you should allow that information to be configurable. The purpose of this technique is to show you how to create a class that performs matching with wildcards. This class can be used to quickly and easily add pattern matching functionality to your application, which saves you time and effort in developing quality software that users really want.

Creating the Wildcard Matching Class

In order to best utilize wildcard matching in your application, you should encapsulate the functionality for matching strings into a single class. That class will handle both the jobs of storing the match characters (such as an asterisk or question mark) and determining if the two strings match. Let's develop such a class and a test driver to illustrate how it is used. Here's how:

1. **In the code editor of your choice, create a new file to hold the code for the source file of the technique.**

In this example, the file is named ch55.cpp, although you can use whatever you choose.

2. **Type the code from Listing 55-1 into your file.**

Better yet, copy the code from the source file on this book's companion Web site.

LISTING 55-1: THE MATCH CLASS

```cpp
#include <iostream>
#include <string>

using namespace std;

class Match
{
private:
    char _MatchMultiple;
    char _MatchSingle;
    string _pattern;
    string _candidate;

protected:

    bool match(const char *pat, const char *str)
    {
        if ( *pat == '\0' )
            return !*str;
        else
            if ( *pat == _MatchMultiple )
                return match(pat+1, str) || (*str && match(pat, str+1));
```

(continued)

LISTING 55-1 *(continued)*

```
              else
                  if ( *pat == _MatchSingle )
                      return *str && (match(pat+1, str+1) || match(pat+1, str));
          return (*str == *pat) && match(pat+1, str+1);
      }
public:
    Match(void)
    {
        _MatchMultiple = '*';
        _MatchSingle   = '?';
    }
    Match( const char *pat, const char *str )
    {
        _MatchMultiple = '*';
        _MatchSingle   = '?';
        _pattern = pat;
        _candidate = str;
    }
    Match( const Match& aCopy )
    {
        _MatchMultiple = aCopy._MatchMultiple;
        _MatchSingle   = aCopy._MatchSingle;
        _pattern       = aCopy._pattern;
        _candidate     = aCopy._candidate;
    }
    Match operator=( const Match& aCopy )
    {
        _MatchMultiple = aCopy._MatchMultiple;
        _MatchSingle   = aCopy._MatchSingle;
        _pattern       = aCopy._pattern;
        _candidate     = aCopy._candidate;
        return *this;
    }

    char Multiple(void)
    {
        return _MatchMultiple;
    }
    char Single(void)
    {
        return _MatchSingle;
    }
    void setMultiple( char mult )
    {
        _MatchMultiple = mult;
    }
    void setSingle( char single )
    {
        _MatchSingle = single;
    }
```

```
void setPattern( const char *pattern )
{
    _pattern = pattern;
}
void setCandidate( const char *candidate )
{
    _candidate = candidate;
}
string getPattern( void )
{
    return _pattern;
}
string getCandidate( void )
{
    return _candidate;
}
bool matches()
{
    return match( _pattern.c_str(), _candidate.c_str() );
}
};
```

The purpose of this class is to see whether or not two strings match, including wildcards if necessary. To accomplish this, we need the following:

▶ A multiple character wildcard

▶ A single character wildcard

▶ An input pattern string

▶ The candidate match string

For example, if we wanted to allow the user to match the string Colour as well as Color so that we could check for British spellings, we would use the following:

▶ Multiple character wildcard: An asterisk (*)

▶ Single character wildcard: A question mark (?)

▶ Input match string: Colo*r

▶ Candidate match string: Either Color or Colour

The result of this should be a positive match. To do this, we built a class that contained member variables for the match characters and strings, and routines to access those match elements. In addition, the class contains a single method, called matches, which indicates if the input and candidate strings match.

3. **Save the source code in the code editor.**

Testing the Wildcard Matching Class

After you create a class, you should create a test driver that not only ensures that your code is correct, but also shows people how to use your code.

The following steps show you how to create a test driver to illustrate various kinds of input from the user, and show how the class is intended to be used.

1. **In the code editor of your choice, reopen the source file to hold the code for your test program.**

In this example, I named the test program ch6_12.cpp.

2. **Type the code from Listing 55-2 into your file.**

Better yet, copy the code from the source file on this book's companion Web site.

LISTING 55-2: THE WILDCARD MATCHING TEST DRIVER

```
string get_a_line( istream& in )
{
    string retStr;

    while ( !in.fail() )
    {
        char c;
        in.get(c);
        if ( in.fail() )
            break;
        if ( c != '\r' && c != '\n' )
            retStr += c;
        if ( c == '\n' )
            break;
    }
    return retStr;
}


int main(int argc, char **argv)
{
    char szPattern[ 80 ];
    char szString [ 80 ];
    bool done = false;

    while ( !done )
    {
        cout << "Enter the pattern: ";
        string sPattern = get_a_line( cin );
        if ( !sPattern.length() )
            done = true;
        else
        {
            cout << "Enter the string: ";
            string sString = get_a_line( cin
);

            Match m(sPattern.c_str(),
              sString.c_str() );
```

```
            if ( m.matches() )
                printf("match\n");
            else
                printf("no match\n");
        }
    }
}
```

The test driver simply gets two strings from the user and uses wildcard matching to see if they match. The pattern string may contain optional wildcards, although the string to match may not. By utilizing the Match class that we developed in Listing 55-1, we check to see if the two strings are wildcard matches of each other.

3. **Save the source code in the editor and close the editor application.**

4. **Compile the application, using your favorite compiler on your favorite operating system.**

5. **Run the application on your favorite operating system.**

If you have done everything right, you should see the following session on your console window:

```
$ ./a.exe
Enter the pattern: A*B
Enter the string: AB
match
Enter the pattern: A*B
Enter the string: AajkjB
match
Enter the pattern: A*B
Enter the string: ABC
no match
Enter the pattern: A?B
Enter the string: AbaB
no match
Enter the pattern:
```

As you can see, the matching class works as advertised.

Part VIII

Utilities

The 5th Wave   By Rich Tennant

"I couldn't get this 'job skills' program to work on my PC, so I replaced the mother-board, upgraded the BIOS and wrote a program that links it to my personal database. It told me I wasn't technically inclined and should pursue a career in sales."

56 Technique

Encoding and Decoding Data for the Web

Save Time By

- ✔ Interfacing with the Internet
- ✔ Encoding and decoding URLs for use on the Internet
- ✔ Creating a URL Codec class
- ✔ Testing that class

The World Wide Web has brought with it a host of new opportunities and a host of new problems. Most applications these days need to be Web-enabled to work directly with Web browsers or Web applications. No matter what kind of application you're developing, odds are that the application will have to interact with the Web or with remote systems that use Web protocols.

The biggest issue in interfacing with the Internet is that of encoding. Encoding is the process of translating characters that cannot be directly used by a system into characters that can. For the World Wide Web, for example, characters such as the ampersand (&), greater- and less- than signs (> and <), and others cannot be directly used. We need to change them into a form that the Web can use. The Web identifies addresses with a Uniform Resource Locator, better known as a URL. One of the rules of working with URLs is that they cannot contain characters such as spaces and slashes, because including them would break many existing browser applications and operating systems. Browsers assume that spaces and slashes indicate breaks in a URL, which is the standard format for Web addresses. There is no way to change the browser, so we must change the string.

The problem is that the C++ library offers no standard way to encode and decode URL strings. The technique for encoding and decoding is well known, but it is new enough that it has not yet made it into the STL or standard C++ library. For this reason, we end up reimplementing the code in each and every application that we write that needs the functionality. This is contrary to the C++ principle of "write once, reuse many times."

Saving time is often about anticipating the needs of your application and planning for them in advance. By planning to Web-enable your code — regardless of whether you expect your application to support the Web (initially, at least) — you save a lot of time in the long-run. It makes sense, then, to create a single, reusable class that will do the encoding and decoding work, one you can insert as needed in the applications you develop. That's what this technique is all about.

Creating the URL Codec Class

In the technical world, a "codec" is a compressor/decompressor, normally used for compressing audio or video formats into a smaller size. However, the concept is very applicable to what we are doing with text because we are working with streams of data that are similar to video and audio formats. For the purposes of this technique, we are going to create a simple class that understands how to encode a string so that it can be used with existing Web browsers. Each character in the string will be examined, and if it is not in a valid format for the Web, will be encoded to use the proper syntax. Here's how it works:

1. **In the code editor of your choice, create a new file to hold the code for the source file of the technique.**

In this example, the file is named ch56.cpp, although you can use whatever you choose. This file will contain the class definition for our automation object.

2. **Type the code in Listing 56-1 into your file.**

Better yet, copy the code from the source file on this book's companion Web site.

LISTING 56-1: DATA ENCODING AND DECODING

```cpp
#include <string>
#include <iostream>

using namespace std;

class URLCodec
{
    string _url;
protected:

    // Convert a hex string to an ASCII rep-
        resentation.
    char htoa (int number)
    {
        if ((number >= 0) && (number <= 9))
            return ('0' + number);
```

```cpp
        else if ((number >= 10) && (number
            <= 15))
            return ('A' + number - 10);
        else
            return ('X');
    }

    // Convert an ASCII string into a hex
        digit.
    char atoh (unsigned char character)
    {
        if ((character >= '0') && (character
            <= '9'))
            return (character - '0');
        else if ((character >= 'A') &&
            (character <= 'F'))
            return (character - 'A' + 10);
        else if ((character >= 'a') &&
            (character <= 'f'))
            return (character - 'a' + 10);
        else
            return (0);
    }

public:
    URLCodec( void )
    {
        _url = "";
    }
    URLCodec( const char *strIn )
    {
        _url = strIn;
    }
    URLCodec( const URLCodec& aCopy )
    {
        _url = aCopy._url;
    }
    URLCodec operator=( const URLCodec&
        aCopy )
    {
        _url = aCopy._url;
        return *this;
    }

    void setURL ( const char *strIn )
    {
        _url = strIn;
    }
    void setURL ( const string& sIn )
    {
```

```
    _url = sIn;
}
string getURL ( void )
{
    return _url;
}

string encode()                         → 1
{
    int index;
    string encoded;

    // Make a copy of the string.
    encoded = _url;

    // Scan the input string backward.
    index = encoded.length();
    while (index--)
    {
        // Check for special characters.
        if (!isalnum((unsigned
          char)encoded[index]))     → 2
        {
            unsigned char special;
            char insert;

            special = (unsigned char)
              encoded[index];
            encoded.erase (index, 1);
            insert = htoa (special %
              16);
            encoded.insert (index,
              &insert, 1);
            insert = htoa (special /
              16);
            encoded.insert (index,
              &insert, 1);
            insert = '%';
            encoded.insert (index,
              &insert, 1);
        }
    }

    return (encoded);
}

string encode_no_xml()                  → 3
{
    int index;
    string encoded;
```

```
    // Make a copy of the string.
    encoded = _url;

    // Scan the input string backward.
    index = encoded.length();
    while (index--)
    {
        // Check for special characters.
        if ((!isalnum((unsigned
          char)encoded[index])) &&
            (encoded[index] != ' ') &&
            (encoded[index] != '<') &&
            (encoded[index] != '>') &&
            (encoded[index] != '_') &&
            (encoded[index] != '\n') &&
            (encoded[index] != '/') &&
            (encoded[index] != '"')  &&
            (encoded[index] != '\''))
        {
            unsigned char special;
            char insert;

            special = (unsigned char)
              encoded[index];
            encoded.erase (index, 1);
            insert = htoa (special %
              16);
            encoded.insert (index,
              &insert, 1);
            insert = htoa (special /
              16);
            encoded.insert (index,
              &insert, 1);
            insert = '%';
            encoded.insert (index,
              &insert, 1);
        }
    }

    return (encoded);
}

string decode()                         → 4
{
    int index;
    string decoded;

    // Make a copy of the string.
    decoded = _url;
```

(continued)

LISTING 56-1 (continued)

```
        // Scan input string forwards
        index = 0;
        while (index < decoded.length())
        {
            // Check for encoded characters.
            if (decoded[index] == '%')
            {
                unsigned char special;

                special = (unsigned char)
                    atoh(decoded[index+1]) *
                    16;
                special += (unsigned char)
                    atoh(decoded[index+2]);
                decoded.erase (index, 3);
                decoded.insert (index, (char
                    *)&special, 1);
            }
            index++;
        }

        return (decoded);
    }
};
```

This class will handle the encoding and decoding of URLs, as well as storing a generic URL string. Each character in the string is examined, starting at the rear of the string and working backwards, so that we can properly interpret characters as we need to.

There are two forms of the encode method shown here:

▶ The first, shown at the line marked → **1**, encodes all characters for the string in standard URL format. This is done at the loop, shown by the line marked → **2**. Each character is checked to see if it is in the valid alphanumeric order, and if not, it is replaced by its hex equivalent.

▶ The second, shown at the line marked with → **3**, does the same thing, but does not encode XML characters that some applications for the Web will need.

If you are working with standard URLs for the Web, use the first version. If you are working with Java applets or .Net applications running on the Web that are expecting valid XML characters, use the second. In any case, you may use the decode method, shown at → **4**, to decode the characters into a human-readable string.

3. **Save the source code in the code editor.**

Testing the URL Codec Class

After you create a class, you should create a test driver that not only ensures that your code is correct, but also shows people how to use your code.

The following steps show you how to create a test driver that illustrates various kinds of input from the user, and shows how the class is intended to be used.

1. **In the code editor of your choice, reopen the source file to hold the code for your test program.**

In this example, I named the test program `ch56.cpp`.

2. **Type the code from Listing 56-2 into your file.**

Better yet, copy the code from the source file on this book's companion Web site.

LISTING 56-2: THE URL CODEC TEST DRIVER

```
int main(int argc, char **argv)
{
    if ( argc < 2 )
    {
        cout << "Usage: ch7_1 url1 [url2
            url3]" << endl;
        cout << "Where: url[n] is the url
            you wish to see encoded/decoded"
            << endl;
        return -1;
    }
```

```
for ( int i=1; i<argc; ++i )
{
    URLCodec url( argv[i] );

    // First, try decoding it.
    string enc = url.encode();        → 5
    string dec = url.decode();
    cout << "Input String: " << argv[i]
      << endl;
    cout << "Encoded: " << enc.c_str()
      << endl;
    cout << "Decoded: " << dec.c_str()
      << endl;

    // Now try decoding the result.
    URLCodec enc_url( enc.c_str() );
    string enc1 = url.encode();
    string dec1 = url.decode();
    cout << "Input String: " <<
      enc_url.getURL().c_str() << endl;
    cout << "Encoded: " << enc1.c_str()
      << endl;
    cout << "Decoded: " << dec1.c_str()
      << endl;
}

    return 0;
}
```

The test driver code above simply allows you to test out the functionality of the encode and decode methods of the URLCodec class. If you enter a string from the command line to the application, it will print out the encoded and decoded versions of the string. There is nothing really magical about this application. As you can see from the listing, the code first tries to encode the string you give it (shown at → 5) and then decodes the result of that encoding to see if they are the same. The second block of code then encodes the result and decodes it to ensure that the code is working properly. When all is said and done, you should see the same input and output to the console.

3. Save the source-code file in the editor and close the editor application.

4. Compile the source file with your favorite compiler, on your favorite operating system.

5. Run the application on your favorite operating system.

If you have done everything right, you can produce a session similar to the one shown in Listing 56-3 on your console window.

LISTING 56-3: OUTPUT FROM THE TEST DRIVER

```
$ ./a.exe "http://this is a bad url"
  "http://localhost/c:/x*.xml"
Input String: http://this is a bad url
Encoded: http%3A%2F%2Fthis%20is%
  20a%20bad%20url
Decoded: http://this is a bad url
Input String: http%3A%2F%2Fthis%20is%20a%
  20bad%20url
Encoded: http%3A%2F%2Fthis%20is%20
  a%20bad%20url
Decoded: http://this is a bad url
Input String: http://localhost/c:/x*.xml
Encoded: http%3A%2F%2Flocalhost%2Fc%3A%
  2Fx%2A%2Exml
Decoded: http://localhost/c:/x*.xml
Input String: http%3A%2F%2Flocalhost%2Fc%3A%
  2Fx%2A%2Exml
Encoded: http%3A%2F%2Flocalhost%2Fc%3A%
  2Fx%2A%2Exml
Decoded: http://localhost/c:/x*.xml
```

Note that input strings on the command line must be enclosed in quotes; otherwise, they will be parsed into separate words on the space breaks.

As you can see, the input is properly converted into the encoded version of the URL string that can be used by Web browsers or servers. The decoded version is what you would expect it to be, in a form that can be used by any application.

Whenever you are exchanging data with a Web-based application, encode the data you send; expect the data you get back to be encoded from the application, too. Prepare your code to deal with encoding and decoding this information. If it turns out that the data does not need to be encoded or decoded, you will have wasted a small amount of time. But if the data does need encoding/decoding, you will have saved a lot of time that would otherwise be spent figuring out why your data looks strange and breaks things.

Technique 57

Encrypting and Decrypting Strings

Save Time By

- Protecting data with encryption
- Understanding and implementing the Rot13 algorithm
- Understanding and implementing the XOR algorithm
- Interpreting output

It would be very nice if we could all trust everyone around us not to view or access our private information. Unfortunately, not everyone is quite as trustworthy as you or I. The fact of the matter is that sensitive information, such as passwords, user names, and credit card numbers, simply should not be stored in a readily readable fashion. If we fail to hide the information in some way, we can be very sure that the information will find its way to every cracker on the Internet and be used in all sorts of evil and insidious ways. Hiding information is a task normally accomplished by *encryption* — translating data from a human-readable format to a non-human-readable format. There are almost as many ways to encrypt data as there are to create it in the first place. Serious encryption methods, such as the RSS or Blowfish encryption algorithms are very complex; they would take pages and pages to explain (and in the end, they'd still be about as hard to understand).

This technique looks at two very simple — but effective — methods of encrypting data from prying eyes: the Rot13 algorithm and the XOR algorithm (XOR stands for "Exclusive Or"). Both methods can defeat casual snoopers, but they're not foolproof; I wouldn't recommend using either method for industrial-strength applications. It is difficult, if not impossible, to add encryption to an application after it's been written. In order to make a secure system, encryption should be included as early in the process as possible. By adding these algorithms at the design phase, you will save time and effort and create a more secure system.

Selecting an encryption method is almost as sensitive an issue as selecting a programmer's editor or compiler. You can save a lot of time by selecting a standard algorithm that provides the level of security your system needs. If you are writing a simple in-house application, XOR encryption is probably more than secure enough. On the other hand, if you are writing a medical-storage application (that is, one that allows access to a database of patient information) that allows access via the Internet, choose a much stronger method, such as the Blowfish algorithm.

Implementing the Rot13 Algorithm

The Rot13 algorithm is really a very simple way of encoding data that makes that data difficult to read, but is almost trivial to decode. The algorithm, as the name suggests, simply rotates characters 13 places in the alphabet. Therefore, an *A* becomes an *N* and so forth. The algorithm wraps around, so anything past *Z* goes back to *A*. The following steps show you how to create a simple class that can both encode and decode Rot13 strings. This class is certainly not industrial-strength encryption, but it will make it difficult for the average person to read your strings.

1. **In the code editor of your choice, create a new file to hold the code for the source file of the technique.**

In this example, the file is named `ch57.cpp`, although you can use whatever you choose. This file will contain the class definition for your automation object.

2. **Type the code from Listing 57-1 into your file.**

Better yet, copy the code from the source file on this book's companion Web site.

LISTING 57-1: THE ROT13 ALGORITHM CODE

```
#include <string>
#include <iostream>

using namespace std;

class Rot13Encryption
{
private:
    string    _encrypt;
protected:
    string rot13(const string& strIn)
    {
        string sOut = "";
```

```
        for ( int i=0; i<(int)strIn.size();
            ++i )
        {
            char ch = strIn[i];
            // the following assumes that
            //   'a' + 25 == 'z' and
            //   'A' + 25 == 'Z', etc.       →1
            if( (ch >= 'N' && ch <= 'Z') ||
              (ch >= 'n' && ch <= 'z') )
                ch -= 13;
            else if( (ch >= 'A' && ch <=
              'M') || (ch >= 'a' && ch <=
              'm') )
                ch += 13;
            sOut += ch;
        }

        return sOut;
    }
public:
    Rot13Encryption(void)
    {
    }
    Rot13Encryption( const char *strIn )
    {
        if ( strIn )
        {
            _encrypt = rot13( strIn );
        }
    }
    Rot13Encryption( const Rot13Encryption&
      aCopy )
    {
        _encrypt = aCopy._encrypt;
    }
    Rot13Encryption operator=( const
      Rot13Encryption& aCopy )
    {
        _encrypt = aCopy._encrypt;
        return *this;
    }
    string operator=( const char *strIn )
    {
        if ( strIn )
        {
            _encrypt = rot13( strIn );
        }
        return _encrypt;
    }
    const char *operator<<( const char
      *strIn )
    {
```

```
        if ( strIn )
        {
            _encrypt = rot13( strIn );
        }
        return _encrypt.c_str();
    }
    string String(void) const
    {
        return _encrypt;
    }
};

ostream& operator<<( ostream& out, const
    Rot13Encryption& r13 )
{
    out << r13.String().c_str();
    return out;
}
}
```

The code in the above listing implements a simple Rot13 algorithm. The bulk of the work is done in the Rot13 function, which simply rotates characters 13 positions in the alphabet. If you look at the code at ➜ **1**, you can see how this works. As the comment in this function specifies, it assumes that the alphabet is contiguous for the character set you are working with. This means that this code will not work on older EBCDIC systems, nor will it work with non-English character sets. Unfortunately, this is true of most text-based encryption algorithms. The other methods of the class, such as the `operator <<` method, are utility functions that can be used to convert the encrypted string for output, or to stream it to an output file.

3. **Save the source file in your text editor.**

This class will handle the Rot13 algorithm. This algorithm works by simply rotating data about in the alphabet. The string is then unreadable by humans, which is the entire point of encryption.

Testing the Rot13 Algorithm

After you create a class, you should create a test driver that not only ensures that your code is correct, but also shows people how to use your code.

The following list shows you how to create a test driver that illustrates various kinds of input from the user, and shows how the class is intended to be used.

1. **In the code editor of your choice, reopen the source file to hold the code for your test program.**

In this example, I named the test program `ch57.cpp`.

2. **Type the code from Listing 57-2 into your file.**

Better yet, copy the code from the source file on this book's companion Web site.

LISTING 57-2: TESTING THE ROT13 ENCRYPTION CLASS

```
int main( int argc, char **argv )
{
    Rot13Encryption r13("This is a test");
    cout << r13.String().c_str() << endl;
    cout <<
        Rot13Encryption(r13.String().c_str())
        << endl;

    return 0;
}
```

3. **Compile the source file, using your favorite compiler on your favorite operating system.**

4. **Run the application in the console.**

If you have done everything properly, you should see the following output on the console window:

```
Guvf vf n grfg                          ➜ 2
This is a test
```

The first output (shown at → **2**) is the rotated version of the string. It remains human-readable, at least up to a point, because the substituted characters are all in the alphabet), but it certainly provides no clue to the semantic content of the text it is encrypting. Thus the purpose of encryption is preserved.

 Encryption is intended to hide the purpose of the text from the user, not to make the text vanish or compress. Note that the string used is embedded in the application; this particular program does not accept any input from the user. It is a very simple test driver.

Unfortunately, Rot13 is one of the most common algorithms in use; hackers know it like the backs of their hands. We need a slightly better approach.

Implementing the XOR Algorithm

The next encryption algorithm we examine is the XOR algorithm. XOR stands for *Exclusive OR*, which means that it uses the mathematical "exclusive or" operator in order to convert text. One property of the exclusive or operation is that a character that is exclusively or'd with another character can be returned to its original state by or'ing it again with the same character. This means that an encryption password can be used to both encode and decode a string using XOR. In this technique, we build a simple class that implements the XOR algorithm and provides methods for encoding and decoding strings.

1. **In the code editor of your choice, reopen the source file to hold the code for the source file of the technique.**

In this example, the file is named ch57.cpp, although you can use whatever you choose.

2. **Append the code from Listing 57-3 into your file.**

Better yet, copy the code from the source file on this book's companion Web site.

LISTING 57-3: THE XORENCRYPTION CLASS

```
class XOREncryption
{
private:
    char    *_encrypt;
    int     _length;
    string  _key;
protected:
    char *do_xor( const char *sIn, int
      length, const string& key)              → 3
    {
        int idx = 0;
        char *strOut = new char[ length ];

        if ( !key.length() )
            return strOut;

        for ( int i=0; i<length; ++i )
        {
            char c = (sIn[i] ^ key[idx]);
            strOut[i] = c;

            idx ++;
            if ( idx >= key.length() )
                idx = 0;
        }
        return strOut;
    }
public:
    XOREncryption(void)
    {
        _encrypt = NULL;
    }
    XOREncryption( const char *strIn, int
      length, const char *keyIn )
    {
        if ( keyIn )
            _key = keyIn;
        if ( strIn )
        {
            _length = length;
            _encrypt = do_xor( strIn,
```

```
length, _key );
    }
}
XOREncryption( const XOREncryption&
  aCopy )
{
    _encrypt = new char [ aCopy._length
];
    memcpy ( _encrypt, aCopy._encrypt,
      aCopy._length );
    _key     = aCopy._key;
    _length = aCopy._length;
}
XOREncryption operator=( const
  XOREncryption& aCopy )
{
    _encrypt = new char [ aCopy._length
      ];
    memcpy ( _encrypt, aCopy._encrypt,
      aCopy._length );
    _key     = aCopy._key;
    _length = aCopy._length;
    return *this;
}
~XOREncryption(void)
{
    delete _encrypt;
}
const char *operator=( const char *strIn
)
{
    if ( _encrypt )
        delete _encrypt;

    if ( strIn )
    {
        _encrypt = do_xor( strIn,
            strlen(strIn), _key );
    }
    return _encrypt;
}
const char *operator<<( const char
  *strIn )
{
    if ( strIn )
    {
        _encrypt = do_xor( strIn,
            strlen(strIn), _key );
    }
```

```
    return _encrypt;
}
const char *String(void) const
{
    return _encrypt;
}
int Length(void) const
{
    return _length;
}
};
```

The code in this class implements a simple XOR algorithm. The main functionality of the class is shown in the do_xor method, shown at ➜ **3**. As you can see, the method takes the input encryption key and XORs it with the string that is provided by the user. The class requires two strings, one that is a "key" used for encrypting or decrypting strings. The second string is the input string to be encrypted or decrypted. Running the algorithm with the same inputs twice results in the original string.

3. **Save the source file in your text editor.**

Testing the XOR Algorithm

The following steps show you how to create a test driver that illustrates various kinds of input from the user, and show how the class is intended to be used:

1. **In the code editor of your choice, reopen the source file to hold the code for your test program.**

In this example, I named the test program ch57.cpp.

2. **Type the code from Listing 57-4 into your file.**

Better yet, copy the code from the source file on this book's companion Web site.

LISTING 57-4: TESTING THE XOREncryption CLASS

```
int main( int argc, char **argv )
{
    Rot13Encryption r13("This is a test");
    cout << r13.String().c_str() << endl;
    cout <<
       Rot13Encryption(r13.String().c_str())
       << endl;

    XOREncryption x1("This is a test",
       strlen("This is a test"), "C++Test");
    cout << x1.String() << endl;
    XOREncryption x2(x1.String(),
       x1.Length(), "C++Test");                    → 4
    cout << x2.String() << endl;
    return 0;
}
```

3. **Compile the source file, using your favorite compiler on your favorite operating system.**

4. **Run the application in the console.**

If you have done everything properly, you should see the following output on the console window:

```
$ ./a.exe
Guvf vf n grfg
This is a test
_CB'E_cJ_                                          → 5
This is a test                                     → 6
```

Note that the above output includes the Rot13 encryption that we developed earlier in this technique for comparison. The strings are all hard-coded into the application, and your output might vary depending on the font and terminal type you are using. The output for the XOREncryption class is shown at → 5 and → 6. Our original string is This is a test and the two lines following it show how that line is first encrypted and then decrypted using the same key. In this case, our "key" is the string C++Test.

The XOREncryption class does not use a string to hold the encrypted version of the input (see → 4 in Listing 57-4), nor does it return the value as a string object. This is because the string class holds only alphanumeric data. The xor operation can result in non-alphanumeric values, and at times can cause the string class to return only a portion of the original string.

Never use a string object to store character buffers that might contain nulls or control characters. String classes assume that the null character terminates the string and will not store any characters past the null.

Converting the Case of a String

Save Time By

✔ Using modern techniques to convert the case of input strings

✔ Using the Standard Template Library's `transform` function

✔ Interpreting output

In the good old days of C programming, converting the case of a string was a simple matter. You just called the `strupr` function and the string was instantly converted to uppercase. Similarly, if you called the `strlwr` function, the string was converted to lowercase. Have things really changed all that much since then? Well, in some ways, things have changed a lot. For example, the following code is not permissible:

```
string myString = "Hello world"
strupr( myString );
```

This code will not compile, since the `strupr` function does not accept a string argument. Nor can you write the following code and expect it to work:

```
strupr(myString.c_str());
```

This code will not compile either; the `strupr` function cannot accept a `const` character pointer — which is what the `c_str` method returns. So how do you write code to convert modern string objects to upper- and lowercase? You could use the brute-force technique, like this:

```
for ( int i=0; i<myString.length(); ++i )
    myString[i] = toupper(myString[i]);
```

This code certainly does work, but it is not very elegant and it does not anticipate all circumstances. It assumes, for example, that the string characters are in contiguous order in memory — which is a bad assumption to make about any Standard Template Library (STL) collection. The entire purpose of the STL is to provide the developer with a way in which to access containers (strings are just containers of characters) without any assumptions about how they are organized in memory. The better choice, of course, is to use an iterator (see Technique 49 for more on iterators). However, the STL provides an even better approach to the whole thing, which is the `transform` function found in the algorithms of the STL. The `transform` function allows you to operate in a container-independent way to modify the individual elements of a container through a conversion function. This saves time because the algorithm has already been written, debugged, and optimized. It also saves time because you can easily extend your conversion functions without rewriting the basic algorithm.

 Always make sure that you are using the most efficient code for your application up front. Rather than trying to implement your own algorithms to work with the Standard Template Library, choose to use the ones in the `<algorithm>` include file as they have been optimized for working with the STL collections.

Implementing the transform Function to Convert Strings

The `transform` algorithm of the Standard Template Library uses a function created by the user of the algorithm to convert each element of a container in some way. The following steps show you how to create a simple `transform` function to convert the case of a string, to either upper- or lowercase. By looking at the technique and how the code is implemented, you will be able to see how to extend the functionality for your own uses in the future. In order to implement this function, we will need to implement a class which does the work of our transformation. The `transform` algorithm accepts two iterators and an object to do its work. Let's take a look at exactly how this is implemented in your own code.

1. **In the code editor of your choice, create a new file to hold the code for the source file of the technique.**

In this example, the file is named `ch58.cpp`, although you can use whatever you choose. This file will contain the class definition for your automation object.

2. **Type the code from Listing 58-1 into your file.**

Better yet, copy the code from the source file on this book's companion Web site.

LISTING 58-1: CONVERSION CODE FOR THE STL STRING CLASS

```cpp
#include <string>
#include <algorithm>
#include <iostream>
#include <vector>
#include <ctype.h>

using namespace std;

// A function for converting a string to
// lowercase.
string convert_to_lowercase( const string&
  sIn )
{
    // First, save a pointer to the
    function.
    int (*pf)(int)=tolower;

    // Next, convert the string.
    string sOut = sIn;
    transform(sOut.begin(), sOut.end(),
    sOut.begin(), pf);

    return sOut;
}

// A function for converting a string to
// uppercase.
string convert_to_uppercase( const string&
  sIn )
{
    // First, save a pointer to the
    function.
    int (*pf)(int)=toupper;

    // Next, convert the string.
    string sOut = sIn;
    transform(sOut.begin(), sOut.end(),
      sOut.begin(), pf);

    return sOut;
}
```

```
string strip_leading ( const string& sIn )
{
    // Find the first non-white-space
       character.
    int iPos = 0;
    while ( iPos < sIn.length() && isspace
( sIn[iPos] ) )
        iPos ++;
    // Copy the rest of it.
    string sOut;
    for ( int i=iPos; i<sIn.length(); ++i )
        sOut += sIn[i];

    return sOut;
}

string strip_trailing ( const string& sIn )
{
    // Find the last non-white-space
       character.
    int iPos = sIn.length()-1;
    while ( iPos >= 0 && isspace( sIn[iPos]
) )
        iPos --;
    // Copy the rest of it.
    string sOut;
    for ( int i=0; i<=iPos; ++i )
        sOut += sIn[i];

    return sOut;
}

// This is a utility class that will convert
// a string to lowercase.
class StringConvertToLowerCase          ➔ 1
{
public:
    string operator()(string s)
    {
        return convert_to_lower_case(s);
    }
};

// This is a utility class that will strip
// leading AND trailing white space.
class StringStripSpace
{
```

```
public:
    string operator()(string s)
    {
        return strip_leading(strip_
           trailing(s));
    }
};
```

This code implements all of the various possible transforms for the `string` class, and throws in several bonus methods for manipulating the strings (such as stripping the leading and trailing characters). In all cases, we will use the `transform` method to actually modify the strings or arrays. As the test driver in this technique illustrates, a single string is no more difficult to convert than is an entire string array. The important functionality here is the class we will be using to convert strings to lowercase, which is the `StringConvertToLowerCase` class shown at ➔ **1**. The `transform` function uses this class to convert strings. As you can see, all of the work is done in a single method, the `operator()` method. This method is called by the `transform` algorithm to do its work, as we will see shortly.

Testing the String Conversions

After you create a class, you should create a test driver that not only ensures that your code is correct, but also shows people how to use your code.

The following list shows you how to create a test driver that illustrates various kinds of input from the user, and shows how the class is intended to be used.

1. **In the code editor of your choice, reopen the source file to hold the code for your test program.**

In this example, I named the test program `ch58.cpp`.

2. **Type the code from Listing 58-2 into your file.**

Better yet, copy the code from the source file on this book's companion Web site.

LISTING 58-2: THE STRING CONVERSION TEST DRIVER

```
int main(int argc, char **argv)
{
    vector<string> stringArray;
    if ( argc < 2 )
    {
        cout << "Usage: ch7_3 string1
            [string2 string3...]" << endl;
        cout << "Where: string[n] is the
            string to convert" << endl;
        return -1;
    }

    // First, do them individually.
    cout << "Individual Conversions: " <<
        endl;
    for ( int i=1; i<argc; ++i )
    {
        cout << "Input String: " << argv[i]
            << endl;
        string sLower =
            convert_to_lower_case( argv[i] );
        cout << "Lowercase String: " <<
            sLower.c_str() << endl;
        string sUpper =
            convert_to_upper_case( argv[i] );
        cout << "Uppercase String: " <<
            sUpper.c_str() << endl;
        stringArray.insert(
            stringArray.end(), argv[i] );   →4
    }

    // Now do the whole array.
    transform(stringArray.begin(),
        stringArray.end(),
        stringArray.begin(),
            StringConvertToLowerCase() );

    // Print them out.
    cout << endl << "Array Conversions: " <<
        endl;
```

```
    vector<string>::iterator iter;
    for ( iter = stringArray.begin(); iter
        != stringArray.end(); ++iter )
            cout << "String: " <<
                (*iter).c_str() << endl;

    cout << endl << "Individual String
        Whitespace Strip Test: " << endl;
    string whiteSpace = "    This is a test
        ";
    string sNoWhite = strip_leading(
        whiteSpace );
    cout << "Stripped String: [" <<
        sNoWhite.c_str() << "]" << endl;
    sNoWhite = strip_trailing( whiteSpace );
    cout << "Stripped String: [" <<
        sNoWhite.c_str() << "]" << endl;

    transform(stringArray.begin(),
        stringArray.end(),
        stringArray.begin(),
            StringStripSpace() );
    cout << endl << "Array of Strings
        Whitespace Strip Test: " << endl;
    for ( iter = stringArray.begin(); iter
        != stringArray.end(); ++iter )
            cout << "String: [" <<
                (*iter).c_str() << "]" << endl;

    return 0;
}
```

3. **Save the source code in your code editor and close the editor application.**

4. **Compile the source code with your favorite compiler, on your favorite operating system.**

5. **Run the program on your favorite operating system.**

If you have done everything right, you should see the output shown in Listing 58-3 in the console window.

LISTING 58-3: OUTPUT FROM THE STRING CONVERSION TEST

```
$ ./a.exe "   This is a test" "This is
    another test  " "   Final Test    "    →2
Individual Conversions:                      →3
Input String:    This is a test
Lowercase String:    this is a test
Uppercase String:    THIS IS A TEST
Input String: This is another test
Lowercase String: this is another test
Uppercase String: THIS IS ANOTHER TEST
Input String:    Final Test
Lowercase String:    final test
Uppercase String:    FINAL TEST

Array Conversions:
String:    this is a test                    →5
String: this is another test
String:    final test

Individual String Whitespace Strip Test:
Stripped String: [This is a test    ]
Stripped String: [    This is a test]

Array of Strings Whitespace Strip Test:
String: [this is a test]
String: [this is another test]
String: [final test]
```

The first line of the output is simply the executable name and the arguments to the program (shown at → 2). As you can see, we are passing in three arguments. The various transformations are then run on each of these arguments. First, we use the individual utility functions (as shown at → 3) to convert each of the input strings. This simply shows that the functions are working properly. The strings are then added to an array (shown at → 4 in Listing 58-2). The transform functions are then applied, converting each string to lowercase (shown in the output at → 5). Finally, just to show how the transformation can be applied to any string, we use the white space removal functions to change the strings to have no leading or trailing white space.

 Keep a library of utility classes around for all of your projects and you will find that you use them automatically — saving time and energy in solving little problems.

Technique 59

Implementing a Serialization Interface

Save Time By

- ✔ Understanding interfaces
- ✔ Understanding serialization
- ✔ Implementing a serialization interface
- ✔ Testing the interface

Implementing interfaces can save you loads of time when you are doing the same thing over and over in your application, or even across applications. In addition, it collects all of the code for a given task in one place, making it quick and easy to change the format of output files or the algorithm used for the functionality of the interface.

If you have ever used Java as a programming language, you're probably already accustomed to interfaces. Simply put, an *interface* is a base class from which you can inherit that provides a given service. The C++ language supports interfaces, although they are slightly different in terms of syntax. Unlike a typical base class, interfaces are less concrete and do not generally allow the application to build upon them, but rather to use them to provide a specific service. In C++, an interface is a pure virtual base class that contains multiple pure virtual methods. A pure virtual method, unlike a regular virtual method, must be overridden by a derived class. For example, an interface might allow your class to print itself out, or save itself to a file, or even allocate its memory from some specialized form of hardware space. This technique shows how to implement an important concept — serialization — as an interface. The most important thing about interfaces, and the way in which they will save you the majority of time, is that if you inherit from an interface, you can pass your object to any function or method that works with objects that implement that interface. So, if you have a function that is used to save all sorts of objects, you can pass your object to the function so long as it implements the Save interface.

Essentially, *serialization* is the capability of an object to write itself to some form of persistent storage. The code that does the job tends to be the same from class to class; the data being written is what changes. Accordingly, serialization lends itself perfectly to the process of creating an interface.

There are two basic steps to implementing an interface in your class:

✔ You must create the actual interface class and identify all areas in which you need input from the derived class. At this stage, you're implementing all the functionality for the interface class — creating it as if it were a main class for your application.

✔ After you've created the interface class, you set up your derived class to inherit from it (and to implement any virtual functions the interface requires).

Implementing the Serialization Interface

The most popular interface is the `serialization` interface. This interface, used by many of the popular class libraries, such as MFC, allows an object to be written to persistent storage (such as a file) so long as it implements a consistent interface. In this example, we will explore how to create a serialization interface and apply that interface to a given class or classes.

1. **In the code editor of your choice, create a new file to hold the code for the interface definition of the technique.**

In this example, the file is named `ch59.h`, although you can use whatever you choose. This file will contain the class definition for your serialization object.

2. **Type the code from Listing 59-1 into your file.**

Better yet, copy the code from the source file on this book's companion Web site.

LISTING 59-1: THE SERIALIZATION INTERFACE CODE

```
#ifndef _SERIALIZE_H_
#define _SERIALIZE_H_

#include <string>
#include <vector>
```

```
#include <iostream>
#include <fstream>

using namespace std;

class SerializeEntry
{
    string _name;
    string _value;
public:
    SerializeEntry(void)
    {
    }
    SerializeEntry( const char *name, const
      char *value )
    {
        setName( name );
        setValue( value );
    }
    SerializeEntry( const char *name, int
      iValue )
    {
        setName( name );
        setValue( iValue );
    }
    SerializeEntry( const char *name, double
      dValue )
    {
        setName( name );
        setValue( dValue );
    }

    SerializeEntry( const SerializeEntry&
      aCopy )
    {
        setName( aCopy.getName().c_str() );
        setValue( aCopy.getValue().c_str()
);
    }
    SerializeEntry operator=(const
      SerializeEntry& aCopy)
    {
        setName( aCopy.getName().c_str() );
        setValue( aCopy.getValue().c_str()
);
        return *this;
    }
```

(continued)

LISTING 59-1 *(continued)*

```
        void setName( const char *name )
        {
            if ( name )
                _name = name;
            else
                _name = "";
        }
        void setValue( const char *value )
        {
            if ( value )
                _value = value;
            else
                _value = "";
        }
        void setValue( int iValue )
        {
            char szBuffer[ 20 ];
            sprintf(szBuffer, "%d", iValue );
            setValue ( szBuffer );
        }
        void setValue( double dValue )
        {
            char szBuffer[ 20 ];
            sprintf(szBuffer, "%lf", dValue );
            setValue ( szBuffer );
        }
        string getName(void) const
        {
            return _name;
        }
        string getValue(void) const
        {
            return _value;
        }
};


class Serialization
{
private:
    long    _majorVersion;
    long    _minorVersion;
protected:
    virtual bool getEntries( vector<
        SerializeEntry >& entries )
    {
        return true;
    }
    virtual string getClassName()
    {
```

```
        return "None";
    }
public:
    Serialization(void)
    {
        _majorVersion = 0;
        _minorVersion = 0;
    }
    Serialization( long major,
      long minor )                          → 2
    {
        _majorVersion = major;
        _minorVersion = minor;
    }
    Serialization( const Serialization&
      aCopy )
    {
        _majorVersion = aCopy._majorVersion;
        _minorVersion = aCopy._minorVersion;
    }
    Serialization operator=( const
      Serialization& aCopy )
    {
        _majorVersion = aCopy._majorVersion;
        _minorVersion = aCopy._minorVersion;
        return *this;
    }

    // Accessors
    void setMajorVersion( long major )
    {
        _majorVersion = major;
    }
    long getMajorVersion( void )
    {
        return _majorVersion;
    }
    void setMinorVersion( long minor )
    {
        _minorVersion = minor;
    }
    long getMinorVersion( void )
    {
        return _minorVersion;
    }

    // Functionality
    bool write( const char *strFileName )  → 1
    {
```

```
        // Note the call to the virtual
          method. This must
        // be overridden in the derived
          class code.

        vector< SerializeEntry > entries;
        getEntries( entries );              → 3

        if ( entries.size() == 0 )
            return false;

        // Try opening the output file.
        ofstream out( strFileName,
          ofstream::out | ofstream::app );
        if ( out.fail() )
            return false;

        // Write out the class name.
        out << "<" << getClassName() << ">"
          << endl;

        // Write out the version informa-
tion.
        out << "\t<VERSION>" <<
          _majorVersion << ":" <<
          _minorVersion << "</VERSION>" <<
          endl;

        vector< SerializeEntry >::iterator
          iter;
        for ( iter = entries.begin(); iter
          != entries.end(); ++iter )
        {
            out << "\t<" <<
              (*iter).getName().c_str() <<
              ">" << endl;
            out << "\t\t" <<
              (*iter).getValue().c_str() <<
              endl;
            out << "\t</" <<
              (*iter).getName().c_str() <<
              ">" << endl;
        }

        out << "</" << getClassName() << ">"
          << endl;

        return true;
    }
};

#endif
```

This code saves a given class to an output stream in standard XML format. It would be simple enough, of course, to modify the class to output in some other format, but for simplicity we will use XML. The important member of the class is the `write` method, shown at **→ 1**. This method writes out the members of a class in XML format, using the member variables of the class to determine the output file and version information. Note that the class keeps track of its own version information so that you can use it to determine whether a persistent version of the class is of the proper version for your application. The version information is defined in the constructor, as shown at **→ 2**.

Take a look at the `write` method; it appears that the code does everything you would expect a `serialization` object to do. The important part of the function is shown at **→ 3**, which is a call to a virtual method called `getEntries`. This method, which must be overridden by any class that uses this interface, returns the individual member variables of the class as a string array. After this method is created for your class, the rest of the functionality of the `serialization` interface will work no matter what the content of the derived classes.

3. **Save the source file and close the file in the code editor.**

As you can see, the serialization class does most of the work by itself. It requires the implementation of only two virtual methods:

- The `getElements` method returns all internal elements of the class that you want saved.

- The `getClassName` method returns the name of the class to use as the root of the XML tree that receives the element data we write out.

In addition, you can specify major and minor versions for the serialized file, so that if you wish to import existing serialized files, you will later on be able to import data created by older versions of the source code and properly default missing values if new ones have been added in the meantime.

 If you are persistently storing data for a class, make sure that you store version information with the data, so you can always know exactly when the data was written and what might be missing or superfluous. As classes change over time, member variables are added or removed. The data stored in a serialized version of older classes, therefore, may have additional or missing data. If you know what version of the class created the serialized data, you will know what data to map into your current member variable set.

Testing the Serialization Interface

After we have defined the `serialization` interface, the next step is to implement that interface for a real class. This allows you to see how the serialization process is used and how much time the interface concept will save in future class implementations. Let's take a look at creating a class with members that need to be stored persistently.

1. **In the code editor, create a new file to hold the code for the test class of the technique.**

In this example, the file is named `ch59.cpp`, although you can use whatever you choose. This file will contain the test code for the technique.

2. **Type the code from Listing 59-2 into your file.**

Better yet, copy the code from the source file on this book's companion Web site.

LISTING 59-2: TESTING THE SERIALIZATION INTERFACE

```cpp
#include "serialize.h"

class MyClass : public Serialization
{
private:
    int       _iValue;
    string    _sValue;
    double    _dValue;
protected:
    virtual bool getEntries( vector
    < SerializeEntry >& entries )          ➞ 4
    {
        entries.insert( entries.end(),
          SerializeEntry( "iValue",
          _iValue ) );                     ➞ 5
        entries.insert( entries.end(),
          SerializeEntry( "sValue",
          _sValue.c_str() ) );
        entries.insert( entries.end(),
          SerializeEntry( "dValue", _dValue
          ) );
    }
    virtual string getClassName( void )
    {
        return "MyClass";
    }
public:
    MyClass(void)
        : Serialization(1,0)               ➞ 6
    {
        _iValue = 0;
        _dValue = 0.0;
        _sValue = "";
    }
    MyClass(int iVal, double dVal, const
      char *sVal)
        : Serialization(1,0)
    {
        _iValue = iVal;
        _dValue = dVal;
        _sValue = sVal;
    }
    virtual ~MyClass()
    {
        Save();
    }
    virtual void Save()
    {
```

```
        write( "MyClass.xml" );
    }
};

int main()
{
    MyClass m1(1,2.0,"One");

    return 0;
}
```

This class simply implements a collection of data, with a string value, an integer value, and a floating point (double) value. The important work takes place in the getEntries virtual function, which builds an array of elements to output for serialization. This method, shown at ➔ **4**, overrides the serialization interface method and will be used for output. After this method is overridden, the remainder of the code works as expected within the interface. Note the use of the SerializeEntry class (shown at ➔ **5**) to hold the data for each element. Because this class can be derived to utilize other data types, the interface concept works even into the future.

3. **Save the source code as a file in your editor and close the editor application.**

4. **Compile the source code with your favorite compiler on your favorite operating system.**

5. **Run the program on your favorite operating system.**

If you have done everything right, the program will create an output file called MyClass.xml in your operating system's file system. This file should contain the following output after the application is run:

```
$ cat MyClass.xml
<MyClass>
        <VERSION>1:0</VERSION>
        <iValue>
            1
        </iValue>
        <sValue>
                One
        </sValue>
        <dValue>
            2.000000
        </dValue>
</MyClass>
```

In the output, you can see that all of the data elements specified in the MyClass class have been output via the serialization interface. This shows that our code works as we specified. Also note that the version information, which we specified in the constructor for the MyClass class (shown at ➔ **6**), is output in the persistent file, so that we can utilize it if we add new members to the MyClass class.

As you can see, the serialization class did exactly what it was supposed to do. In addition, note that the code for the serialization class has virtually no relation to the class from which it is called. This lack of specialization allows us to easily reuse the class as an interface to as many other classes as we want — allowing each of them to serialize the data efficiently.

Also note that if you were suddenly instructed to change the output to a format other than XML, the code needs adjustment in only one place. This saves you time, avoids mistakes, and is in keeping with the best strengths of object-oriented programming.

Creating a Generic Buffer Class

Save Time By

- ✔ Understanding buffer overflow errors
- ✔ Preventing buffer overflow errors from being exploited as a security risk
- ✔ Creating a Buffer class that deals with these errors
- ✔ Testing your class

Buffer overlows occur in a majority of C or C++ programs. Imagine, for a moment, reading data from an input file. The typical C or C++ code might look something like this:

```
char szBuffer[80];
int   nPos = 0;
while ( !eof(fp) )
{
    szBuffer[nPos] = fgetc(fp);
    if ( szBuffer[nPos] == '|' )
        break;
    nPos++;
}
```

This routine is supposed to read in a string from the file, reading until it hits a pipe (|) character or the end of the file. But what happens if the string is longer than 80 characters? Well, in that case, the routine continues to read in the string information, overwriting the memory locations that follow the szBuffer variable. We refer to this problem as a *buffer overflow*. What information is stored in those memory locations? Well, that's hard to say: Maybe there is nothing important there — or maybe an important return address for a function is being overwritten. In the former case, you might never see a problem. In the latter case, the program could easily crash, exposing a serious vulnerability to the outside world.

Problems like this, known as *buffer overflow,* are really quite widespread in the software-development world — but unless they're causing major issues (or haven't been discovered yet), programmers tend to overlook them. Even so, buffer overflow is considered the number-one security problem in software today. Depending on the application, a buffer overflow can crash the application, or simply destroy some vital part of the security wall that prevents an outside user from modifying data within a program. So why are we not doing something about it?

The simple answers look pretty silly: This is the way that we've always written code, the problem is not that serious, and we aren't going to change now. Actually the problem is reasonably easy to fix — and there is no excuse not to do so. This technique shows you how. By eliminating security risks, you will provide a safer application and minimize the amount of time you spend issuing security patches and dealing with customer support nightmares, which will save you a lot of time.

Imagine, for example, rewriting the routine just given so it looks like this:

```
Buffer szBuffer(80);                    → 1
int    nPos = 0;
try
{
    while ( !eof(fp) )
    {
        szBuffer[nPos] = fgetc(fp);
        if ( szBuffer[nPos] == '|' )
            break;
        nPos++;
    }
}
catch ( BufferException& exc )
{
printf("Buffer Overflow!");
}
return 0;
```

Now, this code cannot crash the program. Unlike the earlier code, which used a static array, this program uses a `Buffer` class (see → **1**) to manage the buffer. The `Buffer` class would check to see that the underlying buffer was not overwritten, and prevent memory from getting stomped on. If either condition were to occur, the program would throw an exception — and recover gracefully.

 Catching problems before they occur and spread to odd parts of the program will save you time and frustration later on down the line. If you build your programs as defensively as possible, you will limit the time you have to spend debugging them.

This solution allows programs to behave in that ideal fashion of dealing with problems all by themselves. Perhaps it is not possible to recover completely from an error like this, but at least the program could exit in a safe manner, shutting down all connections and not allowing the operating system to be compromised. This is what software security is all about. The issue, then, is to create a class that implements that generic buffer and protects your data. That is the aim of this technique.

Creating the Buffer Class

The solution we are going to implement for buffer overflows is to create a class that protects the data buffer by allowing access to valid areas of the buffer only. This class overrides the operators that provide access to the individual characters of the buffer, and makes sure that all assignments, copies, and manipulations work only on valid sections of the buffer. Let's create that class now.

1. In the code editor of your choice, create a new file to hold the code for the source file of the technique.

In this example, the file is named `ch60.cpp`, although you can use whatever you choose. This file will contain the class definition for your automation object.

2. Type the code in Listing 60-1 into your file.

Better yet, copy the code from the source file on this book's companion Web site.

Listing 60-1: The Buffer Class

```
#include <stdio.h>
#include <string.h>
#include <stdlib.h>
#include <string>

using namespace std;

class BufferException              → 4
{
```

(continued)

LISTING 60-1 *(continued)*

```cpp
private:
    string _errMsg;
public:
    BufferException( void )                    → 5
    {
        _errMsg = "";
    }
    BufferException( const char *msg )
    {
        _errMsg = msg;
    }
    BufferException( const BufferException&
      aCopy )
    {
        _errMsg = aCopy._errMsg;
    }
    const char *Message()
    {
        return _errMsg.c_str();
    }
    void setMessage( const char *msg )
    {
        _errMsg = msg;
    }
};


class Buffer
{
private:
    // $Member: m_Buffer - This is the
        actual area of allocated memory.
    char *m_Buffer;
    // $Member: m_Size - This is the size of
        the allocated memory.
    int    m_Size;
protected:
    virtual void print_buffer( const char
      *strPrefix )
    {
        printf("%s: [", strPrefix );
        for ( int i=0; i<m_Size; ++i )
            printf("%c", m_Buffer[i] );
        printf("]\n");
    }

    virtual void clear()
    {
```

```cpp
        if ( m_Buffer )
            delete m_Buffer;
        m_Buffer = NULL;
        m_Size   = 0;
    }
    virtual void copy( const Buffer& aBuffer
      )
    {
        m_Buffer = new char[ aBuffer.Size()
          ];
        memcpy( m_Buffer, aBuffer._Buffer(),
          aBuffer.Size() );
        m_Size = aBuffer.Size();
    }
    virtual void allocate( int nSize )
    {
        m_Buffer = new char[ nSize ];
        memset( m_Buffer, 0, nSize );
        m_Size = nSize;
    }

    const char *_Buffer(void) const
    {
        return m_Buffer;
    }

public:
    // Void constructor. No memory is allo-
        cated or available.
    Buffer(void)
        : m_Buffer(NULL), m_Size(0)
    {
        // Clear everything.
        clear();
    }
    // This is a standard constructor.
    Buffer( int nSize )
        : m_Buffer(NULL), m_Size(0)
    {
        clear();
        allocate( nSize );
    }
    // Copy the constructor.
    Buffer( const Buffer& aBuffer )
        : m_Buffer(NULL), m_Size(0)
    {
        clear();
        copy( aBuffer );
    }
```

```
virtual ~Buffer()
{
    clear();
}

// Operators
Buffer &operator=(const Buffer& aBuffer)
{
    clear();
    copy( aBuffer );
    return *this;
}
Buffer &operator=(const char *strBuffer)
{
    // If they are assigning us NULL,
       just clear
    // everything out and get out of
       here.
    clear();
    if ( strBuffer == NULL )
        return *this;

    // Otherwise, we need to set up this
       object
    // as the passed-in string.
    allocate( (int)strlen(strBuffer)+1
      );
    memcpy( m_Buffer, strBuffer,
      strlen(strBuffer) );
    return *this;
}
char& operator[](int nPos)              → 2
{
    if ( nPos < 0 || nPos > m_Size-1 )
        throw BufferException( "Buffer:
          Array index out of range" );
    return m_Buffer[ nPos ];
}
operator const char*()                  → 3
{
    // Just give them back the entire
       buffer.
    return m_Buffer;
}
const char *c_str( void )
{
    return m_Buffer;
}
```

```
// Here come the accessor functions.
int Size() const
{
    return m_Size;
}

// These are memory-based functions.
void Set( char c )
{
    for ( int i=0; i<m_Size-1; ++i )
        m_Buffer[i] = c;
}
void Clear( void )
{
    Set( 0 );
}

Buffer operator()(int nStart,
  int nLength)                          → 4
{
    // Do some validation
    if ( nStart < 0 || nStart > m_Size-1
  )
    {
        throw BufferException("Buffer:
          Array index out of range");
    }
    if ( nLength < 0 || nLength >
      m_Size-1 || nStart+nLength >
      m_Size-1 )
    {
        throw BufferException("Buffer:
          Length out of range");
    }

    Buffer b(nLength+1);
    for ( int i=0; i<nLength; ++i )
        b[i] = m_Buffer[i+nStart];

    return b;
}
};
```

In the code in the listing above, certain elements make it an important step up from the standard C++ character array. First of all, observe the way in which the characters are retrieved using the indexing operator (`[]`). The `operator[]`, shown at ➜ **2**, carefully checks to see whether the index requested is within a valid range. If it is not, it will throw an exception. Similarly, the sub-string `operator()` (shown at ➜ **4**) checks to make sure that all of the characters are in the valid range. Unlike the character array, the `Buffer` class allows you to extract small segments of itself, but protects against those segments being invalid. Because the returned value is a `Buffer` object, this method is safe from overruns. You might notice the conversion operator, shown at the line marked ➜ **3**; it appears to provide a way for the programmer to destroy the string. In fact, because it returns a constant pointer to the buffer, the programmer cannot directly change it without casting the string, a fact that the compiler will be happy to note. The overall idea is that we are preventing the programmer from doing something that will cause problems without thinking about it more than once.

3. **Save the source code in the code editor.**

 Notice that we create our own `Exception` class (shown at the line marked with ➜ **5**) to return errors from the `Buffer` class. It's a good idea to have your own forms of exceptions, rather than using the basic types; that way the programmer can deal with system errors in ways that are different from programmatic solutions.

Testing the Buffer Class

After you create a class, you should create a test driver that not only ensures your code is correct, but also shows people how to use your code. The following steps show you how:

1. **In the code editor of your choice, reopen the source file to hold the code for your test program.**

In this example, I named the test program `ch60.cpp`.

2. **Type the code from Listing 60-2 into your file.**

Better yet, copy the code from the source file on this book's companion Web site.

LISTING 60-2: THE TEST DRIVER FOR THE BUFFER CLASS

```
int main(int argc, char* argv[])
{
    Buffer b1(20);
    Buffer b2;

    b2 = b1;
    b1 = "This is a test";          ➜ 6
    printf("The buffer is: %s\n", (const
        char *)b1);
    b1[2] = 'a';
    printf("The buffer is: %s\n", (const
        char *)b1);
    try
    {
        b1[-1] = 'a';                ➜ 7
    }
    catch ( BufferException& exc )
    {
        printf("Caught the error: %s\n",
            exc.Message() );
    }

    // Test the "sub-buffer" function.
    Buffer b3;

    b3 = b1(0,4);                    ➜ 8
    printf("The new buffer is: [");
    for ( int i=0; i<b3.Size(); ++i )
        printf("%c", b3[i] );
    printf("]\n");


    return 0;
}
```

The above code simply exercises some of the important functionality of the Buffer class. First, we check to see that the assignment operators work as they are supposed to. This is shown at ➜ **6** in Listing 60-2. Next, we test to see whether the indexing logic works properly, as shown at ➜ **7**. If it is working properly, we would expect to see the exception thrown and printed out on the console. Finally, we test the sub-string functions, by extracting a piece of the buffer and making it into a new `Buffer` object (shown at → **8**). If the operator is working correctly, we should see the new buffer be the first four characters of the original string. Let's test it out and see.

3. Save the source file in the code editor and close the editor application.

4. Compile the source file with your favorite compiler on your favorite operating system.

5. Run the application on your favorite operating system.

If you've done everything right, you should see a session similar to this one on your console window:

```
$ ./a.exe
The buffer is: This is a test
The buffer is: Thas is a test
Caught the error: Buffer: Array index out
   of range
The new buffer is: [Thas ]
```

As you can see, the output is exactly what we expected. The error was generated and caught, and the exception information was printed to the console. The sub-string was the characters we expected as well, indicating that both the original assignment and the sub-string operators are correct. By using this class, we can therefore expect to save a lot of time in debugging our applications and in developing applications, because a lot of the functionality exposed makes it quicker to check input data.

As you can see, this code offers greater safety. It sure beats allowing the buffers to be overrun and the memory to be stomped on.

Technique 61

Opening a File Using Multiple Paths

It happens quite often when designing computer software: You ask a user to specify a file to open in your application, and then permit him to choose that file by "browsing" to the correct path. Unfortunately, there is no good way to utilize the underlying operating system to find specific files, especially if you want your application to be portable across various operating systems. It makes more sense, therefore, to build a method for actually looking across all search paths that might exist when you open a file automatically, without worrying about where they are, or how to get at them.

This technique does the job by building a utility class that manages multiple paths for searching files, using that class to find and read whichever file the user specifies. No magic here — just a handy way to utilize the built-in functionality of the C++ Standard Library functions to avoid the problems of using the operating system to find files, since this process is different for each operating system. There is nothing magical about searching various search paths and opening files, but combining the two into a single object provides some power and flexibility that you can utilize in numerous applications — with little effort on your own part. That, of course, is the entire point to building utility classes in C++: You get a lot of bang for your buck.

The new utility class is responsible for three things:

✔ It stores the various paths used for searching and ensures that those paths are all valid.

✔ It uses the input search paths to find a given file when the user specifies one.

✔ It opens the chosen file and returns a stream-object reference to the programmer for use in manipulating the file. The user can then find out where the file is — and read the file from the stream object as needed. The user may not know, or care, where the file they requested is actually located, so long as it can be found along one of the various search paths.

If you are storing various configuration files for your system, it's unlikely that the user will store all the files in one place. For example, if your program has a set of configuration files, a set of definition files, a set of output report files, and so on, the user will probably want them stored in different locations. It's also likely that the user will sometimes forget which ones go where and put them in the wrong places. Rather than making the users do the work of finding all the files, you should define a set of possible search paths for the user. This approach saves time for the user, spares the programmer some grief, makes your application better received, and makes life a bit easier for all concerned. If you require that the user find each file, rather than search for it yourself in the most likely places, you make life harder for the user. If you make life harder for the user, they will use someone else's program.

Creating the Multiple-Search-Path Class

A utility class that allows the user to find a file by using multiple search paths simply makes good sense. The following steps create such a class, called `MultiPathFile`:

1. **In the code editor of your choice, create a new file to hold the code for the implementation of the source file.**

   In this example, the file is named `ch61.cpp`, although you can use whatever you choose.

2. **Type the code from Listing 61-1 into your file.**

   Better yet, copy the code from the source file on this book's companion Web site.

LISTING 61-1: THE MULTIPLE-SEARCH-PATH UTILITY CLASS

```cpp
#include <string>
#include <vector>
#include <fstream>
#include <iostream>
#include <sys/stat.h>

using namespace std;

class DirectoryList
{
private:
    vector< string > _entries;
public:
    DirectoryList(void)
    {
    }
    DirectoryList( const char *strDir )
    {
        _entries.insert( _entries.end(),
            strDir );
    }
    DirectoryList( const DirectoryList&
      aCopy )
    {
        vector<string>::const_iterator
          iter;
        for ( iter =
          aCopy._entries.begin(); iter !=
          aCopy._entries.end(); ++iter )
            _entries.insert(
                _entries.end(), (*iter) );
    }

    bool is_dir( const char *strDir )    → 1
    {
        struct stat st;

        if ( stat( strDir, &st )
          == 0 )                         → 3
        {
            if ( st.st_mode & S_IFDIR )
                return true;
        }
```

(continued)

LISTING 61-1 *(continued)*

```
            return false;
    }

    void addEntry( const char *strDir )
    {
        _entries.insert( _entries.end(),
            strDir );
    }
    void removeEntry( const char *strDir )
    {
        vector<string>::iterator iter;
        for ( iter = _entries.begin();
          iter != _entries.end(); ++iter )
        {
            if ( (*iter) == strDir )
            {
                _entries.erase( iter );
            }
        }
    }
    int count(void) const
    {
        return _entries.size();
    }

    DirectoryList operator+=( const char
      *strDir )
    {
        _entries.insert( _entries.end(),
            strDir );
        return *this;
    }
    DirectoryList operator-=( const char
      *strDir )
    {
        removeEntry( strDir );
        return *this;
    }

    string getEntry( int idx )
    {
        if ( idx < 0 || idx > count()-1 )
            throw "DirectoryList: Array
                Index out of range";

        return _entries[ idx ];
    }
};
```

```
class MultiPathFile
{
private:
    DirectoryList _pathList;
    ifstream      _in;
    string              _path;
public:
    MultiPathFile(void)
        : _path("")
    {
    }
    MultiPathFile( const DirectoryList&
      aPathList )
        : _pathList( aPathList ),
          _path("")

    {
    }
    MultiPathFile( const char *strDir )
        : _pathList( strDir ),
          _path("")
    {
    }

    void addPath( const char *strDir )
    {
        if ( _pathList.is_dir( strDir ) )
            _pathList.addEntry( strDir );
        else
            printf("Invalid path:
                [%s]\n", strDir );
    }
    void removePath( const char *strDir )
    {
        _pathList.removeEntry( strDir );
    }

    bool open( const char *strFileName )  → 2
    {
        for ( int i=0;
          i<_pathList.count(); ++i )
        {
            string sDir =
              _pathList.getEntry( i );
            string sFullPath = sDir +
              strFileName;
            _in.open( sFullPath.c_str(),
              ios::in );
```

```
            if ( !_in.fail() )
            {
                _path = sDir;
                return true;
            }
            _in.clear();
        }

        return false;
    }

    void close()
    {
        _in.close();
    }

    ifstream& file(void)
    {
        return _in;
    }

    string CurrentPath(void)
    {
        return _path;
    }
};
```

3. **Save the source code in the code-editor application.**

The code above breaks down into two classes:

✔ **The** DirectoryList **class:** This class simply maintains a list of various directories in the system and allows the programmer to have a single, consistent way to access directory names. There is nothing really surprising in this class; it is just a wrapper around the Standard Template Library (STL) vector class that does a bit of extra checking to see if a given name is a directory. (See the is_dir method, shown at ➜ **1.**)

✔ **The** MultiPathFile **class:** This is really an extended version of the basic file classes supplied by the STL. It maintains a list of directories to search by using the DirectoryList class to

hold the various directories. When an open request is received via the open method, as shown at ➜ **2**, the class iterates through the various directories in its list and tries to open the file in each one. If the file is found in a given directory, it stores the directory path where the file was found and returns a handle allowing the programmer to access the file.

These two classes (DirectoryList and MultiPathFile) do all of the work of managing the search paths and then utilizing those search paths to open and manipulate the file. Notice the use of stat (a standard C function) shown at the line marked ➜ **3** to check whether an input path is valid and is a directory.

Note that you will need to add search paths to the system using the *path delimiter* (which is the forward or backward slash, depending on the operating system you're working with) appended to the end of the path. That is, you have to enter c:/windows/ rather than simply c:/windows, because the system will not append the delimiter for you. This could easily be fixed, but would require even more code in what is already a fairly long listing.

Testing the Multiple-Search-Path Class

After you create a class, you should create a test driver that not only ensures that your code is correct, but also shows people how to use your code. The following steps tell you how:

1. **In the code editor of your choice, reopen the source file to hold the code for your test program.**

In this example, I named the test program ch61.cpp.

2. **Type the code from Listing 61-2 into your file.**

Better yet, copy the code from the source file on this book's companion Web site.

LISTING 61-2: THE MULTIPLE-SEARCH-PATH TEST PROGRAM

```
void display_file( ifstream& in )
{
    // Display the first 100 characters
    cout << endl;
    for ( int i=0; i<100; ++i )
    {
        char c;
        in.get(c);
        if ( !in.fail() )
            cout << c;
        else
            break;
    }
    cout << endl;
}

int main( int argc, char **argv )
{
    MultiPathFile paths;

    // First, add in all the paths
    for ( int i=1; i<argc; ++i )
    {
        paths.addPath( argv[i] );
    }

    // Now ask them what they want to do.
    bool bDone = false;
    while ( !bDone )
    {
        char szPath[ 256 ];
        char szFile[ 256 ];

        printf("Options:\n");
        printf("(1) Add a new search
          path\n");
        printf("(2) Open a file\n");
        printf("(3) Exit the
          program\n\n");
        printf("What do you want to do?
          ");
        int option = 0;
        scanf("%d", &option );
        getchar();
        switch ( option )
        {
            case 1:                        → 4
                printf("Enter search
                  path to add: ");
                memset( szPath, 0,
sizeof(szPath) );
                gets(szPath);
                if ( strlen(szPath) )
                    paths.addPath(
                      szPath );
                break;
            case 2:                        → 5
                printf("Enter file to
                  open: ");
                memset( szFile, 0,
                  sizeof(szFile) );
                gets(szFile);
                if ( strlen(szFile) )
                    if ( !paths.open(
                      szFile ) )
                        printf("Error
                          finding file
                          %s\n",
                          szFile );
                    else
                    {
                        printf("File
                          found at:
                          [%s]\n",
                          paths.Curren
                          tPath().c_st
                          r() );
                        display_file(
                          paths.file()
                          );          → 7
                    }
                break;
            case 3:                        → 6
                bDone = true;
                break;
            default:
                printf("Invalid
                  Option\n");
                break;
        }
    }

    return 0;
}
```

The above code tests the multiple search paths to open files. When run, the program allows the user to add various search paths to their list of directories to use, then allows them to search for the file using those paths. If the user wants to add a new search path, he enters '1' at the prompt, which falls into the code at → **4**. This code gets a path name from the user and adds it to the search path list. If the user wants to find a file, he enters '2' at the prompt, and the program prompts for the filename to search for (see → **5**). If it is found, it will be printed out along with the path that it was found in. Finally, entering '3' at the prompt terminates the loop and exits the program (see → **6**).

3. **Save the source code in your code editor and then close the editor application.**

4. **Compile the application using your favorite compiler on your favorite operating system.**

5. **Run the application in the console window of your favorite operating system.**

If you have done everything right, you should see a session that looks something like this:

```
$ ./a.exe
Options:
(1) Add a new search path
(2) Open a file
(3) Exit the program

What do you want to do? 1
Enter search path to add: c:/matt/        → 8
Options:
(1) Add a new search path
(2) Open a file
(3) Exit the program

What do you want to do? 1
Enter search path to add: c:/work/        → 9
Options:
(1) Add a new search path
(2) Open a file
(3) Exit the program
```

```
What do you want to do? 1
Enter search path to add: c:/windows/     → 10
Options:
(1) Add a new search path
(2) Open a file
(3) Exit the program

What do you want to do? 2
Enter file to open: DATECL.h              → 11
File found at: [c:/work/]                 → 12

/*
*+------------------------------------------------
    ---------------------------
*| Header.......: DATE
Options:
(1) Add a new search path
(2) Open a file
(3) Exit the program

What do you want to do? 3
```

As you can see, the utility class went through the list of paths I gave it (shown at lines → **8**, → **9**, and → **10**), found the one that matched the filename that was input (shown at → **11**), opened the file, and allowed me to read it. In addition, it returned the path to where the file was found (shown at → **12**); I can output that data to the user of the application. The file is displayed via the `display_file` call in Listing 61-2 at line → **7**.

Improving the class

The class as it stands is very useful, but would benefit from a capability that saves the paths to some form of persistent storage and then reads them back from the storage file at program startup. The user would only have to enter the paths once. In addition, the program does not use relative file paths for some operating systems (such as ~ in Unix), because of the way in which the `open` is done. This could be improved as well.

Part IX

Debugging C++ Applications

The 5th Wave   By Rich Tennant

THAT IT! TARZAN TAKE NO MORE! KEEP GET BAD MESSAGE! WHAT MEAN?! TARZAN TRY EVERYTHING! MAKE TARZAN MAD LIKE CHEETAH! WANT PUT ROLODEX THROUGH SCREEN!

SYNTAX ERROR!

Building Tracing into Your Applications

Technique 62

Save Time By

- ✔ Understanding the benefits of building tracing into your applications
- ✔ Creating a flow trace class
- ✔ Testing the flow trace class
- ✔ Building in tracing after the fact
- ✔ Testing your code

If you have ever tried to debug an application that you didn't write, you know that the biggest challenge is simply figuring out how the program got into its present state to begin with. Quite often, while the individual components of a system are well documented, the overall flow of the system is not. There is no real way for you to know how the program got from the initial entry point to the point at which the problem occurred without stepping through each and every line in the debugger. Given the number of levels in the average production-quality C++ program, it can take hours to get from the beginning of the program to the problem spot. Wouldn't it be nice if you could just look through the source code for potential problems and trace through the code path that you knew the system was taking to get from point A (an entry point into the system) to point B (where the problem occurs)? Of course it would.

In general, what prevents us from having the data we need to trace from one point in the program to the core of the system is a lack of information about the path that is taken. Most debuggers can show you a call stack of how you got somewhere, but that stack goes away when you stop running the program. Worse, because the call stack shows you absolutely everything that goes on, you will often find yourself chasing problems in the system libraries and language code, rather than the more likely problems in your own code. What you really need to know is the path through your code that was used, not every call into the allocation libraries or string functions. This means we need a way to trace through our own code only, and show where we are at any given time.

Of course, the obvious solution here is simply to build a tracing capability into our applications. Okay, how do you go about this? The easiest way is to create a C++ class that can "report" where we are in the program, and to then have that class talk to a "manager" process that can print out a complete trace tree, showing how we got there. That, in a nutshell, is the purpose of this technique.

Implementing the Flow Trace Class

First, we need to implement the definition of the flow trace class. The flow trace class allows us to track what happens in the program, and to quickly and easily display a list of all of the functions that were called from the point the process was begun to when the problem occurred.

1. In the code editor of your choice, create a new file to hold the code for the definition of the source file.

In this example, the file is named `ch62.cpp`, although you can use whatever you choose.

2. Type the code from Listing 62-1 into your file.

Better yet, copy the code from the source file on this book's companion Web site.

LISTING 62-1: THE FLOW TRACE CLASS DEFINITION

```
#include <string>
#include <stack>
#include <vector>

class debugFlowTracer
{
private:
   std::string m_sFlowName;
   std::vector< debugFlowTracer > m_activefunctionStack;
   bool                          m_bRemoved;
protected:
    virtual void AddFlow();
    virtual void RemoveFlow();

public:
    debugFlowTracer(void)
    {
        m_sFlowName = "Unknown";
      m_bRemoved = false;
      AddFlow();
    }

    debugFlowTracer(const char *strFlow)
    {
      m_sFlowName = strFlow;
      m_bRemoved = false;
      AddFlow();
    }
    debugFlowTracer( const debugFlowTracer& aCopy )
    {
      m_sFlowName = aCopy.m_sFlowName;
      std::vector< debugFlowTracer >::const_iterator iter;
      for ( iter = aCopy.m_activefunctionStack.begin(); iter !=
         aCopy.m_activefunctionStack.end(); ++iter )
            m_activefunctionStack.insert( m_activefunctionStack.end(), (*iter) );
    }
```

```
~debugFlowTracer(void)
{
    if ( !m_bRemoved )
        RemoveFlow();
    m_bRemoved = true;
}

std::string Name()
{
    return m_sFlowName;
}

void AddSubFlow( debugFlowTracer& cSubFlow )
{
    // Just push it on top of the active function stack.
    m_activefunctionStack.insert( m_activefunctionStack.end(), cSubFlow );
}
void PrintStack(int iLevel)
{
    std::vector< debugFlowTracer >::iterator iter;
    for ( iter = m_activefunctionStack.begin(); iter != m_activefunctionStack.end(); ++iter )
    {
        for ( int i=0; i<iLevel; ++i )
            putchar ('\t');
        printf("%s\n", (*iter).Name().c_str() );
        (*iter).PrintStack(iLevel+1);
    }
}
};
```

The flow trace object (`debugFlowTrace`) contains a name that you can use for defining specific entry points into the system — such as when the user starts using a feature such as saving a file. It also contains a list of sub-flows, which are simply the functions that are entered when the flow begins. If you start in function one, call function two and four, in which function two calls function three, you would have a trace that looked like this:

```
Function One
    Function Two
        Function Three
    Function Four
```

This listing could be easily generated by the flow trace object.

3. **Save the source code as a file in the code editor of your choice.**

4. **Append the code from Listing 62-2 to your file.**

This will contain the `debugFlowTracerManager` class.

Better yet, copy the code from the source file on this book's companion Web site.

LISTING 62-2: THE FLOW TRACE CLASS AND MANAGER IMPLEMENTATION

```
class debugFlowTracerManager
{
private:
   std::stack< debugFlowTracer> m_functionStack;
   static debugFlowTracerManager *m_Instance;

public:
   static debugFlowTracerManager *Instance()              → 1
   {
      if ( m_Instance == NULL )
         m_Instance = new debugFlowTracerManager();
      return m_Instance;
   }
   void addFlow( debugFlowTracer& cFlow )
   {
      m_functionStack.push( cFlow );
   }
   void removeFlow(debugFlowTracer& cFlow)
   {
      if ( m_functionStack.empty() )
         return;

      // Get the top element.
      debugFlowTracer t = m_functionStack.top();

      // Remove it.
      m_functionStack.pop();

      // If there is anything left, add it.
      if ( m_functionStack.empty() )
      {
         printf("Flow [%s]:\n", t.Name().c_str() );
         t.PrintStack(0);
      }
      else
         m_functionStack.top().AddSubFlow( t );

   }

private:
   debugFlowTracerManager()
   {
   }
   debugFlowTracerManager(const debugFlowTracerManager& aCopy )
   {
   }
   virtual ~debugFlowTracerManager(void)
   {
   }
};
```

```
debugFlowTracerManager *debugFlowTracerManager::m_Instance = NULL;

void debugFlowTracer::AddFlow()
{
    debugFlowTracerManager::Instance()->addFlow( *this );          → 2
}

void debugFlowTracer::RemoveFlow()
{
    debugFlowTracerManager::Instance()->removeFlow( *this );
}
```

The purpose of the `debugFlowTracerManager` class is to keep track of the various flows within the system. Because a flow can really start and end anywhere in the source code of the application, we need a single place to store all of them. This allows us to print them out at the point that gives us the best view of how the processing went. The flow manager contains a single method, `Instance` (shown at **→ 1**), to return an instance of the class. Otherwise, you will notice that the constructors are all private, so that users cannot create an instance of the class. This ensures that there is only a single object of this class in any given application.

Testing the Flow Trace System

After you create a class, you should create a test driver that not only ensures your code is correct, but also shows people how to use your code. The following steps tell you how:

1. **Append the code from Listing 62-3 into your source file.**

   Better yet, copy the code from the source file on this book's companion Web site.

LISTING 62-3: THE FLOW TRACE TEST PROGRAM

```
void func_3()
{
    debugFlowTracer flow("func_3");
}

void func_2()
{
    debugFlowTracer flow("func_2");
    func_3();
}

void func_1()
{
    debugFlowTracer flow("func_1");
    func_2();
}

int main(int argc, char* argv[])
{
    debugFlowTracer mainFlow("main");
    func_1();
    func_2();
    func_3();
    return 0;
}
```

The test driver is constructed to illustrate the way in which the flow manager works. Note that we simply define a `debugFlowTracer` object in each of the functions in the code, and then use the functions as we would normally. The `debugFlowTracer` object attaches itself to the the instance of the manager (shown back in Listing 62-2 at ➝ **2**) and adds itself as a flow when it is created. The manager keeps track of all of the flows, printing them out for diagnostic purposes as they are created.

2. **Save the source code in the source-code editor and close the source-editor application.**

3. **Compile the application using your favorite compiler on your favorite operating system.**

4. **Run the application on your favorite operating system.**

If you have done everything properly, you should see the following output in the console window of your operating system:

```
$ ./a
Flow [main]:
Flow [func_1]:
Flow [func_2]:
Flow [func_3]:
Flow [func_2]:
func_3                              ➝ 3
Flow [func_3]:
```

As you can see, the program indicates what flows are running in the application, and how it got from one point to another. The names of the flows are printed within the square brackets as they are created. When a flow goes out of scope (when the function ends) the sub-flows (calls within that function) are printed out. You can see that in our case, only one of the functions called calls another function. This is shown in the listing at the line marked with ➝ **3**, indicating where func2 called func3. This gives us a good example of tracing and shows us how func3 was called throughout the program.

Adding in Tracing After the Fact

One of the more annoying things in the software world is being told to add something to your application after it has been designed, coded, and released. After all, you say, if it was up to you, the code would have been in there in the first place. Why should you pay for the mistakes of the developers before you? The answer is, because that's the way the world works. Someone comes along, writes a bunch of ugly, unmaintainable code, and then moves on to do it again someplace else. You get to move in and fix the disaster that was left behind.

Fortunately, this isn't really one of those times. It is possible to add in flow tracing after the fact, even automating the process. Let's create a simple little application that will do just that.

1. **In the code editor of your choice, create a new file to hold the code for the implementation of the source file.**

   In this example, the file is named ch62a.cpp, although you can use whatever you choose.

2. **Type the code from Listing 62-4 into your file.**

   Better yet, copy the code from the source file on this book's companion Web site.

A word of warning

Before you use the insertion program, here are a few things you need to know about it:

✔ Consider it a jumping-off point for your own creations. *It is not intended to be used in a production environment.* Using it that way is likely to confuse the program; its interaction with complex programs may require you to update the output. (That is why it does not overwrite your original source.)

✔ It does not handle all cases. Inline code in a class will not be detected and updated.

✔ The code will sometimes detect a function or method when one does not exist. For example, the code will sometimes make this mistake in a macro.

The insertion program will insert tracing objects in most, but not all, of your application functions with the exceptions listed in the notes above. Use it in good health.

LISTING 62-4: A UTILITY PROGRAM TO INSERT TRACING INTO AN EXISTING FILE

```cpp
#include <string>
#include <ctype.h>

void eat_line( FILE *fp, std::string& real_line )

{
    // Just read to the end of the line.
    while ( !feof(fp) )
    {
        char c = fgetc(fp);
        real_line += c;
        if ( c == '\n' )
            break;
    }
}

void eat_comment_block( FILE *fp, std::string& real_line )
{
    char sLastChar = 0;

    // Find the matching comment-close character.
    while ( !feof(fp) )
    {
        char c = fgetc(fp);
        real_line += c;
        if ( c == '/' && sLastChar == '*' )
            break;
        sLastChar = c;
    }
}


std::string get_line( FILE *fp, std::string& real_line )
{
    std::string sLine = "";
    char sLastChar = 0;
    while ( !feof(fp) )
    {
        // Get an input character.
        char c = fgetc(fp);

        real_line += c;

        // Check for pre-processor lines.
        if ( c == '#' && (sLastChar == 0 || sLastChar == '\n') )
        {
            eat_line( fp, real_line );
            continue;
        }
```

(continued)

LISTING 62-4 (continued)

```
// Check for comments.
if ( c == '/'  )
{
   sLastChar = c;
   c = fgetc(fp);
   real_line += c;


   if ( c == '/' )
   {
      eat_line( fp, real_line );
      sLastChar = 0;
      continue;
   }
   else
      if ( c == '*' )
      {
         eat_comment_block( fp, real_line );
         sLastChar = 0;
         continue;
      }
      else
      {
         sLine += sLastChar;
      }
}

// Need to skip over stuff in quotes.

if ( c != '\r' && c != '\n' )
{
   // Here it gets weird. If the last character was
   // a parenthesis, we don't want to allow white space.
   if ( sLastChar != ')' || !isspace(c) )
      sLine += c;
   else
      continue;
}

// A line terminates with a {, a }, or a ; character.
if ( c == ';' || c == '{' || c == '}' )
   break;


sLastChar = c;
}
```

```
    return sLine;
}

std::string parse_function_name( std::string& sLine )
{
    std::string sName = "";


    // First, find the opening parenthesis.
    int sPos = (int)sLine.find('(');

    // Skip over everything that is a space before that.
    for ( int i=sPos-1; i>=0; --i )
       if ( !isspace(sLine[i]) )
       {
          sPos = i;
          break;
       }

    // Now everything backward from that is the name, until
    // we hit either the beginning of the line or white space.
    int sStartPos = 0;
    for ( int i=sPos; i>=0; --i )
    {
       if ( isspace(sLine[i]) )
          break;
       sStartPos = i;
    }

    sName = sLine.substr( sStartPos, sPos-sStartPos+1 );

    return sName;
}


void ProcessFile( FILE *fp, FILE *ofp )
{
    std::string real_line;

    while ( !feof(fp) )
    {
       real_line = "";

       std::string sLine = get_line( fp, real_line );

       // Check for functions/methods.
```

(continued)

LISTING 62-4 (continued)

```
        // Output the "real" line, and then (if we need to) the
        // information we need to embed.
        fprintf(ofp, "%s", real_line.c_str() );
        if ( sLine[sLine.length()-1] == '{' &&
             sLine[sLine.length()-2] == ')' )
        {
            std::string sName = parse_function_name( sLine );
            fprintf(ofp, "\n\tdebugFlowTracer flow(\"%s\");\n", sName.c_str());
        }

    }
}

int main(int argc, char* argv[])
{
    if ( argc < 2 )
    {
        printf("Usage: cppparser filename [filename...]\n");
        exit(1);
    }
    for ( int i=1; i<argc; ++i )
    {
        FILE *fp = fopen(argv[i], "r");
        if ( fp == NULL )
        {
            printf("Error: Unable to process file %s\n", argv[i] );
            continue;
        }

        std::string sOut = std::string(argv[i]) + ".tmp";
        FILE *ofp = fopen(sOut.c_str(), "w");
        if ( ofp == NULL )
        {
            printf("Error: Unable to create output file %s\n", sOut.c_str() );
            continue;
        }


        // Process this file
        ProcessFile( fp, ofp );

        // Finish it up
        fclose(fp);
        fclose(ofp);
    }

    return 0;
```

→ 4

→ 5

There is nothing magical about Listing 62-4. The code takes an input file and writes it out to an output temporary file, appending certain information in the file as it parses the text within the input file. In our case, the code is looking for opening braces (shown at → **4**) to indicate the beginning of a function. When one is encountered, it parses the function name (shown at → **5**) and writes a `debugFlowTracer` object definition into the output file. This creates an automated system for inserting flow tracing into an existing source file.

3. **Save the source code in the source-code editor.**

4. **Create a new file in the source-file editor to use as a test input to the insertion program.**

This file simply acts as test input for the program; it doesn't really have to do anything on its own. For now, just create a file that contains some functions and some class methods.

In this example, the file is named `temp.cpp`, although you can use whatever you choose.

5. **Type the code from Listing 62-5 into your new file.**

Better yet, copy the code from the source file on this book's companion Web site.

LISTING 62-5: A TEMPORARY PROGRAM TO ILLUSTRATE TRACE INSERTION INTO AN EXISTING FILE

```
#include <stdio.h>
#include <string>
#include <iostream>

int func1()
{
    printf("This is a test\n");
}

void func2()
{
    printf("This is another test\n");
}
```

```
class Foo
{
public:
    Foo();
    virtual ~Foo();
};

Foo::Foo(void)
{
}

Foo::~Foo(void)
{
}

int main()
{
    Foo x;
}
```

Don't spend any time studying the code in Listing 62-5; its sole purpose is to provide an input file to test out the parser. If it works properly, we will see an output file which contains `debugFlowTracer` objects in `func1`, `func2`, and the constructor and destructors for the `Foo` object and the main function.

6. **Compile the insertion program with your favorite compiler on your favorite operating system.**

7. **Run the program on your favorite operating system.**

If you have done everything right, you should see a file called `temp.cpp.tmp` created that contains the following text in it:

```
#include <stdio.h>
#include <string>
#include <iostream>

int func1()
{
    debugFlowTracer flow("func1");      → 6
```

```
    printf("This is a test\n");
}

void func2()
{
    debugFlowTracer flow("func2");

    printf("This is another test\n");
}

class Foo
{
public:
    Foo();
    virtual ~Foo();
};

Foo::Foo(void)
{
    debugFlowTracer flow("Foo::Foo");→ 7
```

```
}

Foo::~Foo(void)
{
    debugFlowTracer flow("Foo::~Foo");

}

int main()
{
    debugFlowTracer flow("main");

    Foo x;
}
```

Note that the program properly inserted all of the flow-tracing objects into the existing file. The lines marked → **6** and → **7**, for example, show you that the output is exactly what we wanted and expected.

Technique 63

Creating Debugging Macros and Classes

When you are debugging an application, having a set of techniques and tools that you can drop into an application will aid you in the process of finding and eliminating bugs. These techniques break down into two general categories:

- Macros used to debug techniques
- Classes used in your application to debug the code itself

This technique looks at the sorts of things you can do to build up your own toolbox of debugging techniques and find the ones that work for you. As with most programming, there is no "right" or "wrong" way to debug a problem. There are techniques that work better for some people than others, and it is up to you to discover the ones you like best — and that work most efficiently. By having a library of macros that you can immediately drop into your application, you will save time developing and debugging code.

When it comes to debugging, one size definitely does not fit all. The number of kinds of techniques that people swear by is limited only by the number of programmers using them. To save time for yourself and your application development, you should pick the techniques that work for you and stick with them.

The assert Macro

The first technique we will look at is the assert macro. The assert macro is a simply defined C++ standard macro that evaluates a single argument. If that argument is true, the code continues processing. If the argument is false, the program prints out a diagnostic error message and terminates abruptly. The catch is that the assert macro is only defined when the program is not being compiled in optimized mode. An assert is turned "on" when it is checking values and printing out error messages. Asserts are turned off when they do nothing. In programming parlance, we say that the program is in "debug mode" for `assert` to work, and in "release mode" if asserts are turned off. Let's look at an example of how to use the `assert` macro in your own code.

1. **In the code editor of your choice, create a new file to hold the code for the source file of the technique.**

In this example, the file is named `ch63.cpp`, although you can use whatever you choose. This file will contain the class definition for your automation object.

2. **Type the code in Listing 63-1 into your file.**

Better yet, copy the code from the source file on this book's companion Web site.

LISTING 63-1: USING THE ASSERT MACRO

```
#include <assert.h>
#include <string.h>
#include <stdlib.h>

int func( int v1to10 )
{
    assert( v1to10 >= 1 && v1to10 <= 10 ); → 1

    int divisor = 0;

    switch ( v1to10 )
    {
        case 1:
        case 2:
        case 3:
        case 4:
        case 5:
        case 6:
        case 7:
        case 8:
        case 9:
        case 10:
            divisor = v1to10 * 2;
            break;
    }
```

```
    int retVal = 200 / divisor;
    return retVal;
}

int main(int argc, char **argv)
{
    func(3);
    func(11);
    return 0;
}
```

In the listing above, our function (`func`) accepts an integer value. We expect the input value to be in the range of one to ten, inclusive. Values outside of that range will cause a division-by-zero error in the function, so we want to make sure that the user doesn't supply such a value. The `assert` statement (shown at the line marked → **1**) traps for such a condition and exits the program if the value input is outside the specified range.

3. **Save the file in the source-code editor and close the editor application.**

4. **Compile the source-code file with your favorite compiler on your favorite operating system.**

5. **Run the program on the console window of your favorite operating system.**

If you have done everything correctly, you should see the following output on the console window:

```
$ ./a.exe
assertion "v1to10 >= 1 && v1to10 <= 10"
    failed: file "ch8_1a.cpp", line 7
Aborted (core dumped)
```

The output indicates that the `assert` function triggered and the program exited. The actual text you see will be dependent on your operating system, compiler, and function library, but it will look similar to this. The important aspect is that the `assert` macro tells you what file and line the error occurred on and the assertion statement that failed. This will provide you valuable debugging information for determining how the program failed.

If you compile the source code with optimization on, you will see only the core-dumped message (or your operating system's equivalent of a divide-by-zero error) displayed.

 The `assert` macro is useful during the initial development phase of an application, but it fails to catch run-time errors when the application is released to the user. For this reason, you should never count on `assert` statements to catch all possible errors.

Logging

The next logical type of debugging technique is the logging approach. Logging is the writing of data persistently in your application in order to facilitate debugging and maintenance. Much like a black box on a crashed airliner, logging records the steps the program took so you can understand how it got into the state it's in. Unlike some other techniques, logging can be used in either development mode or user-release mode. You can even turn it on or off at run-time — and even during program execution — to see exactly what is going on. The following steps show you how to implement a logging class.

 When you can turn your logging capability on or off at will, you can zero in on a problem much more quickly — which allows you to filter out extraneous program information and see only what's pertinent to the problem. In this way, logging will save you a lot of time when you're trying to debug a program defect.

1. **In the code editor of your choice, create a new file to hold the code for the source file of the technique.**

In this example, the file is named `ch63a.cpp`, although you can use whatever you choose. This file will contain the class definition for your automation object.

2. **Type the code in Listing 63-2 into your file.**

Better yet, copy the code from the source file on this book's companion Web site.

LISTING 63-2: A LOGGING CLASS

```cpp
#include <iostream>
#include <string>
#include <stdlib.h>
#include <stdarg.h>
#include <fstream>

using namespace std;

class Logger
{
    bool    _bOn;
    bool    _bForceFlush;
    string  _sMessage;
    string  _sFileName;
    ofstream    _file;
public:
    Logger( void )
    {
        _bOn = false;
        _bForceFlush = false;
    }
    Logger( const char *strFileName )      ➔2
    {
        _sFileName = strFileName;
        _bOn = false;
        _bForceFlush = false;
    }
    Logger( const Logger& aCopy )
    {
        _sFileName = aCopy._sFileName;
        _bForceFlush = aCopy._bForceFlush;
        setOn( aCopy._bOn );
    }
    virtual ~Logger()
    {
        Flush();
        if ( _bOn )
            _file.close();
    }

    void setOn( bool flag )
```

(continued)

LISTING 63-2 (continued)

```
    {
        _bOn = flag;
        if ( _bOn )
        {
            _file.open( _sFileName.c_str() );
        }
    }
    bool getOn( void )
    {
        return _bOn;
    }
    void setForceFlush( bool flag )
    {
        _bForceFlush = flag;
    }
    bool getForceFlush( void )
    {
        return _bForceFlush;
    }
    void setFileName ( const char
*strFileName )
    {
        _sFileName = strFileName;
    }
    string getFileName ( void )
    {
        return _sFileName;
    }

    void Log( const char *strMessage )      → 3
    {
        _sMessage += strMessage;
        _sMessage += '\n';
        if ( _bForceFlush )
            Flush();
    }
    void LogString( const char *fmt, ... )  → 4
    {
        char szBuffer[256];
        va_list marker;

        va_start( marker, fmt );       /*
Initialize variable arguments. */

        vsprintf(szBuffer, fmt, marker );

        _sMessage += szBuffer;
        _sMessage += '\n';
        if ( _bForceFlush )
            Flush();
```

```
    }
    void Flush( void )
    {
        if ( _bOn )
            _file << _sMessage << endl;
        _sMessage = "";
    }
};
```

The Logger class can be used to do a more extensive information capture within an application. You can log virtually anything you want, regardless of whether the program is compiled in a debug (development) or release (production) mode. Logging can be turned on or off, even at run-time, allowing you to configure your system whenever you want without recompiling the program. The Logger class accepts a filename in which it will write all of its output (see → **2**), and writes out strings using either a simple string format (see → **3**) or a more complicated formatted output (see → **4**). This makes the logging class ideal for inserting into your program and keeping track of important events for either debugging or customer support purposes.

3. **Save the source file in your code editor.**

Testing the Logger Class

After you create a class, you should create a test driver that not only ensures your code is correct, but also shows people how to use your code. The following steps show you how:

1. **In the code editor of your choice, reopen the source file to hold the code for your test program.**

In this example, I named the test program ch63a.cpp.

2. **Type the code from Listing 63-3 into your file.**

Better yet, copy the code from the source file on this book's companion Web site.

LISTING 63-3: THE LOGGER CLASS TEST DRIVER

```
int main(int argc, char **argv)
{
    Logger log("log.txt");

    // Make the log write things out as it encounters strings,
    // to avoid crashes wiping out the log.
    log.setForceFlush( true );

    // First, see whether the code told us to log anything.
    for ( int i=0; i<argc; ++i )
    {
        if ( !strcmp(argv[i], "-log") )
        {
            log.setOn(true);
            break;
        }
    }

    log.Log("Program Startup Arguments");
    for ( int i=0; i<argc; ++i )
    {
        log.LogString("Input Argument %d = %s", i, argv[i] );

    // Prompt for a string, modify it, and then write it out.
    while ( 1 )
    {
        printf("Enter command: ");
        char szBuffer[ 80 ];
        memset( szBuffer, 0, 80 );
        if ( gets(szBuffer) == NULL )
            break;

        log.LogString("Input String: %s", szBuffer );
        if ( !strlen(szBuffer) )
        {
            break;
        }

        string s = "";
        for ( int i=strlen(szBuffer)-1; i>=0; --i )
            s += szBuffer[i];

        log.LogString("Output String: %s", s.c_str() );

    }

    log.Log("Finished with application\n");
    return 0;
}
```

The above code listing is a simple program that accepts a certain number of input arguments, prints them out, and then prompts the user for some commands. It could do just about anything with either the input arguments or the commands, but that really isn't important for our purposes. Just to modify the string for output, we reverse the characters in the output string. We log the input arguments, as well as the input string and output strings in the command loop. This indicates any potential problems with specific strings.

3. **Save the source file in your code editor and close the editor application.**

4. **Compile the source file with your favorite compiler on your favorite operating system.**

5. **Run the application.**

If you have done everything properly, you should see the following output on your command console:

```
$ ./a -log
Enter command: Hello world
Enter command: Goodbye cruel world
Enter command: Hell o again
Enter command:
```

```
$ cat log.txt
Program Startup Arguments

Input Argument 0 = ./a

Input Argument 1 = -log

Input String: Hello world

Output String: dlrow olleH

Input String: Goodbye cruel world

Output String: dlrow leurc eybdooG

Input String: Hell o again

Output String: niaga o lleH

Input String:

Finished with application
```

As you can see from the above listing, the log file contains all of the arguments, as well as the input and output strings from our session with the command prompts. The input strings are what we typed into the program, and the output strings are the expected reversed text.

As you can see, the application properly logged everything that was coming in and going out. Now, if we had a problem with the code (such as an occasional too-short output string), we could consult the log to look at what the user entered, and figure out why it didn't work in the debugger.

Design by Contract

The final technique that we will look at for use in the debugging of C++ applications is actually one that you build in at the initial coding time, although you can add it after the fact. This technique — called Design by Contract — was primarily created by the Eiffel programming language. In the Design by Contract (DBC) methodology, there are three important parts of any piece of code:

✔ **Preconditions:** These are conditions you take for granted before you can proceed with a process. For example, if you are trying to read from a file, it is important that the file be open first. If you are reading bytes from the file, and it is open, then you must specify a positive number of bytes, because reading a negative number of bytes makes no sense and could therefore lead to problems. Specifying a positive number of bytes, therefore, is a precondition for the process. A precondition is simply an assumption that you have made while you are coding the process. By documenting these assumptions in the code itself, you make life easier for the user of the code, as well as for the maintainer of the code.

✔ **Validity checks:** These are simply "sanity checks" for your object. For example, your object might contain a value that represents a person's age. If that age value is negative, bad things are going to happen when you try to compute that person's year of birth. This should never happen, of course, but it could happen due to programming errors, memory overwrites, or persistent storage errors. By checking the validity of an object each time that you work with it, you insure that the system is always in a known state.

✔ **Post-conditions:** These are conditions that must be logically true after your process has completed. For example, if you are setting the length of a buffer in an object, the post-condition ensures that the length is zero or a positive number. (Negative lengths make no sense and indicate an immediate processing error.) Another good example: A post-condition can check an assumption that a file has been opened — and valid values read in — at the end of a given process. If the file is not open, or there are no valid values in the output list, you know that something you didn't anticipate happened during processing. For this reason, you check these assumptions in the post-condition block of your process.

The purpose of Design by Contract is to eliminate the source of errors before they crop up, which streamlines the development process by making error checking easier and debugging less intrusive. This will save you a lot of time in the long-run by making your programs more robust up front.

Documentation is a valuable asset in understanding code, but it does nothing to fix problems encountered while running the code. If you document the assumptions that your code makes while you're writing it, you not only save those assumptions in one place, but also remind yourself to make the code check for those assumptions at run-time.

So how does it all work? Most DBC (Design by Contract) process controls are implemented via C++ macros. The following steps show you how this could be implemented in your own application:

1. **In the code editor of your choice, create a new file to hold the code for the source file of the technique.**

   In this example, the file is named ch63b.cpp, although you can use whatever you choose. This file will contain the class definition for your automation object.

2. **Type the code in Listing 63-4 into your file.**

   Better yet, copy the code from the source file on this book's companion Web site.

LISTING 63-4: THE DESIGN BY CONTRACT EXAMPLE

```
#include <iostream>
#include <stdlib.h>
#include <string.h>

void abort_program(const char *file, long line , const char *expression)
{
    printf("File: %s Line: %ld Expression Failed: %s\n", file, line, expression);
    exit(1);
}

class DBCObject
{
    long    _magicNo;
public:
    DBCObject( long magic )
    {
        _magicNo = magic;
    }
```

(continued)

LISTING 63-4 (continued)

```
#ifdef _DEBUG
    virtual bool IsValid() const = 0;
#endif
    long Magic(void) const
    {
        return _magicNo;
    }
    void setMagicNo( long magic )
    {
        _magicNo = magic;
    }
};

#ifdef _DEBUG
#define DBC_ASSERT(bool_expression) if (!(bool_expression)) abort_program(__FILE__, __LINE__,
    #bool_expression)
#define IS_VALID(obj) DBC_ASSERT((obj) != NULL && (obj)->IsValid())
#define REQUIRE(bool_expression) DBC_ASSERT(bool_expression)
#define ENSURE(bool_expression) DBC_ASSERT(bool_expression)

#else

// When your code is built in release mode, the _DEBUG flag would not be defined, thus there
    will be no overhead
// in the final release from these checks.

#define DBC_ASSERT(ignore) ((void) 1)
#define IS_VALID(ignore) ((void) 1)
#define REQUIRE(ignore) ((void) 1)
#define ENSURE(ignore) ((void) 1)

#endif

class MyClass : public DBCObject
{
private:
    char *_buffer;
    int   _bufLen;
protected:
    void Init()
    {
        _buffer=NULL;
        _bufLen = 0;
    }

#ifdef _DEBUG
    bool IsValid() const
    {
        // Condition: Buffer not null.
        if ( getBuffer() == NULL )
            return false;
```

```
        // Condition: Length > 0.
        if ( getLength() <= 0 )
            return false;
        // Condition: magic number correct.
        if ( Magic() != 123456 )
            return false;

        // All conditions are correct, so it's okay to continue.
        return true;
    }
#endif

public:
    MyClass(void)
        : DBCObject( 123456 )
    {
        Init();
    }
    MyClass( const char *strIn )
        : DBCObject( 123456 )
    {
        // Precondition: strIn not NULL.
        REQUIRE( strIn != NULL );

        Init();
        setBuffer( strIn );

        // Post-condition: buffer not NULL.
        ENSURE( getBuffer() != NULL );
        // Post-condition: buffer length not 0.
        ENSURE( getLength() != 0 );
    }
    MyClass( const MyClass& aCopy )
        : DBCObject( 123456 )
    {
        // Precondition: aCopy is valid.
        IS_VALID(&aCopy);
        // Precondition: aCopy._buffer not NULL.
        REQUIRE( aCopy.getBuffer() != NULL );
        // Precondition: aCopy._bufLen not 0.
        REQUIRE( aCopy.getLength() != 0 );

        // Set the pieces.
        setBuffer( aCopy._buffer );
        setLength( aCopy._bufLen );

        // Post-condition: buffer not NULL.
        ENSURE( getBuffer() != NULL );
        // Post-condition: buffer length not 0.
        ENSURE( getLength() != 0 );
```

(continued)

LISTING 63-4 *(continued)*

```cpp
}
MyClass operator=( const MyClass& aCopy )
{
    // Precondition: aCopy is valid.
    IS_VALID(&aCopy);
    // Precondition: aCopy._buffer not NULL.
    REQUIRE( aCopy.getBuffer() != NULL );
    // Precondition: aCopy._bufLen not 0.
    REQUIRE( aCopy.getLength() != 0 );

    // Set the pieces.
    setBuffer( aCopy._buffer );
    setLength( aCopy._bufLen );

    // Post-condition: buffer not NULL.
    ENSURE( getBuffer() != NULL );
    // Post-condition: buffer length not 0.
    ENSURE( getLength() != 0 );

    // Return the current object.
    return *this;
}

virtual ~MyClass()
{
    // Precondition: Magic number must be correct.
    REQUIRE( Magic() == 123456 );                                   ➜ 5
    // Pre-condition: length >= 0.
    REQUIRE( getLength() >= 0 );
    // Pre-condition: If length, buffer NOT NULL.
    if ( getLength() )
        REQUIRE ( getBuffer() != NULL );

    // All looks okay; delete the buffer.
    if ( buffer != NULL )           delete [] _buffer;
    _buffer = NULL;
    // Clear the length.
    _bufLen = 0;

    // Post-condition: The magic number is still correct.
    ENSURE( Magic() == 123456 );
    // Post-condition: Buffer NULL.
    ENSURE( getBuffer() == NULL );
    // Post-condition: Length 0.
    ENSURE( getLength() == 0 );                                     ➜ 6



}
```

```
void setBuffer( const char *strIn )
{
   // Precondition: strIn not NULL.
   REQUIRE( strIn != NULL );

   if ( strIn != NULL )
   {
      _buffer = new char[ strlen(strIn) + 1 ];
      strcpy ( _buffer, strIn );
   }
}
void setLength ( int length )
{
   // Pre-condition: Length > 0.
   REQUIRE ( length > 0 );

   _bufLen = length;
}

int getLength( void ) const
{
   // No conditions.
   return _bufLen;
}
const char *getBuffer( void ) const
{
   // No conditions.
   return _buffer;
}
};
```

In Listing 63-4, we use the pre- and post-conditions to insure that valid values are set in our object at all times. Note, for example, in the destructor for the class that our precondition is that the magic number stored in the class be set to the correct values (123456, shown at → **5**) and that at the end of the class the length be zero (shown at → **6**). If either of these conditions is false, the program prints an error message and exits.

As you can see, the code does copious checking to make sure that the object data is always in a consistent state, that the input to the various methods is valid, and that the output from the object processes is valid as well. In the following steps, a very simple test of the code shows exactly how this all works.

3. **In the code editor of your choice, reopen the source file to hold the code for your test program.**

In this example, I named the test program ch63b.cpp.

4. **Type the following code into your file.**

Better yet, copy the code from the source file on this book's companion Web site.

```
int main(int argc, char **argv )
{
   // Program Conditions.
   REQUIRE ( argc > 1 );
   REQUIRE ( argv[1] != NULL );
```

```
// Empty object.
MyClass mc1;

// Object defined from command
line.
MyClass mc2( argv[1] );
// Make a copy of it.
MyClass mc3 = mc2;
}
```

5. Save the source file in your code editor and close the editor application.

6. Compile the source file with your favorite compiler on your favorite operating system.

7. Run the application.

If you have done everything properly, you should see the following output on your command console:

```
$ ./a.exe
File: ch8_1c.cpp Line: 204 Expression
    Failed: argc > 1
```

Okay, it's fairly obvious what happened here: We told the system to check for the number of arguments to the application, and required that there be some arguments, but they weren't there. Let's supply one and see what happens.

```
$ ./a.exe Hello
File: ch8_1c.cpp Line: 99 Expression
    Failed: getLength() != 0
```

Oops! What happened here? We supplied an argument — and the code failed anyway. Looking at the line that failed, we can see that it was the post-condition of the constructor for the class. Aha! We never set the length of the buffer in the constructor, setting only the buffer itself. Let's fix that by adding some to the constructor.

8. In the code editor of your choice, reopen the source file to hold the code for your test program.

In this example, I named the test program ch8_2c.cpp.

9. Modify the code as follows. Replace the existing code in the MyClass constructor with the listing below.

```
MyClass( const char *strIn )
    : DBCObject( 123456 )
{
    // Precondition: strIn not
NULL.
    REQUIRE( strIn != NULL );

    Init();
    setBuffer( strIn );
    setLength ( strlen(strIn) );

    // Post-condition: buffer not
NULL.
    ENSURE( getBuffer() != NULL );
    // Post-condition: buffer
length not 0.
    ENSURE( getLength() != 0 );
}
```

10. Save the source file in your code editor, and then close the editor application.

11. Compile the source file with your favorite compiler on your favorite operating system.

12. Run the application.

If you have done everything properly, you should see the following output on your command console:

```
$ ./a.exe
```

As you can see, there are no errors reported. That significant lack means all the contracts in the code have been satisfied — and the code should encounter no problems when run with the tests we've created.

Of course, to keep this happy arrangement going, you have to exercise some care: Every time you encounter a problem in the system, make sure that you add a test to account for that problem. That is the final piece of the Design by Contract method of debugging and maintenance.

Debugging Overloaded Methods

Save Time By

✔ Debugging overloaded methods

✔ Adding logging to an application

✔ Handling errors

When you are debugging a program, there is nothing quite as frustrating as discovering that all the work you spent tracking down a particular problem was wasted because the method you thought was being called in a C++ class was, in fact, not the code being executed at all. Figuring out which method is being called can be an annoying problem, and careful observation is often needed to see what is really happening, as we will see in this programming technique.

An overloaded method is a method that has the same name as another method in the same class, but contains a different number or type of arguments. (The list of arguments and the return type combine to form a *signature* for the method.)

When you have a class that contains overloaded methods, it is essential that you know which one is being called in each case. Because the number of arguments can be the same for different overloaded methods (only the type of the arguments is different), it can be difficult to tell which method is being called in your application source code. Let's take a look at a class that contains overloaded methods with problems. We will create a class that contains several overloaded methods in this technique, and differentiate them only by the type of argument they accept. You will see that it is not always easy to tell which method is being called in your program. Here's how:

1. In the code editor of your choice, create a new file to hold the code for the implementation of the source file.

In this example, the file is named `ch64.cpp`, although you can use whatever you choose.

2. Type the code from Listing 64-1 into your file.

Or better yet, copy the code from the source file on this book's companion Web site.

LISTING 64-1: CLASS WITH OVERLOADED METHODS

```cpp
#include <iostream>

using namespace std;

class MyClass
{
    int _x;
public:
    MyClass(void)
    {
        _x = 0;
    }
    MyClass(int x)
    {
        _x = x;
    }
    MyClass( const MyClass& aCopy )
    {
        _x = aCopy._x;
    }
    MyClass operator=(int x)              → 4
    {
        setX(x);
        return *this;
    }
    MyClass operator=(double d)          → 5
    {
        setX(d);
        return *this;
    }
    MyClass operator=( const char *str ) → 6
    {
        setX( str );
        return *this;
    }
    void setX( int x )                    → 1
    {
        _x = x;
    }
    void setX( double d )                 → 2
    {
        _x = (int)d;
    }
    void setX( const char *str )          → 3
    {
        int x = atoi(str);
    }
    int getX(void)
    {
        return _x;
    }
};
```

```cpp
void print(MyClass& mc)
{
    cout << "Dump: " << endl;
    cout << "------------------------" <<
        endl;
    cout << "X = " << mc.getX() << endl;
    cout << "------------------------" <<
        endl;
}

int main(int argc, char **argv)
{
    MyClass mc(3);
    print(mc);
    mc = 2.0;
    print(mc);
    mc = 5;
    print(mc);
    mc = "6.34";                          → 7
    print(mc);
}
```

The class shown in our little test program above has three methods that have the same name, setX. These methods take three different types of arguments: The first method, shown at → **1**, takes an integer value; the second method, shown at → **2**, takes a floating point (double) value; the final version of the method takes a string as its argument, as shown at → **3**. In addition, the function has three overloaded assignment operators (operator=, shown at lines → **4**, → **5**, and → **6**). The test driver assigns an object of the MyClass type some various values, 2.0, 5, and "6.34". You would expect that the result of the output in the print statements would be the values assigned at each stage. As we will see, however, the last assignment statement (shown at → **7**) does not work properly. Take a moment and look at the code and see if you can figure out why.

3. **Save the source code in your source-code editor and close the source-code editor application.**

4. **Compile the source code with your favorite compiler on your favorite operating system.**

5. **Run the resulting program on your favorite operating system.**

If you have done everything right, you should see the following output in the console window of your favorite operating system:

```
$ ./a.exe
Dump:
----------------------
X = 3
----------------------
Dump:
----------------------
X = 2
----------------------
Dump:
----------------------
X = 5
----------------------
Dump:
----------------------
X = 5
----------------------
```

Now, something here is obviously not right. We assigned the values to be 3, 2, 5, and 6.34. We should not be seeing the values of 5 in the last two positions. The third position is correct because that was the value assigned just before that print statement. But the fourth position follows an assignment to the string value "6.34". After that is assigned, the value should no longer be 5. So what is going on here?

If we tracked through the code to see what's going on, we'd eventually discover that the problem is in the assignment operator that accepts a string. However, tracing something this specific could take quite a while, because there are numerous ways that this particular bit of code could have been accessed. It's relatively easy to spot the incorrect value when you are looking at the output from the program in this form, because we know what the expected output is and we have a limited number of lines. Imagine, however, having to ransack hundreds of output statements and *thousands* of lines of code — not nearly so easy. So how do we make this task easier to debug?

The next section shows you how.

Adding Logging to the Application

To fix this problem, the best way to handle overloaded methods is to note problems as we encounter them. To do so, we can add some specialized logging to our application to track down which method is failing — and what's going on. The following steps do that:

1. **Reopen the source file for this technique.**

In this example, I called the source file ch64.cpp.

2. **Change the MyClass definition from its existing form to the code shown in Listing 64-2.**

LISTING 64-2: THE MODIFIED MYCLASS LISTING

```
#define LOG(x) (cout << (x) << endl)

class MyClass
{
    int _x;
public:
    MyClass(void)
    {
        setX(0);
        LOG ("Null Constructor: Setting _x
            to 0");
    }
    MyClass(int x)
    {
        setX(x);
        LOG ("Int Constructor: Setting _x
            to x");
    }
    MyClass( const MyClass& aCopy )
    {
        setX(aCopy._x);
        LOG ("Copy Constructor: Setting _x
            to x");
    }
    MyClass operator=(int x)
    {
        LOG("Assignment Operator int");
        LOG(x);
        setX(x);
        return *this;
    }
```

(continued)

LISTING 64-2 (continued)

```
MyClass operator=(double d)
{
    LOG("Assignment Operator double");
    LOG(d);
    setX(d);
    return *this;
}
MyClass operator=( const char *str )
{
    LOG("Assignment Operator str");    → 8
    LOG(str);                          → 9
    setX( str );
    return *this;
}
void setX( int x )
{
    LOG("setX double");
    _x = x;
    LOG(_x);
}
void setX( double d )
{
    LOG("setX double");
    _x = (int)d;
    LOG(_x);
}
void setX( const char *str )
{
    LOG("setX str");
    int x = atoi(str);
    LOG(_x);
}
int getX(void)
{
    return _x;
}
};
```

The code above is substantially the same as the original listing, but it now contains logging statements that can be used in a debug environment to output details about what is going on in the program. As you can see, we have added a LOG statement to each of the methods, so that we are printing out each call and change within the code. For example, in the operator= method that accepts a string argument, we have added lines → 8 and → 9, logging the name of the method and the value we are changing. Let's see what

good this does for us in determining the source of the problem.

3. **Compile the source file with your favorite compiler, on your favorite operating system.**

4. **Run the resulting program on your favorite operating system.**

If you have done everything right, you should see the following output from the program on the console window:

```
$ ./a.exe
setX double
3
Int Constructor: Setting _x to x
Dump:
-----------------------
X = 3
-----------------------
Assignment Operator double
2
setX double
2
setX double
2
Copy Constructor: Setting _x to x
Dump:
-----------------------
X = 2
-----------------------
Assignment Operator int
5
setX double
5
setX double
5
Copy Constructor: Setting _x to x
Dump:
-----------------------
X = 5
-----------------------
Assignment Operator str
6.34
setX str
5
setX double                          → 10
5
Copy Constructor: Setting _x to x
Dump:
-----------------------
X = 5
```

Now, looking at the output from this code makes it pretty obvious where the problem lies — but we can do one more thing to make it even more obvious. We can add asserts to our `setX` functions to verify that what we expect on output is what we really get. We haven't fixed anything yet, but we now know that the reason the value isn't being set is because the `operator=` that accepts a string is sending the proper value to the `setX` that accepts a string, but the value is not being changed (as shown at ➙ **10** in the output listing above). The `assert` will tell us exactly when the value is not changed.

Suppose we modified the `setX` that accepted a string to read like this:

```
void setX( const char *str )
{
    LOG("setX str");
    int x = atoi(str);                    ➙ 11
    LOG(_x);
    assert( _x == x );
}
```

This modification adds a post-condition to the `setX` method that asserts that the value of the variable `x` is equal to the value of the variable `x`.

Wait a minute — we're expecting the output to be the same as the integer value of the string that was input — correct? In this case, the code would fail because the output is not correct; we'd have our culprit. The combination of logging and asserts — built into the overloaded methods — makes the problem easy to find. It also points out a serious problem with overloaded methods: They complicate debugging and maintenance. After we recognize that the problem is a local variable assigned in the method instead of the class member variable `x`, we can fix the problem by removing the local `x` variable shown at ➙ **11** above.

 You don't have to use the features of the language just because they exist. Sometimes it's better not to.

The program will work properly now. What you've seen in this technique is how to trace through the overloaded methods in a class, logging information and assuring that the values coming out of the method are what you expect them to be.

Part X

The Scary (or Fun!) Stuff

The 5th Wave   By Rich Tennant

"CAREFUL SUNDANCE, THIS ONE'S BEEN LOCKED UP AND FORCED TO BETA-TEST POORLY DOCUMENTED SOFTWARE PRODUCTS ALLLL WEEK AND HE'S ITCHING FOR A FIGHT."

Technique 65

Optimizing Your Code

Save Time By
- Making functions inline
- Avoding temporary objects
- Passing by reference
- Postponing variable declarations
- Choosing initialization over assigment

The final stage in any development process is to optimize the code to make it run better, faster, and more efficiently. Of course, in an ideal world, you would be optimizing the code as you went along, but for most applications this simply isn't possible. Instead, developers first get all of the functionality in place, test it, and then optimize it. This technique explores some methods you can use in the post-development phase to optimize your code. While it will never beat developing optimized code in the first place, post-development optimization can still identify and fix many bottlenecks in the code, and give a boost to code that runs just a little too slow.

Making Functions Inline

The first optimization technique that you can use is to make your functions inline code versions. Inline functions and methods are those that are defined at the same time they are implemented, in the class header. An inline function can be considerably faster than its non-inline brethren, but that speed comes at a cost. Inline functions make your program bigger, and can sometimes even make it slower, because they add overhead to the code. An inline function is expanded in place wherever it is called, much like a macro. This can cause the code to grow significantly, because there are many copies of the same code in the program. It could slow loading and executing of the program down, if there are enough of the copies to make the program very large in size. However, in many cases, you can speed up your code significantly by making accessor functions inline. The reason is that the compiler can optimize the code in place, so that procedures that use inline functions are more optimal than they would be with regular function calls. Accessor functions, which provide read and write access to individual data members, are excellent targets for inlining because they are very small and can be optimized readily.

Take a look at the following class:

```
class Foo
{
    string _str;
public:
    Foo(const char *str)
    {
        _str = str;
    }
    string getString(void);
};

string Foo::getString(void)
{
    return _str;
}
}
```

We can improve the efficiency of this method by inlining the method, like this:

```
string getString(void)
{
    return str;
}
```

 Although many modern compilers do this optimization for you automatically, it's always up to you to write the best possible code. Don't rely on the compiler to fix it up.

The rules for inlining are very simple:

✔ Always inline a simple accessor.

✔ Never inline a large method, as the amount of code added to your program far outweighs the savings from the inline.

✔ Inline only when the savings from the function overhead are small compared to the overall savings. In other words, inlining functions that call other functions is generally wasteful.

Avoiding Temporary Objects

If there is a single optimization technique that you should most seriously look at in C++, it's to avoid having to create and delete temporary objects. Every time you pass an object by value, you make a temporary copy of that object. Every time that you write code that casts a basic data type to an object, you create a temporary object. If you want to optimize your code, look through it and remove all temporary object creations. Let's take a look at an example of code that really overdoes it with temporaries, to get an idea of what the problem really is.

1. **In the code editor of your choice, create a new file to hold the code for the implementation of the source file.**

   In this example, the file is named ch65.cpp, although you can use whatever you choose.

2. **Type the code from Listing 65-1 into your file.**

   Better yet, copy the code from the source file on this book's companion Web site.

LISTING 65-1: TEMPORARY OBJECTS

```
#include <iostream>
#include <stdlib.h>
#include <time.h>

using namespace std;

class Integer
{
    int _iVal;
public:
    Integer()
    {
        cout << "Void constructor" << endl;
        _iVal = 0;
    }
    Integer( int iVal )
    {
```

```
        cout << "Normal constructor" <<
          endl;
        _iVal = iVal;
    }
    Integer( const Integer& aCopy )
    {
        cout << "Copy constructor" << endl;
        _iVal = aCopy._iVal;
    }
    ~Integer()
    {
        cout << "Destructor" << endl;
    }
    int getInt() const
    {
        return _iVal;
    }
    void setInt(int iVal)
    {
        _iVal = iVal;
    }
    Integer operator+= ( const Integer& i1 )
    {
        setInt( i1.getInt() + getInt() );
        return *this;
    }
};

Integer operator+( const Integer& i1, const
    Integer& i2 )                          → 3
{
    Integer out;                           → 1

    out.setInt( i1.getInt() + i2.getInt() );
    return out;                            → 2
}

Integer operator-( const Integer& i1, const
    Integer& i2 )                          → 4
{
    return Integer( i1.getInt() -
    i2.getInt() );
}

void  func( Integer i1 )
{
    cout << "Integer Value: " << i1.getInt()
      << endl;
}
```

```
int main(void)
{
    Integer i1(5), i2(3);
    Integer i3;

    cout << "Test plus: " << endl;
    i3 = i1 + i2;
    cout << "Result: " << i3.getInt() <<
      endl;

    cout << "Test minus: " << endl;
    Integer i4 = i3 - i2;
    cout << "Result: " << i4.getInt() <<
      endl;

    cout << "Calling function" << endl;
    func( i4 );
}
```

If we look at the operator+ function that works with the Integer class, you will see that the function accepts two Integer objects by reference. No objects are created here. However, within the object, we create a temporary object that is created locally (see → **1**). This object is then used to set the pieces of the integer from the two Integer objects passed into the function, before being returned to the calling program at → **2**. The result is then assigned to the result variable in the main program (see → **3**). How many temporary objects are being created here? Let's run the program and find out.

3. Save the source file in the code editor and then close the editor application.

4. Compile the source-code file with your favorite compiler on your favorite operating system.

5. Run the program on the console window of your favorite operating system.

If you have done everything correctly, you should see the following output on the console window:

```
$ ./a.exe
Normal constructor
Normal constructor
Void constructor
Test plus:
Void constructor
Destructor
Result: 8
Test minus:
Normal constructor
Result: 5
Calling function
Copy constructor
Integer Value: 5
Destructor
Destructor
Destructor
Destructor
Destructor
```

The output shows each time an `Integer` object is being created and destroyed. Take a look at the `print` statements, especially those between the `Test plus:` statement and the `Test minus:` statement. There is a temporary object created here, and then destroyed.

Look at the difference between the addition operator (shown in Listing 65-1 at the line marked ➜ **3**) and the subtraction operator (shown in Listing 65-1 at the line marked ➜ **4**); notice that the addition operator has some overhead: a void constructor and a destructor call. The subtraction call, on the other hand, has no such constructor call. The only construction is the object in the main function that is being created to hold the result. How does this happen? The answer is, the compiler is optimized to understand that a returned object that is assigned can be created in the actual space that was allocated. Because the compiler can optimize an object that is constructed in a `return` statement, and just

"copy" the memory into the object the result is assigned to, it will save you a lot of time and overhead if you use this optimization. Also notice that if you pass an object by value, rather than by reference — as we do in the `func` function — a copy is made of the object and the various constructors and destructors called. If you are going to pass an object into a function, always pass it by reference. If you do not plan to change the object within that function, pass a constant reference.

Passing Objects by Reference

One of the problems with C++ is that not all of it can be implemented within any single class. That means you either end up with stand-alone functions or other objects that must receive objects in their methods. For example, consider what happens when you pass a stream to a function to output data:

```
int print_my_data(ostream& out)
{
    out << "Dump of my data" << endl
    // Code to dump the data
}
```

In this simple example, we are passing a stream object to a function. Note that the stream is passed by reference, using the ampersand, rather than by value, which would make a copy of the object. Why do we do it this way? Well, suppose you tried to write the code another way, such as this:

```
int print_my_data( ostream out )
{
    cout << "Dump of my data" << endl;
}
int main()
{
    print_my_data( cout );
}
```

You would get a compile error, because the `ostream` class copy constructor is private. Creating a private constructor is one way to avoid having copies made of your objects, but an easier one is to pass the object by reference. This avoids the overhead of a temporary object, avoids the call to the copy constructor and destructor, and avoids the problems with having objects that are modified in the function. Let's look at an example of what I am talking about here.

1. **In the code editor of your choice, create a new file to hold the code for the implementation of the source file.**

   In this example, the file is named ch65a.cpp, although you can use whatever you choose.

2. **Type the code from Listing 65-2 into your file.**

   Or better yet, copy the code from the source file on this book's companion Web site.

LISTING 65-2: PASSING BY REFERENCE

```cpp
#include <iostream>
#include <stdlib.h>
#include <time.h>

using namespace std;

class Integer
{
    int _iVal;
public:
    Integer()
    {
        cout << "Void constructor" << endl;
        _iVal = 0;
    }
    Integer( int iVal )
    {
        cout << "Normal constructor" <<
          endl;
        _iVal = iVal;
    }
    Integer( const Integer& aCopy )
    {
        cout << "Copy constructor" << endl;
        _iVal = aCopy._iVal;
    }
    ~Integer()
    {
        cout << "Destructor" << endl;
    }
    int getInt() const
    {
        return _iVal;
    }
    void setInt(int iVal)
    {
        _iVal = iVal;
    }
};

void func1( Integer i1 )                    → 5
{
    i1.setInt( 12 );
}
void func2( Integer& i2 )                   → 6
{
    i2.setInt(12);
}
int main()
{
    Integer i;

    func1(i);
    cout << "After func1, value = " <<
    i.getInt() << endl;
    func2(i);
    cout << "After func2, value = " <<
    i.getInt() << endl;
}
```

The two functions in this listing both attempt to change the value of the integer value stored in an object passed to them. In the first case (shown at → **5**), the object is passed by value (the entire object is copied before sending it to the function). In the second case (shown at → **6**), the object is passed by reference (the address of the object is passed to the function). You would normally expect the two functions to have the same result because they do the same thing. As we will see when we run the program, however, the two have very different ending results.

3. **Save the source file in the code editor and then close the editor application.**

4. **Compile the source code file with your favorite compiler on your favorite operating system.**

5. **Run the program on the console window of your favorite operating system.**

If you have done everything correctly, you should see the following output on the console window:

```
$ ./a.exe
Void constructor
Copy constructor
Destructor
After func1, value = 0              → 7
After func2, value = 12             → 8
Destructor
```

This code shows that passing a value by reference avoids the overhead of creating a temporary object. More importantly, this approach avoids the problem of making changes that aren't reflected in the original object. Notice that the func1 function does not change the value of the integer variable (shown at → **7** in the output). This is because the function accepts its argument by value, which makes a copy of the original object and modifies that copy, rather than the object itself. The func2 function, shown at → **8** in the output, passes its object by reference, which means that the original object is modified, and the result is reflected in the calling routine.

Postponing Variable Declarations

If you have ever programmed in a language other than C++, you are probably already used to the process of defining a variable before you use it. This was the way to program in C, FORTRAN, and BASIC, so most programmers kept that approach when they moved to the object-oriented C++ language. Doing so is a mistake, however, because it creates potentially unnecessary overhead in the code.

For example, consider the following function:

```
int func( char *ptr )
{
    char *newPtr = new char[200];
    if ( ptr == NULL )
    {
        delete newPtr;
        return -1;
    }

    // Do something with the newPtr
       variable

    return 0;
}
```

The code shows no reason to initialize or define the newPtr variable before we check the input. If this was some class variable that was too large to instantiate efficiently, you'd be wasting a lot of time and memory by defining this variable without knowing whether you'd be using it.

In general, here are the steps you should always follow to optimize the instantiation of variables in a function or method:

1. **First, do any input data validation.**

If the data requires that you exit the function, do so before you create any variables locally.

2. **Pass the data to existing classes as appropriate.**

If the data you are using must be passed into a constructor or other method of a class, break the constructor for that class into two parts, validation and initialization.

For example, consider the following code for a class that tries to open a file:

```
int  open_the_file(const char *strName)
{
    // See whether the input character
       string is valid.
    if (strName==NULL || strName[0]==0)
        return -1;
```

```
    // Construct the object.
    fileHandle fh(strName);
    // This will check to see if the
       file already exists.
    if ( !fh.Exists() )
       return -1;
    // Now, we can do the "expensive"
       operation of
    // opening and reading the file.
    if ( fh.Open() == false )
       return -1;
    // Read the file...
}
```

In this example, we first check all input for validity. If it isn't valid, there is no cost to the `fileHandle` object being created. If the input is valid, we then pass the validation onto that object. First, we simply set the filename into the object and see whether that file exists. Then we try to open the file — which will buffer the data for it and do the overhead (that is, getting the operating system to open the file). Only then, if all those things work, do we actually *read* the file, which costs the most time.

Choosing Initialization Instead of Assignment

The final optimization technique to look at is initializing data (rather than assigning data in constructors for classes). Under normal circumstances, the member data for a class is first constructed (using default constructors), and then assigned values based on input to the constructor (or defaults provided by the programmer). The problem with this approach is that the initialization is really done twice — first in the constructor and then in the assignment. This is wasteful, and leads to program slowdowns.

To see how to make this improvement, follow these steps:

1. **In the code editor of your choice, create a new file to hold the code for the implementation of the source file.**

   In this example, the file is named `ch65b.cpp`, although you can use whatever you choose.

2. **Type the code from Listing 65-3 into your file.**

   Better yet, copy the code from the source file on this book's companion Web site.

LISTING 65-3: INITIALIZING VERSUS ASSIGNING

```
#include <iostream>
#include <string>

using namespace std;

class Point
{
private:
    int _x;
    int _y;
public:
    Point(void)
    {
        cout << "Point: void constructor
            called" << endl;

        _x = 0;
        _y = 0;
    }
    Point( int x, int y )
    {
        cout << "Point: full constructor
            called" << endl;
        _x = x;
        _y = y;
    }
    Point( const Point& p )
    {
        cout << "Point: copy constructor
            called" << endl;
```

(continued)

LISTING 65-3 *(continued)*

```
        _x = p._x;
        _y = p._y;
    }
    Point& operator=( const Point& p )
    {
        cout << "Point: operator= called" <<
          endl;
        _x = p._x;
        _y = p._y;
        return *this;
    }
    int& X()
    {
        return _x;
    }
    int& Y()
    {
        return _y;
    }
};

class Line
{
    Point _p1;
    Point _p2;
public:
    Line(void)
    {
    }
    Line( int x1, int x2, int y1,
      int y2 )                              → 9
        : _p1(x1,y1),                       → 10
          _p2(x2,y2)
    {
    }
    Line( const Point& p1, const Point &p2 )
    {
        _p1 = p1;
        _p2 = p2;
    }
    Point& TopLeft()
    {
        return _p1;
    }
    Point& BottomRight()
    {
```

```
        return _p2;
    }
};

int main()
{
    // First, create some points.
    Point p1(0,0);
    Point p2(10,10);

    // Now create some lines.
    cout << "Line 1: " << endl;
    Line l1( 0,0, 10, 10);
    cout << "Line 2: " << endl;
    Line l2( p1, p2 );
}
```

In this case, we are using a very simple set of classes that implement a point and a line. Notice that in the Line class, there are two separate constructors. One takes four data values, indicating the starting and ending x and y coordinates (see → **9**). The second takes two point objects to define the same coordinates, as shown in → **10**. The difference in the two constructors is how the data is assigned to the internal member variables in the two cases. In the first case, the two points in the Line class are initialized within the initialization line of the constructor code. In the second case, the two points are initialized by assignment within the constructor body. As we will see when the program runs, these two choices have very different results.

3. Save the source file in the code editor and then close the editor application.

4. Compile the source-code file with your favorite compiler on your favorite operating system.

5. Run the program on the console window of your favorite operating system.

If you have done everything correctly, you should see the following output on the console window:

```
$ ./a.exe
Point: full constructor called
Point: full constructor called
Line 1:                                    → 11
Point: full constructor called
Point: full constructor called
Line 2:                                    → 12
Point: void constructor called
Point: void constructor called
Point: operator= called
Point: operator= called
```

Notice that in the first case (shown at → **11**), we construct the two points as a part of constructing the line. This is as expected because the `Line` object contains two point objects. However, those two objects are constructed using the full constructor for the `Point` class, using the data values we passed in. This means there is no additional overhead for creating the points. In the second case, shown at → **12**, however, we not only have the two `Point` objects being created, but also the overhead of two assignment statements. This means that twice as much work is being done. If you initialize things using the initialization process in C++ constructors, you avoid the overhead of the assignments.

Technique

66

Documenting the Data Flow

Save Time By

- ✔ Learning how the code operates
- ✔ Improving the readability of your code by documenting the data flow
- ✔ Adding an undo system
- ✔ Testing your code

Beginning programmers are often afraid to make adjustments to existing code for fear of destroying the code's functionality. Existing code is simply part of life in the programming world, and you can't be afraid to just dig in and make changes to the code base. Other than to offer simple encouragement, I can't really give you any advice on how to work with existing code; however, I can give you ideas on how to make your code easier to work with.

If you want to save a lot of time for yourself and all of the programmers who come after you, document the flow of data through the system. Most programmers document how the code works, or how you interface to the objects in the system. This is a nice thing, but the problems that crop up in coding are normally related to data, not code. In this technique, we are going to explore the most important part of the programming system, the data flow.

Learning How Code Operates

If you really want to know how the code in a system operates, just watch how it manipulates data. The surest way to do so is to keep track of all changes in a system. Although we normally think of an object-oriented system as having member variables and methods to access those variables, there is really no reason to do things this way. We can simply implement a system that stores the data in properties and then accesses those properties through standard methods of the property manipulation class rather than through the parent class. The following steps show you this exact process, implementing a property holding class and providing methods to track the changes to the data as it goes through the system.

1. **In the code editor of your choice, create a new file to hold the code for the implementation of the source file.**

In this example, the file is named `ch66.cpp`, although you can use whatever you choose.

2. **Type the code from Listing 66-1 into your file.**

Better yet, copy the code from the source file on this book's companion Web site.

LISTING 66-1: IMPLEMENTING PROPERTIES AS A CLASS

```cpp
#include <map>
#include <string>
#include <iostream>
#include <stack>
#include <stdlib.h>

using namespace std;

class State
{
    string _name;
    string _value;
public:
    State(void)
    {
        _name = "";
        _value = "";
    }
    State( const char *name, const char
      *value )
    {
        setName( name );
        setValue( value );
    }
    State( const State& aCopy )
    {
        setName( aCopy.getName() );
        setValue( aCopy.getValue() );
    }
    void setName( const char *n )
    {
        _name = n;
    }
    void setName( const string& n )
    {
```

```cpp
        _name = n;
    }
    string getName(void) const
    {
        return _name;
    }
    void setValue( const char *v )
    {
        _value = v;
    }
    void setValue( const string& v )
    {
        _value = v;
    }
    string getValue( void ) const
    {
        return _value;
    }
};

class Properties                              → 1
{
    map<string, string> _props;
    stack<State>        _previous;            → 2

public:
    Properties(void)
    {
    }
    Properties( const Properties& aCopy )
    {
        map<string, string>::iterator iter;
        for ( iter = _props.begin(); iter !=
          _props.end(); ++iter )
            _props[ (*iter).first ] =
                (*iter).second;
    }
    virtual ~Properties()
    {
    }

    void setProperty( const char *name, int
      value )
    {
        // First, see if its there
        if ( _props.find(name) !=
          _props.end() )
        {
            State sold(name, _props[name].
              c_str() );                       → 3
```

(continued)

LISTING 66-1 *(continued)*

```
            _previous.push( sold );
        }
        else
        {
            State sold(name, "");
            _previous.push( sold );
        }
        char szBuffer[20];
        sprintf(szBuffer, "%d", value );
        _props[name] = szBuffer;
    }
    string getProperty( const char *name )
    {
        return _props[ name ];
    }
}
```

Okay, there's nothing particularly special about this code — it simply allows you to add new properties to an object, modify them as you see fit, and retrieve them. It also keeps track of all of the changes to a given object, which would allow you to log those changes, or even implement an undo system. To give you an idea of how simple it would be to add functionality to a system based on this object, the next step adds an undo method for the Properties object. The Properties class, shown at ➜ 1, keeps track of a list of properties for other objects. Within the class, the State class (shown at ➜ 2) is used to maintain a list of the various values for each property. When a value is changed, a new State object is created with the old value and stored (see ➜ 3). This will allow us to implement undo very simply.

3. **Add the following code to the class listing:**

```
void undo()
{
    if ( _previous.empty() )
        return;
```

```
    // Pop off the last change
    State s = _previous.top();
    _previous.pop();

    // Apply it
    _props[s.getName()] = s.
        getValue();
}
```

Here, because we're tracking all changes to the object anyway, undoing one of those changes is trivial. Adding this sort of code to the system at the outset — rather than trying to build it in later — makes for a very robust system that's also easy to debug.

4. **Save the source code in your code editor.**

Testing the *Properties* Class

After you create a class, you should create a test driver that not only ensures your code is correct, but also shows people how to use your code. The following steps tell you how:

1. **In the code editor of your choice, reopen the source file to hold the code for your test program.**

   In this example, I named the test program ch66.cpp.

2. **Type the code from Listing 66-2 into your file.**

   Better yet, copy the code from the source file on this book's companion Web site.

LISTING 66-2: THE PROPERTY TEST PROGRAM

```
int main()
{
    Properties p;

    p.setProperty( "x", 12 ); ➜        4
    cout << "x = " << p.getProperty
        ("x").c_str() << endl;
```

```
    p.setProperty( "x", 13 );                    → 5
    cout << "x = " <<
        p.getProperty("x").c_str() << endl;
    p.undo();                                     → 6
    cout << "x = " <<
        p.getProperty("x").c_str() << endl;
}
```

The test program simply creates a Properties object and adds a new property called x to it (shown at → **4**). We print out the value of that property, then change it → **5**. The value is then printed out again to verify the change. At this point, we undo the last change for the Properties object by using the undo method at → **6**. We would then expect the value of x to be its previous value, 12, rather than the current value of 13.

3. **Save the source code in the source-code editor and close the editor application.**

4. **Compile the source code with your favorite compiler on your favorite operating system.**

5. **Run the program on your favorite operating system console.**

If you have done everything properly, you should see the following output from the program on the console window:

```
$ ./a.exe
x = 12
x = 13
x = 12
```

As we expected, the value of x changes from the last set value, 13, to its previous setting of 12 due to the undo function call. The undo functionality, besides being useful in a program by itself, also shows you how to track changes to data within the program. This ability will make it very simple to debug applications by seeing exactly how things changed over time.

As you can see, the system properly stores the information for the properties and easily implements the undo system. This type of object could easily be dropped into a "regular" object to replace the entire member variable list.

 Tracking and documenting the data flow within an application is the single most important thing you can do for programmers, maintainers, debuggers, and customer support personnel. Data flow is what the user cares about and the QA department uses to validate your system. By making it easy to see what changes and when it happens, you save yourself immense amounts of time later on in the development process.

Technique 67

Creating a Simple Locking Mechanism

Save Time By

- ✔ "Locking" functionality in an application
- ✔ Creating a locking mechanism
- ✔ Testing the locking mechanism

From time to time, programmers must "lock out" the functionality of a given application. There are many possible reasons for this necessity: If you're running a multithreaded application, for example, you need to keep multiple threads from hitting the same function at the same time. Or perhaps you're writing an application in which a resource (such as a hardware device) can be accessed only at certain times.

"Locking" a program means denying the program access into a given block of code until a certain condition occurs. Not unlike a finite-state machine, a lock mechanism can force a system into certain transitions (movements from one state to another) only when they are ready to happen — which ensures a predictable outcome and avoids unforeseen circumstances. Locking mechanisms save time for the developer by reducing hard to reproduce errors and problems that can only be tested in multi-user environments.

There are many ways to implement locking in an application. Most operating systems provide heavyweight critical-section handlers that can be used to lock only small pieces of code at the hardware level. These mechanisms, however, are intended only for serious multithreading; they impose too much overhead in terms of processing time, memory required, and code required, for the average application to utilize. What is really needed is a more lightweight system — with little or no overhead — that you can use to lock global resources within your application code at run-time. Filling that need is the purpose of this technique.

 Portability is one big advantage of implementing and employing your own locking mechanism instead of a system-level lock. Using your own locking mechanism allows your code to port easily from system to system without requiring extensive rewrites (often necessary when you use a new compiler or operating system). Even if you choose to use the underlying system support to lock your application, you should wrap that functionality in your own class so it's the only place you have to make changes when you move to a new operating system, compiler, or version of the library code.

Creating the Locking Mechanism

Giving your code the appropriate locking functionality is pretty straightforward. The following steps show how to create a class that does the job:

1. **In the code editor of your choice, create a new file to hold the code for the implementation of source file.**

In this example, the file is named ch67.cpp, although you can use whatever you choose.

2. **Type the code in Listing 67-1 into your file.**

Better yet, copy the code from the source file on this book's companion Web site.

LISTING 67-1: THE SIMPLE LOCKING-MECHANISM CLASS

```cpp
#include <string>
#include <vector>

using namespace std;

class LockException
{
    string _msg;
public:
    LockException(void)
    {
        _msg = "Lock Exception";
    }
    LockException( const char *msg )
    {
        _msg = "Lock Exception: ";
        _msg += msg;
    }
    LockException( const LockException&
      aCopy )
    {
        _msg = aCopy._msg;
    }
    const char *Message(void)
    {
        return _msg.c_str();
    }
    void setMessage( const char *msg )
    {
        _msg = msg;
    }
};

class Lock
{
private:
    static bool _bLock;                    → 1
    bool        _isLocked;
public:
    Lock(void)
    {
        _isLocked = false;
    }
    Lock( const Lock& aCopy )
    {
        _isLocked = aCopy._isLocked;
    }
    virtual ~Lock()
    {
        unLock();
    }
    bool setLock()
    {
        if ( !_isLocked )
        {
            if ( _bLock == false )
            {
                _bLock = true;
                return true;
            }
        }
        return false;
    }
    bool isLocked(void)
    {
        return _bLock;
    }
    void unLock( void )
    {
        if ( _isLocked )
        {
            if ( _bLock == true )
            {
                _bLock = false;
            }
        }
    }
};
bool Lock::_bLock=false;                    → 2
```

The above listing consists of two classes: the Lock class, which implements the actual locking mechanism, and the LockException class, which implements an exception holder for any locking errors. The Lock class works by maintaining a single global variable (bLock, shown at ➜ **1**) that is used to see whether or not the lock is active. All instances of the Lock class use the same variable to track their locking states, so the Lock class is really useful only for a single lock in your application. The Lock class just checks to see whether or not the variable is set; if so, it will not allow another lock to be implemented. The destructor clears the lock (shown at line marked ➜ **2**) so that a lock cannot be maintained indefinitely. Alternatively, the user can set and clear the lock manually, by using the setLock and unLock methods.

You will notice that the code uses a single static Boolean data member (shown at line marked with ➜ **2**) to maintain its state. This is necessary because the Lock class must be accessible across different objects; otherwise the entire purpose of the class is defeated. Using static data members is not always a good idea — doing so makes inheritance from the base class harder to implement — but such an approach can also solve some pretty thorny problems.

3. **Save the source file and close the code editor.**

Testing the Locking Mechanism

In order to illustrate how the locking code works and why it works, you should create a test driver that shows how to use the code and what the expected results will be. The following steps show you how.

1. **In the code editor of your choice, reopen the existing file to hold the code for your test program.**

In this example, I named the test program ch67.cpp.

2. **Type the code from Listing 67-2 into your file.**

Better yet, copy the code from the source file on this book's companion Web site.

LISTING 67-2: THE LOCK TEST DRIVER

```
Lock gLock;

void func1()
{
    Lock l1;

    if ( l1.isLocked() )
        throw LockException("Unable to acquire lock\n");
    else
        printf("Able to acquire lock\n");
}

void func2()
{
    if ( gLock.isLocked() == false )
        gLock.setLock();
    else
        gLock.unLock();
}
```

```
int main(int argc, char **argv)
{
    if ( argc < 2 )
    {
        printf("Usage: ch7_7 [ lock | unlock ]\n");
        printf("Where: lock indicates that the program should first set the global lock and\n");
        printf("       unlock indicates that the program should not first set the global
          lock\n");
    }

    if ( !strcmp ( argv[1], "unlock" ) )
    {

        // Note that in this order, the two functions will work properly.
        try
        {
            func1();
        }
        catch ( LockException& exc )
        {
            printf("unlock: Exception trying to lock: %s\n", exc.Message() );
        }

        func2();
    }
    else
        if ( !strcmp ( argv[1], "lock" ) )
        {
            func2();                                                            → 3
            try
            {
                func1();                                                        → 4
            }
            catch ( LockException& exc )
            {
                printf("lock: Exception trying to lock: %s\n", exc.Message() );
            }
        }
        else
            printf("Unknown argument %s\n", argv[1] );

    return 0;

}
```

The test driver code simply exercises the various locking functions. If you pass in a command line argument, it will either lock (pass in `lock`) or unlock (pass in `unlock`) the global lock object. If a lock is requested, and cannot be granted, it throws an exception that should be displayed on the console.

3. **Save the source file in the code editor and close the editor application.**

4. **Compile and link the application on your favorite operating system, using your compiler of choice.**

If you have done everything right, you should see the following output appear on your shell window:

```
$ ./a.exe
Usage: ch7_7 [ lock | unlock ]
Where: lock indicates that the program
    should first set the global lock and
        unlock indicates that the program
    should not first set the global lock

$ ./a.exe lock                          → 5
lock: Exception trying to lock: Lock
    Exception: Unable to acquire lock

$ ./a.exe unlock                        → 6
Able to acquire lock
```

Note that the three possible scenarios for running the program are shown in the output:

🖒 If you invoke the program with no arguments, it prints out the usage of the program and exits.

🖒 If you attempt to set the lock, the program first sets a lock (as shown at → 3) and then sets a local lock within a function (shown at → 4). Because the global lock is still in operation, the lock in `func2` fails and throws an exception.

🖒 If you run the program to unlock, it succeeds as expected and prints out the fact that it could acquire a lock.

In the first run of the program (the `lock` case, shown at the line marked → 5), we have first locked the global lock in the function `func2`. This causes the call to `func1` to fail, because it cannot get access to the lock.

In the second run of the program (shown at the line marked → 6), we call the `func1` function first so the program can get the lock and continue. The `lock` object goes out of scope and releases the lock before the second function (`func2`) is called — so `func2` can also get access to the lock and successfully proceed.

This code illustrates another use of the static data member in C++, besides the typical use of keeping track of data within a class. Used properly, static data members can be used to communicate between functions, methods, or instances of objects — even across thread boundaries.

Creating and Using Guardian Classes

Save Time By

✔ Protecting functionality with guardian classes

✔ Creating a guardian class

✔ Testing your class

A *guardian class,* as its name implies, is a class that "guards" its contents from the world of application developers. Guardian classes are often used when memory is being allocated, or when a hardware device needs to have specific inputs validated for it. Because a memory allocation needs to be matched with a de-allocation, a guardian class is the ideal solution: it wraps the transaction in a single class. Guardian classes, as shown in this technique, can also be used to make existing functionality memory-safe, exception-safe, and (most importantly) error-proof.

Consider, for a moment, the standard C-style function `fopen`. This function is used with the C library to open a file for input, output, or both. The `fopen` function has the following prototype:

```
FILE *fopen(
    const char *filename,
    const char *mode
);
```

The basic idea is that you pass in a file name and a "mode" parameter, and the function opens the file in any operating system. The function then returns to you a pointer to an internal structure used for working with the file. At this point, you can perform basic file operations: You can write to, read from, seek within, and close the file as needed.

Although they are not the least bit object-oriented in design, you can use the `fopen` and related functions safely in your C++ code. Unfortunately, C-style functions do not tend to have a great deal of error checking, nor are they forgiving. If `fopen` fails, it returns a NULL pointer. If you then pass this NULL pointer to another function expecting a FILE pointer, it crashes the application. This is where guardian classes work best. In terms of code stability and robustness, however, consider the following snippets of code:

```
(1)    FILE *fp = fopen(NULL, NULL);     → 1
(2)    FILE *fp = fopen("myfile.txt",
       "z");                             → 2
(3)    FILE *fp = fopen("myfile.txt",
       "r");                             → 3
fprintf(fp, "This is a test");
fclose(fp);
(4)    FILE *fp = fopen("myfile.txt",
       "w");                             → 4
try {
    call_a_function_that_might_throw_excep-
    tions();
}
    catch(...)
    {
        printf("Error in function\n");
            return -1;
        }
        fclose(fp);
```

All these functions suffer from various — and serious — problems related to the file-handling functions provided with C:

✔ Example (1 shown at → **1** crashes. The `fopen` function does not understand how to deal with `NULL` values in either the name or the mode parameter.

✔ In example (2) shown at → **2**, the `mode` parameter may not be `z`. Mode parameters are well defined, and must be one of a certain list of characters. Typically, the list is `r`, `w`, and `a`. The behavior in such a case is unknown — and will probably result in the file not being opened.

✔ Example (3), shown at → **3**, is a crash waiting to happen: Because the programmer did not check for the return value from `fopen`, the `fprintf` function call will crash — and so will the program — if the file pointer is `NULL` .

✔ Example (4), shown at → **4** has a serious problem: If the function call for `call_a_function_that_might_throw_exceptions` throws an exception, then the function will return without closing the file — creating a memory leak and leaving a file open (both on disk and in memory). At best, the open file will not be written properly to disk; at worst, it might be partially written and corrupted.

All these problems can — and should — be prevented. There is no excuse for allowing a simple file-open routine to cause your program to crash. Because the file-handling functions are so fragile, you should wrap them in a guardian class to ensure that the programmer cannot make mistakes, that no memory is leaked, and that the functions are protected from invalid values. This technique shows you how to set up this essential safeguard.

 Whenever you run across a piece of code that is unsafe to use in any manner other than the way specified by the programmer, wrapping that code in a guardian class will save you a lot of time trying to track down problems. If the program simply crashes with no diagnostics, you have to step through every single line in the application to figure out what went wrong. If (instead) you get into the habit of wrapping any would-be leaks or crashes in a code that insulates the underlying technology from the possibility of error, you won't see this kind of error in your application.

Creating the File-Guardian Class

The heart of this technique is the creation of a file-guardian class called `FileWrapper`. To create it, follow these steps:

1. **In the code editor of your choice, create a new file to hold the code for the implementation of source file.**

In this example, the file is named `ch68.cpp`, although you can use whatever you choose.

2. **Type the code from Listing 68-1 into your file.**

Better yet, copy the code from the source file on this book's companion Web site.

LISTING 68-1: THE GUARDIAN-CLASS SOURCE CODE

```
#include <stdio.h>
#include <string.h>

typedef enum
{
    Read = 0,
    Write = 1,
    ReadWrite = 2,
    Append = 3
} FileMode;

class FileWrapper
{
    FILE    *_fp;
    char    *_name;
    FileMode _mode;

    virtual void Init()
    {
        _fp = NULL;
        _name = NULL;
    }
    virtual void Clear()
    {
        if ( _fp )
        {
            printf("File %s is now closed\n", _name );
            fclose(_fp);
            _fp = NULL;
        }
        if ( _name )
            delete [] _name;
        _name = NULL;
    }

public:
    FileWrapper(void)
    {
        Init();
    }
    FileWrapper( const char *name, const FileMode& mode )
    {
        Init();
        setName( name );
        setMode( mode );

    }
    FileWrapper( const FileWrapper& aCopy )
```

(continued)

LISTING 68-1 *(continued)*

```
    {
        Init();
        if ( aCopy._name )
            setName( aCopy._name );
        if ( aCopy._mode )
            setMode( aCopy._mode );
    }
    FileWrapper operator=(const FileWrapper& aCopy)
    {
        Clear();
        if ( aCopy._name )
            setName( aCopy._name );
        if ( aCopy._mode )
            setMode( aCopy._mode );
    }
    virtual ~FileWrapper( void )
    {
        Clear();
    }

    virtual void setName( const char *name )
    {
        if ( name )
        {
            _name = new char[ strlen(name)+1 ];
            strcpy( _name, name );
        }
    }
    virtual void setMode( const FileMode& mode )
    {
        _mode = mode;
    }

    virtual bool open()
        if ( _fp != NULL )
        {
            fclose(_fp);
            _fp = NULL;
        }
        char *mode = NULL;
        switch ( _mode )
        {
            case Read:
                mode = "r";
                break;
            case Write:
                mode = "w";
                break;
            case ReadWrite:
                mode = "r+";
                break;
```

→ 6

```
            case Append:
                mode = "a";
                break;
        }
        if ( mode == NULL )
            return false;

        _fp = fopen( _name, mode );
        if ( !_fp )
        {
            printf("Error opening file %s\n", _name );
            return false;
        }
        printf("File %s is now open\n", _name );
    }
    virtual char getc()                                          → 7
    {
        if ( _fp != NULL )
            return fgetc(_fp);
        return 0;
    }
    virtual bool eof()
    {
        if ( _fp != NULL )
            return feof(_fp);
        return true;
    }
    virtual bool putc( char c )                                  → 8
    {
        if ( _fp != NULL )
            return fputc(c, _fp) == c;
        return false;
    }
    virtual bool puts( const char *s )                           → 5
    {
        if ( _fp == NULL )
            return false;
        if ( s == NULL )
            return false;
        return (fputs( s, _fp ) != EOF );
    }

    virtual bool close()
    {
        if ( _fp == NULL )
            return false;
        Clear();
        return true;
    }
};
```

The code above doesn't really do anything that the standard C functions don't already do for you. The `puts` function, for example, does exactly what the `puts` method (shown at ➜ **5**) method does with one very important difference. If the file is not open, or the string is NULL, the `puts` method in the class above checks for the error and returns an error code. The `puts` function, on the other hand, crashes the application if either of those conditions is true.

Note also the `open` function, shown at the line marked ➜ **6**. The mode problem cannot exist in this class, as it did in the `fopen` function, because we pass in an enumerated value that must be one of a list of valid values. If it is not, an error occurs.

3. **Save the source code in the code editor.**

Note that we have replaced the problematic "mode" parameter of the `open` class with a safer, more secure enumeration that we can validate. Also notice that all the various read and write functions (shown at lines ➜ **7** and ➜ **8**) work, whether or not the file was successfully opened.

Testing the File-Guardian Class

After you create a class, you should create a test driver that not only ensures that your code is correct, but also shows people how to use your code. The following steps tell you how:

1. **In the code editor of your choice, reopen the source file to hold the code for your test program.**

In this example, I named the test program `ch68.cpp`.

2. **Type the code from Listing 68-2 into your file.**

Better yet, copy the code from the source file on this book's companion Web site.

LISTING 68-2: THE FILE-GUARDIAN TEST PROGRAM

```
int func2()
{
    throw "This is bad!";
}

int old_func()
{
    FILE *fp = fopen("anoldfile.out", "w");
    if ( fp == NULL )
        return -1;

    fprintf(fp, "This is a test\n");
    try
    {
        func2();
    }
    catch ( ... )
    {
        printf("An error occurred\n");
        return -2;
    }

    printf("Closing file\n");
    fclose(fp);
    return 0;
}

int new_func()
{
    FileWrapper out("anewfile.out", Write);
    if ( out.open() == false )
        return -1;

    out.puts("This is a test\n");
    try
    {
        func2();
    }
    catch ( ... )
    {
        printf("An error occurred\n");
        return -2;
    }

    out.close();
    return 0;
}
```

```
int main(int argc, char **argv)
{
    if ( argc < 2 )
    {
        printf("Usage: ch7_9 filename\n");
        return -1;
    }

    FileWrapper fw(argv[1], Write);

    // Note that we do not check the
        results.
    fw.open();                              → 9

    // Write out all the arguments.
    for ( int i=2; i<argc; ++i )
    {
        fw.puts ( argv[i] );                → 10
    }

    // Note that we don't call close.

    // Now test the various functions.
    old_func();
    new_func();

    return 0;
}
```

The test driver simply opens an output file (shown at **→ 9** in Listing 68-2), writes out any arguments from the command line to the file (shown at **→ 10**) and then finishes. In addition, it uses two functions to illustrate how the old-style and new-style functions are used. If you look at the output, you will see that when the exception is thrown the new-style file routines properly close the file, whereas the old-style functions do not. This is an important difference, especially if you are writing to a file throughout your application as in the case of a log file.

3. **Save the source code in the code editor and then close the editor application.**

4. **Compile the source code with your favorite compiler, on your favorite operating system.**

5. **Run the program on your favorite operating system's console.**

If you have done everything properly, you should see the following output from the program on the console window:

```
$ ./a.exe test.out this is a test of the
    emergency broadcast system
File test.out is now open
An error occurred
File anewfile.out is now open
An error occurred
File anewfile.out is now closed
File test.out is now closed
```

As you can see, the new file was properly closed, as was the test.out file. These files were both created via the new functionality. The old-style file, however, was never closed, because the exception was thrown and the fclose statement was never executed.

You should also see two files created in your file system, anewfile.out and anoldfile.out. If you look at the contents of the files, you should see the following.

```
$ cat anewfile.out
This is a test

$cat anoldfile.out
```

The anewfile.out file has the text we expected. The anoldfild.out file, on the other hand, is empty.

 Depending on your operating system and settings, you may or may not see text in the anoldfile.out text file. This uncertainty alone makes it worthwhile to close the files. Some operating systems flush data as it is written to them to the disk. Others keep it in memory until the file is closed, or there is enough data to write out a full buffer. You do not want to rely on the operating system to determine this, if the data being written is important to you.

Working with Complex Numbers

Save Time By

✔ Understanding complex numbers

✔ Creating a complex numbers class

✔ Testing your class

The mathematical world deals with complex numbers all of the time. A *complex number* is simply a combination of a "real" number (that is, a floating-point value), and an "imaginary" number (i — the square root of -1 — or a multiple of i). Complex numbers are usually written out in the form $x + yi$, where x is the real number and y is the multiplier of the imaginary number.

You might not believe it, but some folks think they never need to know anything about complex math — and never expect to use a complex number in your applications. Okay, complex numbers are rarely used in applications — but when they *are* needed (in scientific projects, for example), they can be tricky to work with. Creating a class that deals with these numbers in advance of working on such a project is to your advantage. Understanding the fundamentals of complex mathematics can be tricky; you just need a class that does the work for you so that you don't have to think about it.

If you attempt to become an expert in all the expert subject matter in every application you work on, you will quickly find yourself not only frustrated, but buried in work. Sometimes it's best just to accept that others know the science or business of the area better than you ever will. In such cases, you save a lot of time by finding a good set of classes that do the work of the expert subject matter — and then working on the rest of the application. It is more important that you have an excellent suite of tests to validate your classes than it is that you have the ability to write them from the start. Save time and energy, and work on the test suite rather than the class. This technique shows you how.

Implementing the Complex Class

Most versions of the Standard Template Library have a complex template in the `<complex>` header file. However, this is not universal — and using this template means loading in the entire STL when you link your application. If all you need is a complex-number class, you'd be better off creating your own class.

First, we need to implement the definition of the complex number class. The following steps show you how.

1. In the code editor of your choice, create a new file to hold the code for the implementation of source file.

In this example, the file is named `ch69.cpp`, although you can use whatever you choose.

2. Type the code from Listing 69-1 into your file.

Better yet, copy the code from the source file on this book's companion Web site.

LISTING 69-1: THE COMPLEX CLASS DEFINITION

```
#include <math.h>
#include <stdio.h>
#include <iostream>

using namespace std;

class Complex
{
private:
        double real;
     double imaginary;
protected:
        // mathematical functionality
     void add(const Complex &a, const Complex &b);
        void subtract(const Complex &a, const Complex &b);
     void multiply(const Complex &a, const Complex &b);
        void negative();


public:
        Complex();
     Complex(double realValue, double imaginaryValue);
     Complex( const Complex& aCopy );

     Complex operator=(const Complex &a);

        // accessor functions
     double magnitude() const;
        double get_real() const;
     double get_imaginary() const;

};
```

This listing is simply the class definition. In complex terms, the $x + yi$ part maps to the real and the imaginary terms in the code. As you can see, we support constructors and accessors to get back the real and imaginary portions of the complex number.

The next step is to do the actual implementation of the class. This will not include any external operators, because they "live" outside of the class definition itself.

3. **Append the code from Listing 69-2 into your file.**

Better yet, copy the code from the source file on this book's companion Web site.

LISTING 69-2: THE COMPLEX CLASS IMPLEMENTATION

```cpp
// constructors
Complex::Complex()
{
    real = imaginary = 0;
}

Complex::Complex(double realValue, double imaginaryValue)
{
    real = realValue;
    imaginary = imaginaryValue;
}

// Copy constructor
Complex::Complex( const Complex& aCopy )
{
    real        = aCopy.real;
    imaginary   = aCopy.imaginary;
}

// accessor functions
double Complex::magnitude() const
{
    return sqrt(pow(real,2) + pow(imaginary,2));
}

double Complex::get_real() const
{
    return real;
}

double Complex::get_imaginary() const
{
    return imaginary;
}
```

```
void Complex::add(const Complex &a, const Complex &b)                      → 1
{
     real = a.get_real() + b.get_real();
     imaginary = a.get_imaginary() + b.get_imaginary();
}

void Complex::subtract(const Complex &a, const Complex &b)                 → 2
{
     real = a.get_real() - b.get_real();
     imaginary = a.get_imaginary() - b.get_imaginary();
}

void Complex::multiply(const Complex &a, const Complex &b)                 → 3
{
     real = a.get_real()*b.get_real() - a.get_imaginary()*b.get_imaginary();
     imaginary = a.get_real()*b.get_imaginary() + a.get_imaginary()*b.get_real();
}

void Complex::negative()
{
     imaginary = -imaginary;
}

// assigns one complex number to another
Complex Complex::operator=(const Complex &a)
{
     real = a.get_real();
     imaginary = a.get_imaginary();

     return *this;
}
```

The above listing is the implementation of the code that we defined in the class definition. These two listings could, and often are, split into two files. The class definition is placed in a header file, and the class implementation is placed in a source file. For simplicity, we are placing them all in the same file for this technique. The functionality for the underlying complex variable class is implemented in the add (shown at → **1**), subtract (shown at → **2**) and multiply (shown at → **3**) methods that are protected methods of the class. This is necessary so that we can override the operators +, –, and * later on.

Finally, we need to implement the utility functions for this class — in particular, the external operators that allow us to override the mathematical operations, as well as the streaming operator that allows us to output a complex number simply. These functions are implemented separately because they are not a part of the class itself, but rather they are global functions that can reside anywhere.

4. **Append the code from Listing 69-3 into your file.**

Better yet, copy the code from the source file on this book's companion Web site.

LISTING 69-3: THE COMPLEX VARIABLE UTILITY METHODS

```
Complex operator+(const Complex &a, const Complex &b)
{
     Complex c(a.get_real() + b.get_real() , a.get_imaginary() + b.get_imaginary());

     return c;
}

Complex operator-(const Complex &a, const Complex &b)
{
     Complex c(a.get_real() - b.get_real() , a.get_imaginary() - b.get_imaginary());

     return c;
}

Complex operator*(const Complex &a, const Complex &b)                             ➞ 4
{
     Complex c(a.get_real()*b.get_real() - a.get_imaginary()*b.get_imaginary(),
   a.get_real()*b.get_imaginary() + a.get_imaginary()*b.get_real());

     return c;
}

ostream& operator<<( ostream& out, const Complex& aComplex )
{
     out << aComplex.get_real() << "+" << aComplex.get_imaginary() << "i";
     return out;
}
```

The operators simply construct new `Complex` objects by using the components of the input `Complex` object. For example, in the `operator*` code, shown at ➞ **4**, the multiplication result is computed by multiplying the two real parts of the complex variables input, subtracting the two imaginary parts multiplied together, and assigning the result to the real portion of the returned variable.

Testing the Complex Number Class

After you create a class, you should create a test driver that not only ensures that your code is correct, but also show people how to use your code. The following steps tell you how.

 If you provide a test suite with your class-definition file, application programmers can determine right away whether any changes they've made to the class have broken things. In addition, this arrangement gives the developer of the original code a simple way to run regression tests (suites of tests which indicate whether previous functionality is still working) when problems occur.

1. **In the code editor of your choice, re-open the source file to hold the code for your test program.**

In this example, I named the test program `ch69.cpp`.

2. **Type the code from Listing 69-4 into your file.**

Better yet, copy the code from the source file on this book's companion Web site.

LISTING 69-4: THE COMPLEX-NUMBER TEST PROGRAM

```
int main( int argc, char **argv)
{
    Complex c1( 2.0, 1.0 );                                          → 5
    Complex c2( 3.0, 3.0 );

    Complex c3 = c1 + c2;                                            → 6
    Complex c4 = c1 * c2;
    Complex c5 = c2 - c1;

    cout << "C1 " << c1 << endl;                                     → 7
    cout << "C2 " << c2 << endl;
    cout << "C3 " << c3 << endl;
    cout << "C4 " << c4 << endl;
    cout << "C5 " << c5 << endl;

    // Output the pieces
    cout << endl;
    cout << "Real" << "\t" << "Imaginary" << endl;
    cout << c1.get_real() << "\t" << c1.get_imaginary() << endl;
    cout << c2.get_real() << "\t" << c2.get_imaginary() << endl;
    cout << c3.get_real() << "\t" << c3.get_imaginary() << endl;
    cout << c4.get_real() << "\t" << c4.get_imaginary() << endl;
    cout << c5.get_real() << "\t" << c5.get_imaginary() << endl;

    return 0;
}
```

Listing 69-4 simply exercises the various components of the Complex class functionality. We create a few Complex objects at the block of lines shown starting at → 5. Our next set of tests exercises the mathematical operators to add, subtract and multiply the Complex objects, as shown in the block of lines starting at → 6. We then output the results for each of the objects, using the streaming operator (<<) to illustrate how the formatting is done, and check the results. This is shown in the block starting at → 7. Finally, we use the accessor routines to print out the real and imaginary portions of each object.

3. **Save the source code as a file in the code editor and then close the editor application.**

4. **Compile the source code with your favorite compiler, on your favorite operating system.**

5. **Run the program on your favorite operating system's console.**

If you have done everything properly, you should see the following output from the program on the console window. Note that in this listing C3 is the sum of C1 and C2, C4 is the product, and C5 is the difference. We should see that reflected in the output:

```
$ ./a
C1 2+1i
C2 3+3i
C3 5+4i
C4 3+9i
C5 1+2i

Real    Imaginary
2       1
3       3
5       4
3       9
1       2
```

The components listed above are simply the objects from our test driver. Because C1 is equal to $2 + 1i$ and C2 is equal to $3 + 3i$, we would expect that if we added the two objects, we would get $5 + 4i$, which is exactly what is shown for the value of C3 (the sum of C1 and C2). As we expected, we get the results we should. Likewise, in the bottom listing of real and imaginary, C3 is the third entry and has a real component of 5 and an imaginary component of 4, as expected.

As you can see, the output is what we would expect from the `Complex` number class. We can now drop

this class into our application and use it — because it has no real ties to any other classes.

A class is useful in an inverse proportion to the number of other classes it has to include. Cumbersome is bad. If you create a class that drags in an entire library of functionality just to use a single function in that library, people will avoid it. If (instead) you create a class that does a single task — such as representing complex numbers — and have that class stand alone, people will tend to use it in their applications.

Technique 70

Converting Numbers to Words

Save Time By

- Understanding the value of converting numbers to words
- Understanding the basic logic of such a program
- Creating a conversion class
- Testing your conversion class

If you go into a bank and ask for a cashier's check, your bank computer system will print the check for the appropriate amount; look closely at that check and you'll see that it has the entire amount spelled out in English. For example, if I got a cashier's check for $1,200.60, the check would read *One thousand two hundred dollars and sixty cents.* This is not an unusual use for a software program, and the ability to translate numbers to words can be applied in many different types of applications, from education to finance.

The design of the codesystem that performs this kind of translation is very interesting. The process we go through for this is always done the same way. We break the number — no matter how large — down into hundreds, and then parse the results into English. For example, if you are given the number 123,456, you look first at the 123 and append a thousand to it — resulting in *one hundred twenty-three thousand.* Further, within a block of hundreds, you will always look at numbers from one to twenty, then multiples of ten, then multiples of a hundred. For example, you will list the numbers from one to nineteen for a given hundred, then it is twenty, twenty-one, thirty, thirty-one, and so forth.

A process that breaks something into smaller pieces — and then assembles the pieces into larger components — should naturally make you think about objects. In this case, you can see that there are objects for the one-to-twenty conversion, the twenty-and-up conversion, and the hundreds conversion. The thousands conversion is really just a variant of the hundreds. All these cases have a common set of things to look at:

- the specific range of the value
- convert that range into a string

Let's look at an example, because this is all rather confusing to explain and much easier to show. If we start with the number 123,456 and want to convert it to English, we would do the following:

1. First, we break the number down into the highest unit, in this case thousands. So, the first part of our given number produces the number 123, with a unit of *thousand*.

2. Next, we split off the hundreds. So, we have *one hundred*.

3. The next step is to look at the tens unit. If this number were zero, we would skip it. In this case, it is a two, so the number is twenty. An important exception here is the number one. In this case, we have to apply special English rules (i.e. eleven, twelve, thirteen) and skip the ones digit. So, because the second digit is a two, we now have *one hundred twenty*.

4. Finally, we look at the ones digit. In our case, it is a three, so we have *one hundred twenty three*.

5. Append the units from step 1: *one hundred twenty three thousand*.

6. Repeat for the next block. If we are under a thousand, we skip the units part. Put both blocks together to produce: *one hundred twenty three thousand four hundred fifty six*.

From an object-oriented design viewpoint, the process shows that its cases have some elements in common elements — as well as some elements that are discrete for different cases. This suggests that we have a common base class, and then derived classes that manage those discrete elements. Furthermore, we can build some of the elements from the base classes to create new extended classes, such as when we create thousands from ones and tens.

This technique shows you how to convert numbers into written English.

 Always take a step back from the problem when you are trying to do an object-oriented design. Doing so gives you the opportunity to see the problem from a big-picture perspective, which often allows you to break it down into small components much more easily. When you see all the pieces, you can also usually see the overlap between them — which can be factored into your base classes.

You can save a lot of time in the long-run by getting the design right from the beginning. Understanding how all the pieces fit together is essential to getting that design right.

Creating the Conversion Code

The first step toward implementing the system is to create the base classes used to build the application. The following steps show you how. The base classes represent the number ranges we are going to use to parse the existing number into digits and convert those digits into words.

1. **In the code editor of your choice, create a new file to hold the code for the implementation of source file.**

   In this example, the file is named ch70.cpp, although you can use whatever you choose.

2. **Type the code from Listing 70-1 into your file.**

   Or better yet, copy the code from the source file on this book's companion Web site.

LISTING 70-1: THE CONVERSION BASE CLASSES: SOURCE CODE

```cpp
#include <vector>
#include <string>
#include <iostream>

using namespace std;

class RangeEntry
{
    long _lMin;
    long _lMax;
    long _lIncrement;
public:
    RangeEntry(void)
    {
        _lMin = 0;
        _lMax = 0;
        _lIncrement = 1;
```

```
}
    RangeEntry(long min, long max, long inc=1)
    {
        _lMin = min;
        _lMax = max;
        _lIncrement = inc;
    }
    RangeEntry( const RangeEntry& aCopy )
    {
        _lMin = aCopy._lMin;
        _lMax = aCopy._lMax;
        _lIncrement = aCopy._lIncrement;
    }

    RangeEntry operator=(const RangeEntry& aCopy )
    {
        _lMin = aCopy._lMin;
        _lMax = aCopy._lMax;
        _lIncrement = aCopy._lIncrement;
        return *this;
    }

    // Accessors
    long Min()
    {
        return _lMin;
    }
    long Max()
    {
        return _lMax;
    }
    long Increment()
    {
        return _lIncrement;
    }

    bool InRange( long lVal)
    {
        if ( lVal >= Min() && lVal <= Max() )
            return true;
        return false;
    }

    virtual string getString(int iVal)
    {
        return "Unknown";
    }

};

class OnesRangeEntry : public RangeEntry
{
```

(continued)

LISTING 70-1 *(continued)*

```cpp
public:
    OnesRangeEntry(void)
        : RangeEntry(0,19,1)
    {
    }

    virtual string getString(int iVal)
    {
        switch ( iVal )
        {
            case 1:
                return string("one");
            case 2:
                return string("two");
            case 3:
                return string("three");
            case 4:
                return string("four");
            case 5:
                return string("five");
            case 6:
                return string("six");
            case 7:
                return string("seven");
            case 8:
                return string("eight");
            case 9:
                return string("nine");
            case 10:
                return string("ten");
            case 11:
                return string("eleven");
            case 12:
                return string("twelve");
            case 13:
                return string("thirteen");
            case 14:
                return string("fourteen");
            case 15:
                return string("fifteen");
            case 16:
                return string("sixteen");
            case 17:
                return string("seventeen");
            case 18:
                return string("eighteen");
            case 19:
                return string("nineteen");
        }
        return string("");
    }
};
```

```
class TensRangeEntry : public RangeEntry
{
public:
    TensRangeEntry(void)
        : RangeEntry(20,90,10)
    {
    }

    virtual string getString(int iVal)
    {
        int iDigit = iVal / 10;
        switch ( iDigit )
        {
            case 1:
                return string("ten");
            case 2:
                return string("twenty");
            case 3:
                return string("thirty");
            case 4:
                return string("forty");
            case 5:
                return string("fifty");
            case 6:
                return string("sixty");
            case 7:
                return string("seventy");
            case 8:
                return string("eighty");
            case 9:
                return string("ninety");
        }
        return string("");
    }
};

class HundredsRangeEntry : public RangeEntry
{
public:
    HundredsRangeEntry(void)
        : RangeEntry(100,1000,100)
    {
    }

    virtual string getString(int iVal)
    {
        OnesRangeEntry ore;

        int iDigit = iVal / 100;

        string s = ore.getString( iDigit );
        s += " hundred";
```

(continued)

LISTING 70-1 *(continued)*

```
            return s;
        }
};

class ThousandsRangeEntry : public RangeEntry
{
public:
    ThousandsRangeEntry(void)
        : RangeEntry(1000,999999,1000)      ➜ 1
    {
    }

    virtual string getString(int iVal)
    {
        HundredsRangeEntry hre;
        TensRangeEntry tre;
        OnesRangeEntry ore;

        int iDigit = iVal / 1000;
        int iNum = iDigit;
        string s = "";
        if ( hre.InRange(iDigit) )           ➜ 2
        {
            s += hre.getString( iDigit );
            iDigit = iDigit - (( iDigit/100 ) * 100);
        }

        if ( hre.InRange(iNum) )
        {
            s += " ";
            s += tre.getString( iDigit );
            iDigit = iDigit - (( iDigit/10 ) * 10);
        }

        if ( ore.getString( iDigit ).length() )
            s += " ";
        s += ore.getString( iDigit );
        s += " thousand";

        return s;
    }
};
```

These base classes "know" how to convert a single string into a series of words that describe a number. However, because there are differences for thousands, hundreds, and single digit values, we need a set of classes to do each of these. After we have created the three basic ones (digits, hundreds, thousands), we can then parse any number up to one million. If we wanted to parse numbers over one million, of course, we would need to add a new class, and so forth for each further magnitude we want to handle.

The important thing is how the higher level classes (thousand, for example) call the lower level classes (hundred, ones) to process the smaller numbers. For example, take a look at the `ThousandsRangeEntry` class. The class contains a range value that it processes, numbers between 1000 and 999999 (shown at → **1**). Within the `getString` method, which converts the number into a human readable string, the class then uses the hundred, ten, and one digit parsing classes to do its work (see lines beginning at → **2**). We don't duplicate a lot of code and we don't have to go searching through the code to see which piece broke when there is an exception. For example, if we wanted to properly hyphenate output strings (thirty-five, instead of thirty five) we would just modify the tens class.

3. Save the source code in your code editor.

The next step is to implement the processing object that gathers up all the individual conversions into the output text string.

4. Reopen the source file in the code editor.

5. Append the code from Listing 70-2 to the source file.

LISTING 70-2: THE CONVERSION CLASS: SOURCE CODE

```
class NumberToWords
{
private:
    vector< RangeEntry *> _entries;

protected:
    virtual void InitializeToDefaults()
    {
        _entries.insert( _entries.end(),
            new OnesRangeEntry() );          → 3
        _entries.insert( _entries.end(),
            new TensRangeEntry() );
        _entries.insert( _entries.end(),
            new HundredsRangeEntry() );
        _entries.insert( _entries.end(),
            new ThousandsRangeEntry() );
    }

public:
```

```
NumberToWords( void )
{
    InitializeToDefaults();
}
virtual ~NumberToWords(void)
{
    vector< RangeEntry *>::iterator
        iter;
    for ( iter = _entries.begin();
        iter != _entries.end(); ++iter )
        delete (*iter);
}
string Convert( int iVal )
{
    string sRet = "";
    while ( iVal > 0 )                 → 4
    {
        bool bFound = false;

        vector< RangeEntry *>::itera-
            tor iter;
        for ( iter =
            _entries.begin(); iter !=
            _entries.end(); ++iter )
        {
            if ( (*iter)->InRange(
                iVal ) )
            {
                if ( sRet.length()
                    )
                    sRet += " ";
                sRet += (*iter)-
                    >getString( iVal
                    );

                iVal = iVal - (
                    (iVal / (*iter)-
                    >Increment()) *
                    (*iter)-
                    >Increment());
                bFound = true;
                break;
            }
        }

        if ( !bFound )
            iVal = 10;

    }
    return sRet;
}
};
```

The main parts of the NumberToWords class are the entries (shown at ➜ **3** in the Listing 70-2) and the Convert method. The entries are simply extensions of the base RangeEntry class that process given ranges of the value being converted (the iVal parameter). The number is broken down by the increment of each range (thousands, hundreds, tens, ones) and each entry is called to process that particular unit. This continues until the input value is reduced to a value of zero. The loop to process the value is shown at ➜ **4**.

Testing the Conversion Code

After you create a class, you should create a test driver that not only ensures that your code is correct, but also shows people how to use your code. The following steps show you how.

1. **In the code editor of your choice, re-open the source file to hold the code for your test program.**

   In this example, I named the test program ch70.cpp.

2. **Type the code from Listing 70-3 into your file.**

   Better yet, copy the code from the source file on this book's companion Web site.

LISTING 70-3: THE NUMBER-CONVERSION TEST PROGRAM

```cpp
int main()
{
    NumberToWords nw;
    string s1 = nw.Convert(123);
    cout << "String: " << s1 << endl;
    string s2 = nw.Convert(1);
    cout << "String: " << s2 << endl;
    string s3 = nw.Convert(23);
    cout << "String: " << s3 << endl;
    string s4 = nw.Convert(807);
    cout << "String: " << s4 << endl;
    string s5 = nw.Convert(123456);
    cout << "String: " << s5 << endl;
}
```

The purpose of our little test driver is simply to show that the class works with all of the exceptional cases that exist for numeric conversions. For example, we want examples of ones, tens, hundreds, and thousands. We also want a simple example that requires the code to check all of its conditions, such as 23.

3. **Save the source code in the code editor and then close the editor application.**

4. **Compile the source code with your favorite compiler, on your favorite operating system.**

5. **Run the program on your favorite operating system's console.**

If you have done everything properly, you should see the following output from the program on the console window:

```
$ ./a
String: one hundred twenty three
String: one
String: twenty three
String: eight hundred seven
String: one hundred twenty three thousand
    four hundred fifty six
```

As you can see from the output listing, the code works properly. All of the various scenarios are handled correctly and the output is in expected English. As mentioned previously, possible enhancements to the application would be extending the classes to process millions, billions, and so forth, or adding hyphens, if desired.

Technique 71

Reducing the Complexity of Code

Programmers know the best program design is always simple. In fact, among programmers, the KISS principle has become a cliché: "Keep It Simple, Stupid." To keep things simple, you have to follow three basic principles when writing and maintaining code:

- Componentizing
- Restructuring
- Specializing

By following these few simple processes when you develop and debug your code, you can drastically cut down on your maintenance time. In this technique, we will look at these four pillars of programming simplicity — and examine how to apply them.

A Sample Program

Imagine, for a moment, that you're working on a program that parses input files for words. This sort of program might be used to get a list of words for a spell-checker or a stop list for an indexing program. In text indexing, a stop list gives the program a list of words to ignore when placing them in the index. The code for this type of program is shown in Listing 71-1. Its obviously a very simple, stripped-down program, but it illustrates the basic idea of what we're trying to accomplish.

LISTING 71-1: THE ORIGINAL WORD-PARSER PROGRAM

```cpp
#include <stdio.h>
#include <string.h>
#include <vector>

using namespace std;

void my_func( std::vector< char *>& words )
{
   FILE *fp = fopen("myfile.txt", "r");
   if ( fp == NULL )
      return -1;

   while ( !feof(fp) )
   {
      char szBuffer[ 81 ];
      memset( szBuffer, 0, 80 );
      if ( fgets( szBuffer, 80, fp ) == NULL )
         break;

      // Parse the line
      char szWord[80];
      memset ( szWord, 0, 80 );
      int pos = 0;

      for ( int i=0; i<(int)strlen(szBuffer); ++i )
      {
         switch ( szBuffer[i] )
         {
            case ':':
               if ( strlen(szWord) )
               {
                  char *str = new char[strlen(szWord)+1];
                  strcpy( str, szWord );
                  words.insert( words.end(), str );
                  szWord[0] = 0;
                  pos = 0;
                  memset ( szWord, 0, 80 );
               }
               break;
            default:
               szWord[pos] = szBuffer[i];
               pos++;
               break;
         }
      }
   }

   fclose(fp);
}
```

→ 1

```
int main(int argc, char **argv )
{
   std::vector< char *> words;
   my_func( words );

   std::vector< char *>::iterator iter;
   for ( iter = words.begin(); iter != words.end(); ++iter )
      printf("Word: %s\n", (*iter) );

   return 0;
}
```

The code above is supposed to read lines in from a file, parse them into words, and store the words in an array. It is assumed that the lines have a specific format: word1:word2:word3 followed by a carriage return. Given an input like that, the assumption is that the program will produce a list that contains word1, word2, and word3. The code accomplishes this by stepping through each character in the line, looking for a colon (:) and taking whatever precedes it as a word. You can see this code in the loop shown at ➜ **1**.

This code generally works, except it has a rather severe bug — it will skip words at the end of a line — and anyway the real issue is that this code is hard to maintain. If we add a new separator to the line (for example), what happens? If someone comes along and has no idea what the code does, is it at all intuitive? The first step to making things better is to separate it into components.

If we run the program with an input file that looks like this

```
word1:word2:word3
line2:word2:word3
line3:word3:word4
```

the program will then parse the individual lines into

```
Line1:
word1
word2

Line2:
line2
word2
```

The problem is shown by the fact that the word3 from line 1 and word3 from line 2 are not shown.

Componentizing

Componentizing is my own term for the process of splitting something up into components. In our code, there are two major components, a file component and a parser component. Components differ from functions, methods, or classes. A *component* is a single functional element — that is, a collection of code that accomplishes a single task or deals with a single area such as a file or parsing text. Componentizing simplifies your code by reducing the amount of cohesion between the various units of a module, and by limiting the areas in which you need to search for a given piece of functionality. If we are looking for something that reads from or writes to a file, we look in the file component. We wouldn't bother to look in the parser component, because that has nothing to do with reading or writing from a file. We have not yet split our class into components, we are merely identifying the different units in the current code.

The next step toward making our code simpler is to break it down into separate components. Let's identify and split out the pieces into their own componentized classes. Our new structure will contain two separate classes. This is how you do it.

1. In the code editor of your choice, create a new file to hold the code for the implementation of source file.

In this example, the file is named `ch71.cpp`, although you can use whatever you choose.

2. Type the code from Listing 71-2 into your file.

Better yet, copy the code from the source file on this book's companion Web site.

LISTING 71-2: THE COMPONENTIZED SAMPLE PROGRAM

```cpp
#include <stdio.h>
#include <string.h>
#include <vector>
#include <string>

using namespace std;

class ParserFile                        → 2
{
private:
    FILE *fp;
public:
    ParserFile(void)
    {
        fp = NULL;
    }
    ParserFile( const char *fileName )
    {
        if ( fileName != NULL )
            fp = fopen( fileName, "r" );
    }
    string getLine()
    {
        string s = "";

        if ( fp == NULL )
            return s;

        char c = 0;

        while ( !feof(fp) && c != '\n' )
        {
            c = fgetc(fp);
            if ( c != '\n' && c != '\r' && c !=
              EOF)
                s += c;
        }
```

```cpp
        return s;
    }
    bool eof()
    {
        if ( fp == NULL )
            return true;
        return feof(fp);
    }
};

class Parser                            → 3
{
private:
    char delimiter;
    vector< string > words;
public:
    Parser(void)
    {
        delimiter = ';'; // default
    }
    Parser( const char& delim )
    {
        delimiter = delim;
    }

    void clear()
    {
        words.erase( words.begin(),
            words.end() );
    }

    bool parse( const string& in )
    {
        string sWord = "";

        if ( delimiter == 0 )
            return false;
        if ( in.length() == 0 )
            return false;

        for ( int i=0; i<(int)in.length(); ++i )
        {
            // End of word or string?

            if ( in[i] == delimiter)
            {
                words.insert( words.end(),
                    sWord );
                sWord = "";
            }
            else
```

```
        {
            sWord += in[i];
        }
    }

    if ( sWord.length() )
        words.insert( words.end(), sWord );


    return true;
  }

  int num()
  {
    return words.size();
  }
  string word( int idx )
  {
    string s = "";
    if ( idx < 0 || idx >
(int)words.size()-1 )
        return s;
    s = words[idx];
    return s;
  }
};


int main(int argc, char **argv )
{
    ParserFile pf( "myfile.txt" );
    Parser     p(':');

    while ( !pf.eof() )
    {
        p.clear();

        if (p.parse( pf.getLine() ) == true )
        {
            printf("Parsed:\n");
            for ( int i=0; i<p.num(); ++i )
                printf("Word[%d] = %s\n", i,
                    p.word(i).c_str() );
        }
    }

    return 0;
}
```

Note that this code does not do anything different from our original code listing. It has simply been restructured to be more componentized. The logic and functionality remain the same. The code to read a file into individual lines has been moved into the `ParserFile` class (shown at→ **2**). This class does more error-checking for input, and has specific methods to read the file and return individual lines, but it is otherwise functionally equivalent to the previous example code. Likewise, the `Parser` class (shown at → **3**) still parses a given line, but is no longer reliant on any file input to do its work. It is now a simple parser class that takes in a string and breaks it down into words, using a developer-supplied delimiter, in place of our hard-coded colon of the first example.

Looking at the main program, you can see how much cleaner the interface is, and how much simpler it is to read. It should also be considerably easier to debug, because each piece of the code is in a separate component, meaning that when a problem is encountered, only that component needs to be checked out.

Restructuring

Restructuring (also known as *refactoring*) is the process of going back through code and eliminating redundancy and duplicated effort. For example, let's consider the following snippet of code (not from our example, just a generalized piece of code):

```
int ret = get_a_line();
if ( ret == ERROR )
    throw "Error in get_a_line!";          → 4
ret = get_words_from_line();
if ( ret == ERROR )
    throw "Error in get_words_from_line!";
ret = process_words();
if ( ret == ERROR )
    throw "Error in process_words!";
```

This code is prime territory for refactoring. Why? Because the code contains multiple redundant statements, namely the exception handling (throw lines, such as the one shown at ➜ **4**) To do this, follow these steps.

1. **Examine the code for similar looking statements or processes.**

   In our case, the code that is similar is the check for the return code and the throwing of the exception string.

2. **Extract the redundant code and factor it into a routine of its own.**

   In this case, we can factor the code into a single routine:

```
void CheckAndThrowError( int retCode,
   const char *name )
{
   if ( retCode == ERROR )
      throw name;
}
```

3. **Replace the existing code with the calls into the refactored code.**

```
CheckAndThrowError( get_a_line(),
   "get_a_line");
CheckAndThrowError(get_words_from_line(
   ),
      "get_words_from_line" );
CheckAndThrowError(process_words(),
      "process_words" );
```

4. **If necessary, after the code is refactored, re-examine it for other similarities.**

   In this example, we might consider logging the error within the `CheckAndThrowError` function. This isn't really a refactoring case, but rather an observation of what might make the code more complete.

Specialization

Programmers have a habit of writing code that is generalized to the extreme. Why write a routine that can break down a string into four parts at particular boundaries, when you can write a generalized routine that can handle *any* number of segments — of any length each? Sounds great in theory . . .

One sad lesson — normally learned when debugging programs — is that generalization is really a pain in the neck. It causes vastly more problems than it solves, and it never turns out that your code is general enough to handle *every* single case that comes its way. So you hack the code to make it work; it ends up littered with special cases.

Take a look at an example of generalization and how it can get you into trouble. Going back to our original code, assume that your input file has very long strings in it — not really a valid input file at all. Suppose it looked something like this:

```
This is a really long sentence that doesn't
   happen to have a colon in it until it
   reaches the very end like this: do you
   think it will work?
```

If we run our first example program on this input file, it will crash, because we will overwrite the end of the word allocated space. This happens because we generalized the input to handle any sort of file, instead of making it specific to the kind of input we were expecting. We could easily change our code to handle a bigger string, but instead, we should follow the rules of specialization:

✔ **Make sure that input files are clearly marked as valid input to the program:** In nearly all cases, your program-specific input should contain a version and type identifier. We haven't added this to this simple example, but it would make sense to modify the `ParserFile` class to read in a beginning line containing version information.

✔ **If your input is fixed-length, check the length before you start loading the data:** If you have an input file that is supposed to contain words of no more than 80 characters, then any time you have not encountered a delimiter within 80 characters, you should abort the input process and print out an error message for the user. If the word length is not fixed, then you should never use a fixed-length buffer to store it.

We already fixed this one in the `ParserFile` class by using a string in place of the fixed size buffer.

✔ **Reject data in any format you do not understand:** This precept is a little easier to understand with an example. Let's suppose that you are reading in a date from the command line or in a graphical user interface. Dates have so many formats that it is almost not worth enumerating them all. However, if you are given a date that is given as 1/1/04, there are numerous ways to interpret it. For example, it could be in M/D/YY format, and be January 1, 2004. Alternatively, it could be in D/M/YY format — which would still be January 1, 2004, but would change the interpretation. There is no reason to keep the ambiguity. Either force the user to enter in a single format, or use a control that specifies the format.

This one really has no issue in our `ParserFile` class, because we aren't dealing with specific data sizes.

If you follow these guidelines, you will cut down on the number of bugs you receive — which makes it easier to debug problems that you do encounter in your application.

Index

D

T

BUSINESS, CAREERS & PERSONAL FINANCE

0-7645-5307-0

0-7645-5331-3 *†

Also available:

- ✒Accounting For Dummies †
  0-7645-5314-3
- ✒Business Plans Kit For Dummies †
  0-7645-5365-8
- ✒Cover Letters For Dummies
  0-7645-5224-4
- ✒Frugal Living For Dummies
  0-7645-5403-4
- ✒Leadership For Dummies
  0-7645-5176-0
- ✒Managing For Dummies
  0-7645-1771-6

- ✒Marketing For Dummies
  0-7645-5600-2
- ✒Personal Finance For Dummies *
  0-7645-2590-5
- ✒Project Management For Dummies
  0-7645-5283-X
- ✒Resumes For Dummies †
  0-7645-5471-9
- ✒Selling For Dummies
  0-7645-5363-1
- ✒Small Business Kit For Dummies *†
  0-7645-5093-4

HOME & BUSINESS COMPUTER BASICS

0-7645-4074-2

0-7645-3758-X

Also available:

- ✒ACT! 6 For Dummies
  0-7645-2645-6
- ✒iLife '04 All-in-One Desk Reference For Dummies
  0-7645-7347-0
- ✒iPAQ For Dummies
  0-7645-6769-1
- ✒Mac OS X Panther Timesaving Techniques For Dummies
  0-7645-5812-9
- ✒Macs For Dummies
  0-7645-5656-8

- ✒Microsoft Money 2004 For Dummies
  0-7645-4195-1
- ✒Office 2003 All-in-One Desk Reference For Dummies
  0-7645-3883-7
- ✒Outlook 2003 For Dummies
  0-7645-3759-8
- ✒PCs For Dummies
  0-7645-4074-2
- ✒TiVo For Dummies
  0-7645-6923-6
- ✒Upgrading and Fixing PCs For Dummies
  0-7645-1665-5
- ✒Windows XP Timesaving Techniques For Dummies
  0-7645-3748-2

FOOD, HOME, GARDEN, HOBBIES, MUSIC & PETS

0-7645-5295-3

0-7645-5232-5

Also available:

- ✒Bass Guitar For Dummies
  0-7645-2487-9
- ✒Diabetes Cookbook For Dummies
  0-7645-5230-9
- ✒Gardening For Dummies *
  0-7645-5130-2
- ✒Guitar For Dummies
  0-7645-5106-X
- ✒Holiday Decorating For Dummies
  0-7645-2570-0
- ✒Home Improvement All-in-One For Dummies
  0-7645-5680-0
- ✒Knitting For Dummies
  0-7645-5395-X

- ✒Piano For Dummies
  0-7645-5105-1
- ✒Puppies For Dummies
  0-7645-5255-4
- ✒Scrapbooking For Dummies
  0-7645-7208-3
- ✒Senior Dogs For Dummies
  0-7645-5818-8
- ✒Singing For Dummies
  0-7645-2475-5
- ✒30-Minute Meals For Dummies
  0-7645-2589-1

INTERNET & DIGITAL MEDIA

0-7645-1664-7

0-7645-6924-4

Also available:

- ✒2005 Online Shopping Directory For Dummies
  0-7645-7495-7
- ✒CD & DVD Recording For Dummies
  0-7645-5956-7
- ✒eBay For Dummies
  0-7645-5654-1
- ✒Fighting Spam For Dummies
  0-7645-5965-6
- ✒Genealogy Online For Dummies
  0-7645-5964-8
- ✒Google For Dummies
  0-7645-4420-9

- ✒Home Recording For Musicians For Dummies
  0-7645-1634-5
- ✒The Internet For Dummies
  0-7645-4173-0
- ✒iPod & iTunes For Dummies
  0-7645-7772-7
- ✒Preventing Identity Theft For Dummies
  0-7645-7336-5
- ✒Pro Tools All-in-One Desk Reference For Dummies
  0-7645-5714-9
- ✒Roxio Easy Media Creator For Dummies
  0-7645-7131-1

SPORTS, FITNESS, PARENTING, RELIGION & SPIRITUALITY

0-7645-5146-9

0-7645-5418-2

Also available:
- Adoption For Dummies
  0-7645-5488-3
- Basketball For Dummies
  0-7645-5248-1
- The Bible For Dummies
  0-7645-5296-1
- Buddhism For Dummies
  0-7645-5359-3
- Catholicism For Dummies
  0-7645-5391-7
- Hockey For Dummies
  0-7645-5228-7

- Judaism For Dummies
  0-7645-5299-6
- Martial Arts For Dummies
  0-7645-5358-5
- Pilates For Dummies
  0-7645-5397-6
- Religion For Dummies
  0-7645-5264-3
- Teaching Kids to Read For Dummies
  0-7645-4043-2
- Weight Training For Dummies
  0-7645-5168-X
- Yoga For Dummies
  0-7645-5117-5

TRAVEL

0-7645-5438-7

0-7645-5453-0

Also available:
- Alaska For Dummies
  0-7645-1761-9
- Arizona For Dummies
  0-7645-6938-4
- Cancún and the Yucatán For Dummies
  0-7645-2437-2
- Cruise Vacations For Dummies
  0-7645-6941-4
- Europe For Dummies
  0-7645-5456-5
- Ireland For Dummies
  0-7645-5455-7

- Las Vegas For Dummies
  0-7645-5448-4
- London For Dummies
  0-7645-4277-X
- New York City For Dummies
  0-7645-6945-7
- Paris For Dummies
  0-7645-5494-8
- RV Vacations For Dummies
  0-7645-5443-3
- Walt Disney World & Orlando For Dummies
  0-7645-6943-0

GRAPHICS, DESIGN & WEB DEVELOPMENT

0-7645-4345-8

0-7645-5589-8

Also available:
- Adobe Acrobat 6 PDF For Dummies
  0-7645-3760-1
- Building a Web Site For Dummies
  0-7645-7144-3
- Dreamweaver MX 2004 For Dummies
  0-7645-4342-3
- FrontPage 2003 For Dummies
  0-7645-3882-9
- HTML 4 For Dummies
  0-7645-1995-6
- Illustrator CS For Dummies
  0-7645-4084-X

- Macromedia Flash MX 2004 For Dummies
  0-7645-4358-X
- Photoshop 7 All-in-One Desk Reference
  For Dummies
  0-7645-1667-1
- Photoshop CS Timesaving Techniques
  For Dummies
  0-7645-6782-9
- PHP 5 For Dummies
  0-7645-4166-8
- PowerPoint 2003 For Dummies
  0-7645-3908-6
- QuarkXPress 6 For Dummies
  0-7645-2593-X

NETWORKING, SECURITY, PROGRAMMING & DATABASES

0-7645-6852-3

0-7645-5784-X

Also available:
- A+ Certification For Dummies
  0-7645-4187-0
- Access 2003 All-in-One Desk Reference For
  Dummies
  0-7645-3988-4
- Beginning Programming For Dummies
  0-7645-4997-9
- C For Dummies
  0-7645-7068-4
- Firewalls For Dummies
  0-7645-4048-3
- Home Networking For Dummies
  0-7645-42796

- Network Security For Dummies
  0-7645-1679-5
- Networking For Dummies
  0-7645-1677-9
- TCP/IP For Dummies
  0-7645-1760-0
- VBA For Dummies
  0-7645-3989-2
- Wireless All In-One Desk Reference
  For Dummies
  0-7645-7496-5
- Wireless Home Networking For Dummies
  0-7645-3910-8